D0890226

HOLY BONES, HOLY DUST

CHARLES FREEMAN

HOLY BONES
HOLY DUST

HOW RELICS SHAPED THE HISTORY
of MEDIEVAL EUROPE

YALE UNIVERSITY PRESS
NEW HAVEN AND LONDON

For information about this and other Yale University Press publication, please contact:
U.S. Office: sales.press@yale.edu   www.yalebooks.com
Europe Office: sales@yaleup.co.uk   www.yalebooks.co.uk

Set in Arno Pro by IDSUK (DataConnection) Ltd
Printed in Great Britain by TJ International Ltd, Padstow, Cornwall

Library of Congress Cataloging-in-Publication Data

Freeman, Charles, 1947–
    Holy bones, holy dust : how relics shaped the history of medieval europe/Charles Freeman.
       p. cm.
    ISBN 978–0–300–12571–9 (cl:alk. paper)
    1.   Relics–History–To 1500.   2.   Christian saints–Cult–History–To 1500.
    I.   Title.
    BX2333.F74 2011
    235'.2–dc22

                                                                                          2010044321

A catalogue record for this book is available from the British Library.

10 9 8 7 6 5 4 3 2 1

For my son Tom

Contents

CONTENTS

Illustrations

13. Ambrogio Brambilla, *Speculum Romanae Magnificentiae* (1575), British Museum. © The Trustees of the British Museum.

14. Luca Signorelli, *St James the Greater with a Living and a Dead Pilgrim* (*c*.1508), Museum of Fine Arts, Budapest. © Szépművészeti Múzeum, Budapest.

15. Interior of Sainte-Chapelle, Paris.

16. Louis IX exhibiting a relic of the True Cross and the crown of thorns, Cambridge, Corpus Christi College, MS 16, f.142v. Reproduced by permission of the Masters and Fellows of Corpus Christi College, Cambridge.

17. Hieronymous Bosch, *Death and the Miser* (1485–90), National Gallery of Art, Washington D.C. Image courtesy of National Gallery of Art, Washington D.C.

18. Giotto, 'The Descent into Hell', detail from *The Last Judgement* (1305), Scrovegni Chapel, Padua. © The Art Archive/Scrovegni Chapel Padua/Alfredo Dagli Orti.

19. Domenico Ghirlandaio, *Funeral of Saint Fina* (1470), Chapel of Saint Fina, Duomo di San Gimignano. © The Art Archive/Duomo di San Gimignano/Gianni Dagli Orti.

20. Gentile da Fabriano, *The Crippled and the Sick Cured at the Tomb of Saint Nicholas* (1425), National Gallery of Art, Washington D.C. Image courtesy of National Gallery of Art, Washington D.C.

21. Tintoretto, *The Stealing of the Body of Saint Mark* (*c*.1562–66), Galleria dell'Accademia, Venice. © akg-images/Erich Lessing.

22. Paolo Veneziano, Ferial Altarpiece (detail), *Finding the Body of St Mark* (1345), Museo di San Marco, Venice. Scala, Florence.

23. Gentile Bellini, *Procession in St Mark's Square* (1496), Galleria dell'Accademia, Venice.

24. Gentile Bellini, *Miracle at the Bridge of San Lorenzo* (1500), Galleria dell'Accademia, Venice. Scala, Florence.

25. Reliquary of the True Cross, Scuola Grande di San Giovanni Evangelista, Venice. Image courtesy of Scuola Grande San Giovanni Evangelista, Venice.

26. Lucas Cranach the Elder, *Christ and the Virgin Interceding for Humanity before God the Father* (1516–18), Museum of Fine Arts, Budapest. © Szépművészeti Múzeum, Budapest.

Maps

Preface

THE LONG queues lining up in Turin in the summer of 2010 to venerate a piece of cloth that is claimed by many to be the shroud in which Jesus was buried show just how powerful the attraction of the relic remains in the Christian world. The Turin Shroud is one of several shrouds and veils related to Jesus or his mother Mary that have been venerated as relics over the centuries. It may have been one of those shrouds derided by the Protestant reformer John Calvin in 1543 when he noted that none of them conformed to the Jewish burial practice of wrapping the head separately, as confirmed by the description of the discarded headcloth in the tomb (John 20:7).[1]

The Turin Shroud only came to prominence when a photograph taken in 1898 showed the haunting image of an apparently crucified man. Radiocarbon testing, analysis of the blood stains (which show a blood type that only originated in the early Middle Ages) and fragments of plants and rock from Palestine suggest that the Shroud was created there, like other known relics, between AD 1260 and 1390, but every single test has been challenged by those who claim that the image could only have been made in the first century, perhaps even through a burst of radiation prefiguring the Resurrection of Christ. There remains enough doubt about the process through which the image may have been created to allow believers to continue their veneration. The Catholic Church itself refuses to comment on the authenticity of the Shroud, saying that this is purely a scientific question.

Relics were immensely important to medieval life, yet their role has consistently been underestimated or even, in some histories of the medieval Church, virtually ignored. Certainly they are not given the prominence that they deserve. It is quite extraordinary that there has been no full-length study of medieval relics in English. Yet the material is overwhelming, not only in many books of medieval miracles and the legends of the saints who effected them, but in continuing cults and sacred objects that are still venerated today.

I was recently exploring a church in a hill town in the Italian Marche with some Protestant friends who were used to bare altars. It had on its high altar a lifesize statue of Saint Martin, two glass-fronted cases of relics of other saints and only a candle in a lamp to show that a consecrated host, the 'real' body and blood of Jesus Christ, was among them. In the remainder of the church there was a single example of Christ on a crucifix on a side wall and another box of relics. Images of the Virgin Mary, usually with the baby Jesus, were more popular than any other and the two were shown perched on the roof of a model of Mary's house from Nazareth, the relic of which was to be seen at nearby Loreto. In the Middle Ages, an age when the Bible stories were not even available in vernacular languages, there was ample scope for the imaginative use of the bodies, whole or fragmented, of holy men and women to inject vitality into everyday spiritual life. Unless one gets within this mentality – one in which a variety of spiritual forces, some favoured by the Church, others by local communities, others by local magnates or royalty, worked together sometimes in consensus and sometimes in opposition – medieval religion does not make much sense. It was, in effect, a polytheism that endured long after the traditional pagan gods of the Mediterranean had been expelled. It is centred on an extraordinary variety of objects that were treated as sacred.

There was, in essence, a community of the supernatural in which most medieval people lived. It is alien to our own 'scientific' times and therefore risks giving the impression that this was a world where credulity ruled. My approach will instead be inspired by that proposal by Robert Orsi in his book *Between Heaven and Earth*, in which he explores the relationship of Catholics with their saints through the reminiscences of his own family.[2] Most of his relations had saints whose personalities, experiences and sufferings reflected their own. Orsi shows how the building up of this group of imaginary friends gave a psychological balance to their lives that it would be unwise to dismiss. One major theme of my book is an exploration of how the tribulations of life, combined with the very specific burden of dread laid by the medieval conception of the afterlife, drove the helpless masses into a world 'between heaven and earth', the only part of their lives that they could fashion for themselves.

This is, of course, only one part of the story. Relics fulfilled many other functions, as prestige items, money-spinners, talismans against disaster and as the focus of community identity. They are so common as a backdrop to everyday spiritual activity that they are often mentioned only in documents in passing. It is, in fact, one of the most remarkable features of the cults that they were accepted at every level of life, among rich and poor, king and serf, theologian and the illiterate, without challenge. Traditions of rational enquiry, such as developed in the medieval period, left the status of relics as miracle-workers undisturbed.

Of course, to shift one's consciousness into the supernatural, the space 'between heaven and earth', is to lessen one's attention to the immediacy of the natural world, and this had its own effects. It is beyond the scope of this book to assess how European society might have been shaped if the cults had not been destroyed in some parts of Europe in the sixteenth century. Their destruction is only one of the reasons why, from the seventeenth century onwards, the vitality of the Protestant north and its breakthroughs in science contrasted with the stagnant intellectual life of Italy and Spain. I have tried to view the cults as an integral part of everyday life in the Middle Ages and not beyond.

As there is no precedent for a history of relics from the 380s to 1600, it proved very difficult to find a suitable structure for the book. My editors at Yale, Heather McCallum and Rachael Lonsdale, have been enormously important in helping to define a structure that works and keeping the focus on relics at the forefront of a very complex millennium in European history. They deserve very special thanks for giving time to the book over and beyond what I could have expected. I am also grateful to Martin Llewellyn who read the text 'in house' and made helpful comments. Two anonymous academic readers confirmed or challenged some of my assertions and suggested further reading that I had missed.

Religious imagery flourished in the medieval world and, as relics and miracles were such an important part of it, we were overwhelmed with material for the illustrations. I have tried to present a variety from different contexts and here the Yale picture researcher Sophie Sheldrake has been wonderful in digging out my choices from churches, medieval archives and picture galleries throughout Europe. Richard Mason has done a meticulous job as copy-editor, spotting many grammatical errors and even correcting some of my dates. Tami Halliday has brought the finished text up to the standards expected of Yale University Press. All remaining errors are my own.

Like any wandering enthusiast within the churches of Catholic Europe, I had long been aware of the importance of relics but I had never focused on them until this book began to mature in my mind. Awareness of their power has given a much broader dimension to my understanding of the medieval churches I visit. In the past three years, my wife Lydia has become used to my peering in dusty corners of churches, and explaining the importance of now obscure saints whose bones lie before us. She has been a steady and delightful companion in these excursions but with Paris as the home of the wonderful Sainte-Chapelle and not far from Chartres it has not all been hard work. Two good and erudite friends, Anthony Stanton and Manjula Salomon, have read the final version and given further comments. My friend Julian Barker keeps me on my toes on all matters theological as we explore medieval churches and, often medieval, pubs in my native Suffolk.

When I was talking about this book to my children, my son Tom reminded me of the days when we faced together the challenge of homework projects on medieval Europe set by the English National Curriculum in History. A good many times we scrambled over the remains of medieval castles and he was taken in search of remote county churches. We visited the Bayeux Tapestry together. So this book is dedicated to him in memory of those days before he took up the more modern pursuits of occupational psychology and jazz drumming. I hope he enjoys it.

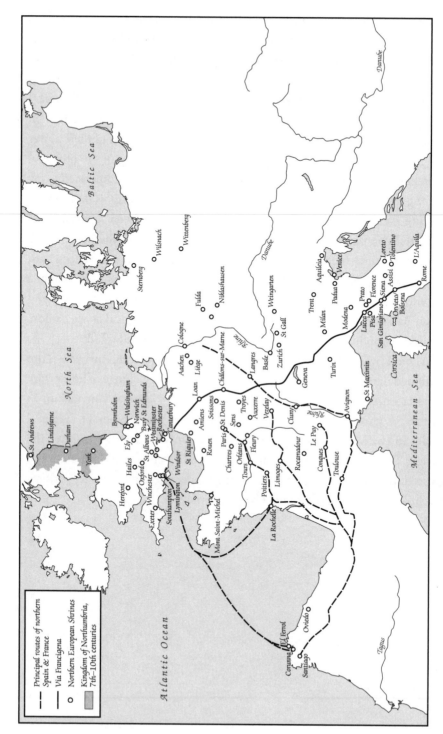

Map 1: The major medieval shrines and pilgrimage routes of northern and central Europe

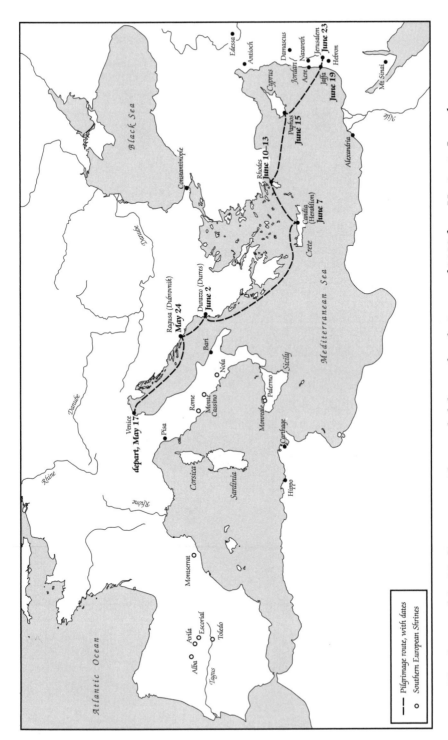

Map 2: The shrines of the Mediterranean with recorded dates of a pilgrimage of 1458 from Venice to Jerusalem

Prologue: The Making of a Martyr

THE FIRST downward slice of the sword glanced off the archbishop's skull and cut through to the shoulder bone, almost severing the arm of one of his attendants as the weapon fell. Two more slashing cuts on his head followed and the archbishop slumped dying to the ground. Then the top of his head was sliced off and finally the exposed brains were scraped out from the skull and scattered on the cathedral floor.

The shockwaves of the outrage, committed on 29 December 1170, spread across Europe. For the man who had just been murdered by four knights sent from the court of King Henry II was the Archbishop of Canterbury, Thomas Becket, and he had been cut down on the cold floor of his own cathedral. Rumours were soon spreading that he had been killed on the orders of the king and that he was a martyr not only for his own beliefs but for all those who upheld the privileges of the Church over those of the State.[1]

For six years Thomas had been in France, in self-imposed exile after falling out with Henry, and had only returned to his diocese a few days earlier. He had faced a tumultuous welcome. An unscrupulous and rapacious local family, the de Brocs, had ravaged his lands and even occupied the archbishop's palace while he had been away. They had made themselves deeply hated. Now a joyful procession of monks and clergy led Thomas through the crowds to his cathedral where hymns and the fanfare of trumpets greeted him. Those chroniclers who, after his death, described Thomas's arrival knew how to craft the accounts as portents of his impending fate. 'For wherever the archbishop passed', recorded Herbert of Bosham:

a throng of paupers ran up to him in a group, some prostrating themselves on the road, others tearing off their garments and spreading them on the road, crying out again and again: 'Blessed is he who comes in the name of the Lord'. . . . If you had seen it . . . you would have said without question that the Lord was for the second time approaching his passion and that He who once died at Jerusalem to save the whole world had come again to die at Canterbury for the English Church.

Thomas was not wholly innocent, however. Always an arrogant man, he had proved obsessive about preserving his privileges. In the previous June, King Henry II had arranged the coronation of his son, another Henry (young King Henry), at Westminster Abbey. Shared rule had been a device used successfully by the French kings, although in this case the young Henry was to die before his father. Thomas was still in exile at the time, so it was the Archbishop of York, supported by the bishops of London and Salisbury, who carried out the anointing. When he heard the news, Thomas's temper got the better of him. Just before he left France, he excommunicated the three bishops for usurping his prerogative as Archbishop of Canterbury to preside at the coronation. It was extraordinarily provocative for Thomas to declare war on the senior bishops of the Church of which he claimed to be head, just when a reconciliation between Henry and himself, arranged by Pope Alexander III and allowing him to return to England, seemed in place.

The news that Thomas, now back in Canterbury, had excommunicated the three bishops and thus, in Henry's eyes, invalidated the coronation, reached the king while he was at Bur-le-Roi in his Norman territory. It was the final straw in a relationship that had long been in tatters. Thomas had been appointed Henry's chancellor after a dramatic rise from relatively humble beginnings. When he appointed him archbishop in 1162, Henry expected him to continue to put the king's business first. He had forgotten that Thomas had studied Church law in Paris and Bologna, and Thomas now decided that his commitment to the Church took precedence. At a time when the Crown had been trying to extend its powers into Church affairs, Thomas declared himself a defender of its privileges. For Henry, the betrayal was unforgivable.

'A man who has eaten my bread, who came to my court poor, and I have raised him high – now he draws up his heel to kick me in the teeth' was

Henry's furious response to the news of the excommunications. 'Thomas has shamed my kin, shamed my realm, the grief goes to my hearts, and no one has avenged me.' His words struck a chord in a fractious court. Tensions were heightened when, a few days later, the excommunicated bishops themselves arrived. It was now that four barons, Reginald FitzUrse, William de Tracy, Hugh de Morville and Richard Brito, all important men, decided to act. On 26 December 1170 they left Normandy and on the 28th they arrived at Saltwood Castle in Kent, where they knew that its owners, the de Broc family, would welcome them. It appears that their aim was no more than to arrest Thomas and bring him to the young King Henry as a prisoner.

The next day the barons gathered an armed detachment from the garrisons of neighbouring royal castles and surrounded Canterbury. They announced that they were on king's business: the citizens were ordered to stay indoors as the barons and twelve knights entered the hall of the archbishop's palace to confront Thomas. They had left their arms outside. Thomas had just finished dining but appeared from a private chamber to meet them. The knights demanded that he absolve the excommunicated bishops and go with them to the new king. Thomas refused and the barons withdrew and this time they armed themselves. They barged their way back into a palace that had now been shuttered against them. Thomas drew back into the main body of the cathedral but he made no attempt to barricade the doors behind him. There were taunts and scuffling, and then what had been an attempt simply to hold Thomas captive degenerated into the vicious attack that led to his death. Either FitzUrse or de Tracy struck the first blow and de Tracy the second. Brito sliced open the skull and a clerk of Hugh de Morville scattered the brains. The murderers went on to ransack Thomas's palace.

Today a police investigation of the murder would move through an ordered ritual. In a sense this was what happened in 1170, but it was a ritual of a very different kind. The focus now was on the proof of Thomas's sanctity. There was no doubt in the minds of the shocked monks and other onlookers that Thomas was a martyr. Benedict of Peterborough, a monk who was a witness to the events, believed that the ransacking of the palace was an imitation of the division of Christ's clothes at his Crucifixion and in itself a sign from God that a martyrdom had taken place. One could always tell a martyr by the serenity of his countenance and the preservation of his features, however gruesome the reality of his death. So, as Benedict goes on to describe, with Thomas, 'while blood in the likeness of a crown, perhaps in a sign of sanctity, lay around his head, his face nevertheless seemed entirely freed from blood, except for a thin line, which descended from the right temple to the left cheek crossing his nose'. When Thomas later appeared in visions, Benedict tells us, those experiencing them described him in the same way, even though they had not seen him lying dead.

Of course it was not only appearance that made a martyr. Miracles were supposed to be made possible through the medium of his body. When Nikon, a popular preacher in the Peloponnese who went by the name 'Ho Metanoeite' ('Repent Ye'), died in about 1000, the waiting crowds, summoned by the saint himself to his deathbed, set upon the corpse:

> One hastened to carry away something from the squalid locks on the blessed man's head, another something from the hairs in his beard, still another a patch from his old cloak and from his goatskin outer garment. And so it was a great and illustrious thing for all to carry way some of the things touching the skin of the holy remains, for relief from sufferings and every sort of disease.[2]

In the same way there was no time to be lost in accumulating as many parts of Thomas as there were to be had, and crowds soon gathered:

> As he lay still on the pavement then, some daubed their eyes with blood, others who had brought little vessels made away with as much as they could, while others eagerly dipped in parts of their clothes they had cut off: later no one seemed happy with themselves unless they had taken something away, however insignificant, from this precious treasure.[3]

His *pallium*, the stole that was a symbol of Thomas's office, and his outer garment were soaked in blood and these were later given to some poor. Benedict condemns them for selling the relics on, not for the act itself, but because they charged far too little for such precious objects. Relics were part of the medieval economy, with a monetary as well as a spiritual value.

Rumours now went around that Thomas's body had been removed and destroyed by the de Brocs. They were said to have hung it up as if he was a felon or thrown it into a drain. Destroying a saint's body was a well-known way of stifling the beginning of a cult – it could hardly prosper without something tangible to venerate. The monks were taking no chances. They gathered up the body as soon as they could and buried it without washing or embalming it. As the corpse of a martyr, its own blood had given it perfume and no spices needed to be added. While stripping the body, however, the monks found a hair shirt worn against the skin. Thomas's arrogance and high living had been legendary, but this sign of austerity had a powerful effect on those who saw it.

The first miracles followed shortly afterwards. A witness to the murder who had dipped his shirt in the saint's blood took it home that night to his paralysed wife. She asked that the blood be mixed with water and she be washed with it. Her paralysis was cured immediately. Ampoules containing the diluted blood were soon circulating. 'Innumerable sick' were cured, those on the point of death survived and the blood 'even succeeded in bringing some back from the dead'.

At first the cathedral was closed as it had been polluted by the violation of the murder, but by 2 April access to the crypt was given to pilgrims. By December 1171, when the upper church was reopened, another fifteen cures had been reported and the pilgrims had begun to flock in. The miracles were recorded in a large book where they were publicly read out in the chapter house. One John of Salisbury told some interested enquirers in France that 'both in the place of his passion and before the high altar, where he spent the night before burial, and at the place of burial, the paralyzed are cured, the blind see, the deaf hear, the mute speak, the crippled walk, the fevered are relieved, the possessed are freed from the devil, and the sick are cured from diverse illnesses'. Eventually there were two volumes with a total of four hundred miracles from the shrine at Canterbury alone. Thomas's enemies were not convinced. They accepted that apparent miracles had taken place but these had been caused by the magical practices of the monks, not by the will of God. Magic, effected either by angels or devils, pervaded the medieval world. As even devils were able to perform apparently good deeds to mislead the unwary, sorting out the genuine contributions of a saint was always a challenge.

As the list of miracles lengthened, the prior of Canterbury felt confident enough to send a petition to the Pope for Thomas's canonisation and so receive formal recognition that Thomas had indeed gone straight to the glory of heaven. 'Thomas, of holy memory, once archbishop of Canterbury, who accepting the supreme penalty in defence of the Church's liberties, attained the crown of martyrdom, as the virtues of the miracles which God is working through him makes manifest.' Pope Alexander III needed no further encouragement. Here was his opportunity to promote a saint who would attract all those distrustful of the ambitions of secular governments. He appointed two cardinals to study the authenticity of the miracles and in February 1173 he announced the canonisation.

Henry II had been outmanoeuvred. He was shattered by the news of the death of Becket, perhaps because he had some residual affection for the man who had once been so close to him, but he was also horrified at what his outburst had led to. He condemned the murderers and they were ashamed enough to seek penance from the Pope himself. All four were ordered to take a pilgrimage to the Holy Land from which none are known to have returned. Henry tried to present a doctored version of his own role to the Pope, but it was swamped by eyewitness accounts from Canterbury and popular revulsion. The Pope issued a personal interdict on him and Henry was forced into making major concessions to the Church. He would no longer impede appeals on Church matters to the Pope, and the secular courts surrendered their right to judge clerics.

Henry's final gesture was the most effective of all. He made a pilgrimage to Thomas's shrine at Canterbury and did penance there. Every time he returned to England from abroad he visited the shrine. He made the final approach on his bare feet and submitted to being flogged by the monks. Whether his remorse was genuine or merely a public relations stunt, some form of reconciliation had at last been made. By now, however, the cult of Thomas Becket had spread throughout Europe. Within ten years Thomas could be seen prominently displayed on a mosaic in Monreale Cathedral in Sicily, and churches dedicated to Thomas are to be found throughout Catholic Europe.

The original burial place of Thomas was soon judged to be unworthy of him. The bodies of saints must be encased in marble rather than stone, and above ground where the shrine can be a focus for worship. An opportunity was given when the choir of Canterbury was burned down in 1174. By this time the Gothic style had been born in France (see Chapter 12 below) and it was copied at Canterbury in what was the first major example in England. The columns of the circular chapel at the east end of the cathedral drew on rose-pink marble from Tournai interspersed with white limestone. This was a deliberate re-enactment of Thomas's scattered blood and brains. The shape, the corona, stood for his martyr's crown while the extensive window-glass told of his martyrdom and miracles.[4]

In 1218 Archbishop Stephen Langton made an announcement that spread across Europe. The corona was finished. In the summer of 1220 there would be a grand *translatio*, the ceremony in which a saint's bones are moved, usually to a more prestigious part of a church or cathedral, and in Thomas's case, the corona. *Translationes* were always commemorated annu-ally and the date, 7 July, ensured that Thomas would be honoured by pilgrims on each anniversary at a time when settled seas and dry roads would allow them to reach Canterbury. The body was exhumed. By this time the flesh had decayed, but the recovered bones were now wrapped in silk. Langton shrewdly kept back a few small ones 'for distributing to great men and churches for the honour of the martyr'. The festivities, conducted by the archbishop in the company of twenty-four other bishops and archbishops in the presence of the young King Henry III and the papal legate, lasted two weeks. A banquet for 33,000 pilgrims was held four days before the *translatio* and on the day itself wine ran in the streets. The cathedral was still paying off the debt four bishops later.[5]

In return, the long-term revenues of what became by far the wealthiest shrine in England were immense. In the first years after Thomas's death, offerings at the shrine brought in 28 per cent of the total income of a cathe-dral that was already well endowed. In the year of the *translatio*, revenues from the shrine amounted to £1,142, two-thirds of the income. Three hundred years later, the Venetian ambassador visited the shrine and reported back home. 'The shrine is entirely covered with plates of pure gold. But the gold is scarcely visible beneath a profusion of gems, including sapphires, diamonds, rubies and emeralds ... exquisite designs have been carved all over it and immense gems worked intricately into the patterns.'[6] As we shall see, the successes of the shrine depended hugely on their glamour and glitter in an age where most communities were remote and living stan-dards were still well below those of the Roman empire.

The story of Thomas's transition from haughty archbishop to martyr and through this to the glorification of his relics in a golden shrine echoes, if at an elevated level, thousands from the Middle Ages. In classical Latin, the word *reliquiae* refers specifically to the physical remains or ashes of a dead human being, but by the end of the sixth century, in the *Dialogues* of Pope Gregory the Great, for instance, it was used in this sense to include everything from the foreskin of Jesus discarded at his circumcision, the hair or milk of the Virgin Mary, the bodies of Apostles – but also anything that may have been associated with them; their clothes, for example, or even any object that had touched them, *brandea* as they were known. The instruments of the Crucifixion, the Cross itself, or the lance that had pierced Jesus's side, might appear to have been contaminated by their role in the killing of the Son of God, but they too were assumed to have a sacred power. Even the thirty pieces of silver given to Judas could be seen in Rome. Wood, human hair, lances, shrouds and veils, all claiming to be the authentic originals, emerged in the centuries that followed the fall of the Roman empire. So the assembled body parts of Thomas were taking their place in a long-established tradition of the veneration of sacred objects. A web of shrines covered the European landscape and created a layer of consciousness of the sacred that it is the purpose of this book to explore.

CHAPTER ONE

How the Christian Relic Emerged

Mᴇᴅɪᴇᴠᴀʟ Cʜʀɪꜱᴛɪᴀɴɪᴛʏ had its distinctive qualities but it shared many of the features of the polytheistic religions that had been traditional to the Mediterranean for many centuries before Christ. The creation of an altar or shrine over the body of a 'hero' was a very ancient practice. Achilles had so honoured his beloved friend Patroclus before his own death in the Trojan War. Homer tells how:

> 'In tears' the mourners 'gathered their gentle comrade's white bones,
> All in a golden urn, sealed with a double fold of fat,
> And stowed the urn in his shelter, covered well
> With a light linen shroud, then laid his barrow out.'[1]

Later generations created a tomb for the mythical Achilles, and Alexander the Great visited it when he arrived in Asia in 334 on his conquest of Persia. He took some 'relics' in the shape of Achilles' supposed armour from the shrine's temple with him as a talisman. In 475 ʙᴄ the Athenian general Cimon conquered the Aegean island of Skyros for his city. He had been alerted by an oracle that he would find 'a coffin of a great corpse with a bronze spear-head by its side and a sword'. This would be the body of none other than Theseus, the founder-king of Athens. The bones were uncovered and brought back for honoured burial in Athens.[2]

'Heroes', namely saints and martyrs, translated easily into the Christian world. Early Christian commemorative rituals were close to those already followed in the pagan world. In fact, one of the difficulties in charting the spread of early Christianity is that practices at the tombs of martyrs echoed those at pagan shrines. Recent archaeological work is stressing how much of Christianity took place in cemeteries, away from the instutional elite.[3] So in Egypt, the bodies of saints were approached with similar questions to those offered to pagan oracles, on business affairs, marital issues, pregnancies and foreign travel. There was also a long tradition of healing shrines in the ancient world. Epidaurus, one of the most prestigious of the shrines of the healing god Aesclepius in the Greek Peloponnese, maintained a sanctuary that no one might enter before being purified. Ritual sacrifices were made to the god before the afflicted visitor bedded down in a dormitory alongside Aesclepius' temple. The inscriptions from Epidaurus and other ancient healing shrines show that 'miracle' cures were expected, often after Aesclepius had appeared to the visitor in a dream with advice or a remedy. The Christian shrine of Saints Cyrus and John at Menouthis near Alexandria seems to have operated in just the same way.

Similarly, pilgrimages to sacred shrines were not a specifically Christian practice. Christian pilgrimages did, of course, have 'Christian' destinations, predominantly the Holy Land or Rome, but visitors to oracle sites, such as Delphi, or sanctuaries such as that of Artemis in Ephesus or Aesclepius at Epidaurus, were surely pilgrims too, as were those Jews scattered by the diaspora who returned to Jerusalem. They had undertaken a journey; it had a sacred purpose, and lifted them out of the routines of everyday life. The shrines they visited may have had as deeply emotional an impact on them as would the later opulent churches of the Christian relic cults.[4] So the bodies of saints may represent a very different kind of religious tradition but they were often presented in contexts that would have been familiar. Although many pagan temples were destroyed by Christian mobs, others were converted into Christian churches. Gregory the Great (Pope 590–604) asked no more than that pagan buildings be blessed with holy water and supplied with relics before Christians began to use them.

Christianity did, however, bring with it a major shift in the way miracles were perceived. One of the principal achievements of the ancient Greeks was to suggest that the workings of the natural world might be understood at a complex level that did not depend on the intervention of the gods. The philosopher Aristotle can be seen as the founder of this approach in the fourth century BC. It was grasped by Aristotle and those in the tradition of intellectual enquiry he initiated, that if an earthquake took place or a person suffered an epileptic fit there might be a natural cause that did not require the direct involvement of a god or gods. Aristotle, who has been seen as 'probably the most significant figure in the history of Western thought up to the end of the sixteenth century',[5] went further in trying to understand the underlying purpose of the natural world. All would eventually be understood through patient enquiry, the accumulation of empirical evidence (again Aristotle was a pioneer here) and reflection on it. There might be no place for miracles. Aristotle's world was presided over, in fact, by an Unmoved Mover who made no direct interventions at all.

This 'rational' approach lasted well into the second and third centuries AD, and even in the fourth century it pervades the works of many of those involved in theological debate. Of course, it was only a tiny, if brilliant and influential, elite who ever thought this way, and the potency of the sacred remained part of everyday life for the majority. The rise of a more authoritarian empire in the fourth century, as the barbarian tribes closed in and the Christian emperors used their adopted religion as a means through which to establish their authority, challenged the untrammelled use of reason. Whereas pagan philosophy had flourished on free debate, Christians taught the overwhelming power of a God who demanded obedience. The Christian mind conceived the sphere of heaven encircling the earth, where heaven was a place of perfection in contrast to the unstable and decaying material world. There was a major shift of attention away from interest in the natural world – it was to last until the sixteenth century. This was understandable if the need was now to comprehend the mind of God. John Chrysostom, the brilliant but severe preacher who was Bishop of Constantinople in the early fifth century, is typical in asking God to clear his mind of secular learning so that he might be open instead to 'the reception of divine words'. This is the beginning of the shift of the educated elite into the world of the Christian supernatural.

Reason depends on axioms, the foundations from which logical thought progresses. Axioms are considered incontrovertible but what is seen as 'incontrovertible' may vary with the historical context. Once it had become axiomatic that there was one supreme God, expressed in a Trinity of God the Father, Christ the Son and the Holy Spirit, the doctrine laid down in law by the Christian emperor Theodosius in AD 381, it was not irrational to say that

God could change the world at will. Nothing that exists or happens can be against nature 'because nothing is impossible for God, when everything that exists is the will of God, and whatever God wills has singular existence'.[6] Philastrius, bishop of the Italian city of Brescia, writing at the end of the fourth century, subverted the empirical tradition in his analysis of the causes of earthquakes. 'There is a certain heresy concerning earthquakes, that they come not from God's command, but, it is thought, from the very nature of the elements. Paying no attention to God's power, the heretics presume to attribute the motions of force to the elements of nature like certain foolish philosophers, who, ascribing this to nature, know not the power of God.'[7] So Christians assumed that God could intervene in the material world and rational explanations of natural phenomena were now seen to be 'heretical'. With the abeyance of the Aristotelean tradition, there were no restraints on belief in the miraculous and it was at the shrines that miracles happened, often on a daily basis.

There was a further development, one that was totally alien to the pagan world. Christ had preached in the Gospels that the saved would be separated from the unsaved and those rejected would burn eternally (Matthew 13:38). Four centuries later the theologian Augustine had gone further and argued that as a result of the sin of Adam, the 'original sin' passed down to all generations of humanity, none deserved to escape the wrath of God. As an old man, Augustine preached that salvation was always unjustified but it might be granted, somewhat capriciously it seems, through the grace of God. His ideas brought a tragic quality to human existence but Augustine appears indifferent to this. In the melancholic final chapters of his *City of God* he seems almost to revel in the fact that the vast majority of his fellow human beings will suffer for eternity. It is one of the great paradoxes of western theology that in the Middle Ages Augustine's texts became almost as authoritative as the Scriptures. It is still hard to grasp the devastating impact of his views on eternal punishment. For many centuries to come, the Church leaders followed Augustine in revelling in the vileness of human nature, the certainty that most would be punished for the genes of original sin they could not avoid inheriting.[8]

There might, however, be a way out. Pagan philosophers such as Plato had argued that the 'Supreme Good', God, could not be swayed by prayer or sacrifice. By contrast Christians believed that God, or Christ in his role as

judge, could, despite starting from a position of anger due to his outrage over the sin of Adam, be prevailed upon by the minority of souls who had already been saved – and were with him in heaven – to save others. In this sense the Christian God was a much less rational and less stable deity than that conceived by the philosophers – He was, even if only in rare circumstances, amenable to pressure. The mother of Christ, the Virgin Mary, was the obvious intercessor, the most likely of all to be listened to, but those who had suffered as martyrs or had led exemplary lives would also play their part if pleaded by sinners to do so, and the bodies of such martyrs and saints acted as the medium through which heaven could be reached. Nothing could ensure success, of course, because, as Augustine argued, no sinner deserved it, but the remote possibility explains the many accounts of the outbursts of emotion, hysteria and self-abasement that accompanied the exposition of relics. The saints might just succeed in persuading God or Christ to relent.

There needed, however, to be a focus for the veneration of saints and martyrs. With the granting of toleration to Christians by the emperor Constantine in AD 313, the bodies of martyrs from the second- and third-century persecutions of Christians could be brought out into the open, and it became the custom to place them in the central altar of the new basilicas. A verse from the Book of Revelation (6:9) – 'I saw under the altar the souls of them that were slain for the word of God and the testimony which they held' – endorsed the practice, thus providing an effective link between Scripture and the veneration of Christian martyrs. Those bodies that had not been moved remained in cemeteries where the tradition continued of the bereaved visiting them on the anniversary of their deaths. There is a fascinating homily preached by John Chrysostom at a martyrs' festival in which he sets out his advice for the veneration of a martyr:

Stay beside the tomb of the martyr; there pour out fountains of tears. Have a contrite mind; raise a blessing from the tomb. Take him as an advocate in your prayers and immerse yourself perpetually in the stories of his struggles. Embrace the coffin, nail yourself to the chest. Not just the martyrs' bones, but even their tombs and chests burn with a great deal of blessing. Take holy oil and anoint your whole body – your tongue, your lips, your neck, your eyes.[9]

So evolved a distinct role for relics that went beyond anything known in the pagan world. They were linked to the Christian narrative, to the events and personalities described in the Gospels or to the years of persecution. They had a dual power. They were a medium through which a saint or holy figure such as the Virgin Mary could be reached and called on to intercede for the salvation of sinners. Relics were also objects through which miracles could be effected. These might be benign as in a cure, or malign, as in the striking down of pagans and other malefactors.

There are so many other levels of experience that will emerge in this book. The saints have personalities. Some, such as the Virgin Mary, play many different nurturing and protective roles. Others have had specific experiences during their earthly lives, some of which can be historically verified, though most are legendary, that appeal to the supplicant at the shrine. In medieval Europe, the shrines of the saints became objects of awe in themselves. The reliquaries are golden and studded with jewels, the shrine dominates the landscape. So the pilgrim comes to see a form of theatre, and is enriched by the flamboyant processions and expositions of the relics on their feast days. The relic reaches out to the supplicants, the supplicants infuse the relics with their hopes. There are the makings of an enduring relationship, sometimes at an intimate level as when a statue of the Virgin Mary offered her breasts to Bernard of Clairvaux to suck, or when a communicant receives the body and blood of Christ in the Eucharist.

It remains hard to know exactly where the power of relics is to be found and the parameters within which they exercised their authority.[10] Something of the answer may lie in the way that relics were displayed and dramatised as symbols of spiritual and political power. This was a development of the late fourth century AD.

CHAPTER TWO

The Incorruptible Flesh
of the Martyrs

It WAS in the city of Milan, the Roman Mediolanum, northern Italy, in the 380s AD that Christian relics first became part of a dramatic display. Since the late third century, the vast Roman empire had been divided into separate territories, usually two, a Latin-speaking west and a Greek-speaking east, to make defence more manageable. Each had their own emperor, although the two often collaborated in fighting off threats. The western emperors were based in Milan rather than in Rome, which was too far south from the threatened northern borders.

In the summer of AD 386, however, Milan was in crisis. The fourteen-year-old emperor of the west, Valentinian II, had found himself in deadlock with the city's bishop, Ambrose. Ambrose had been a provincial governor, not even a baptised Christian, when made bishop in 374, at a time when there was a great deal of unrest in the Christian community over rival interpretations of doctrine. He was a powerful man. He soon brought order to his fractured congregation and then emerged as a formidable defender of the Church, against pagans, heretics and the emperors who tried to thwart him.[1]

Ambrose and Valentinian were fighting over control of San Lorenzo, one of the churches in the city that the imperial family claimed was theirs to use. Ambrose had opposed them because, in his eyes, Valentinian and his redoubtable mother Justina were heretics, clinging to the Arian doctrine, which preached that Christ was subordinate to God the Father. Ambrose was a fervent believer in the doctrine that Father and Son were 'one in substance', and thus equal with each other, declared at the First Council of Nicaea that had been presided over by the Emperor Constantine in 325. Ambrose must have felt that history was on his side as Theodosius I, the

15

emperor of the eastern half of the empire, had also declared Arianism heretical in 381 and imposed legislation to support the Nicene alternative and suppress the Arians. He had included the Holy Spirit with Father and Son as the third in a Trinity.

In January 386 Valentinian tried to break the deadlock. Ignoring the initiative of his co-emperor Theodosius in the east, he promulgated a law preserving the Arian faith in the western empire. On the face of it Ambrose was vulnerable, but Valentinian's own position in the empire was also weak. He was still only fourteen and he had already been challenged by a usurper, Maximus, who now controlled Britain and Gaul. The barbarian tribes hovered along the northern frontiers of the empire, only held in check by determined forays against their bases. Unrest in Milan could not be risked. Within the city Ambrose had built up his own enthusiastic congregations, and when Valentinian used his troops in an attempt to seize a church at Easter 386, they were met by a crowd whipped up by the bishop. Rather than risk a massacre, Valentinian withdrew, but it was a humiliating climbdown. Milan remained tense and Ambrose searched for a dramatic coup to push home his advantage.

Again the coup centred on a church. Ambrose was just completing a large new basilica, the Basilica Ambrosiana. Something of his dominating personality can be sensed from its dedication, as this is the first Christian church known to have been named after its founder. Now it was ready for consecration and the reception of the bones of saints. Milan had experienced little persecution and there was hardly any record of buried martyrs. Yet Ambrose now surprised everyone by announcing that he knew where some local martyrs were buried, and a procession was organised to find them. It followed with great anticipation where Ambrose led it, to a small martyrs' memorial outside the city. Here the bishop ordered digging to begin and sure enough two bodies began to emerge. Ambrose later told his sister that the bones were intact with much blood on them. They now had to be given authenticity and Ambrose had prepared for this. He pushed forward some victims of demonic possession, and a devil, confronted by the awesome power of saintly remains, cried out from one of them that the bodies were indeed those of martyrs. It named them as Gervasius and Protasius. Some old men were then produced to claim that they recognised these names as those of martyred Christians from many decades before. The bodies were loaded up onto a cart and the procession then set off back into the city with its sacred cargo. There was more excitement when a blind man rubbed a cloth on the bones and then on himself and his sight was restored. Ambrose, in a sermon two days later when the bones were installed in the new basilica, claimed that their miraculous power confirmed that the Nicene version of the Trinity was the correct one.

Milan had a sophisticated intellectual elite and Ambrose was widely mocked by the court and more educated citizens. How could anyone know that he had not planted the bodies as well as the 'possessed' bystanders who had been paid to scream out at the right moment? The miracle was simply too opportune and surely the claim that it showed that God favoured one doctrine over another was pure manipulation. However, in a series of impassioned sermons, with hymn chanting to match, Ambrose grasped the protective power of the revealed martyrs for the city. Those who scoffed were no better than the Jews who had questioned the miracle of the blind man being healed by Jesus (John 9:13–23). The Jews were always a safe target and Ambrose's dramatic presentation quelled his critics. Valentinian and Justina had been openly defied and Maximus soon exploited their weakness. The next year he moved into Italy, forcing Valentinian and Justina to flee to the east. Theodosius came to their support, counter-attacked and entered Milan. However, Ambrose was now sure of imperial approval from a fellow Nicene. Despite having his own conflicts with Theodosius, Ambrose still lies near the high altar of his basilica with the bodies of his martyrs beside him.

Ambrose had created a precedent that was to be of vital importance in establishing cults in early medieval Europe. This was to dramatise relics so that they became a public demonstration of sacred power. And this power could be channelled to achieve the ends of the celebrant who controlled it. Ambrose was manipulating centuries-old rituals of display in a completely new context, the proclamation of the majesty of God, and here Nicene orthodoxy, as supreme even over an emperor.

Ambrose was treading on dangerous ground. In the same year, Theodosius issued a law forbidding corpses to be brought for burial within city walls. Dead flesh was disgusting and dangerous. The risk of contamination had always been recognised and Theodosius was doing no more than reaffirming custom and good sense. As the scoffing of Ambrose shows, the use of body parts to effect miracles also went deeply against the traditions and instincts of Greek and Roman society. The philosophers had long taught that the appetites and desires of the living body subverted the effectiveness of rational thought and contemplation. The use of bodies as a medium through which miracles could be achieved was beyond comprehension to anyone with an educated mind.

Christianity overcame these inhibitions through a development of an idea that was unique to it: there had been an original state of a spiritual flesh that had been lost at the Fall of Adam and Eve from Paradise. 'Our sacred books tell us', writes Augustine, 'that this human flesh of ours was differently constituted before man's sin . . . it was possible for this flesh never to suffer death. . . . This condition changed after man's sin, and man's flesh became what it has always been known to be in this distressful situation of mortality.' So there is a spiritual immortal form of human flesh from before the Fall, and a physical mortal one from after it.[2] Augustine is here, as so often, inspired by the Apostle Paul. Paul saw Christ as acquiring a spiritual body after his Resurrection that would act as the 'first fruits' for others. 'As in Adam all men die [i.e. lose their original spiritual flesh], so in Christ all will be brought to life.' And so, too, will those who follow Christ. Christ 'will change our lowly body into the likeness of his glorious body, by the power which enables him even to subject all things to himself' (Philippians 3:20). So joining the Christian community gives one the chance to regain a pre-fallen state of one's flesh and the hope of eternal life in heaven. Paul makes it clear, in fact, that no one can enter heaven without the fallen mortal flesh being transformed. 'The perishable cannot possess immortality . . . the trumpet will sound and the dead will rise immortal and we shall be changed. This perishable being must be clothed with the imperishable, and what is mortal must be clothed with immortality.' (1 Corinthians: 15)

The question that buzzed around the early Christian communities was whether this transformation from mortal to immortal could begin on earth before death. In 2 Timothy 2:18, we are told that there were Christians who believed that their resurrection had already taken place on earth, although they are condemned for this. Others believed that it was through receiving the body and blood of Christ at the Eucharist that one's mortal body could move towards the ultimate transformation. In the words of Ignatius, Bishop of Antioch, the capital of the province of Syria, at the beginning of the second century AD, the Eucharist is referred to as 'the medicine of immortality and

an antidote, that we not die, but live forever in Jesus Christ'. At the end of
the second century Irenaeus, Bishop of Lyons, asks 'How can they affirm
that the flesh is incapable of receiving life eternal, which flesh is nourished
from the body and blood of the Lord and is a member of him [sic].' There
was a widespread belief that the Eucharist allowed believers to embark on
the transition from a physical to a spiritual body even before death, through
the absorption of Jesus's body.

The process of transformation could be subverted by too much food and
sex. Fasting, for instance, helped maintain the body in a more spiritual form.
Tertullian, an austere Latin-speaking Christian from Carthage, who was
known for the rigidity of his views and power of his eloquence, assures his
listeners in his *Treatise on Fasting* that 'they who are in the [mortal] flesh
cannot please God'. Anyone who cares too much for the pleasure of the flesh
is doomed. Through the 'strait gate of salvation will slenderer flesh enter;
more speedily will lighter flesh rise [to heaven]; longer in the sepulchre will
drier flesh retain its firmness.'[3] In other words, abstinence creates a body
already primed to enter heaven. The ascetic Church Fathers, some writing
from their desert retreats, linked gluttony to lust. The spirituality of the body
would be lost if it was contaminated through intimate contact. Augustine
makes the same point in his *De sancta virginitate*. The good features of
marriage, such as the procreation of children, are merely temporal. Those
who adopt a life of virginity, on the other hand, achieve 'participation in the
life of angels and a foretaste of perpetual incorruption in the corruptible
flesh'.[4] Even if resurrection in the flesh could not be achieved during one's
lifetime, one could make progress towards it.

The process of transformation from a physical to a spiritual body could
also be achieved through martyrdom. The experience was emotionally
devastating for the early Christians who witnessed it. It involved not only
death but horrific mutilations of the martyrs' bodies when these were burnt,
crushed or mauled by animals in the arena. Yet these sufferings were recast
as providing an abrupt and glorious way of transforming the physical
remnants of the body into a spiritual entity.

There is a fascinating early example of this belief in a letter from Ignatius,
Bishop of Antioch. Ignatius had been arrested for refusing to sacrifice in
honour of the emperor and was being taken off to Rome for judgement and
certain martyrdom, perhaps about AD 107. The Christian community in

Rome had some influential members who were prepared to plead with the authorities that Ignatius should not be killed. Ignatius himself was having none of it. Foreseeing the ravages of wild beasts in the arena he enthused: 'Let me be ground by the teeth of wild beasts, that I may be found the pure bread of Christ.' Here the actual martyrdom itself is the means by which the body becomes the spiritual bread, transcending the material body that has been completely eliminated by the beasts.

A century later, in the early third century, Tertullian echoes this in suggesting that the very experience of martyrdom allows one to transcend the world of mortal flesh. The transformed body would not feel pain. 'The leg does not feel the chain when the mind is in the heavens.' So there are stories of martyrs rejoicing in the midst of their pain, of Lawrence, martyred in Rome in 258, asking to be turned over onto the other side as he was roasted on the grid. The glory of martyrdom anaesthetised any suffering experienced by the flesh that had itself moved beyond normal material sensation. This gave the martyr's body its sacred quality. John Chrysostom, Bishop of Constantinople, recorded the story of a martyr by the name of Drusus who was burned to death. 'And the smoke which rose up stifled the demons who were flying up there, put the devil to flight, and purified the air.'

The belief also developed that the body itself had become so transformed that it would remain uncorrupted by the torments of the persecutors. The Old Testament provided a precedent in the three men thrown into the fiery furnace by Nebuchadnezzar (Book of Daniel, Chapter 3), which told how they were able to dance about in the furnace without harm. The story was often represented on early Christian sarcophagi, as was the body of Jonah vomited from the whale and shown reclining naked on the shore, to make the point that the body is unblemished despite its ordeal. In the New Testament, Luke 21:18–19 proved a particularly influential text. 'Some of you will be put to death. . . . But not a hair of your head shall be lost. By standing firm you will win true life for yourself.'

Soon persecution stories were being written to reaffirm the incorruptible body as a reality. Two surviving accounts of martyrdoms in Smyrna, the trading port in Asia Minor (the modern Izmir), make the point. Polycarp, the bishop of the city, was especially revered because it was claimed that he had met John the Evangelist at the beginning of his life. His martyrdom took place about AD 155. When Polycarp was being burned, it was recorded that 'the fire took the shape of a vaulted room, like a ship's sail filled with the wind, and made a wall round the martyr's body, which was in the middle not like burning flesh but like gold and silver refined in a furnace. Indeed we were conscious of a wonderful fragrance, like a breath of frankincense or some other costly spice.' The 'birthday' of the martyrdom was celebrated each year and the bones were seen as 'more valuable than precious stones and purer than wrought iron'.[5]

The martyrdom of Pionius, a victim of the persecutions under the emperor Decius in AD 250, ends with the scene at the funeral pyre in which a body is transformed:

> After the fire had been extinguished, those of us who were present saw his body like that of an athlete in full array at the height of his powers. His ears were not distorted; his hair lay in order on the surface of his head; and his beard was full as though with the first blossom of hair. His face shone once again – wondrous grace! – so that the Christians were all the more confirmed in the faith, and those who had lost the faith returned dismayed and with fearful consciences.[6]

As the saints and martyrs were destined for heaven in any case, they did not have to wait for the Last Judgement. They could bypass the stench of decomposition that ordinary mortals suffered and which early Christian texts saw as one of the main evils of hell.

One could always recognise an unearthed corpse as that of a saint by the wholeness of his or her body. The fifth-century historian Sozomen records how the body of the Old Testament prophet Zachariah had turned up in Palestine after its discoverers had been alerted to the tomb by a dream. The centuries during which it had been buried had made no difference to the body. 'The prophet appeared sound; his hair was quite closely shorn, his nose was straight, his beard moderately grown, his head quite short, his eyes rather sunken, and concealed by the eyebrows.'[7] Similarly Sulpicius Severus, a devotee and biographer of St Martin of Tours, surveyed the remains of his hero who had died in AD 397. 'His body was white as snow: so much that people remarked: Who could believe that he had ever worn sackcloth or been covered with ashes. In fact, it seemed that the full glory of the coming resurrection and the new nature of the transfigured body was being displayed.' The triumph over putrefaction was complete and it was said that the flesh would exude sweetness – a foretaste of the atmosphere that would be found in heaven. The body did not even have to be that of a martyr to possess flesh that had potency.

Four centuries later an eastern theologian, John of Damascus, provided his own reflections on the bodies of the saints in a treatise that would also become influential in the west. In his *Exposition of the Orthodox Faith* John has to explain how dead bodies can effect miracles. They are not dead at all, says John, merely asleep, and this is because, as saints, God dwells in them. '. . . . For how [else] could a dead body work miracles? How, therefore, are demons driven off by them, diseases dispelled, sick persons made well, the blind restored to sight, lepers purified, temptations and troubles overcome, and how does every good gift from the Father of lights come down through them to those who pray with sure faith?' Such corpses have become, in effect, spiritual treasures. Although the law forbids the touching of a dead body, these bodies, John assures us, can be touched because of the life still in them. Speaking to doubters of the tradition that oil and fragrance exuded from their bodies, John tells how 'the Master Christ made the remains of the saints to be fountains of salvation to us, pouring forth manifold blessings and abounding in oil of sweet fragrance. For if water burst in the desert from the steep and solid rock at God's will and from the jaw-bone of an ass to quench Samson's thirst, is it incredible that fragrant oil should burst forth from the martyrs' remains?'[8]

The corpse that is not decayed and exudes fragrant oil provides a good example of the difficulties of writing about this subject. There is some fragmentary evidence that bodies of martyrs or holy men or women were honoured by the addition of spices that may have helped preserve them (as Christ's body would have been if it had remained in the tomb). However, we are entering a world where there are thousands of accounts of undecayed bodies, resurrections of the dead, healings and the opportune deaths of those who have offended the dead saint or the monastery or church that he, or she, was protecting. There was a readiness to interpret events in a certain way, see what was not strictly there or believe that an illness had genuinely been cured. We are in the realms of faith, impossible perhaps to define with any certainty, in which observations are slanted to maintain the fiction of these bodies' spiritual and physical wholeness.[9] We are between heaven and earth.

What Ambrose had done was to force these ideas into the open. Gervasius and Protasius were, he had claimed, martyrs. Therefore their bodies held a sacred power, the blood of martyrdom still lingering on them. They had already achieved a spiritual form that prefigured the way they would appear among the saints at the Last Judgement. Meanwhile, they were able to bring miracles on earth and act as intercessors in heaven. This is because they had achieved a quality that took them beyond the physical world.

Ambrose's coup also set a precedent for the bishop as initiator and guardian of a shrine in the Latin west. Central to this was the open display of the saint's body in the centre of a church, close to or underneath the altar. So when Alexander, the bishop of the north African town of Theveste, brought out his own saints, buried after martyrdom, he could rejoice: 'Where once long rest had robbed them from our gaze, they now blaze with light on a fitting pedestal, and their gathered crown now blooms with joy. . . . From all around the Christian people, young and old, flow in to see them, happy to tread the holy threshold, singing their praises and hailing with outstretched hands the Christian faith.'[10] Setting this all up was the purpose of the *translatio*, one of the most important rituals in any saint's acceptance as an intercessor who was available, visibly at least, to all.

CHAPTER THREE

Creating a Christian Landscape

'ALL WE, the faithful, worship the cross of Christ as his staff: his all-holy tomb as his throne and couch: the manger and Bethlehem, and the holy places where he lived as his house . . . we reverence Sion [Jerusalem] as his city; we embrace Nazareth as his country; we embrace the [river] Jordan as his divine bath'. So enthused Leontius of Byzantium, writing in the early seventh century, on the experience of pilgrimage to the Holy Land.[1]

The fourth century, after the granting of toleration to Christianity by the emperor Constantine in 313, brought the first explosion of interest in the biblical sites of Palestine. The cave of the Nativity and the manger itself were on show in Bethlehem by 320. Within the walls of Jerusalem, the site of the Temple, destroyed by the Romans in AD 70, was left unsanctified as a reminder of the wrath that God had bestowed on the Jews for their part in the Crucifixion of Christ, but relics were honoured in the church of the Holy Sepulchre, the great basilica built by Constantine on what was assumed to be the site of the tomb of Christ, and hence of the Resurrection. Legend tells how Helena, the mother of Constantine, had found the True Cross there while on pilgrimage in Palestine in 326. Sixty years later a wealthy Spanish pilgrim, Egeria, described how a fragment of it, preserved in a silver-gilt casket, was venerated each Easter in Jerusalem by being kissed by the faithful. A hundred years later pilgrims were bringing small flasks of oil and watching how the oil bubbled over as these touched the Cross.[2]

It is Egeria, too, who describes a phenomenon that was to become ubiquitous in the Christian world, the development of opulence in the decoration of shrines. As she entered Constantine's basilica she was overcome: 'the decorations are too marvellous for words. . . . They are beyond description, and so is the magnificent building itself . . .'. Under the supervision of Helena it had been adorned 'with gold, mosaic and precious marble, as much as his [Constantine's] empire could provide, and this not only at the Great Church, but at the Anastasia [site of the Resurrection], and the other Jerusalem sites as well'. After Constantine had given tolerance to the Christian communities in 313, he had adopted the pagan practice of transferring vast resources into the building of temples for the Christian world.

There were many Christians who were horrified by this development. Grand places for worship had never been part of Christian teaching. Deep in the early Christian imagination was the belief in the soul as a pilgrim in itself, a stranger in this world on a journey which, one might hope, led to heaven.[3] So the journey should be inwards, not outwards into the corrupt real world. The ascetic Church Fathers warned that even in Jerusalem there were charlatans and prostitutes. However, sheer curiosity about where Jesus had preached, been crucified and had risen again, and the excitement of travel, won out. By the end of the fourth century AD the inhibitions had faded, pilgrimage to Palestine was commonplace, and virtually every site or happening in the Gospels had been pinned down. When the scholar Jerome, a cantankerous ascetic, famous for his translation of the Hebrew Scriptures into Latin, arrived on pilgrimage with his companion and patroness, the aristocratic Roman Paula, they carried out a meticulous search for the Christian past. 'On entering the Tomb of the Resurrection [in Jerusalem] Paula kissed the stone which the angel removed from the sepulchre door, then like a thirsty man who at last comes to the water he has so long yearned for, she faithfully applied her mouth to the very shelf on which the Lord's body had lain. Her tears and lamentations there were known to all Jerusalem – or rather to the Lord himself to whom she was praying.' The spot where the Holy Spirit had descended at Pentecost, the Mount of Olives and the place where the Ascension took place were all identified. In Bethlehem the field where the angels had announced Jesus's birth to the shepherds, the site of the massacre of the Holy Innocents and the cave of the Nativity could be seen. When Paula kissed 'the' manger, she had a vision of the baby Jesus, Joseph and the visiting shepherds.[4]

Rome's own Christian past was more fragmentary than that of Jerusalem, of course, and it could not claim any direct link to Christ's life on earth. So the aura that suffused Jerusalem would always be lacking. By the middle of the second century AD, the supposed burial place of the Apostle Peter, by tradition the first bishop of Rome, was being honoured on the Vatican Hill, and Constantine had built another richly decorated church, the first St Peter's, over it. The putative site of Paul's martyrdom, on the road from Rome to the port of Ostia, had also been commemorated by a shrine, and in the 380s this was also transformed into a vast basilica. There were other famous Roman martyrs who had been buried, according to custom, outside the city walls. These included Lawrence, by tradition roasted to death on a grid, and Agnes, a virgin who resisted the advances of the son of the Roman prefect, and these were now also honoured. In the catacombs, the long passageways that ran through the soft tufa rock outside the city, there were thousands of other Christian burials, many of them of martyrs from the persecutions of the third and early fourth centuries.

The practice of *translatio*, the transferring of relics from one site to another, was already well established in Rome. Helena had brought back part of the True Cross to Rome and its headboard, the *titulus*, was installed in Santa Croce. She was later said to have also shipped the *Scala Sancta*, the steps up which Jesus had ascended to Pilate's palace. These were installed close by her son Constantine's church of Christ the Redeemer, now St John Lateran.

As Rome accumulated its collection of relics, it refused to pass any on. An inscription set up by Damasus (Pope 366–84) outside the catacomb of San Callisto records how he would have liked to have been buried there himself but 'I feared to disturb the holy remains of these godly souls.'[5] There had always been ancient fears of disturbing the dead, but it was also believed that distributing relics would lessen the sacred power of the city itself and its popes at a time when their authority in the wider Christian world was still weak. In the late sixth century Pope Gregory the Great did condescend to send a demanding Byzantine princess some shavings from the chains that had shackled Paul in prison, but normally enthusiasts had to make do with *brandea*, sacred objects, in this case cloths that had touched the tombs, or even lamp oil from the shrines of martyrs. The use of *brandea* was an important development that had scriptural support. In Mark's Gospel (5:25–34) the woman with the issue of blood had touched Christ's clothes and he could feel the power coming out of him through the cloth towards her. Peter's shadow was also potent enough to cause miracles (Acts 5:14–15). In Acts 19:11–12, when 'handkerchiefs and scarves which had been in contact with his [Paul's] skin were carried to the sick, they were rid of their diseases and the evil spirits came out of them'.

While Rome refused to dilute the power of its martyrs by sending pieces of their bodies abroad, Bishop Ambrose in Milan had a very different approach. He grasped that relics could be a means of exercising personal power, especially through the ancient practice of gift exchange. Giving and receiving gifts was a means of proclaiming status and establishing links with fellow members of the Roman elite. Ambrose extended the range of appropriate gifts to include relics. He sent off dust and bloodstains from the bodies of Gervasius and Protasius to his admirers and inspired a network of elite relic collectors who reinforced each other's collections. So here was a new explosion of holy sites, places that, unlike Jerusalem and Rome, had had little or no contact with the events of Jesus's life or the legendary afterlives of the Apostles.

A leading member of the coterie was Paulinus, a Roman aristocrat who had renounced his estates in Gaul, Spain and southern Italy (like Ambrose he had been a provincial governor in Italy). He now dedicated his energies to creating a shrine around the body of St Felix, a martyr of the third-century AD persecutions, at Nola in central Italy. Paulinus became bishop of the settlement. He celebrated his relationship with Felix in a large number of poems, a new one written each year, and adopted him as a father figure and patron, whose renunciation of the world provided an incentive for his own. The shrine was glorified with buildings that were hung with curtains and lamps, and Paulinus also decorated the walls with stories from the Old Testament for those who could not read. A ritual was soon in place by which pilgrims would bring ampoules of oil, pour them into the open holes above the tomb of Felix, and then refill them from the base when the oil would be found miraculously mixed with holy dust.[6]

By now, nearly four hundred years after the Crucifixion, remains of the disciples were appearing. Ambrose helped Paulinus add a package of relics that included something of the Apostles Andrew and Thomas and part of the body of the Evangelist Luke to the bones or dust of Gervasius and Protasius. None of their martyrdoms had been recorded in the Scriptures but there were legendary accounts of their achievements dating from the second century AD onwards. From Melania, an aristocratic connection who had renounced her vast estates and made for Jerusalem, Paulinus obtained a fragment of the Cross. In his turn he benevolently scattered relics. He celebrated the extension of the Christian landscape with his customary eloquence (he was one of the last great writers of classical prose): 'Wherever a drop of dew has fallen on men in the shape of a particle of bone, the tiny gift from a consecrated body, holy grace has brought forth fountains in that place and the drops of ashes have begotten rivers of life.'

Ambrose was a gifted orator, ready to create a case for the veneration of martyrs with whatever powers of rhetoric he could muster (in an age when rhetoric was at the core of education). So was another of the recipients of his largesse, Vitricius, Bishop of Rouen in Gaul. When relics arrived from Ambrose in AD 396, Vitricius preached a sermon on *Praising the Saints* that was a further public demonstration of the raised status of relics. He stressed the transformed context in which the Church now flourished. We are living in new times, he told his congregation. The age of persecution is over and we are now enriched by the passion of the saints. 'No torturer now has oppressed us, yet we carry the trophies of the martyrs. In this time there is no outpouring of blood, no persecutor pursues us, yet we are filled with the joy of triumphs. So we must immerse ourselves in tears, and release our great joy in lavish weeping.'[7] Vitricius announced that the saints whose bones he was welcoming had chosen this site themselves and arranged for the building to be ready for them. In return, they must be welcomed with acclamations as if they were an emperor arriving in one of his cities (in the ceremony of *adventus*). So the carrying of relics in a ceremonial procession became part of the ritual of a cult that gradually created a network of shrines wherever Christianity spread.

A number of currents had flowed together to create the Christian shrine. There was an intense interest in the rediscovery of the Christian past, especially the world of the disciples and the early martyrs. There were ancient traditions of veneration that were being transferred into a Christian context. The shrines were beginning to become centres of opulent decoration. They were places of pilgrimage but also the sites where miracles might be hoped for. The relic of a particular saint had become the medium through which intercession through the pleadings of that saint to God might be made. The development of the Augustinian theology of original sin, and the likelihood of eternal punishment for most, gave this a special charge. Shrines were emotional places with much spiritual capital tied up in them, which might be released to the lucky visitor. Yet there were still those who were suspicious of their power.

CHAPTER FOUR

The Battle for Acceptance

THIS ENTHUSIASM for relics was bound to arouse hostility and ridicule from non-Christians. A traditional pagan view had always been that a god who had to rely on the miraculous to show his power was degrading himself. The emperor Julian (r. 361–63), who had converted back to paganism from a Christian background, put it in his *Against the Galileans*. 'You Christians have filled the whole world with tombs and sepulchres, and yet in your scriptures it is nowhere said that you must grovel among tombs and pay them honour.' He taunted the Christians for introducing a new form of polytheism through their adulation of so many saints and martyrs. Another critic of Christianity, Eunapius of Sardis (*c*.345–after 414), poured scorn on the way Christians 'collected the bones and skulls of criminals who had been put to death for numerous crimes . . . made them out to be gods, and thought they themselves became better by defiling themselves at their graves. "Martyrs" the dead men were called, and ministers of a sort, and ambassadors of a sort to carry men's prayers.'[1]

Many Christians were also opposed to this new wave of enthusiasm for relics. It offended those who had received a more traditional education in rational thought, had little foundation in Scripture, and, as the pagan critics had pointed out, fragmented worship among the bones of a mass of different ascetics, prophets and martyrs in effect preserved polytheism.[2] Whatever Christians said about relics being a medium through which a saint would intercede with God or Christ, the new practices threatened to diminish the status of Christ. Basil of Caesarea, one of the great saints and theologians of the east, saw the *martyria* as completely unnecessary. 'As the sun does not need the lamplight, so also the church of the congregation can do without the remains of the martyrs. It is sufficient to venerate the name of Christ, for the Church is his bride, redeemed by his blood.'[3]

One of the protagonists of the traditional view was a Gallic clergyman called Vigilantius who was active in the early fifth century AD. The only record of Vigilantius' arguments comes from the vicious condemnation of them by one of the enthusiasts for relics, Jerome, in his letter *Against Vigilantius*.[4] Vigilantius argued that the saints were actually in heaven and they could just as easily intercede for sinners from there. One did not have to attend a shrine to gain access to them. 'Is it the case that the souls of the martyrs love their ashes and fly around them, as if they were not able to hear if they were absent when someone came to pray?' Wherever the souls of the martyrs might be, any dead body is corrupted and unclean, whether it is of a saint or not. Vigilantius goes on to ridicule the practice of wrapping up bits of dust in fine cloth and then putting them in a precious vessel. He wonders whether the saints are in a position to intercede in any case. He quoted the Book of Revelation's assertion that the saints were waiting under the altar for their voices to be heard by God. If so, they were not at hand for intercessions.

Vigilantius faced stern opposition and it is important to pinpoint its roots. One bond that bound together the enthusiasts for relics was a deep personal asceticism, a rejection of worldly desires. Paulinus had married and had a child, but Ambrose, Vitricius and Jerome were fixated with virginity and maintaining the purity of their own bodies. Celibacy was the subject of one of Ambrose's first works after his baptism as a Christian in 374, and he aroused a great deal of opposition in Milan when he tried to get young girls to leave family life and commit themselves to perpetual virginity. Jerome was the author of a prurient letter on the dangers of lust to a young girl, Eustachium, to whom he was a counsellor. He dwells with loving detail on the pleasures of sex that he asks her to renounce.

The ascetic was by nature a solitary, keeping him or herself apart from physical contact. Vigilantius suggested that relics provided some kind of compensation for this bleak withdrawal from the world and human company. The martyr or saint could play the role of an imagined friend, but the relationships we read of border on the perverse. In the vituperative letter he sent to Vigilantius, Jerome revealed himself. 'I love chaste flesh, virginal and fasting. I love a flesh that knows it is going to be judged: I love the flesh which is, for Christ, at the hour of martyrdom, broken, torn to pieces and burned.' Jerome seems to need his flesh but only in a form that tears it apart and takes it above everyday carnal desire. His contemporary, John Chrysostom, Bishop of Constantinople, had similar desires. He had become obsessed with the works of St Paul and now wanted physical contact with his mentor. 'Would that it were now given me to throw myself round the body of Paul, and be riveted to the tomb, and to see the dust of that body that "filled up that which was lacking" after "Christ", that bore "the marks" that sowed the Gospel everywhere yea, the dust of that body through which he ran to and fro everywhere, the dust of that body through which Christ spoke, and the Light shone forth more brilliant than any lightning, and the voice started out, more awful than any thunder to the devils!'[5]

Faced with cravings like this, Vigilantius can be forgiven for arguing that asceticism led to losing oneself in the realms of fantasy. One of his targets was Martin of Tours, a rare case of an ascetic who maintained his lifestyle even when made a bishop. Martin had continually claimed to be in personal touch with demons, angels, the Virgin Mary and the Apostles Peter and Paul. For more down-to earth clerics, such as Vigilantius, this was simply embarrassing.

In his counter-attack Jerome was preoccupied with humiliating Vigilantius. He lost his chance to offer any effective justification of relics, although he was quoted in later centuries for his belief that the bones should never be worshipped in themselves but only as a means of preserving the memory of the martyrs. It is rather Vitricius who attempted a more sophisticated response in the sermon of welcome he gave in Rouen to the sacred dust that Ambrose had sent him. Vitricius seems particularly concerned with Vigilantius' claim that saints cannot be in two places. He counters him with an elaborate theological justification in which he argues that there is a composite spiritual body, of Christ and all who live in him. The martyrs and saints are part of that spiritual body. 'By their righteousness they are made companions of the Saviour, by their wisdom his rivals, by the use of limbs concorporeal, by blood consanguineous, by the sacrifice of the victim sharers in the eternity of the cross.' Any part of this spiritual community, even a sliver of a bone from a single martyr, has exactly the same substance as the whole. So Ambrose's fragments, and any others he passes on to others, have the same power as the saint enjoys in heaven. The inscription on the tomb of Martin of Tours, who died on 8 November 397, around the same time as this sermon, echoes Vitricius. 'Here lies Martin, the bishop of holy memory, whose soul is in the hand of God; but he is [also] fully present here, made manifest through every grace of miracles.'

Vitricius concludes his oration with a burst of rhetoric that links the temporal world to the eternal. 'It is toward these jewels that we should set the sails of our souls; there is nothing fragile in them, nothing that decreases, nothing which can feel the passage of time. The blood which the fire of the Holy Spirit still seals in their bodies and in these relics shows that they are extraordinary signs of eternity.' Against this fervent and emotive outburst, Vigilantius was fighting a rearguard action. Sealing the Holy Spirit into the relics for eternity was to make them as precious and as immutable as gold.

We are lucky enough to be able to trace the process through which the rational misgivings of Christians and pagans alike were subsumed by the adulation of relics through the long career and extensive writings and sermons of the theologian Augustine of Hippo (AD 354–430).[6] The extraordinary breadth of Augustine's mind, the insights of his theology and his determination to provide a coherent structure of thought for the Church allowed him to dominate his generation. Yet this was just the problem. Christianity depended on the Scriptures, not on the theology of any one man, however brilliant. Augustine soured with age, his contempt for his fellow human beings grew, but he resolutely refused to let anyone through the barriers he had erected around his theology.

Augustine's education, in Carthage, could not have been more traditional. In his early years, he appears typical of the educated pagan elite in his application of reason to the problems that confronted him. Even after his conversion to Christianity, which eventually took place in 386 under the influence of Ambrose, and in Milan, where Augustine had become the city orator, Augustine continued to distrust the miraculous. His views can be seen in his treatise, *On True Religion*, written in 390. Here Augustine argued that the creation of the world, and its recreation at the Resurrection of Christ, could be seen as miracles, wondrous events, in themselves. Similarly, God had put in place the laws by which the natural world operate. It was the day-to-day miracles, miracles within the miraculous as it were, that aroused his scepticism. He accepted that in the early Church dramatic events had been needed to advertise the power of Christ, but now that the Church was well established 'these [biblical] miracles were no longer permitted to continue in our time, lest the mind should always seek visible things, and the human race should be chilled by the customariness of the very things whose novelty had inflamed them'. Too many miracles would simply limit the impact of the Christian drama. In 400 Augustine told an enquirer that those coming for baptism might first be attracted by stories of miracles but that the Scriptures offered a sounder and more reliable guide to Christian faith.

Then gradually a change takes place. By now Augustine had returned to his native north Africa and become a priest and then bishop of the coastal city of Hippo, where he was to remain until his death in 430. One can detect the drift in his thought away from its original rational underpinning, especially after he became obsessed with original sin in the 390s. Increasingly he decries curiosity, the driving force of intellectual progress, to the extent of calling it a sin and an example of man's fallen state. He turns towards faith as the guarantor of belief and the authority of the Church as sufficient enough as a foundation for doctrine.[7] Yet Augustine was still hesitant to applaud the miraculous. He, too, was confronted by the arrival of pieces of the ubiquitous Gervasius and Protasius, at a country estate near Hippo, but, in contrast to Paulinus and Vitricius, Augustine preached that the primary function of the saints was to give example to the living through the stories of their endurance and readiness to die for their faith. He spoke with distaste of 'hypocritical monks' who went a round selling the limbs of martyrs (evidence in itself that a trade in relics was already established).

It was the bones of St Stephen that proved a catalyst for Augustine's adoption of the miraculous. Stephen, the earliest recorded martyr, was stoned to death by the Jews in c. AD 34 when he proclaimed that he had a vision of Christ at 'God's right hand' (Acts 7). Now, nearly four hundred years later, a priest by the name of Lucian had a dream in which the rabbi Gamaliel, who is recorded in the Acts of the Apostles as a teacher of Paul, told Lucian where to find Stephen's corpse. John, the Bishop of Jerusalem, gave help, one of many bishops who boosted their prestige by being present at the uncovering of a lost saint or martyr. There were no doubts that it was the right body because as it came into sight there was a series of earth tremors, a marvellous scent and the healing of no fewer than seventy-three people within an hour of the discovery. This ritual of rediscovery, in which a favoured Christian is alerted by a dream to a martyr's body, then the identification is confirmed by miracles, was to become common in medieval Europe.

The remains of 'Stephen' were soon divided up and they spread fast across the empire. An ivory plaque from Constantinople shows his right arm arriving in the eastern capital in about 420, where it was welcomed by the emperor Theodosius II and his pious sister Pulcheria. Other fragments ended up on the island of Minorca where their origin as the bones of a man martyred by the Jews appears to have been a signal for the breakdown of what had been a healthy relationship of the local church with the Jewish community. A series of confrontations led to the burning of the local synagogue. Stephen was clearly having his revenge on his murderers.

Pieces of Stephen arrived in north Africa about 418, and in the final chapters of his magisterial *City of God* Augustine dwells on the outburst of miracles they have effected in the cities close to him. A brother and sister had been inflicted by a curse from their mother that had given them some form of trembling disease, and they had been wandering the Mediterranean looking for relief. Stephen had granted it. A little boy was playing in the square in front of a shrine to Stephen. A runaway ox cart knocked him down and he was close to death. His mother snatched him up and put him in the shrine, and he survived. Those close to death were revived and there was even a resurrection of a dead boy whose body had been laid on the martyr's tomb. Others sources, a surviving miracle list of St Stephen, for instance, dwell on the frenzy that relics inspired in some. A noblewoman from Carthage, Megetia, travelled to Stephen's shrine at nearby Uzalis. She was so overcome with the experience that she beat her body against the tomb, broke the grille that protected it, pushed her head inside the tomb and laid it on the relics, drenching them with her tears. The enthusiasm of Jerome and John Chrysostom for contact with saintly flesh lived on.

The fragments of Gervasius and Protasius also exercised their power in Augustine's Hippo. A demon had entered a young man and reduced him almost to a corpse. When he clutched the shrine to the two martyrs, the demon shrieked out but as it left the man it tore out one of his eyes. The eyeball was popped back into the socket, bound up, and with the help of the martyrs he was totally cured. In contrast to his earlier restraint Augustine now demands publication and proclamation of these miracles. There is a dramatic account in *The City of God* of one Innocentius, about to go under the knife for the removal of a fistula. Everyone, including Augustine, gathers at his house in fear on the day of the operation. When the surgeons arrive, the fistula has miraculously disappeared. One Innocentia, a woman of high status, who might have wanted to keep to herself her miraculous cure from breast cancer, effected when the sore was touched by newly baptised women in Carthage, is berated by Augustine. 'I was indignant that so astounding a miracle, performed in so important a city, and on a person far from obscure, should have been kept a secret like this; and I thought it right to admonish her and to speak to her with some sharpness on the matter.'[8] Augustine goes on to argue that the stories of miracles must be told and retold, just as one drives gravel down into a path until it is firmly embedded there. The effects of miracles are lost if they are not publicised. Like Ambrose, he knew that the effective churchman also had to be a confident impresario, not only displaying his relics openly as Ambrose had done but proclaiming their miracles.

Augustine's sudden enthusiasm for the miraculous arose from his belief in the possibility of transforming human flesh into the spiritual form that Adam and Eve had enjoyed before the Fall, and which Christ himself had showed after his Resurrection. In *The City of God* Augustine claimed that by effecting miracles the relic of a martyr showed that God recognised its faith:

What do these miracles attest but the faith which proclaims that Christ rose in the flesh and ascended into heaven with the flesh? . . . . God may himself perform them [miracles] by himself, through that wonderful operation of his power whereby, being eternal, he is active in temporal events; or he may effect them through the agency of his servants [i.e. the saint in his relics and, Augustine adds, angels] . . . . Be that as it may, they all testify to the faith in which the resurrection to eternal life is proclaimed.'[9]

Whatever the reality of the decaying bones and nauseous flesh that may have made up the actual relics being hawked around the Mediterranean, they were symbols of faith and the miracles they effected were a proclamation of their authenticity in the eyes of God.

As the most important theologian of his age, and one who had increasing confidence in his authority, Augustine is able to provide an intellectual justification for his beliefs that is far above that of the ordinary worshipper. However, his justifications simply reinforced what was by now popular feeling. In fact, his drift towards the acceptance of miracles might well be the result of popular pressure. By the fifth century the martyrs had become the celebrities of their day. Theodoret, Bishop of Cyrrhus in Syria, vividly describes the way a new mood has gripped the empire with the demise of philosophy. 'The philosophers and the orators have fallen into oblivion; the masses do not even know the names of the emperors and their generals; but everyone knows the names of the martyrs, better than those of their most intimate friends.'[10] Augustine's theological support meant that there was a consensus between popular feeling and theology that was vital in consolidating the cults at every level of Christian society.

The masses were unable to speak for themselves, but in the western empire this adulation may well have been rooted in the growing insecurities of a disintegrating empire. The last emperor who had effectively maintained the borders was Valentinian I, who had died in AD 375. From then on, barbarian armies were penetrating the Roman provinces. Alaric and his Goths sacked Rome in 410. Even though the Goths were Christians (most of the tribes had been converted by missionaries in the mid-fourth century) and spared the churches, the shock was felt by Christian and pagan alike. There was a gradual process of dislocation, its end symbolised by the abdication of the young emperor Romulus Augustulus in 476. Yet in the eastern part of the Mediterranean the empire survived, in new forms perhaps but as deeply attached to its Christian relics as was the west.[11]

CHAPTER FIVE

The View from Byzantium

The city is more amazing than all other cities in the world for its gold and silver, marble and lead, tapestries and silks, and is far more glorious than all other glories of the world because of the bodies of the saints which it possesses, and especially on account of the most precious relics of our Lord Jesus Christ which are believed to be greater there than in all the other parts of the world.

So enthused an eleventh-century traveller who had journeyed from Europe to Constantinople, the city that the emperor Constantine had founded on the ancient site of Byzantium.[1] Constantinople had been officially dedicated in AD 330 and the beginning of a distinct 'Byzantine' empire is often dated from this moment. As the Roman empire in the west crumbled under barbarian pressure, Constantinople emerged as the largest city in its surviving territories. Its attractions lay in its superb defensive position, a peninsula on the 'European' coastline overlooking the Bosporus and entrances to the Black Sea, and a fine harbour, the Golden Horn. Constantinople had no Christian heritage and the only church Constantine had completed in the city before his death in 337 was his mausoleum, the Church of the Twelve Holy Apostles, of whom Constantine rather presumptuously numbered himself number thirteen. Relics of the Apostle Andrew, Timothy the disciple of Paul, and the Evangelist Luke were transferred to the church.[2]

There are records of other early relics arriving in Constantinople while Constantine was emperor. The largest part of the True Cross discovered by his mother Helena remained in Jerusalem, but later legends told of how she sent a piece of it to her son in his new capital together with two of the original nails. According to different sources, Constantine embedded these either in his horse's bridle, his helmet or his diadem. The fifth-century historian Socrates tells how Constantine placed the fragment of the Cross inside the statue of himself which stood on a porphyry column in the Forum in Constantinople. Later reports tell of how the crosses of the two thieves crucified with Jesus, the twelve baskets into which the loaves and fishes were gathered, and the axe that Noah had used to construct the ark were also placed near the column.

The Byzantine emperors still saw themselves as Roman emperors rightfully entitled to the lost provinces of the west and, under the emperor Justinian (r. 527–65), had even regained parts of Italy, including Ravenna. They had also taken the leading role in defining Christian orthodoxy, despite opposition from the popes in distant Rome who claimed primacy over the whole Christian Church in both east and west. Theodosius I, emperor between 379 and 395, had set the trend by transforming his capital into a Christian city at a time when its citizens were still largely pagan. It was from Constantinople that he proclaimed the Nicene Trinity as orthodoxy, condemned the Arians, probably a majority of the Christian population, as heretics, called two conferences, one in 381 and one in 383, to confirm his decisions, and by the 390s had launched a campaign against paganism. The more fanatical of Theodosius's officials and local bishops demolished other pagan sanctuaries in the east on their own initiative, often causing outrage and disruption that shocked the emperor. Most dramatically of all, Theodosius had announced through his Church Council of 381 that Constantinople stood second only to Rome in the ecclesiastical hierarchy, a promotion that infuriated people in the older Christian cities of the east, Alexandria and Antioch, as much as it did the Romans.[3]

This all had its effect on the choice and accumulation of relics for Constantinople. In the fragmenting western empire, it was the bishops such as Ambrose who pioneered shrines; in the east it was the emperor. Theodosius I developed the precedent set by Constantine in his capital of using relics to confirm the sacred status of the ruler and he tied this in with the orthodoxy that he was establishing through law. When he condemned the Arians Theodosius expelled the remains of Macedonius, a former Arian bishop of the city, from a church founded in his memory and replaced them with those of a 'Nicene' bishop of the city, Paul the Confessor, who, it was said, had been strangled by Arians. The bones of martyrs, among them St Phocas, who had offered himself up for death in the Diocletian persecution at Sinope on the Black Sea (c.303), were brought in. The bones of the Old Testament prophet Samuel arrived from Palestine along with those of Joseph, the son of the Patriarch Jacob, and Zacharias, the father of John the Baptist. They were carried in procession from the Holy Land, landed at the jetty at nearby Chalcedon and then welcomed into the city by the Patriarch and the city officials.

By the early fifth century under Theodosius's son Arcadius and his grandson Theodosius II (r. 408–50), a ritual of welcome had evolved. The ivory relief that shows the arm of St Stephen being carried into the city in a box by two bishops on a chariot has citizens standing in ordered ranks watching the procession. The reliquary is received by Pulcheria, the pious elder sister of Theodosius II who had acted as his regent when he was a boy. Behind her, the church that will receive the arm is still being finished. The arm was eventually given a place in a chapel next to the main throne room of the imperial palace. The name *Stephanos* has the same root in Greek as the word for 'crown' or 'diadem', and in later reigns the relics were brought in to the throne room as part of the ritual of the coronation. Theodosius II and Pulcheria had paid their own respects to Jerusalem, donating, for instance, a diamond-studded gold cross that was to be erected at Golgotha, the site of the Crucifixion, and a grant for the poor of Palestine in exchange for their relic of Stephen.

The devout Pulcheria was a powerful force in Byzantine politics and remained influential throughout the reign of her brother. The use of relics was crucial in the way she presented herself and maintained her prestige. She had welcomed 'Stephen' and built a church for him; she did the same for relics of the Roman martyr Lawrence and the prophet Isaiah. In 435 she had a dream that led her to the astonishing discovery in Constantinople of relics of the Forty Martyrs of Sebaste (in Armenia), soldiers who had been frozen to death in a lake for their Christian beliefs. A magnificent ceremony was held at which their remains were welcomed and placed in a vase in the church of St Thrysus, another martyr, from Alexandria. Another great festival took place in 438 when the bones of the former bishop of the city, John Chrysostom, who had outraged so many by his outspoken attacks on the luxuries of the imperial court that he had been exiled in 404, were returned. He had never lost his following among the poor who had applauded his sweeping denunciations of the rich. Thirty years on, Pulcheria saw how his bones could be used to link Byzantium rulers to the masses, and she laid on a great spectacle. As the remains crossed the Bosporus they were welcomed by the faithful who crowded the waterways in the boats that glowed with lit torches.

One bishop who was still alive, and thus not so malleable as the bones of John Chrysostom, was Nestorius, appointed Bishop of Constantinople in 428. Pulcheria had a deep devotion to the Virgin Mary and had welcomed the movement that had been gathering pace in the eastern Church to 'promote' her to a new title, *Theotokos*, 'Mother of God'. Nestorius preferred the less elevated 'Bearer of Divinity'. He further offended Pulcheria by criticising her for combining her life as a professed virgin with so much public activity. Pulcheria hit back by encouraging her supporters to barrack Nestorius in his own cathedral and, when Mary was indeed proclaimed *Theotokos* at the Council of Ephesus in 431, the bishop was exiled. Now a thanksgiving to the Virgin was required.[4]

Altogether Pulcheria built three churches to the Virgin in the city. The most prestigious was built in the suburb of Blachernae at the north-western end of the walls overlooking the harbour. Relics were needed for these churches, of course. As the Virgin Mary was believed to have fallen asleep and then been assumed intact into heaven, relics were hard to come by. Luckily her robe appeared. One account told how it had been found in a chest belonging to a pious Jewish descendant of hers. The discoverers had some scruples about taking it from its owner but they beseeched the Virgin Mary for approval. 'It is to thy city that the robe is being transferred, the city which is the Queen of all other cities, whose first charge it has always been to honour anything of thine.' The assent of the *Theotokos* was given. There was a rival account of how the Virgin's coffin had been found preserved in Jerusalem, in the garden of Gethsemane. The robe had been left behind in the coffin when she had been assumed into heaven, and it passed from there to Constantinople. The most prestigious of Pulcheria's acquisitions was an icon of the Virgin painted by the Evangelist Luke that Theodosius II's wife Eudocia had brought back from Jerusalem. The *Hodegetria* (literally 'She who shows the way') became the most famous icon in Constantinople.

Pulcheria incorporated these relics into ceremonial displays. One later account by two Spanish visitors to Constantinople tells how each Tuesday twenty men wearing long red robes would enter the church where the *Hodegetria* was stored. The icon indicated which one of the twenty was favoured to pick it up, and when it was lifted the frame would then weigh almost nothing. Next the icon was carried from the church and paraded around one of the squares in the city. It would bow from side to side towards those it favoured. (There are identical descriptions of statues of deities behaving in this way in ancient Egypt.) Clergy would touch the image with pieces of wool that were then handed out to the crowd.

The *Theotokos* had clearly chosen Constantinople as her home, and Pulcheria never missed an opportunity to link her own imperial status, as Augusta, 'the revered one', to the Virgin. She even had her own image mounted in the church of the Blachernae and left her imperial cloak covering its altar. Nestorius's successor as bishop, Proclus, created ritual chants in honour of Mary using the same rhetoric of adulation that would be addressed to an emperor. The famous *Akathistos Hymn* to Mary ('the hymn that is said standing'), which may have its origins in the fifth century, also uses imperial themes. When the choir chants 'Hail to you [Mary], through whom the trophies of victory are assured. Hail to you, through whom the enemies are vanquished', the singers are using the same words that were addressed to Tyche, the pagan goddess of Fortune, the earlier protectress of the city. When Mary was believed to have saved the city from destruction in an assault on the city's walls in the seventh century, the hymn was to come into its own and it remains important in the eastern churches.

On Theodosius's death in 450, Pulcheria took as her consort a soldier, Marcian, who respected her long-preserved virginity. They presided together at the Council of Chalcedon of 451 that defined the relationship between the humanity and divinity of Christ, and this gave them both further prestige. Pulcheria died in 453, but the *Theotokos* continued as a major protectress of Constantinople. Over the decades, other relics appeared in Constantinople. They included the remains of Simeon Stylites, the ascetic superstar who had perched for years on a pillar in the Syrian desert, and a copy of the Gospel of St Matthew that had been found clasped in the hands of St Barnabas (the companion of Paul), whose body had been discovered in his native Cyprus. In the later sixth century, during the reign of Justin II

(r. 568–78), the hair of John the Baptist and another fragment of the True Cross appeared in the city.

When these relics arrived they were displayed in the finest church in Constantinople, the majestic Santa Sophia, rebuilt in its final form in 563. The basilica dominated the city, as it still does today, its dome as if suspended from heaven, and its lamps glowed across the Bosporus so 'as to show the returning seafarer the way to the living God'. The relic would remain displayed here until a patron, usually a member of the imperial family, built a shrine for it, whereupon it would be transferred. Among Santa Sophia's permanent collection were the trumpets that had sounded around the walls of Jericho and the wellhead on which Jesus had sat while talking to the Samaritan woman.

However, the security of the Byzantine empire was not to last. In the seventh century it was to be shattered and the contours of Mediterranean politics, religion and society were transformed. In 602 the emperor Maurice had been deposed by a minor army officer with the name of Phocas. The usurpation encouraged the emperor of neighbouring Persia, Khusro II, to declare war on the Byzantine empire and invade Syria. In 610 Phocas, weakened by his lack of legitimacy and defeat by the Persians, was in his turn overthrown by Heraclius, son of the exarch of Carthage, whom the Senate had invited to Constantinople. Heraclius knew how a Christian emperor-to-be should present himself. He arrived with reliquaries and icons of the Virgin Mary on the masts of his ships and was crowned by Sergius the Patriarch of Constantinople in the chapel where St Stephen's arm was kept. Phocas was put to death.[5]

Despite this divine support Heraclius's prospects did not look good. The Persians had now reached into Cappadocia in Asia Minor while another enemy of the empire, the Avars, were raiding across the Danube. Then, in a massive advance, the Persians struck through Palestine, capturing Jerusalem in 614 and sweeping on through Egypt and Libya. At Jerusalem they sacked the city and took the True Cross as booty. In Asia Minor the Persians even reached Chalcedon and held the western shoreline of the Bosporus as the Avars launched an assault on Constantinople itself. Heraclius was away on campaign but Sergius galvanised the support of the Virgin Mary. The Byzantine fleet defeated its enemies at a spot where it was overlooked by the church of the *Theotokos* in Blachernae, and when an icon of the Virgin was displayed on the walls of the city the Avars' attack was blunted. The city survived intact and the *Akathistos* became Constantinople's hymn of triumph.

The combined blows of the failure of the attack, the defeat of a second Persian army on its way to Constantinople and an advance by Heraclius into Mesopotamia, were so devastating that it was now the humiliated Khusro who was murdered in his palace and the Persians sued for peace. The eastern boundaries of the Byzantine empire were restored and Heraclius celebrated his triumph by parading the regained True Cross through his territory before returning it to Jerusalem. Later generations gave him the accolade of 'the first crusader'. The battle between Heraclius and Khusro is vividly recorded in the thirteenth-century *Golden Legend*, a famous account of the lives of saints and their relics (see below, p. 131), and is portrayed on the frescoed panels of Piero della Francesca's *Legend of the True Cross* in the church of St Francis in Arezzo, central Italy. The Holy Lance, which had pierced Christ's side while he was on the Cross, and the Holy Sponge, which had been soaked in vinegar and offered to Christ on the Cross, were taken back to Constantinople with other relics of Christ's Passion. However, the Arab invasions now swept across the eastern Mediterranean and the True Cross itself also had to be brought back to Constantinople when Jerusalem fell in 638.

With the explosion of Islam, the Byzantine empire had lost vast quantities of territory and, after further losses to the Arabs, had to regroup itself around a core of Asia Minor and the Balkans. It was not only the loss of so much territory that made this a troubled time. Constantinople suffered from new outbreaks of plague and earthquakes, a major one occurring in 740, and much of the city fell into ruin. Then the Byzantine armies experienced defeats from the Arab forces. Fear that this was some form of divine retribution for unknown failings sparked off the campaign against icons, the painted boards that carried the faces of Christ, the Virgin Mary or saints.

The Greek word *eikon* simply means 'image', but many icons such as the *Hodegetria* had ancient lineages that gave them sanctity in themselves and thus they had become hard to distinguish from other relics.[6] The campaign against images was launched in 726 through an edict issued by the emperor Leo III demanding that they be destroyed. He was responding to pressure from the dispirited soldiers who noted how their Islamic enemies specifically forbade sacred images and remained victorious. The only unifying symbol now permitted was the Cross, which had traditionally been carried before the army and the appearance of which would, according to the Evangelist Matthew, announce the return of Christ. The campaign began with the removal of an icon of Christ from the palace gate and its replacement by a Cross.

It is still hard to pinpoint the forces that sustained the iconoclasm. Perhaps the strongest was the belief that images focused worship away from the central figure of Christ and so threatened the purity of the Church (a view that eastern theologians like the much-respected Basil of Caesarea had held), but there were political undercurrents rooted in ancient disputes between factions in the Church which helped prolong the controversy. The bitterness of the debates encouraged John of Damascus (see above, p. 22) to formulate a defence of images that became highly valued in both the eastern and western Churches.[7] In his *On the Divine Images* John sees images, like relics, as forms of Christian experience that hover somewhere between the secular and the divine. The Jews did not allow images, but as Jesus had broken with Judaism and taken on human flesh, it was fitting for images to record this. Images serve to bring the believer closer to God. John makes the important distinction between direct adoration of God, which evokes awe at his majesty and thanksgiving for all he has given, and mere veneration of material objects that are part of his creation.

John's views were enthusiastically endorsed by the Council of Nicaea of 787 that upheld the importance of images against the iconoclasts during a lull in the campaign. 'When these icons are before our eyes, the hearts of those who fear the Lord rejoice; faces bloom, the disheartened soul turns cheerful, singing along with David, the forefather of Him who is God: "I remembered God and rejoiced." ' With the final victory over the iconoclasts proclaimed by Empress Theodora in 843, the status of both relics and icons was preserved. The great Dominican theologian of the thirteenth century, Thomas Aquinas, absorbed John's works and it was through Aquinas that they entered the western tradition. They provided the most sophisticated rationale available for the continued veneration of all these objects in medieval Europe. So, although the west completely avoided the controversy and the popes even encouraged the making of icons in Rome during the eighth century, John's views helped support a reassertion of the importance of relics and images by the Catholic Church during the west's own outbreak of iconoclasm at the Reformation.

Despite these upheavals, the Byzantine empire was more manageable than it had been. With the loss of Alexandria and Jerusalem to the Arabs in 638 the religious status of Constantinople within the empire was now unchallenged. The fragments of the True Cross were used alongside the relics of the Virgin Mary as defenders of the city. One smaller sliver was paraded with the army in the seventh century and again, alongside the robe of the Virgin, to counter an attack by the Slavs in the ninth century. It was placed in a special reliquary that was then hung around the neck of an official who marched in front of the emperor and so provided a talisman for the troops.

Within the imperial palace the power of the relics of the Passion was pervasive. The most sacred of all Christian relics had become linked to the most sacred family in the empire. The Book of Ceremonies from the tenth century mentions three crosses within the palace chapels, possibly the True Cross and those of the thieves crucified alongside Christ. These took the central role in public rituals. In late July each year the Cross was put on display within the palace. It was venerated first by the emperor, then it was taken to one of the reception rooms where members of the Senate paid their respects. A procession around Constantinople followed to 'cleanse and sanctify all places and houses of the god-guarded and imperial city: and not only the buildings, but also the walls of the city and its suburbs'. Eventually, it was returned to the emperor's main audience hall, the *Chrysotriklinos*, and was placed on his throne before 'sanctifying and cleansing' the palace itself.

Once these sacred tasks had been finished, the Cross was placed in the church of the Virgin of the Pharos ('the lighthouse'). This church was somewhere in the centre of the palace complex and by the tenth century it had become the most opulent shrine in Constantinople. One account describes it as 'so rich and noble that there was not a hinge nor a band nor any other part that was not all of silver, and there was no column that was not of jasper or porphyry or some other rich precious stone'.[8] Another describes the white marble wall of the exterior that was so beautifully made that it appeared to be a single sheet of marble. Entering inside the chapel was, it was said, like coming into heaven. The chapel held the Holy Lance as well as the True Cross.

It was in this chapel that relics directly associated with Christ, those at the top of the hierarchy, were displayed when they arrived. One of the most prestigious was the Mandylion. This is first heard of in Edessa in the sixth century and purported to go back to the dawn of Christian history. Abgar, the King of Edessa, had written to Jesus asking to be cured of leprosy. Jesus had sent him back a letter promising a visit from one of his disciples, along with an image of himself on a cloth. It was this image, the Mandylion, a word having no known other meaning, that had survived and was given in 944 to the Byzantines as a ransom for two hundred Muslim prisoners after campaigns close to Edessa. The Mandylion was an *acheiropoietos*, an image 'not made by human hands', a type of relic that held enormous sanctity because of its provenance but could also be used as evidence by iconophiles that Christ himself had approved images. Rome was also to have its own example, a true icon, a *Vera Iconica*, apparently the cloth with which Christ's face was wiped as he dragged his Cross to Golgotha.[9]

When the Mandylion arrived in Constantinople in 944 it was taken by sea along the walls of the city to the church of the Blachernae. It rested here and then was taken in an imperial procession through the Golden Gate. It 'entered the city with high psalmody, hymns and spiritual songs and boundless light from torches . . . [so] that because of this the city would receive holiness and greater strength, and would thus be kept safe and remain impregnable forever.' A lame man who saw the image as it entered the city was immediately cured. The Mandylion was then given a service of welcome in Santa Sophia before being displayed on the imperial throne in the palace and then transferred to the Chapel of the Pharos. When Edessa itself was eventually captured, the original letter of Jesus to Abgar was found and was added to the imperial collection. The Keramion, a brick that had touched the Mandylion and received its own miraculous image, Christ's purple robe, his leather sandals, the reed that he held, the sheets in which he was wrapped in the tomb, the Crown of Thorns and an iron shackle with which he was bound were also to be found in the chapel. Nicholas Mesarites, who made a list of the relics in the chapel in about 1200 noted how the Crown was still fresh and green and unwithered, smooth to the touch, for it had been given immortality as a result of its contact with Christ's head. The right arm of John the Baptist was another treasure.

Yet the *Theotokos* remained the protectress of Constantinople and her relics were displayed whenever the city was threatened. In 924 the emperor Romanos was forced into abject negotiations when a Bulgarian army under 'tsar' Symeon reached the city walls:

So the emperor . . . entreated the all-hymned and immaculate Mother of God to soften the hard and inflexible heart of the arrogant Symeon and to persuade him agree to peace. Therefore, having opened the holy casket in which was stored the sacred robe of the holy Mother of God, the emperor took this and wore it like an unbreachable breastplate, and with his faith in the irreproachable *Theotokos* which protected him like a helmet, he left the church fortified with these secure weapons. Having arranged the troops about him with shields and weapons, he went to the set meeting-place to talk to Symeon.[10]

Peace was indeed made, even if at the cost of the emperor having to give Symeon 'magnificent gifts'.

Constantinople's impregnable position meant that it had always survived intact. Its walls had not been breached since the late second century AD, when the emperor Septimius Severus had taken the city after a long siege. With the protection of the Virgin and the relics of the Passion sanctifying the emperors, the city had become confident about its survival. Despite all its territorial losses and the natural calamities that had weakened it, this was by far the largest and richest city in the Mediterranean world. No one would have imagined that in the thirteenth century a resurgent Christian Europe would launch a successful challenge to its pre-eminence in the Christian world and sack it.

CHAPTER SIX

Bishops, Magic and Relics in the Post-Roman World

W HILE THE empire in the east successfully transformed itself and survived, in the west the Roman empire collapsed in the fifth century. There was a scramble by war leaders to carve up the abandoned territories. Most were heirs of the barbarian tribes that had gradually dislocated the provincial administration of the empire. Even though many of these had absorbed 'Roman' lifestyles, much of what can be called civilisation – urban life, trade, high levels of craftsmanship, literacy – vanished as living standards slumped, often to below those of pre-Roman Europe. Gregory the Great was so appalled by the devastation and collapse he saw around him that he believed that the last times were on the way, and the reign of the Anti-Christ predicted in the Scriptures was about to begin. 'Towns are depopulated, fortified places destroyed, churches burnt, monasteries and nunneries destroyed; fields are deserted by men and the earth forsaken by the ploughman gapes desolate. No farmer dwells here now; wild beasts have taken the place of throngs of men.' It would not be until the eighth century and the stabilisation of central Europe under Charlemagne that any form of recovery would be possible.[1]

The first Christian dioceses were based within the walls of decayed Roman cities. Here there were the remnants of traditional allegiances, buildings that might be converted and some rudimentary means of protection. So in England, the dioceses of Canterbury, Rochester, Lincoln and York, still prominent today, all originated within former Roman cities. Then there were the monasteries, common in eastern Christianity since the early fourth century but only known in the west from the fifth. About 220 are known in the Gaul of AD 600, a hundred in the same period in Italy. They were usually independent and relied on the protection of kings or local aristocrats for their security as well as their own saints. Benedict, the founder of western monasticism, who died c.550, lay buried in his last foundation, Monte Cassino in central Italy, always ready like any effective saint to use miracles to defend his abbey against enemies.

There was little outreach from these centres of religious power to the local population in the impoverished countryside, largely because the Roman taxation systems that had bound the masses to administrators had disappeared. More transient loyalties had taken their place and this affected the spread of Christianity. When the missionary-monk Augustine, who took his name from the great theologian, arrived at Canterbury from Rome in 597, all ten thousand subjects of King Aethelbehrt 'converted' to Christianity when he did, but then lapsed as quickly on the king's death in 616. (Kings at this time were always kings of peoples – rex Francorum, 'king of the Franks' – not territories.) Vast areas of northern Europe remained unconverted and in much of the rest the Church had to acquiesce in the continuing pagan mentalities of the mass of the population to survive. In Ireland, semi-legendary figures such as Patrick sowed seeds of Christianity that spread organically from family to family and from one small tribal group to another. Ireland had never been part of the Roman empire and had no martyrs but, during the sixth century, sites that claimed to be the tombs of holy men became the focus of Christian worship. Each had its own territory whose boundaries were marked by crosses or inscriptions. The Irish words for 'saint' and 'relic' draw on pre-Christian terms for tribal divinities and talismans.[2]

As the idea of veneration of the dead spread, the Christian Church could tap into its own heritage of saints and martyrs. Most provinces of the empire had known some persecution, so there were bodies of martyrs to be rediscovered. Many dioceses gave special honour to their first bishop, even if he was often a purely legendary figure. Some of these figures were given a heritage that celebrated them as colleagues of the Apostles or Evangelists who had come to western Europe after the Crucifixion. So there was a loosely defined network of saintly figures who successfully meshed themselves into the Christian communities of the post-Roman world.

Without an emperor to imprint Christianity from a central court as in Constantinople, the expansion of Christianity in the western Mediterranean took place within communities suffused by magic, 'magic' being used here to describe all forms of exercise of control by human beings over nature which are linked to supernatural forces, Christian or pagan. Christians had traditionally condemned the *magi*, the magicians, but as they themselves believed, with the theological endorsement of Augustine, that God intervened through miracles and that angels and demons also existed, in practice they were as committed as pagans were to the presence of supernatural forces that might act for good or ill. When in his *On the Divination of Demons* Augustine railed against augury and divination, it was not because he was being 'rational' but because these were arts of the devils that he knew existed. 'Sometimes they [the demons] foretell future events which they recognise in advance through natural signs that cannot reach the senses of man.'[3] It was believed that, after Satan and his angels had been expelled from heaven, they lurked in the upper regions of the air. Droughts, tempests or floods that emanated from this region were usually the work of the Devil. 'One should not be surprised that the devil, thrown from heaven, can excite storms in the atmosphere', as Pope Gregory the Great put it. Another Christian source tells how astrologers tracking the movements of the stars are hoodwinked, 'not knowing that it is not the course of the stars, but the operation of demons that regulate these things; and those demons, being anxious to confirm the error of astrology, deceive men to sin by mathematical calculations'. This, then, is the reason for condemning astrology and being suspicious of mathematics.[4]

As a result many Christian miracles deal with the direct confrontation with devils in their ethereal homes. 'The ability to detect, see, resist, repel, or exorcise demons constituted one of the most regular and potent proofs of sanctity in late antique Christianity.'[5] The monks of Iona told a legend that angels had come down to confer with Columba, the founding saint of their monastery. When, after his death, a drought struck, it was important to open up the airways so that rain could get through. The monks gathered up the white tunic of the saint in which he had died and some of the books he had transcribed himself, went up the hill where the angels had landed, shook out the tunic and read from the books. The devils were overcome and torrents of pent-up rain were soon released.

It was always difficult, therefore, to draw a boundary between Christian and pagan magic. In her fascinating study, *The Rise of Magic in Early Medieval Europe*, Valerie Flint argued that the boundaries shifted into paganism in that shrines gradually absorbed many elements of what had been pagan magic.

The exercise of practices that had originally been condemned by Christians were now made acceptable by being Christianised. A typical example from the sixth century tells of the wife of one Serenatus who suddenly becomes dumb. The local diviners, *harioli*, a term of condemnation in Roman law, try to treat her by placing herbs on her, but to no effect. Along comes a Christian who throws away the herbs and applies oil and dust from the tomb of St Martin, at which the woman's speech is restored. Neither healing takes a 'scientific' approach so it is really a question of power, with the saints taking on roles that pagans had traditionally used and for which they had been condemned. Flint also shows how the roles of angels, notably Michael the Archangel, are expanded to cover such skills as divination that Christians had traditionally forbidden. She argues that the adoption of magic was a deliberate policy to make the process of conversion less disruptive and cement loyalties of the former pagans. In effect, she goes further than merely describing a redistribution of magical powers to conclude that 'magic was allowed to rise in importance in the early medieval west as a result of profound and careful thought and for the good it could do'.[6]

This would explain how many early Christian shrines in western Europe were ancient sacred sites. Gregory's famous letter to Abbot Mellitus, sent when Mellitus was on his way to join the monk Augustine in England in 601, tells him that if pagan shrines are 'well-built, it is essential that they should be changed from the worship of devils to the service of the true God. . . . Take holy water and sprinkle it in these shrines, build altars and place relics in them.' One form of magical practice takes the place of another on a site that the local community has long considered sacred. In about 700 a monk rejoices that Christian worship is taking place in buildings 'where once the crude pillars of the same foul snake and stag were worshipped with coarse stupidity in profane shrines'.[7] Even so, it is extraordinary that the pagan gods were never dislodged as patrons of the days of the week, so that we still talk of Woden or Thor's day and have calendar months that are rooted in the world of the classical emperors (July/Julius Caesar, August/Augustus).

Christian worship embraced not only 'temples', but trees, springs, groves and large stones. The archaeological evidence shows how Christian burials take place within mounds and earthworks from the prehistoric and Roman past. In France even today there are some six thousand springs considered by tradition to be 'holy'. The treasure within the burial mound of a pagan

Anglo-Saxon king at Sutton Hoo in Suffolk, England, was left unmolested by Christians even though memories of the wealth of the recently completed tomb must have been vivid. The plateau of the Hemmaberg above the River Sava became a thriving pilgrimage destination in the fifth century, its churches of Christian relics built above ancient healing springs, while the histories of other springs were recast to tell how they first gushed out at the command of a passing saint. The great Gothic cathedral of Chartres in France encloses an ancient spring.[8]

Valerie Flint's acquiescence in and approval of 'the rise of magic' was in dramatic contrast to the views of that earlier chronicler of the coming of Christianity, Edward Gibbon, the leading historian of the Enlightenment and the scourge of superstition whose Decline and Fall of the Roman Empire was published between 1776 and 1789. Gibbon would have agreed with Flint that Christian 'magic' was on the rise, and even with her thesis. 'The ministers of the catholic church imitated the profane model which they were impatient to destroy. . . . The most respectable bishops had persuaded themselves that ignorant rustics would more cheerfully renounce the super-stitions of paganism, if they found some resemblance, some compensation, in the bosom of Christianity.'[9] However, the spread of Christianity attracted some of his most withering prose. Whatever one's religious beliefs, it is impossible not to be enthralled by Gibbon's language:

> The satisfactory experience, that the relics of saints were more valuable than gold or precious stones, stimulated the clergy to multiply the treasures of the church. Without much regard for truth or probability, they invented names for skeletons, and actions for names. The fame of the apostles, and of the holy men who had imitated their virtues, was darkened by religious fiction. To the invincible band of genuine and primitive martyrs, they added myriads of imaginary heroes, who had never existed, except in the fancy of crafty or credulous legendaries. A superstitious practice, which tended to increase the temptations of fraud, and credulity, insensibly extin-guished the light of history, and of reason, in the Christian world.[10]

An influential challenge to Gibbon's views, and especially the idea that the rise of Christianity involved compromise with vulgar popular religion, was made in the historian Peter Brown's The Cult of the Saints, based on a series of lectures given in 1978.[11] Brown eloquently argued that the spread of the cults suggested by the archaeological and the limited literary evidence represented a new and more positive phase of religious belief, characterised by 'radically new forms of reverence, shown to new objects in new places, orchestrated by new leaders'. They represented the highest spiritual aspirations of the age and had a healthy effect, because a cult provided a 'human' mediator between God and man that made the spiritual more easy to accept. As the elites, bishops and rulers, enthusiastically endorsed the cults, they provided a way of bringing rich and poor, ruler and subject, closer together. The shrines themselves acted as social refuges, their aura of sanctity and healing making them havens in a violent and disintegrating world. Unlike an irascible living ascetic, 'dead' relics were a constant and stable presence. In short, the cults represented 'new forms of the exercise of power, new bonds of dependency, new, intimate hopes for protection and justice in a changing world'. The reverence shown towards shrines 'was not a luxuriant undergrowth of credulity or neo-paganism. It involved learning an etiquette toward the supernatural.'

Later writers have not been quite so enthusiastic as Brown.[12] More recently the emphasis has been on detailing the rivalries between shrines, the deliberate use of one saint politically, essentially as protector of one dynasty, city or faction against another in this early post-Roman period. The result is to highlight the fragmentation of early medieval Christianity and downplay its coherence as a single force inexorably absorbing pagan populations.

A telling example of the political use of a saint comes from the most successful kingdom of central Europe, that of the Merovingians founded by Clovis I, king of the Franks (r. 481–511). (Their name derives from Clovis's grandfather, Merovech.) It came to cover much of ancient Gaul and even extended north of the Rhine and southwards over the Alps. Clovis's conversion from paganism to Catholicism, as the Christianity of Ambrose can now be called, was a vital moment in the Christianisation of Europe. It was said that his coronation was sanctified by oil provided from above by the Holy Ghost himself – in such quantities that there was still some left for other coronations, the last recorded one being that of Louis XIV in 1638. The historian of the period, Gregory of Tours, acquiesces in accepting the brutal victories of Clovis as a sign of divine support against his rivals. It was not a healthy development. Far too many medieval rulers would follow the precedent, go to war and then, if successful, claim that God had supported them, and might continue to do so in further ventures.[13] The Merovingian dynasty lasted some 250 years, even though the dynasty was marked by continual infighting as rival members of the family quarrelled over their inheritances.

One well-documented conflict was between a member of the royal family and her local bishop.[14] It was common for the women of the royal family to leave their husbands later in life and adopt an ascetic lifestyle. Queen Radegund, one of the wives of Clothair, a son of Clovis, had especially good reasons for doing so. She was from a defeated royal family of Thuringia and had been forced into her marriage. She 'escaped' when her husband murdered her brother. She imposed intense suffering on herself, including burning a cross onto her arm, and then founded her own nunnery at Poitiers. To maintain her status, she was determined to keep it independent of the jurisdiction of Maroveus, the local bishop. In the tussle between the two that followed, relics became the weapons. Maroveus had the body of Hilary of Poitiers, a fourth-century theologian known for his dogged defence of the Nicene Trinity when Arianism was still popular, in his cathedral. Radegund had to trump him. Using all her regal authority, she dispatched delegations to Constantinople, the capital of the Byzantine empire, and Jerusalem. The finger of St Mammes, a third-century child-martyr from the coastal city of Caesarea, was sent back from Palestine. In case there was any doubt about the division of a saint's body, the finger detached itself ready for dispatch as the messenger arrived to take it. St Mammes was no match for St Hilary, but from Constantinople the queen received a triumphant tribute. In addition to some remains of eastern saints, she was given a fragment of the True Cross in a reliquary decorated with gold and jewels. 'What Helena had done in the East [by finding the True Cross in Jerusalem], Radegund did for Gaul', relates the nun Baudovinia, the queen's biographer. Radegund had brought the sophistication and spiritual power of the east into the more rugged world of Merovingian Gaul. The precious gift arrived back in Poitiers.

The bishop was furious and attempted to stop the fragment being installed in her nunnery. Radegund appealed to her royal contacts to get the bishop overruled. Maroveus is recorded as going off to sulk in his villa and, in his absence, it was the bishop and clergy of nearby Tours who organised the grand reception of the relic. The poet Venantius Fortunatus, later himself a bishop of Poitiers, wrote processional hymns, the *Vexilla Regis* and

Pange Lingua, for the occasion, hymns that are still used in the Catholic Church today. The clergy carried the relic into the chapel where it was to be stored along with other relics, 'those precious gems which Paradise holds and which Heaven hoards'. Sick and possessed people were soon being admitted to be healed as if, it was said, they were supplicants at a royal court. Radegund herself gained such status through her coup that she became a person of spiritual power and influence in her own right and even began to effect her own miracles. (She was canonised in the ninth century.) When she died in 587, her initiative was lost as her nuns split into their own quarrelling groups and the focus of local worship shifted back to the city tomb of Hilary.

One of Radegund's visitors was Gregory, the Bishop of Tours. As they were talking Gregory noticed an oil lamp that was leaking. Radegund replied that it was merely that the power of the True Cross was swelling the volume of the oil, a display of its force that echoed similar miracles in Jerusalem. This was, however, a minor miracle in comparison to those that were to take place in Gregory's own city, Tours, at the shrine of St Martin.

Martin was a soldier in the Roman army who gave, as a charitable gesture, half of his cloak to a beggar. That night he had a vision of Christ wearing the cloak himself and this provided the incentive for baptism. (The cloak re-emerged as a relic in its own right during the seventh century.) Martin was profoundly ascetic and became notorious (or respected) for his ragged appearance. The vast majority of bishops in the west in the fourth and fifth centuries were from aristocratic landowning backgrounds (so inaugurating a tradition that lasted into the nineteenth century). Mosaics show them dressed in silk, and they were disgusted when Martin did not smarten himself up when elected bishop. Nevertheless he had a large popular following and had attained some celebrity for miracles that involved the destruction of pagan shrines. (Martin was a contemporary of Ambrose and lived in a period when the Roman empire, now Christian, was still intact and there was effective secular authority supporting the Church in its confrontations with paganism.)

Martin had died in 397 in the nearby village of Candes. Immediately, Poitiers and Tours squabbled over which town should have his body. It was the opportunist citizens of Tours who managed to smuggle it out at night through a window of the chapel and convey it in triumph up the River Loire to their city. It joined fragments of Protasius and Gervasius that were already honoured there. Candes remained an important focus for pilgrims (the place where Martin's body lay is still shown to visitors), while at the nearby monastery of Marmoutier, which Martin had founded, his admirers 'licked and kissed and moistened with their tears each spot where the blessed man had sat or prayed or where he had eaten food or laid his body to rest after his many tasks'.

Tours gained its importance as the centre of a road network and from its position on the Loire, which acted as the traditional boundary between northern and southern Gaul. By the 450s, when the empire was still officially in place but the Arian Visigoths already controlled Aquitaine to the south, Martin, the former soldier, was being trumpeted as the vanguard of Catholic resistance to these heretics. A new church was built outside the city walls to house his sarcophagus. Clovis I visited it before his conversion and believed that the psalm being chanted as he entered, 'For thou hast girded me with strength into battle: thou hast subdued under me those who rose up against me' (Psalm 18:39), legitimated his conquests of his enemies. Once he had defeated the Arian Visigoths, he lavished the plunder of his victory on the shrine. It is recorded that when the new shrine for Martin was completed the sarcophagus proved too heavy to move, but an angel disguised as an abbot appeared to help transfer the remains. The new shrine was decorated with murals, and the adulatory life of Martin by Sulpicius Severus composed soon after Martin's death was put in verse to make it easier to memorise.

During the next century, the cult of Martin was one of several patronised by the Merovingian kings although they did not make the city itself one of their strongholds. It now emerges as an important centre of healing, the best documented of its time. Gregory, Bishop of Tours, was the impresario who gave the shrine this role. Gregory came from a Gallo-Roman aristocratic family. He was an outsider to Tours – his appointment as bishop was through his royal connections – and he had every reason to be apprehensive over his welcome by a congregation that had not elected him. He delayed moving to his new diocese and then fell ill when he arrived. 'A sharp pain penetrated my entire stomach and went down into my intestines.' It was through drinking water mixed with the dust from Martin's tomb that he was cured. Already he carried with him the relics of one Julian, apparently an early Gallic martyr. When Gregory brought these into Martin's church a brilliant flash of light convinced him, and he hoped others in his new congregation, that Martin had welcomed Julian and by association, himself, into the diocese. Gregory cannily used the miracles of his saint to give evidence of God's support for his authority.

Gregory soon began to compile one of those important propaganda documents vital to the success of any shrine, the miracle list of his patron. Its details make the shrine by far the best documented from this period. He tells how pilgrims came from the neighbouring provinces, though never much further, and that many of them were from elite backgrounds. This was before the age of lengthy pilgrimages, but Gregory may well have been exaggerating the importance of his shrine by raising the status of his visitors. When other preachers appeared in the city with their own relics, Gregory quickly saw them off. He had to quash any competition to Martin's supremacy as the protector of Tours, and hence to his own authority.

Gregory was typical of his generation in believing that sickness and disability were the results of sin. And the list of sins was growing. The *Penitentials*, texts that first developed in Celtic Ireland in the sixth century, listed every possible transgression, including an imaginative range of esoteric sexual practices, and the appropriate penance demanded by the priest to whom confession was made. When reconciliation with God had not taken place, divine punishment was administered.[15] Gregory records some of the 'offences' that had crippled or blinded his pilgrims: the repairing of a fence during Lent or on a Sunday, baking on the night before a Sunday or gathering hay on a Sunday. A rash on a woman's face was a double blow, not only to the recipient's physical comfort but because, as Gregory said, it was God's way of shaming her before the community. Gregory warned his congregation that sexual intercourse just before Sunday would lead to children who would be born crippled or suffer epilepsy or leprosy. Only a saint with direct access to God could hope to reverse the terrible consequences of sin, and Gregory, as the city's bishop, was the one and only gatekeeper.

In an echo of Epidaurus, the shrine of the god Aesclepius in the Peloponnese, supplicants would often sleep at the tomb of Martin and receive his help through dreams. A crippled nun was healed after she dreamt that the saint had stroked her limbs; another woman experienced the saint untangling and straightening her twisted fingers. Often, however, healing took place during the liturgy or on the feast day of the saint, perhaps in similar form to the emotionally charged evangelical healing ceremonies of today.

In Gregory's accounts a successful miracle involved much more than the relief of suffering. The transition from sickness to health involved the acceptance of a sinner back into the religious community. The transition was marked not just by the healing but by the transformation of the flesh as a result. Here the argument of Augustine that miracles confirm the future physical resurrection of the body was given a material form. Gregory often described the unhealed body as dry and lifeless. So the bones in one man's leg were 'twisted like ropes'. When the healing occurred the body itself took on new life. Watching the withered hand of a boy being restored, Gregory commented that 'you might think that a sponge that had long since been dry had been immersed in water and was thirstily soaking up the water'. This was spiritual flesh as it would be when it was received into heaven at the Last Judgement. The opposite occurred when a saint was offended. Gregory recorded that a man who had stolen from a shrine of St Julian became so hot that 'smoke poured from his body as if from a furnace'. This was a warning to all of his coming eternal punishment in the fires of hell.

So here was a new development in the cult of relics. It is not simply the body of the saint that is uncorrupted, but a relic now has the power to affect the flesh of those who come into contact with it and give them new life of a spiritual kind. A physical body could be transformed, either to a state of perfection or to one of disintegration according to the merits of the supplicant. The idea that a saint could punish miscreants who offended him went right back to the beginnings of Christian history when the Apostle Peter, for instance, struck dead Ananias and Sapphira (Acts of the Apostles 5).

What is perhaps the most engaging miracle of St Martin happened some centuries later, possibly in the ninth century, when Tours was facing raids from the Normans. It was decided that the body of Martin needed to be moved eastwards, and the city of Auxerre was chosen. Here an early bishop of the city, St Germanus, was the local saint and the two bodies were laid beside each other. The problem now was how to work out the respective contribution of each saint when miracles took place, especially if fair offerings were to be made to the most effective. The solution was to bring in a leper whose disease had spread so horribly that his whole body was ravaged and he was close to death. He was made to lie down for the night between the two bodies. In the morning the side next to Martin was totally healed and that beside St Germanus was still as disfigured as it had been. This might have been chance and so the leper was made to lay down the other way around for the second night. The next morning he was completely cured. William of Malmesbury, who recorded this story in the early twelfth century, noted that the Auxerre clerics explained that the natural hospitality of their own saint was such that he 'yielded to the honour of such a welcome stranger'. It was as if the saints were creating their own community.

If so, it was a community that was benefiting from revived trade in the Mediterranean. The trade is poorly documented. Most of it, spices, incense and silks from the east, exchanged, it appears, for pagan slaves from northern Europe, was perishable. Relics from the east must have been crammed in among bulkier goods. What information survives of this cross-Mediterranean relic trade has been gleaned from a study of the collections at Sens, in northern Gaul, and Chelles, near Paris, the site of an important convent. The fragments in the collections can often be dated from the scripts on the tags attached to them that also note their provenance.[16]

Understandably, many of these relics came from other shrines in Gaul, yet a surprising number of relics in these two collections come from cities of Asia Minor. Some of these cities had Christian histories that went back to the first century AD, when they had been visited by Paul and other early missionaries, so they offered good hunting grounds for relics of martyrs. When this region saw a collapse in urban life in the seventh century, the trade with the west in relics was diverted to Constantinople. There were also trading links with the Islamic world, the dominant power in the Holy Land, Syria and Egypt after the seventh century. These again had all been important early centres of Christianity. By the eighth century, a fifth of all relics arriving in Gaul came from Palestine. Sens had 'the Lord's cradle' and a relic of the cantankerous St Jerome from Bethlehem. The 'Apostles' Table', some manna and the prophet Elias came from other parts of the Holy Land.

There were more devious means of acquiring a protective saint.[17] In the seventh century some enterprising monks from Fleury, a monastery on the River Loire, led by their abbot, went in search of a top-class saint. The Lombard invasions of the sixth century had reached down into central Italy as far as Monte Cassino, the burial place of St Benedict of Nursia, the founder of the Benedictine rule. Benedict's achievements had been well publicised by Pope Gregory the Great, who had portrayed him as the exemplar of the man of God whose miracles centred on his everyday care for his fellow human beings. Benedict's bones had already proved their worth by protecting the monastery from one attack and a fire, but the monks of Fleury shamelessly declared that the site had been abandoned in the disruptions and that Benedict needed rescuing. They spirited away Benedict's body and that of his sister Scholastica and carried them back in triumph across the Alps. One account tells how the bones shed fresh blood on the linen in which they were wrapped and were so light that the horse carrying them could not feel the burden. These unscrupulous *furta sacra*, 'holy thefts', were then justified when the saint began to show his appreciation through miracles, as Benedict did. He emerged as a fierce defender of the privileges of his new monastic home.

The monks of Monte Cassino would not give in so easily. Even though they could not produce Benedict's bones, they claimed that his body had infused the earth where it had been buried and so his protection remained. The papacy was petitioned by both sides and each site received a declaration, from different popes, that they had the saint in their possession. The looted 'Benedict' still lies in the crypt at Fleury. His arrival in Frankish territory gave a boost to the Benedictine rule. Charlemagne's son, Louis the Pious, later decreed that it should be the standard rule for all monasteries in his empire, and the Benedictines spread from there to become the most influential Order in Europe.

These last two chapters have highlighted one of the most remarkable features of the story; the way in which both highly authoritarian and centralised states such as Byzantium and diffuse localised rural communities are both able to find a meaning for Christian relics. In Byzantium they are used as prestige objects for the emperors and as a protective force for their capital. In the west they are used for reasons of prestige, to consolidate the authority of a local bishop, but they also provide a focus for the community. They are the health centres, offering cures for both spiritual and physical disabilities. Peter Brown's thesis that such relics offer an arena for spiritual etiquette is attractive but they also establish rivalries with each other, one episcopal or royal patron exercising his impresarial skills against another. Similar narratives were being rehearsed across the channel, in Anglo-Saxon England.

CHAPTER SEVEN

'A barbarous, fierce and unbelieving nation'

GREGORY, BISHOP of Tours, was also the most important historian of his times and he records its many upheavals and conflicts. His *History of the Franks* bristles with narratives of civil wars between rival members of the Merovingian dynasties.[1] The emerging Anglo-Saxon kingdoms of England were also racked with conflict. Relatively little is still known of Anglo-Saxon England. Even the process by which the newly arriving peoples, Angles, Saxons and Jutes, from what is now Germany and Denmark, reached and settled within the native English population is hotly disputed. Yet by the end of the seventh century a number of kingdoms whose courts appear to have been the main initiators and protectors of Christianity have emerged. By the same date there was a network of bishops that transcended the fluctuating boundaries of local rulers and recognised the seniority of the Archbishop of Canterbury.[2]

Martyrs had been few in Roman Britain. Later Christians recorded only three: St Alban, martyred in the Roman city of Verulamium, now St Albans, in the persecutions of the third century AD, and his two companions. Christianity then appears to have disappeared in England until the arrival of Augustine at Canterbury in 597. Augustine was in trepidation of the 'barbarous, fierce and unbelieving nation'.[3] His baptism of the Anglo-Saxon king Aethelbehrt followed and, as Christianity spread, it was the Anglo-Saxons who provided an array of their own spiritual leaders who achieved sainthood (in the sense of leaving bodies or objects associated with them that brought about miracles). Their cults were still localised, usually linked to a specific territory. The names of 140 holy men and women from the seventh and eighth centuries are recorded and of these 120 are associated with minsters, a term first used in seventh-century texts to denote a settled community with a daily ritual of prayer. The saint is protected by the reverence of those living around his shrine; he or she offers protection to the community in return. In some cases there is evidence of a defined territory beyond the community for which the saint takes responsibility, as was also to be found in Ireland.

One of the most potent and evocative symbols of Anglo-Saxon England is the stone cross. Stone working was one of those skills that had declined dramatically with the fall of the Roman empire, but the skill re-emerged in the seventh century.[4] The crosses found within the kingdoms of Mercia and Northumbria are rich with iconography that is probably copied from smaller jewelled crosses. Some of these were undoubtedly reliquaries, similar to that owned by Queen Radegund in Poitiers. Perhaps the most remarkable poem of the period, the *Dream of the Rood* ('crucifix'), possibly by the seventh-century Anglo-Saxon poet Caedmon, describes a dream in which a Cross is seen as bedecked by gems and gold, as if the poet has seen an actual reliquary. The Cross speaks to the dreamer of how it bore the body of Christ in the drama of the Crucifixion. Christ is given an Anglo-Saxon identity in so far as he is portrayed as a dead warrior who was honoured as such by his companions (the Apostles) when he was taken down from the Cross. After his body was removed the Cross was buried, but then the 'thanes' (aristocratic warrior companions) of Christ rediscovered it. 'Now has the time come when they will honor me far and wide, men over earth, and all this great creation, will pray for themselves to this beacon. On me God's son suffered awhile. Therefore I, glorious now, rise under heaven, and I may heal any of those who will reverence me.'[5] The creation of the Cross as a personality in its own right suggests that relics were becoming part of a wider Christian imagination. The dreamer goes on to lament his own loneliness on earth; his friends have died but they are in heaven, and he now calls upon the Cross to fetch him and take him to join them in their feasting.

This echoes what we know of the Anglo-Saxon period in which Christianity becomes inextricably linked with the warrior culture. 'The Christ of the early Middle Ages, it has often been remarked, was a god far more comfortable on the battlefield than in the heart, a war leader rather than a lover, an all-powerful warrior and king of heaven rather than a pitiable victim of human sin, his Cross not so much an instrument of torture as a weapon of victory, "a trophy".'[6] In this period social and 'heroic' status seems to be as important a factor as personal saintliness in defining those who were worthy of devotion or whose relics held sacred power. Ancient traditions of the ruler as sacred remained powerful.[7]

There was, for instance, the haughty Wilfrid (c.633–709), the son of a noble family from Northumbria. Wilfrid had entered a monastery while young and then had studied in Canterbury, Gaul and Rome. He was ostentatious in his lifestyle, always travelling with a vast retinue, far greater than that of a king, and was known for his arrogance. He was eventually consecrated Bishop of Northumbria but was deposed and reappointed as kings reacted in different ways to his flamboyance. He built a vast church at Hexham that was proclaimed to be a recreation of St Peter's in Rome, with subterranean passageways that echoed the catacombs, quarrying the stone from the wall that the Roman emperor Hadrian had built in the second century AD to mark the limits of his empire.

When Wilfrid died there was genuine concern among his supporters as to whether God would recognise this worldly man as a saint, but on the first anniversary of his death a great white arc appeared in the sky and they knew they were safe. This was always a crucial moment in the history of a saint's cult. Unless God showed unequivocally that he or she was in heaven, then any chance of his protection would be lost. For the next three hundred years, Wilfrid's shrine at Ripon produced miracles. When the monastery at Oundle, where he had died, was attacked by barbarians, Wilfrid sent an angel with a golden cross to defend it. All those attackers who did not make a sign of the cross in time were struck blind and easily killed off by the defenders.

Wilfrid was an aristocratic bishop, similar perhaps to those in Gaul, but here without a lineage rooted in centuries of Roman culture. The conflicts of Anglo-Saxon England gave special prominence to martyred warrior kings. Oswald (c.604–42) is typical. He had been converted to Christianity in Ireland, had returned to his native Northumbria and had then overthrown the local king and become king himself. Before the victory over his rival, Oswald had set up a wooden cross, no doubt as a protective charm. His success gave it an aura of sanctity. Splinters were prised off, mixed with water and then fed to humans or animals as cures. The moss scraped off the cross proved as effective. On one occasion Oswald showed his piety by ordering the distribution of fine foods to the poor while at dinner. He had been inspired by his dinner guest, Aidan, Bishop of Lindisfarne, who grasped his arm in approval of Oswald's generosity. Aidan's gesture gave Oswald's arm its own sanctity and when Oswald was killed by the pagan king of Mercia in 642, it was cut off and preserved as a separate relic in a silver container at Bamburgh in Northumberland. The battlefield where Oswald died had such resonance that the soil on which his body fell was scooped up and mixed with water. Eventually there was a hole as deep as a man's height. If the soil was smeared on a lamp post, it would guard against fire. Oswald's severed head had been placed on a stake and this, too, produced healing splinters. While the chronicler of Oswald's life, the Venerable Bede, claims that it was his lifestyle that earned him his sanctity, echoes of ancient pagan customs of hero worship were now being absorbed into Christianity.

Bede is our main source for the period. His *The Ecclesiastical History of the English People* (731) is an accomplished account, much superior to Gregory's history of the Franks (whose Latin has been described by a twentieth-century commentator as 'guilty of every conceivable barbarity').[8] It tells of the triumph of the Northumbrian (Anglo-Saxon or English) Church over the native Britons, whom Bede treats contemptuously not least because of their heretical impulses. It is a driven narrative whose sophistication does much to obscure its biases and exaggerations (although these are difficult to evaluate because there are few other sources with which to compare the *History*). Bede follows Gregory's *History of the Franks* in watching out for and highlighting military victories as a sign of God's support for his chosen people, and his heroes are known through their sanctity and their continuing miracles.

The belief that the sanctity of a person is confirmed by his or her body remaining incorruptible after death reappears in Bede's account of Queen Aethelthryth (often known as her 'Roman' name Etheldreda). Aethelthryth was another woman from a royal family who had founded her own nunnery, in this case on land she owned at Ely in eastern England. She died in 679 of a cancer that had eaten into her jaw, and she was buried in a simple wooden coffin. Sixteen years later, her successor as abbess decided that Aethelthryth's body needed to be given greater reverence and a search was made for a stone coffin. A marble one was found at Granchester near Cambridge. It fitted her body exactly. When the original coffin was opened the body was found as intact as the day she had been buried. Better than this, the physician who had attended her in her last illness testified that he had made a large incision in her cancerous jaw that was still unhealed when she had died. Now it was so well healed that only a tiny scar could be seen. The body had been recomposed in a healed form. Bede noted that her preserved body was also 'proof that she has remained uncorrupted by contact with any man'. Everything was in place for a *translatio* and Aethelthryth's, which took place in 695, is the earliest English one of which we have record (and an indication that the Anglo-Saxon kingdoms were now borrowing rituals from France). Needless to say, the new shrine in which the coffin was housed became a major focus for miracles. The original wooden coffin kept its potency and was helpful with eye problems if one rested one's head on it, while the cloths in which the body had been wrapped proved good at expelling demons from those possessed by them.

Sainthood in this period was certainly a flexible concept. The reverence given to the regal Aethelthryth, the warrior-king Oswald and the arrogant and wealthy Wilfrid emphasises the importance of social status. The boundaries between secular and sacred power have become permeable. In contrast, the figure of Cuthbert (born *c*.635) is saintly in a more conventional sense of the word.[9] Cuthbert's vocation to a life of spirituality came after a stranger on a white horse appeared and healed his damaged knee. Cuthbert joined a monastery and eventually arrived as prior of the monastery on the island of Lindisfarne. Lindisfarne had been founded by the Irish missionary St Aidan, another of Bede's heroes in 635. Aidan had died leaning against a wooden buttress in the church, a buttress that survived intact during two burnings down of the church and that became a relic in itself, splinters being taken off and mixed with water to effect cures.

When Cuthbert was prior, he would often disappear for long periods of solitary prayer and he died on the smaller island of Farne in 687, tended by a single carer within walls that, when he looked out, would only allow him to see the sky. He wished to be buried here, but the monks brought him back to the main island of Lindisfarne. The body was first placed in a stone coffin and then, eleven years later, transferred into a wooden coffin that was given an elevated position in the church. Coming only three years after the *translatio* of Aethelthryth, this suggests that 'elevating' a saint was now a standard practice. Remarkably, large parts of the coffin, which was decorated with images of Christ, the Virgin Mary, the Apostles and the Evangelists, survive (and are now in the Treasury of Durham Cathedral). Naturally enough, the body was found uncorrupted and Bede tells that its limbs were flexible and it looked as if it was merely sleeping. The clothes in which the body had been buried were still 'wondrously bright'. The new prior, Eadberht, was reported by Bede to have burst into song at the sight, comparing the sparing of Cuthbert's body from corruption with the unblemished body of the Old Testament Jonah after he had been vomited from the whale.

Bede, however, does let us into a secret. He knew something of embalming. In a commentary on the Song of Songs he wrote: 'Myrrh and aloes refer to the continence of the flesh, because the nature of these aromatics is that the bodies of the dead, when anointed with them, do not decay.' There was, of course, the biblical precedent of the women coming to Christ's tomb with spices to anoint his body. When Cuthbert's remains were inspected in 1104, the examiner described how cloth had been 'glued' to the entire body. There is circumstantial evidence that when a holy man died, the ceremony of laying him to rest included the anointing with spices, and it could be that the incorruptible state of the body was often the result of this.

Cuthbert's body remained in Lindisfarne for two hundred years. Then, when the Viking invasions threatened in 875, the monks took it onto the mainland. The coffin was carried from place to place (it seems, in fact, from one of the monastery's estates to the next), but any attempt to take it beyond the boundaries of Northumbria was thwarted. When it was put on a boat to Ireland, a tempest drove it back. Cuthbert's reputation spread across England and he even appeared in a vision to Alfred the Great, the king of Wessex between 871 and 899, and promised him that he would drive out the Viking invaders and become ruler of the whole country. It was never to be, but Alfred sent his grandsons north to pay homage to Cuthbert at Chester-le-Street, close to Durham, where the body was temporarily settled. One of these, Edmund, records how he laid two Greek stoles in the uncorrupted body of Cuthbert and, extraordinarily, there still survives at Durham a much-faded silk showing the prophet Jonah which is certainly from the Byzantine east. Eventually, at the end of the tenth century, the coffin and its retinue arrived on the high spur of Durham that is wound round by the River Wear. Here the coffin halted on its wheeled carriage and even a crowd of helpers could not move it on. This was where the saint had decided he must rest. Although the monks fled with their saint back to Lindisfarne during the Norman Conquest, when England was more peaceful Cuthbert was returned to Durham and his body has never left the great Norman cathedral where he, and the Venerable Bede, both lie.

The shrine is bare today, merely a stone with *Cuthbertus* on it, but an account of 1383 shows how over the centuries it was encumbered by an extraordinary collection of offerings that were placed on the steps surrounding it.[10] Ostrich eggs, a rib of the later Anglo-Saxon king, Edward the Confessor, some scorched bones of the martyr Lawrence, milk from the Virgin Mary, St Cecilia's tooth, two griffins' claws, a piece of Moses's rod, bread blessed by Jesus and some wood from a tree in the Garden of Paradise were among the panoply. This is truly a shrine whose contents stretch credulity – one cannot imagine that no one questioned the authenticity of the fingernails of St Malachy, manna found in the Virgin Mary's tomb, a wimple belonging to her mother, St Anne, or the vestment of St John the Evangelist.

Such an impressive accumulation reflects how Durham became the great medieval pilgrimage centre of northern England, rivalled in the rest of the country only by the cult of the Virgin Mary at Walsingham and Thomas Becket's shrine at Canterbury. The wonderful eighth-century *Lindisfarne Gospels*, illustrated on the skins of some five hundred calves, were probably created for Cuthbert's original shrine and travelled with him. His shoes were kept outside the coffin to act as miracle-workers for those who touched them, while hairs from his head were available for distribution to churches that asked for them. In the twelfth century Cuthbert appeared in a vision ordering that one of his vestments be attached to a staff and be taken into battle whenever the Palatinate, the region governed by the Bishop of Durham, was threatened. In 1513 the Duke of Norfolk carried this banner into battle against the Scots at Flodden, and the Scottish army was annihilated. It was little wonder that Cuthbert's shrine had so great a following, and no other English saint had so many churches dedicated to him as Cuthbert – his only rival is Becket himself.

There has always been an air of mystery about the world of the Anglo-Saxons simply because so little is known about them. Christianity wove itself into a world where warriors and saints laid equal claim to holiness, where pagan traditions became entwined with the Gospels to create Christ the warrior god leading his armies. There was a tenacity of worship, the beginnings of a Christian artistic and literary culture, a few centres of scholarship and achievement. Perhaps the most persistent theme was the sacredness of the rulers. Among the later Anglo-Saxon kings were Edmund (r. 855–70), a martyr against the invading Danes, and Edward the Confessor (r. 1042–66), the title 'Confessor' recognising the sanctity of his rule. Both were to have fine shrines – Edmund at Bury St Edmunds, Edward the Confessor at Westminster – which would carry their memory on into Norman and Plantagenet England. Added to the shrine of Cuthbert at Durham, this was an important and enduring legacy.

CHAPTER EIGHT

The Great Consolidator

CHARLEMAGNE (742–814) is the first 'great' figure to emerge from the confusion of what has often been called the 'Dark Ages'.[1] 'Dark' is appropriate partly because so little evidence survives and partly because what does survive suggests an age of profound insecurity with severely debased standards of living. The relics of saints were now pervasive in the Christian parts of Europe. Even when he was still a boy, such relics were important to Charlemagne. He often talked of how he had been present as a seven-year-old at the *translatio* of the body of Saint Germain, a sixth-century Bishop of Paris, to the church of Saint-Germain-des-Prés. As an adult, Charlemagne wore a necklace with two crystal amulets containing pieces of the True Cross and the hair of the Virgin Mary. In the palace chapel he built at his winter capital, Aachen, the most stable of his courts, there was a dress belonging the Virgin, Jesus's swaddling clothes, a cloth used during John the Baptist's beheading, and the waistcloth Jesus wore before his Crucifixion. Charlemagne also used his adulation of relics as a means of distinguishing his own empire from that of the Byzantine east. The *Libri Carolini* of 792, an official statement on religious policy, reflects the views of Charlemagne on the Byzantine Church. 'They, the Greeks, place almost all the hope of their credulity in images [e.g. icons] but it remains firm that we venerate the saints in their bodies or better in their relics or even in their clothing, in the ancient tradition of the fathers.' The Byzantine empire had, of course, its own massive collections of relics, but the conflicts over icons must have given the west the impression that they were preoccupied by images. For Charlemagne, the bones of saints were more potent than mere pictures of them, not least because they appeared to provide a more effective way of maintaining contact with heaven.[2] His words suggest, too, that the 'ancient tradition' of veneration is deeply rooted.

The early years of Charlemagne's reign are ones of conquest. He had succeeded jointly with his brother Carloman in 768 but became sole ruler of the Franks when Carloman died in 771. Almost immediately he confronted the pagan Saxon tribes who were raiding Gaul from the north. Churches were often a casualty of the raids, and in January 775 Charlemagne ordered his warriors 'to overwhelm in wars the infidel and faithless Saxon people and to continue until they had either been defeated and subjugated to Christianity or were completely annihilated'. The campaigns were vicious as the Saxons proved extraordinarily resilient, rising in revolt as soon as Charlemagne was campaigning elsewhere: 4,500 Saxon prisoners were beheaded in one massacre in 782.

The violence behind the conversion of Europe is all too often concealed behind tales of literate and charismatic Irish missionaries lightening the darkness of uncouth barbarians. The reality is often somewhat different. Christianity has always to be seen within a specific historical context. In these centuries Christ was envisaged as a warrior god, fully justified in using his power to coerce recalcitrant pagans. Charlemagne was his instrument. 'If there is anyone of the Saxon people lurking among them unbaptized and if he scorns to come to baptism and wishes to absent himself and stay a pagan, let him die', as the *Capitulary*, the set of administrative rules for Charlemagne's new conquests in Germany, put it in 785.

Between these campaigns, Charlemagne defeated the Lombards, the most powerful kingdom of northern Italy, and crowned himself their king. He pushed back the Arabs into Spain (in a campaign that was to be elaborated in medieval legend), and then in 792 gained enormous plunder from a defeat of the Avars of western Hungary. Although the Hungarian plain was too extensive and unprotected for him to hold, he was now without effective enemies and had enlarged his inherited territory by a half. In late 800 he entered Rome and, after he had prayed at the shrine of Peter, the Pope, Leo III, placed a crown on his head and proclaimed him an emperor and the new protector of Rome.

It was an irrevocable shift in the structure of Mediterranean power. Latin-speaking Rome had long been isolating itself from the Greek-speaking east, had stood clear of the iconoclasm controversy and, even before the reign of

Charlemagne, had begun seeking relations within northern Europe. Now Latin Christendom was consolidating itself. For the first time for four hundred years western Europe had an effective ruler linked to the Latin Church, and hence the Byzantine empire had a rival.

The 'real' Charlemagne eludes us. The biography by his contemporary Einhard, written a few years after his death, is too concerned with relating him to Roman emperors to reveal his personality, although we know he was extrovert and exulted in being at the centre of a throng. In many ways he was a typical Frankish warrior. He loved being on horseback and had a passion for hunting. However, he must have had a determination, energy and charisma that raised him well above his fellow aristocrats. At seven foot, as a study of his bones has confirmed, he towered above them physically as well. He was ruthless in his campaigns, striking quickly and rewarding his warriors so that they felt tightly bound to him so long as victories came. The plunder from his conquests and the slow revival of a European economy in which northern Italy and western Europe were united gave him immense resources and he used them with energy. Charlemagne's policy of *correctio*, a bringing into line of his peoples under a centralised Christian rule, had a dynamic that was in contrast to the more leisurely rituals of the Byzantine empire. His patronage of the arts fostered the so-called 'Carolingian renaissance' in what were essentially the first stirrings of intellectual life since the collapse of the Roman empire. It was the length of Charlemagne's reign, from 768 to 814, that consolidated his empire, although the impetus of the regime faltered in the final ten years.

Charlemagne's title evoked memories of the Roman empire itself and there were certainly echoes of Roman imperialism, in his coins, for instance, but his passion for conversion of pagans showed how far this was an imperialist Christian state. In his *Admonitio Generalis* of 789 Charlemagne compared himself with the biblical king Josiah who founded and implemented the Book of Law. Charlemagne was powerful enough to maintain himself as head of his own Church, and the hierarchy of bishops and monasteries gave him channels of control that proved much more effective than the allegiances of landed aristocrats. Both clergy and laity were ordered to centre their lives on Christian worship and preaching. Clergy and secular leaders travelled together on administrative visitations. Charlemagne's status within the Church was reinforced by the introduction of tithes, a tax of a tenth of produce that went to the Church and added to its wealth and support for the regime. For the first time since the fall of Rome, there was serious discussion of theology at the court and an insistence on the education of the aristocratic elite and clergy.

Shrines were alternative centres of power that could be exploited against central rule by local religious and secular leaders, especially through the emotionally charged processions of the *translatio*. Charlemagne's response was to legislate to bring them under control. At the Synod of Frankfurt, a Council of all the bishops of his empire held in 794, Charlemagne ordered that no new shrines be set up unless they were churches commemorating a deceased person of exemplary behaviour. In 813 it was decreed that the bodies of saints could only be moved in a *translatio* under the auspices of 'the prince' (Charlemagne), a bishop or a Council. In newly absorbed areas such as Bavaria, Charlemagne confiscated shrines from the defeated nobles and placed them under the direct control of his bishops. This was the first period in post-Roman Europe that there was sufficient wealth for relics to be housed appropriately in spectacular churches, and the emperor set the tone by his palace chapel at Aachen that he modelled on the imperial church of San Vitale in Ravenna, Italy. Charlemagne ordered that every altar should have relics and he also made it obligatory for oaths either to be sworn in a church or over the Gospels or relics. The throne in the chapel at Aachen had compartments for the storing of relics and so any oath sworn on it carried the double weight of sacred and secular obligation.

We can see the emphasis on ordered display of relics in a remarkable document, the 'Plan of St Gall', which survives in the library of the monastery founded on the site of the hermitage of St Gall (a companion of the Irish missionary St Columbanus), in present-day Switzerland. The plan dates from the 820s, shortly after Charlemagne's death, and is the earliest known architectural drawing from the Middle Ages (with no equivalent until the thirteenth century). The plan never served as the basis for any building at St Gall and it is probably an idealised version of what a monastery should look like. The abbey church is modelled on the typical basilica of the early church, with an apse at either end and a narrow transept.[3]

It is the way that the altars holding relics are arranged that is of special interest, and here the dedications of the altars appear to relate to the relics that St Gall held in its collection. At the eastern end, set into the apse, is the altar to Paul, and at the western end that to Peter. In the centre of the church, in the nave between these two, is an altar of the Holy Cross and behind this, near the western end of the church, an altar dedicated jointly to John the Evangelist and John the Baptist. (There was a similar joint dedication of the two Johns in St John Lateran in Rome, the cathedral church of the popes.) In front of the apse dedicated to Paul are altars to the Virgin Mary and St Gall himself, in a place of obvious honour, and, immediately before these, altars to St Benedict, the founder of the Order, and St Columbanus. Then on each side of these two, in the transepts, come the Apostles. There are relics of Philip, James and Andrew. On each side of the nave, at ordered intervals along the walls, are four altars and these are reserved for the relics of saints and martyrs who are placed lower in the hierarchy than the Apostles. Stephen, Martin, the Holy Innocents and, jointly, Lucy (a martyr from Syracuse in Sicily, deeply venerated in Rome) and Cecilia are on one side; and Lawrence, Maurice (see below), Sebastian and, jointly, Agatha, another martyr from Sicily, and Agnes are on the other. In effect, the church is used to recreate a Christian Order that is flexible enough to incorporate the local saint in a prominent position.

Charlemagne himself used relics as gifts as a means of binding his senior courtiers to him, echoing here the example of Ambrose. One of the emperor's companions, Angilbert, the consort of his daughter, and abbot of St Riquier in Picardy, rejoiced in the vast array he had accumulated with the help of God 'and the assistance of my glorious lord, the great emperor'. They were housed in a vast abbey church that Charlemagne provided for him. The most original and imposing feature of the church was the western facade, probably the earliest grand facade in church architecture. Here, in 800 in the case of St Riquier, was re-enacted the imperial Roman ceremony of *adventus*, the welcome of an emperor, Charlemagne himself. The facade represents an arched and richly decorated city gate. A similar ceremony of welcome was held at the facade for the arrival of the new relics.[4]

Angilbert neatly grades the relics according to their importance but, for him, in contrast to the hierarchy of the St Gall relics, it is their origin that counts. Those coming from Rome, through Hadrian I (Pope 772–95, and a close friend of Charlemagne), were the most prestigious. Rome had gradually relaxed its ban on distributing relics as it realised the advantages of buying support with them. So, when the Synod of Whitby met in Northumberland in 663–64 and Rome wanted to make sure the assembled clergy voted to accept the authority of Rome, relics of the Apostles Peter and Paul, Lawrence and Gregory the Great were sent north. A cross with a golden key made from the fetters that had bound Peter and Paul in prison was given to the wife of King Oswy in recognition of her piety. It worked, and England accepted papal authority more easily than many of the countries of mainland Europe. Next in the hierarchy after Rome were relics that Charlemagne had acquired through embassies he had sent to Jerusalem and Constantinople. After them came relics from the rest of Italy, Germany, Burgundy and Aquitaine. Angilbert was meticulous about authenticity and he liked to have documents or attached tags as guarantees of his relics' provenance.

Similarly, much of the collection at Sens in France came as a personal gift from Charlemagne when the church was dedicated there in 809. They represented the full sweep of Christian history. The church of the Holy Sepulchre in Jerusalem, under the rule of the Arabs since the seventh century, provided a fragment of the Sepulchre itself. (Charlemagne had been given administrative control of the church by the Caliph Harun-al-Rashid who may have felt that Latin protection was worth having against any future expansion of the Byzantine empire. The Caliph sent Charlemagne relics, in addition to a set of keys to the city and an elephant.) There was a stole that had belonged to the Virgin Mary and the somewhat less prestigious 'relic' of 'a pebble from the River Jordan'. Parts of many early saints included John the Baptist, the Apostle Peter and the martyr Stephen. The Desert Father, Anthony, and Pachomius, the founder of monastic communities in the Egyptian desert in the early fourth century, commemorated the ascetic tradition. Relics of Pope Gregory the Great were included as were those of his contemporary, Isidore, Bishop of Seville, a scholarly bishop associated with the eradication of Arianism in Spain.

Then there were fragments of more exotic saints. Maurice, a Nubian legionary stationed in Switzerland under the empire, who refused to order the killing of Christians and who was executed in his turn, was applauded as a model Christian soldier. (As late as 1916 'his' sword and spurs were used at the coronation of Austro-Hungarian emperors.) Another martyr was Anastasius, a Persian who had converted from Zoroastrianism to Christianity in the early seventh century, travelled to Jerusalem and then had been decapitated by his fellow countrymen when they attacked the city. Angilbert was generous enough to send a relic of the Apostle Andrew from his own cache at St Riquier. Chelles, another collection formed at this time, included among its treasures some of the water of the Tigris and Euphrates rivers gathered, it was said, just as they flowed out of Paradise, and a piece of the stone on which Moses was standing when he saw God, together with a list of saints as comprehensive as that at Sens.

The favoured shrines were thus providing a perspective on Christian history that stretched back through time to Moses and other figures of the Old Testament. This represents a dramatic enlargement of Christian consciousness, mirroring the reopening of the Mediterranean world to travel and trade in this century. Charlemagne also reinforced the supremacy of his own kingdom over its conquered neighbours by gathering the relics of Frankish martyrs and allocating them to new churches such as in Saxony, thus confirming Christian sovereignty over conquered pagan territory.

One feature of Charlemagne's empire was the growth of wealthy monasteries that based their prestige on the saint whose body they honoured. His father, Peppin, had set a pattern by enriching the shrine of Saint Germain with the estates of the dispossessed Merovingians. The most forceful Anglo-Saxon missionary of the period was Wynfrith, the 'Apostle of Germany' (675–754), better known as Boniface, from the Roman name he adopted. Boniface was a contemporary of Bede and shared his view that the bringing of Christianity to the pagans should be an heroic endeavour. Although historians have recently downgraded Boniface's role as the first missionary to this area, the legend of his achievement remains powerful. Boniface's mission to the Germans was dramatically inaugurated in 723 by beginning to cut down a great oak tree venerated by the pagan natives at Geismar (in modern Thuringia). He called upon the pagan gods to avenge their shrine if they had power to do so, but the tree miraculously fell of its own accord. The timbers were used to build a new church dedicated to the Apostle Peter. Thirty years of preaching across Germany followed and Boniface set up a hierarchy of dioceses, each one acting as a springboard for further expansion. He believed that the Christian world should be publicised through the status of its missionaries and he travelled in style. This was his undoing. In June 754 his retinue was set upon by a band of pirates as it reached the North Sea coast. They were after treasure and threw aside the liturgical manuscripts Boniface was carrying with him as they rummaged through his chests. One of the texts survives with cuts in it, perhaps when it was held up to defend its owner from the slashing swords that killed him.

Whatever the motives of the pirates, Boniface had become a martyr and his body had to be appropriately housed. The church chosen was that of the monastery at Fulda (near modern-day Itesse in Germany) that Boniface had himself founded ten years earlier on the site of an ancient Merovingian fort in the forest of Buchonia. Although it followed a Benedictine rule, Boniface had shrewdly placed the monastery under the direct protection of Pope Hadrian and it benefited from immense patronage from local nobles as Christianity spread through Germany or was imposed there by Charlemagne. There was one fraught episode during the Saxon wars when the monks had to flee with their precious relic but, as the empire settled, a great church grew up around the crypt where Boniface's body still lies. Endowed with estates able to provide the large numbers of skins of cattle and sheep needed for parchment, and thus the copying and writing of texts, Fulda became one of the most important centres of Carolingian learning.

After Charlemagne's defeat of the Lombards, the Pope was also able to profit from more settled conditions, and Hadrian and Charlemagne became close to each other, although Charlemagne never paid more than lip service to the spiritual authority of any Pope.[5] Hadrian was able to regain many papal estates in Italy and to plough back the income into the glorification of his native city, especially its major shrines, St Peter's, St Paul's, St Lawrence's, and the opulent basilica of Santa Maria Maggiore that now boasted the manger from Bethlehem among its relics. Charlemagne provided the massive timbers needed for the reroofing of these churches, and in return Hadrian sent him 'mosaic, marbles, and other materials from floors and walls' from Rome and Ravenna for the building of the palace chapel at Aachen.

Hadrian also addressed the problem of the catacombs that still housed a vast number of bones. These had already been raided by the Lombards in the dying days of their kingdom and now further looting was taking place; shepherds were using the tunnels as shelters for their flocks and many of the passageways were beginning to fall in. Hadrian ordered cartloads of bones to be moved into the city. In the church of Santa Maria in Cosmedin he created a vault with niches into which relics could be stored for veneration. It still exists. Pope Paschal I (r. 817–24) continued the policy and the churches of Santa Cecilia in Trastevere and San Prassede were created for the bones of these native Roman saints brought in from the catacombs to the sites of what were believed to have been their original homes in the city.

This more relaxed policy stimulated a direct demand for relics from Rome, and Charlemagne and his successors cast themselves as saviours of the Roman Christian heritage. An imperial document of 802 praises the Carolingians not only for rescuing 'the relics of blessed martyrs from Rome but for giving them special veneration in reliquaries of gold and precious stones'. The connection continued after Charlemagne's death in 814. In 823 Charlemagne's grandson, Lothair, himself to be emperor of the Franks from 840 to 855, visited Rome where a vicious battle for the papacy was going on between rival candidates. Lothair backed the winner, Eugenius II, but named the price of his support. He insisted that the Franks should always be consulted in future papal elections and that the body of St Sebastian, a victim of persecution under the first-century emperor Domitian, should be released to him as a gift. He then allocated it to Hilduin, the Bishop of Paris and arch-chamberlain to the court, who had travelled with Lothair, and it was carried back to a monastery at Soissons.

Hilduin's fellow bishops were furious at this endowment. The embarrassed Pope Eugenius quickly announced that Sebastian had never been moved at all and was still in Rome, but it was too late to stop other courtiers wanting their own 'Roman' relics. In Rome a deacon, Deusdona, set up a black market in the trade. He had unlimited access to the poorly guarded catacombs and each year raided a different suburb of the city. As soon as the looted relics had safely crossed the Alps they were brought out into the open and processed towards the collector who had bought them.[6]

One of Deusdona's clients was Einhard, the biographer of Charlemagne (and in fact, the historian who coined the title *Carolus magnus*, 'Charlemagne') and now private secretary to his son, Louis. Einhard was an exceptional man, known for his learning and eloquence as well as his honesty. He had been instrumental in securing a smooth succession to Charlemagne and so was equally respected by the new emperor, Louis the Pious. Louis had granted him estates along the River Main, traditionally a border zone of the Roman empire which had only become Christianised under Charlemagne. This was Boniface's country and his burial place at Fulda was not far north of Einhard's estates. It was already a major pilgrimage site.

Einhard provides an outstanding example of a man who knew exactly how to link the power of the saints to his personal prestige. First he had to get hold of some top-class relics. In 827 he put in an order to Deusdona for

Saints Marcellinus and Peter, two well-known martyrs from the persecution of Diocletian. The recent death of Pope Eugenius provided the power vacuum Deusdona needed in which to locate and snatch the bodies. As soon as they were safely over the Alps, out they came from their wrappings and they were paraded on their journey northwards.

Einhard was a fervent believer in continuing Charlemagne's policy of *correctio*, the imposition of order through the Church, and for him this involved building new churches on his estates. He first brought his relics to the remote town of Michelstadt, then he moved them to his estate at Mulinheim, on the Main itself, which was much more accessible. His 'excuse' was that at Michelstadt the reliquary had begun oozing blood which he chose to interpret as a sure sign that the saints were unhappy there. Now the saints showed their pleasure at their new home and miracles began to be reported.

Yet Einhard knew that he had to establish a momentum of miracles that could get his shrine established, and here he proved to be an adept opportunist. In 828 he heard rumours that Hilduin had planted a thief in the retinue accompanying the saints from Rome, and that part of Saint Marcellinus had gone missing and then had reappeared at Soissons. Hilduin was temporarily in disgrace for supporting Louis's sons against their father and he was forced to disgorge his gains. Einhard made the most of it. The regained relics were brought up to the royal court at Aachen and Louis and his queen Judith met them with gifts. Miracles started happening and Einhard began a shrewd distribution of fragments of the relics to favoured courtiers. Then he carried out a *translatio* of the recovered relics from Aachen to Mulinheim that drew out adoring crowds as the relics passed. By the time Einhard had reunited his purchase, his prestige had soared. 'At present the courtiers are mostly talking about the signs and miracles happening in Einhard's house by means of his saints', the palace librarian recorded.[7] Einhard was soon at work compiling a miracle list for his shrine in which he stressed how pilgrims were coming from all over the region for cures.

Einhard was still not satisfied. He had wider ambitions: to use his saints to bring the empire closer to Rome. He had been very conscious that Hilduin had, in the body of Sebastian, a more prestigious saint than his two. Hilduin had now been seen off but something more dramatic needed to be done if the undeveloped Christianity of the region was to be given order. In Rome,

Pope Paschal I had set the model for a relic shrine at the church of San Prassede where he had brought the bones of 2,300 saints that he had collected from the catacombs. Typically for the time, he had placed them in a crypt. In 830 Einhard began building a new church at Mulinheim that was directly modelled on San Prassede, no less than an echo of Rome-on-the-Main. It had its effect. Within seven years of Einhard's death, Mulinheim was known as Saligenstadt, 'the holy place'.

Einhard had used relics to enhance his own prestige. While bishops had been the traditional instigators of shrines, he had shown that courtiers were now able to do the same. Yet he manipulated his cult to strengthen his position against a rival, Hilduin, and to shape the form that Christianity would take in this newly Christianised region through providing a direct link to Rome. The boundaries between the use of relics for religious and political purposes had become blurred, another sign of how flexible such relics had become as vehicles of personal ambition and religious strategy.

A few voices dared to protest against the relic cults. Claudius, Bishop of Turin from 817 to 827, stands out as an outspoken maverick. He was one of the small elite who had received an intensive education in the Christian classics, notably those by Augustine, but he revived the almost forgotten tradition of Vigilantius in that he argued that believers should forge a direct relationship with God and Christ that had no place for images, relics or even intercession by the saints. Holy men and women could have spiritual power during their lives, but this faded as soon as they had died. Claudius ridiculed any icon that represented the Christian story. Just because Mary remained a virgin did not mean that virgins should be given special veneration. He even deplored the making of the sign of the cross. God called on men to carry the cross, not to adore it. Furthermore, it was pointless for a priest to require a penitent to make a pilgrimage to Rome, when repentance could be done as easily in any monastery. The popes only held special power in so far as their lives were modelled on those of the Apostles; the power of Peter had passed to all bishops, not only to the bishops of Rome. Hardly surprisingly, Claudius was condemned by that great collector of relics, Pope Paschal I, and he remains a lone voice.

CHAPTER NINE

Hope and Desperation in a Disordered World

THE FRAGMENTATION that followed as Charlemagne's empire disintegrated saw the end of relic cults as expressions of imperial patronage, but there was now an urgent need for their help in protecting vulnerable institutions in an age of disorder. It was as if they sprung back against the pressures of Charlemagne's control and took on new roles. Once again we see the astonishing flexibility in the way in which cults could be manipulated to respond to new challenges. Paschasius Radbertus (785–865), the abbot of the Benedictine monastery of Corbie (in northern France), provides some sense of this awakening. 'Never before have so many and so great things been done by the relics of saints since the beginning of the world, for everywhere saints in this kingdom and those brought here excite each other to song even as cocks at cockcrow'.[1]

The ease with which relics were adapted to new functions can be seen in the kingdom of West Francia, which was formally separated from the Carolingian empire in 843. It stretched from Flanders and Champagne in the north to Toulouse and Gascony in the south. Central control was never strong and by the time a new dynasty emerged – the Capetians, founded by the Count of Paris, Hugh Capet, who was proclaimed king in 987 – allegiances to the monarchy were weak. As authority disintegrated, the last remnants of the Carolingian structure of government, the counts, were easily outmanoeuvred by local warlords. 'Evil doers had sprung up like seeds and wicked men ravaged the vineyard of the lord like thorn bushes and briars choking the harvest' as one bishop put it.[2] These built up their own power bases and protected themselves in newly built castles.

It was the monasteries that suffered most from these depredations but, in the late tenth century, they responded imaginatively through the 'Peace of

God' movement, an attempt to restore what the monks saw as the divine order instituted by heaven. In practical terms, the movement, which was strongly supported by the local bishops, was a desperate attempt to force the rampaging nobles to reject the use of violence. It is first recorded in Aquitaine in south-western France, an area where Hugh Capet's authority was especially weak. The monasteries here, notable among them St Martial of Limoges, St Geraud of Aurillac and St Julian of Brioude, had built up extensive but scattered estates. They were thus especially vulnerable to unrest and land-grabbing and had every reason to join in common cause to protect themselves. They knew they could rely on the support of the peasantry who had most to lose from having their bodies harassed or their lands taken over by power-hungry nobles, and the movement was supported by mass popular enthusiasm.

It was now that the saints and their relics came into their own. Studies of the monastic liturgies, especially that of the abbey of St Martial at Limoges in central France, show how they were given a heightened presence in worship in this period. Illuminated manuscripts highlight their role as intercessors by showing them assembled around Christ, often in song, with their faithful followers gathered on earth. Studies of the lives of saints show that whereas in Carolingian times they often did not include any miracles, by the tenth century books of miracles were the most popular form of hagiography. When a saint's feast day took place, there was a formal reading out of all the miracles he or she had effected.[3]

An important mark of the new status of saints is the appearance of reliquaries in which their remains were displayed, not only on an altar, but in processions through the surrounding neighbourhood. One of these survives from this period, the reliquary in which was placed the head of the child martyr St Foy, a Gallic girl killed by the Romans when she was twelve. The reliquary is of gold and studded with gems and is partly reworked from a Roman original. It aroused enormous devotion. Writing in 1010, Bernard d'Angers described how 'the crowd of people prostrating themselves on the ground was so dense it was impossible to kneel down. . . . When they saw it [the reliquary] for the first time, all in gold and sparkling with precious stones and looking like a human face, the majority of the peasants thought that the statue was really looking at them and answering their prayers with her eyes.'[4] The custom was for pilgrims to circulate three times around the statue in the hope of protection for their coming journey on to the shrine of St James at Compostela, but the miracle lists that date from the eleventh century suggest St Foy was particularly good at curing blindness. She was also so adept at 'begging' jewellery off pilgrims that women were warned not to bring theirs with them.

The relics of St Martial and St Geraud are among those known to have been encased in gold statues. It was as if the reality of fractured bones and decayed flesh had to be glorified in gold and precious stones if its true value as the body of a saint could be recognised. There was a further innovation. From the eleventh century, reliquaries might also be made in the shape of the bone or body part they held – an arm for a saint's arm, for instance. There was an intriguing use of arm reliquaries. At the end of the Mass the celebrant gave the congregation a blessing before they left. That given by a bishop was of a much higher status that that by a mere priest, and congregations often felt they had been badly done by. Yet if the priest held up an arm reliquary and blessed the congregation with that, it was believed to have the same effect as if the bishop himself had been there.[5]

The advantage of placing a relic in a portable reliquary was obvious. It could be carried outside the monastery, so adding to the flexibility and range of relic cults. The *Vercelli Homilies*, an early example of English prose dating from this period, the late tenth century, show how relics are used as a Christian substitute for the ancient fertility rituals on the so-called Rogation days in the spring when God's blessings on the land were called for in return for penitence. 'We must carry holy relics that are the remains of holy men, of their hair or parts of their body or clothing, and with all these holy things we must go humbly around our land in these holy days. And our cattle and our homeland and our woods and all our goods we must commend to God. . . .'[6] We know that the St Foy reliquary could be taken out by the monks for a whole day and they would stop at ancient sacred places, wells or crossroads, and these gained their own healing powers while the relic was resting there. It presided over the councils of the community, was hurried to the site of any disaster and once, when there was a riot in the cloisters at Conques in south-eastern France, it was thrust in the faces of the rioters.

St Martial was one of the most prominent advocates of 'the Peace of God' movement, and his status was elaborated to create the legend that he was a relation of the Apostle Peter who was present during Christ's Passion and at the foundation of the Church at Pentecost. Martial's 'legend' was actually ghostwritten in the eleventh century by Ademar of Chabannes, a monk of St Martial. Ademar was deeply embarrassed when his cover was blown by an Italian monk, Benedict of Chiusa, and Ademar was forced to respond by building forgery upon forgery to such effect that the legend became accepted as the truth from the eleventh century onwards. It was not until the 1920s that the fabricated manuscripts were decoded and Benedict of Chiusa was vindicated. So throughout the Middle Ages, Martial's status as a friend of the Apostles remained intact.[7]

The 'Peace of God' was enforced through councils, normally called by the local bishop at a moment of special crisis. In 994 crops in the region around Limoges had been ravaged by disease and to counter it the body of St Martial 'was raised up [from his tomb] so that everyone was filled with immeasurable joy, and all sickness ceased: and a pact of peace and justice was sworn by the duke and his princes . . . with the huge crowd of people filling all the places to within twelve miles around the city, rejoicing under open brilliant skies'.[8] Some councils were responses to events such as solar eclipses that were taken as portents of doom; others were related to the heightened expectations at the first millennium or the year 1033, the thousandth anniversary of the Crucifixion. Relics played an important part. One account from the ancient Pyrenean town of Rodez, tells how the bishop called a council to which all the surrounding monasteries were asked to bring their relics. 'These reliquaries were marshalled in array under tents and pavilions, in the pastures of St. Felix situated about a mile from the city.' The gold reliquary of St Foy is recorded among them, as well as three others, one dedicated to the Virgin Mary, the others to two bishops. At some councils relics were thrown into a heap and surrounded by thorns, a 'humiliation', as it was termed, that could only be reversed if all present swore on the relics that they would keep the peace. In another case, recorded from Bourges in central France in 1038, all the attending males over the age of fifteen swore over the relics of St Stephen that they would actively confront anyone who broke the oath.

The oaths normally confirmed that the lands and clergy of the monastery would be protected, but many included the harvest, vineyards, mills, granaries, goods being carried in carts and, in one case, even bees. One can even see the councils as a means of organising poor relief by ensuring that the more powerful did not corner food supplies. The penalty for breach of the oath was excommunication. This was an important deterrent now that noble families were consolidating their relationships with favoured monasteries and expecting to be buried there from generation to generation. Anyone excommunicated could be refused burial and so the relationship would be broken.

The Peace of God movement marks important shifts in medieval society, especially in the emergence of a more clearly defined clerical elite due to their initiatives as protectors of their lands. It was during this period that clerical celibacy was advocated (it was a condition laid down by the council held at Anse in 994 and officially extended to the whole western Church in 1049) and the role of the laity in Church affairs diminished. At a council held at Bourges in 1031, it was decreed that lay people could no longer appoint their own priests without the consent of the local bishop. Increasingly the Church claimed that it, rather than the State, had the right to judge its own, later the major cause of contention between Thomas Becket and Henry II.

The enhanced authority of the clergy was recorded by one of the few contemporary historians of these events, Rodulphus Glaber of the prosperous abbey of Cluny, who notes how integral relics were to the process. 'The bishops and abbots and other devout men of Aquitaine summoned great councils of the whole people to which were borne the bodies of many saints and innumerable caskets of holy relics . . . [and the people] came rejoicing and ready, one and all, to obey the commands of the clergy [sic] no less than if they had been given by a voice from heaven speaking to men on earth'. In short, the 'councils' of West Francia provide the first evidence of relics as mass drama, the gathering of crowds in a heightened state of tension in the hopes of not only bringing peace to their region but appeasing God in time before the Last Judgement that many feared was imminent. When 'the bishops raised their crosiers to heaven', at one council, 'all present stretched their palms to God', shouting with one voice "Peace! Peace! Peace!": this was the sign of their perpetual covenant which they had vowed between themselves and God.[9] Rodulphus Glaber noted, too, that for the first time crowds of ordinary peasants and women were among the 'innumerable multitude of people from the whole world', setting off to pilgrimage at Jerusalem in 1033.

Tied in with the breakdown of order was a rise in millennium fervour. The year 1000 and later 1033, the thousandth anniversary of the Crucifixion, aroused intense disquiet that the end of times was near: perhaps the thousand years of rule by the Antichrist predicted by John in the Book of Revelations was about to begin. Every event became charged. So at Orléans in central France in 999 an icon of Christ on the Cross began weeping tears and crowds flocked to see it. The next year much of the city burned down. It was then remembered how Jesus had wept over Jerusalem and predicted its destruction (Luke 19:41–44). Sure enough, news reached Europe in 1009 that the Holy Sepulchre in Jerusalem had been vandalised. Tragically, the story was soon put about that the caliph had been incited to do this by the Jews. Rodulphus Glaber tells how Jews were driven from their homes, some massacred and others forced to suicide 'so it was that after this very proper vengeance [sic] had been taken, very few of them were to be found in the Roman world'.

While many of the laity appeared to become closer to the clergy in this age of apparent crisis, a different aspect of millennium fervour was a growing disgust with the increasing power of the Church. It was rooted in the wealth of the Church and the distancing of the clergy from their flocks. When Bernard of Chiusa publicly accused Ademar of forging his life of St Martial to boost the wealth of his monastery, he was wildly applauded by onlookers. Demands for a return to the teachings of the Gospels and poverty of the Apostles appear at just this time. Ominously, these demands were soon declared heretical by the authorities and therefore the eleventh century sees the revival of systematic persecution by the Church. The very first judicial burning of heretics in Europe for which there is firm evidence involved a dozen clerics at Orléans who challenged the validity of an ordained priesthood, the sacraments and the miraculous events of Christ's life. They died at the stake in 1022.[10]

The heightened tensions and fears of the age are also visible in the arts. Whereas in the Carolingian period Christ had been portrayed as a warrior, now, by the tenth century, the focus shifts to his role as judge. The Old English poem *Christ III*, which is dated to about 940, describes how the Cross of Christ, here portrayed with Christ hanging on it drenched in blood, 'shall bring calamities and afflictions on men, on them who, working iniquity, rendered not thanks to God. . . . He is minded to exact a return with rigour when the red [e.g. bloody] cross shines brightly over all in the place of the sun. . . . Thus it shall go hard on the stern day of the great judgment with them who, defiled by deadly sins, shall behold the scars, the wounds, and anguish of the Lord.' The Gero crucifix, still in Cologne where it was commissioned in the late tenth century, is the first to show Christ on the Cross, not triumphant but slumped in death. The Christ in tears in Orléans represents his suffering at the hands of sinful humanity. In 1010 Ademar had his own vision of Christ weeping on the Cross, one that had such a devastating impact that it was twenty years before he could talk of it.[11]

The new mood of desperation is reflected in the prayers that survive that tell of the inner pain of guilty sinners. In about 1075, a supplicant recorded his anguish in a prayer to the Virgin Mary. 'O most sweet and holy ever-Virgin Mary, I stand grieving before the face of your piety, confounded beyond measure by the abominations of my sins; I have become filthy, deformed, and horrible to the angels and all the saints. I am extremely frightened of the judgement of eternal damnation. . . . Where can I flee from the face of your Son, our Lord and judge . . . If he should judge me justly for my actions, it would have been better for me that I had not been conceived, or killed as soon as I was born . . .[12] These prayers are important not simply because of their obvious authenticity, but because they explain so much of the intensity of emotion that accompanied visits to the shrines and which is otherwise unrecorded. The medieval church did nothing to encourage the faithful that they would escape hell and, in fact, in so far as it followed Augustine, taught of the innate sinfulness of humanity that God had every right to punish.

One of the most noticeable developments of the eleventh century is the focus on an inner core of saints close to Christ: the Virgin Mary, Apostles, disciples and Evangelists.

As this prayer suggests, the Virgin Mary becomes the most prominent. An annual procession in Rome on the eve of each 15 August in which an icon of Christ was taken to the church of Santa Maria Maggiore where it 'met' an icon of the Virgin Mary painted by the Evangelist Luke had become more elaborate every year since its inauguration in the late seventh century. From the year 1000 and probably at the direct instigation of the Holy Roman Emperor Otto (r. 996–1002), the rituals spread north and are found at the opulent abbey at Cluny from where they travel even to England. At Cluny the procession including the solemn carrying of relics included a vial containing the milk of the Virgin.[13]

Other cults of those close to Christ were also growing. The body of Mark the Evangelist was being venerated in Venice by the ninth century (see

Chapter 13). The body of Mary Magdalen had, according to a legend first recorded in the eleventh century, been found on the coast of Provence in the mid-eighth century and taken from there northwards to a new home at Vézelay in Burgundy (see Chapter 18). The story of St Martial as close friend of Christ and the Apostles, created by Ademar of Chabannes, first appears at the same time at Limoges (and a grand new basilica was dedicated to him in 1028). In England the legend that Joseph of Arimathea, who had provided the tomb in which Jesus was buried, came to Glastonbury with the Holy Grail, the cup used by Jesus at the Last Supper and then by Joseph to catch the blood of Jesus as he hung from the Cross, appears not much later. Relics of the Apostle Andrew, three fingers of the saint's right hand, the upper bone of an arm, one kneecap and one of his teeth, were said to have been brought to what is now the town of St Andrews in Scotland in the fourth century. Legend tells how King Angus of the Picts, facing an army of Saxons in 832, had a vision of a diagonal cross, the saltire, similar to that on which tradition tells that Andrew was crucified. From then on he becomes a patron saint of Scottish nationalism, evoked as a protector by the medieval champions of Scotland against the English William Wallace and Robert the Bruce. Just outside Paris, there was the shrine of St Denis. This had originally been created in honour of a third-century Celtic martyr of this name, but in 836 Hilduin, the abbot of St Denis, claimed that Denis was none other than the Dionysius who had been converted by Paul in Athens (Acts 17:34), and so he 'upgraded' the cult by extending it two hundred years back in time to a completely different individual.

One of the most important new cults, in the sense that it is still vital today, was that of the Apostle James ('Santiago' as the Spanish corruption of Saint James makes it) at Compostela in north-western Spain.[14] The Visigothic rulers, successors of the Roman empire in the fifth century, had been driven northwards by the advance of the Arabs through the peninsula in the early eighth century. The embattled Christian kingdom had an urgent need for a saint who could be used as a figurehead to confront the invaders. As early as the seventh century, a legend had emerged that James had shown a special interest in the peninsula. It told how he had gone to preach in Spain after the Crucifixion but had returned to Judaea where he had been beheaded by Herod Agrippa in AD 44. There was then a miraculous *translatio* of his headless body in a boat without sailors or a rudder that carried it back to Spain. In the ninth century a hermit, Pelagius, dreamed that he knew where the grave was. A light had shown him the exact spot at Compostela in Galicia, and there the Apostle was found. The head was discovered later and rejoined the rest of the body. The shrine gains prominence in the tenth century. The earliest French pilgrim known to have made the trip to the shrine of St James of Compostela is Bishop Gottschalk of Le Puy in 951.

So although the ninth and tenth centuries might seem to have been a period of breakdown, there was no lack of imaginative responses. The most prestigious saints from the Christian past in Europe – the Apostles James and Andrew, Mary Magdalen, the Evangelist Mark – received new shrines that were to become of lasting importance in the medieval world and beyond. The clergy consolidated themselves as a defined class, again using relics to support their role. Relics had also become portable and so could be used flexibly to make a show of spiritual power when there were large gatherings. Up to now the bishops had been the focus and coordinators of Christian worship, but now the monks began to emerge as the ideal of Christian life, even though the contrast between their professed asceticism and the wealth of the monasteries created new tensions.

It was a period, too, when parishes were establishing their own identity often through their own shrines, churchyards and, as one can still see from the many stone examples that survive from the twelfth century, baptismal fonts. No longer did one have to go to the local bishop to be welcomed into the Church. Each new altar needed its own relics and these could either be brought in or appropriated from remains of the local holy men and women of the past. Rodulphus Glaber echoes Paschasius Radbertus: 'When the whole world was clothed in a white mantle of new churches . . . the relics of many saints were revealed by various signs where they had long been hidden. It was as though they had been waiting for a brilliant resurrection and were now, by God's permission, revealed to the gaze of the faithful; certainly they brought much comfort to men's minds.'[15] In a time of social and religious change, the persistence of the cults was an important form of stability, anchoring Christianity to the emotional needs of the masses.

CHAPTER TEN

Cults and the Rise of Anti-Semitism

T HE OUTBURST of 'vengeance' against Jews in 1009 was a stark reminder
that they had long been vulnerable to Christian prejudice and hostility. As
far back as the second century AD, the Jews had, collectively, been accused of
the murder of Jesus, the Son of God, in effect deicide. By the fifth century
they had been excluded from public life. Their close-knit communities made
them easy to scapegoat and attack. In the 1090s there had been massacres of
the Jewish populations of several European cities by passing crusaders.
Guibert of Nogent records how, in Rouen, northern France, the crusaders
'herded the Jews into a certain place of worship, rounding them up by force
and guile and without distinction of age or sex put them to the sword'. In this
chapter we will tell the story of one cult that was born within this climate of
suspicion.

A community of Jews had been brought to England by William the
Conqueror after his successful invasion of England in 1066. The community
originated in Rouen where Jews had long acted as moneylenders and
changers. These European Jews were a well-educated group and have been
seen by medievalists as 'culturally far superior to their Christian counter-
parts',[1] largely due to their deep-rooted traditions of education and skills in
literacy and numeracy. They settled first in London but by 1159 nine other
Jewish communities are known in England. One of these, numbering about
two hundred, was in Norwich, in eastern England, home of a flourishing
trade with north-western Europe and Rouen itself.

The Jews were attractive to the Norman elite. Unlike the native English
many could speak French. They could loan money without breaking the rules
against usury to which Christians were subject, and change into English

coinage the silver that was flooding into England as payment for wool. As a result they had the special protection of the king or, outside London, the local sheriff, the king's representative. In Norwich the sheriff occupied the castle that the Normans had built to impose their authority. The Jews clustered in the streets very close by to it and, in addition to their normal commercial activities, had forged some links with the lively artisan community.

Norwich was also made the centre of a new diocese of East Anglia. In 1091 Herbert of Losinga became bishop and he founded a cathedral in the city with a Benedictine monastery (known in such a case as a priory) along-side it. The buildings were ready for occupation in 1101 although the great cathedral church was only finished in 1145, long after Herbert's death. Herbert was a forceful character, a preacher and a teacher, who believed personal example was more important than using the miraculous as a means of getting his way. His cathedral was dedicated then (as now) to the Holy Trinity and not to any named saints. It is not even known whose relics were there.

At Easter 1144 a twelve-year-old boy, William, who was an apprentice tanner in Norwich, disappeared and was later found dead in a local wood.[2] Soon rumours began going around that he had been taken by the local Jews who had ritually tortured and crucified him and then dumped his body. William's family were among the first to make the accusations. The women of the family had the habit of receiving visions and these apparently included some that predicted the murder of William or saw him in heaven. The women were known for their piety and the monks at the cathedral priory were sympathetic to the story. When miracles were reported, the boy's body was brought into the monks' own cemetery. The miracles then ceased and there is little evidence of any hostility against the Jews. No one was ever found guilty of William's murder. Here, it seemed, was a potential cult that had never become active.

In about 1150, however, a monk newly arrived at the priory, one Thomas of Monmouth, produced the first part of *The Life and Passion of St. William, the Martyr of Norwich*. He added to it over the years, with the final additions appearing as late as 1173. The *Life* provides a compelling insight into the creation of a cult that seems to have originated in the mind of Thomas. He began by describing the holiness of little William. He then claimed that he had personally investigated the murder. He had been given an eyewitness account of the wooden structure on which the Crucifixion had taken place, had heard tell that the body was still uncorrupted when the monks had transferred it to their cemetery, and he had been able to inspect the body's wounds. Thomas also had the support of his bishop, William de Turbeville, who saw the cult of William as a means of gaining revenue for the cathedral and, in particular, publicised any miracles that brought benefits to his clergy.

However, William de Turbeville and his literary monk faced opposition. The sheriff, John de Chesney, the king's own representative in Norwich, would give no support to the cult. He recognised its anti-Semitic undertones and knew it might arouse a backlash against the Jewish community that he was responsible to the king for protecting. Furthermore, John's own family was supporting the rival cult of St Faith at the nearby shrine of Horsham St Faith. The monastery at Horsham had been founded in 1105 by two English pilgrims who had visited the shrine of St Foy in Conques and brought back two of its monks, and presumably some relics, with them. It had been given the blessing of Pope Alexander III in 1163 and so was a serious rival to a local saint who had no international contacts or papal support.

The opponents to the cult of William assembled their case. It was not certain, they said, that the Jews had murdered William, and how could William de Turbeville and Thomas expect to set up their cult without any higher ecclesiastical approval. Others complained that saints always came from families of good social status whereas William was no more than 'a poor and neglected little fellow', hardly one that God would have chosen for a saint (an interesting reflection on how sainthood and social status were still seen to go hand in hand). Thomas retaliated with the example of Christ's poverty and the story of the Holy Innocents. Some challenged the miracle record. Thomas hit back: the miracles actually confirmed William's sanctity by recording his innocence, virginity and martyrdom.

Thomas had a clear strategy. His immediate aim was to get William's body transferred from the monk's cemetery to a more prestigious site within the priory. It was the prior, Elias, who had to be won over to this and Elias proved obdurate. Thomas was not to be deterred. He told Elias that he had received visions from the founder of the monastery and cathedral, Bishop Herbert of Losinga. In them Herbert had specifically requested that William's body be transferred to the priory.

Elias finally gave way but he was grudging and set his conditions. The body was to be laid, not within the priory church or cathedral, but in the monks' chapterhouse, a most unusual place for a relic to be placed. The monks met there on a daily basis so it would have been difficult to provide access for pilgrims. Elias allowed the stone floor to be cut away for the sarcophagus to be lowered into it but he insisted that the sarcophagus must not protrude above ground. There was to be no showing off of this disputed saint. On the sixth anniversary of William's death, the Wednesday after Palm Sunday in 1150, after Lauds, six sympathetic monks at last brought William's body into the chapterhouse. Now the 'martyr' was to make his own protest against the attempts to demean his sanctity. Each time the stonemasons tried to sink the sarcophagus to ground level, it popped up again. Once again Elias had to give way in face of such obvious divine intervention but he insisted that a carpet and a candle laid beside the grave be removed.

Next the miracles began. The sub-prior had a vision in which the carpet and candle were required to be returned. Then, in October 1150, Elias died and Thomas went so far as to suggest that it was because he had insulted the memory of William. The cult gathered momentum as many more miracles were reported. In 1151 the priory chapter, now without Elias as their prior, agreed that the body be moved again, to a space south of the high altar in the priory church. In April 1154 a fourth *translatio* took place when the bones were moved into the chapel of the martyrs in the cathedral itself.

Thomas's cult had succeeded because of a focused campaign by a small group of dedicated monks who had the support of their bishop and were able to exploit an undercurrent of anti-Semitism. The cult never attracted many pilgrims. The vast majority of recorded visitors came from Norwich and the larger towns of Norfolk, the county of which Norwich is capital. Only ten pilgrims are recorded as coming from outside the diocese of East Anglia. Yet it may have been this cult that led to accusations of ritual murder of children by Jews that became part of the anti-Semitic folklore of medieval Europe. In England within twenty years further child martyrdoms attributed to the Jews were recorded at Gloucester, Bury St Edmunds and Bristol. William's cult was still active in the sixteenth century (when all English cults were dissolved at the Reformation). In Loddon church in Norfolk a painted panel of about 1500 shows William spreadeagled on a scaffold with Jews surrounding him, one of whom is collecting his blood in a bowl. As we shall see (Chapter 19),

Jews were closely linked to the abuse of Christian blood, including that of Christ himself.

There is, in fact, little evidence for further hostility to the Jewish community in Norwich in the 1150s, but in England as a whole there was growing antagonism to the Jews during the reign of Henry II (r. 1154–89). The contemporary historian William of Newburgh complained that Henry's continuing royal support for the Jews disfigured his reign. The payment of interest was, naturally, unpopular, and so was the seizing of lands used as security when loans were not repaid. Many of the borrowers were from the aristocratic elite or from monasteries, influential people whose opinions carried weight. They could draw on support from the Church when the Third Lateran Council of March 1179 stressed that contact with Jews could lead to spiritual contamination; even lodging with a Jew was enough to ensure excommunication.

Henry II's authority was respected enough to prevent any direct violence against the Jews. With his death in 1189, the hostility exploded. On the very day of the coronation of his successor King Richard I, Richard the Lionheart, the Jews had assembled to pay their own respect when the mob set upon them, slaughtered many and rampaged through Jewish properties. The violence spread through the rest of England during 1190 with attacks on Jews in Norwich, Bury St Edmunds and other cities. The horrific climax came in York. Led by barons who were heavily indebted to the Jews, a crowd attacked Jewish homes. The Jews eventually took refuge in York castle and then committed mass suicide when their position became hopeless. Another group who offered to convert to Christianity were massacred after they had surrendered. The crowds swarmed on to York Minster where the records of debts were kept and burned them. Although the royal authorities did restore order, punish some of the instigators and offer some continuing protection for the surviving Jews, all Jews were expelled from England in 1290 and were only allowed to return in 1655. The cult of St William plays a small but telling part in this tragic story.

CHAPTER ELEVEN

Fervent Christian Pilgrims

THE ELEVENTH century was a period in which newly built churches and newly discovered saints were spreading across the landscape. Most Christians could now find all they needed – baptisms, daily Mass, marriage (solemnised in the church porch) and burial – within their local parish. However, while in this sense Christians were more firmly rooted in their local Christian community, other forces were encouraging them to leave. The growth of the European economies, the revival of sea routes and the development of new tracks across Europe saw the first long-distance pilgrimages for even humble Christians. The Latin term *peregrinus*, an outsider, a traveller who arrives from foreign parts, the origin of the English 'pilgrim', is very apt.[1]

The stirring of desire for a medieval pilgrimage can be traced back to the tenth and eleventh centuries. A document of 813 mentions only Rome and Tours as pilgrimage destinations. A century later a life of Gerald of Aurillac, who died in 909, adds the shrine of St Martial at Limoges to the list. There were scattered reports of pilgrims reaching Jerusalem, but there are only three known narrative accounts of actual journeys between 600 and 1000, although these suggest that there was a Latin community in Jerusalem, still enjoying Muslim protection and offering hospitality to western travellers. There was, however, a burst of activity in 1033, the millennium of the Crucifixion, when, in the heightened tension of the era 'an innumerable multitude of people, from the whole world, greater than any man could hope to see, began to travel to the Sepulchre of the Saviour at Jerusalem'. These included aristocrats and bishops – as well as more humble pilgrims, and women, the first time this had ever happened records our contemporary source, Rodulphus Glaber. Such was the enthusiasm that 'many even wanted to die there rather than return to their own country'.

The mass pilgrimage was something new. Earlier pilgrimages were usually by aristocrats and bishops with large retinues and many objectives. The Venerable Bede tells how Benedict Biscop of Northumbria, the abbot of Wearmouth, would make frequent trips to Rome in the late seventh century. After one of these he escorted back the new Archbishop of Canterbury, the Greek Theodore of Tarsus, who had never been to England before and needed time on the road to talk over his new job. On another Biscop brought back an enormous haul of materials and skilled workers: 'a wealth of holy books, a venerable gift [from the Pope] of relics of the blessed martyrs of Christ, architects for the building of his [new] church, glassmakers to build and decorate its windows', even 'masters of the chant' to help him celebrate the liturgy. There were images specifically to help those who could not read to learn of the 'works of our Lord and Saviour'. There were also treasured letters from the Pope granting Biscop's church its own privileges.[2] Bede gave thanks that his abbot took on all these tasks and so left the monks in peace to pray.

The pilgrimages of the eleventh century onwards catered for much more immediate and emotional needs, above all the desperation for salvation that a pilgrimage to a favoured saint or shrine might bring. It was Jerusalem above all that haunted the Christian imagination. The Book of Revelation provides the image of Jerusalem as the glittering city that descends to earth. The famous pilgrimage of Constantine's Mother, Helena, to the city was evoked in fresco and text throughout the Middle Ages. Many mosaics from the fifth and sixth century onwards, especially in Ravenna and Rome, show Jerusalem resplendent in precious stones. In the eighth century, legends appeared that told of a king of the Latins who would recreate the Roman empire in its original glory and then ascend into heaven from the place of Christ's Crucifixion. Medieval maps, such as the celebrated *Mappa Mundi* in Hereford Cathedral, place Jerusalem at the centre, as 'the navel of the world'. As the site of the Crucifixion and Resurrection, Jerusalem can be seen as a special kind of relic, an earthly city that, like the body of a saint, was a means through which intercession might be made to heaven.

The city had become accessible in the eleventh century as a new land route opened up through Hungary to the Holy Land. Although Jewish and

Christian communities had been able to live in Jerusalem in comparative peace, stories that Muslims had damaged buildings sacred to Christianity began filtering back to Europe, including that of 1009 which had led to retaliation against Jews. Such stories inspired the mass pilgrimage of 1033 and later provided one of the incentives that led to the proclamation of the First Crusade (1096–99) to regain the city more than sixty years later. It was a difficult journey. One account of a German pilgrimage that set out in 1064 under the leadership of Gunther, Bishop of Bamberg, has the party continually attacked by 'pagans' as it made its way. An abbess was raped and killed. Hungarians, Bulgars and Turks all harassed them, while the Greeks of Constantinople treated them with disdain. When the group reached the eastern Mediterranean the magnificence of their array first drew amazed crowds, but eventually the lure of plunder was too much and they were attacked and forced to take refuge in the city of Ramleh (in today's Israel). Luckily, the local military leader, 'the King of Babylon', grasped that there was more to be made out of wealthy passing pilgrims by protecting them and so encouraging others to follow, and he saw them safely through to Jerusalem.[3]

Few could hope to reach Jerusalem in this period, but one response to the longing to do so was to recreate the church of the Holy Sepulchre that Constantine had built to include the tomb of Christ and the surrounding area, in the west. From the eleventh century onwards some sixty-five churches and monasteries in Europe have evidence of sepulchre cults, among them the town of San Sepolcro in Tuscany, founded by two hermits.[4] There is a fine eleventh-century copy of the domed shrine itself in the basilica of Aquileia in northern Italy. Other copies are known in Venice and Florence. In Bologna in the twelfth century the complete sanctuary of the church was recreated including Calvary itself and the courtyard where Pilate condemned Jesus to death. Perhaps the most elegant recreation is the much later, mid-fifteenth century, Chapel of the Holy Sepulchre in San Pancrazio, Florence, by the Renaissance architect and humanist Leon Battista Alberti.

At the end of the eleventh century the crusading movement provided the impetus for sending a military expedition to regain the Holy Land for Christianity.[5] Although 'the age of crusades' is now seen to include the conquest, or reconquest, for Christianity of Sicily, Spain, the Baltic and, internally, the Cathars in the Albigensian crusade, Pope Urban II, the instigator of the 'First' Crusade (to the Holy Land), cleverly framed Jerusalem as the greatest prize. If this city was brought back within Christianity, it would usher in 'the last days' promised in the Book of Revelation, and so provide the keys to heaven. Moreover, those who reached Jerusalem, or even died en route, would earn a plenary indulgence, the remission of all penalties for sin.[6]

The attraction of the indulgence lay in the fear of eternal damnation that Augustine and many of his successors in the medieval Church taught was the inevitable and deserved punishment for most members of a sinful humanity. Augustine's bleak forecast of perpetual suffering had been partially lightened by the doctrine of purgatory, a halfway house where punishment after death was painful but not eternal. The length of the period during which the soul was being 'purged' depended, of course, on the gravity of one's sins, but it could be shortened by undertaking spiritual enterprises as penance before death. It was these that earned an 'indulgence'. They did not relieve guilt but allowed remorse to be shown through arduous undertakings, such as crusades and other pilgrimages and the visits to certain shrines. So it was with a promise of salvation if they succeeded, that the crusaders set off. They were lucky. It was a moment of political vacuum in the region and rivalries between Muslim rulers prevented a united response to their invasion. Eventually Jerusalem was taken in 1099. The medieval concept of just war was flexible enough to portray the bloodbath of Muslims and Jews that followed as God's confirmation of justice. 'It suffices to say', wrote Raymond of Aguilers, 'that in the Temple and porch of Solomon, they rode in blood to their knees and up to the reins of their horses. With the fall of the city, it was a delight to see the devotion of the pilgrims before the Lord's Sepulchre, how they clapped their hands, rejoicing and singing a new song to the Lord. . . . This day, I say, saw the abolition of all paganism, the confirmation of Christianity, the renewal of our faith.'[7]

Once the route to Jerusalem had been secured, it was possible for the more intrepid pilgrim to go further still. One of the 'new' cults of medieval Europe was that of Katherine of Alexandria. The legend is only recorded for the first time in the ninth century and describes Katherine as a noblewoman of the third or fourth centuries who refused to renounce her faith and confounded pagan scholars with her learning. Fifty of them were so over-come with her arguments that they converted to Christianity, as did the wife of the emperor Maxentius who visited her in prison. Katherine resisted attempts to take her virginity. After escaping torture on a wheel (the wheel recoiled at its task and exploded, killing four thousand pagans in the process), she was finally beheaded.[8]

In the 1030s three of Katherine's fingers appeared in a monastery in Rouen. They had been purchased from a Greek monk who told how they had come from the monastery in the Sinai desert founded on the site of Moses's Burning Bush. The story went that her body had been carried by angels to a mountain above the monastery, and so the monastery, now St Catherine's, became a focus for pilgrimage.

Pilgrims (males only, women could not stay at the monastery) took three weeks to cross the Sinai desert by camel to reach the monastery and, as *Mandeville's Travels*, a fourteenth-century compilation of an English knight's travel experiences, recounts, they passed the tombs of Abraham, Isaac and Jacob at Hebron, as well as the cave where Adam and Eve lived after they had been banished from paradise.[9] Then there were two gruelling climbs, up the mountain where Moses had received the Ten Commandments and further still to the spot where the body of Katherine had come to rest. The pilgrims would descend to venerate her body in its alabaster tomb in the monastery itself. A monk would produce the bones and more oil would exude from them as he stirred them about. This was distributed in small quantities to the pilgrims who were also shown the head of Katherine with the wrapping in which the angels had transferred it. Despite the lack of any evidence for her existence, Katherine was to become one of the most popular of medieval saints, easily recognisable in paintings for her opulent dress and the broken wheel beside her.

During Pope Urban II's campaign of 1095 to enthuse the crusaders he added other indulgences as rewards for visiting and protecting local churches. Unfortunately, his initiative was all too successful, especially as the right to grant indulgences was extended to bishops. Soon bishops were freely handing out indulgences and outbidding each other in their generosity. Pope Innocent III spoke at the Fourth Lateran Council of 1215 of 'the indiscreet and excessive indulgences which certain prelates of the churches grant'. Innocent limited the period of remission to a year for those present at the dedication of a new church, and forty days to those visiting a church on each anniversary of the dedication. In Rome the scale of indulgences varied with the distance the pilgrim had come (see further p. 101 below). Still, it was hard to avoid inflation. In his first months as Pope, only a year after Innocent's intervention at the Fourth Lateran Council, Honorius III granted a plenary indulgence to Francis of Assisi for each visit to a church the saint had rebuilt. Honorius's cardinals were so taken aback by his profligacy that they persuaded him to restrict the indulgence to a single day each year. The shrine of the Holy Blood, set up by Henry III in 1247 (see below, p. 188), had an indulgence of six years and one hundred and sixteen days attached. This had been reached by adding together fifty-seven separate episcopal grants.

Other routes became popular during the second half of the tenth century. New roads were opening through Italy on the way to that other great pilgrimage destination, Rome. The Roman *Via Aurelia* that ran down the western coast of Italy had been abandoned as malarial but there was now the *Via Francigena* that led the pilgrim from France, down to Piacenza on the northern Italian plain and then to Lucca and so to the 'eternal city'. Archbishop Sigeric's account of his return from Rome to his diocese at Canterbury in 993 along this road lists eighty separate stopping places, all ready to offer him hospitality.[10] One of the towns that came into being on this route was Siena, hitherto remote from the road network of the Roman empire, but now set to become one of the major Italian city-states. The crossing of the Alps was especially hazardous, but the eleventh-century priest, Bernard of Aosta, was heroic in his endeavours to protect pilgrims as they made their way across. He remains commemorated in the two passes where he set up hostels (the Great and Little St Bernard Pass) and the St Bernard dog that rescues travellers lost in the snow and carries a welcome tot of brandy.

The most popular relic for those who reached Rome was a veil that was believed to show the face of Christ, wiped by one Veronica as he struggled with his Cross towards Calvary. The word 'Veronica' is a corruption of *Vera Iconica*, 'the true likeness', and there is no one of this name in the Gospels so the legend of a specific woman called Veronica must be a later development. The earliest reference to the veil only appears in the late twelfth century, but Pope Innocent III established its veneration as a public cult in the early thirteenth century and by 1300, when the veil was displayed in St Peter's during the Holy Year, it drew enormous crowds. It even makes a guest appearance in Dante's *Divine Comedy*.[11]

It must have been an extraordinary experience to visit Rome. The third-century Aurelian walls still defined the city – and even stand to this day – but within them the settlement, the overcrowded *abitato*, had shrunk to a core in the bend of the River Tiber that frequently flooded. Many of the great classical buildings still stood, some virtually complete like the Pantheon, by now the church of Santa Maria Rotondo, but others were in ruins. Some had been incorporated into fortresses built by rival factions, while others, such as the Colosseum, were being quarried for stone. Although several ancient churches were restored in a building spree in the twelfth and thirteenth centuries, the only newly built church was the Gothic Santa Maria sopra Minerva of 1280. It was in the cemetery here that the body of Catherine of Siena was buried after her death in 1380 and then transferred into the church when miracles began. Although the veil might have been the most prestigious relic in Rome after 1200, there was, of course, a much older tradition of pilgrims visiting the relics housed in the seven major basilicas of the city, St Peter's, St Paul's, St John Lateran, Santa Maria Maggiore, St Lawrence, Santa Croce in Gerusalemme and St Sebastian on the Via Appia.[12]

Bewildered pilgrims had to try to sort out the jumble of ruins that confronted them and to fit Christianity into hazy memories of a classical past. The church of Santa Maria in Trastevere had been built, the legend went, to commemorate a miraculous gush of oil on the day of Christ's birth. Santa Maria in Ara Coeli, on the side of the Capitoline Hill, was believed to stand where the emperor Augustus had had a vision of the Virgin and Child, while there was even a legend that Janus, the son of Noah, had founded Rome after the flood and that all Roman emperors had been descended from him. There was still some prejudice against the pagan past. The Bishop of Tours, Hildebert of Lavardin, visited Rome in the early twelfth century, acknowledged the achievements of ancient Rome but concluded: 'I prefer this present disgrace to those triumphs.' It was not until the fifteenth century that the revival of classical texts allowed the ancient city to be given back its true history.

The decay did nothing to lessen the aura of Rome and, after 1204 and the looting of Constantinople's collection by the Crusaders (see p. 125–9), it had the largest collection of relics in the Christian world. While the basilica of St Peter on the Vatican hill had been the original focus of the pilgrim, from the eleventh century it was rivalled by the papal palace of the Lateran at the southern end of the city. This had been an imperial palace where Constantine had built the massive church to Christ the Redeemer, now dedicated to the two Johns of early Christian history, John the Baptist and John the Evangelist (and so St John Lateran). The heads of both Peter and Paul were preserved on the altar in gold reliquaries. From the Old Testament there were the Tablets of Moses, the Ark of the Covenant, the rod with which Aaron created snakes (see below p. 149) and some manna. From the New Testament there was the tunic of the Virgin Mary, clothes of John the Baptist including his hair shirt, the five loaves and two fishes from the feeding of the five thousand, as well as the table on which the Last Supper had been eaten. In a chapel in the palace, there was the foreskin of Jesus as well as his umbilical cord, alongside a relic of the Cross. Close by the Lateran, the *titulus*, the name board from the Cross, was to be found in Santa Croce in Gerusalemme while another legendary acquisition of Helena, the steps up to Pilate's palace that Christ had ascended, the *Scala Sancta*, had been incorporated into the palace. In the chapel at the top was an icon of Christ said to have been painted by Luke the Evangelist.

Churches in Rome had a reputation for opulence. Even in the fourth century AD the pagan historian Ammianus Marcellinus had noted the wealth of the popes and their flamboyant lifestyles. *The Treatise of Garcia of Toledo* of about 1100 gives a satirical account of a visit of the Archbishop of Toledo to the court of Pope Urban II. The archbishop brings with him relics of saints Albinus and Rufinus but these names are fronts for what he has really brought: 'relics of Saints Silver and Gold' intended for 'a shrine of Saint Cupidity' in Rome! The historian paints a picture of a luxurious papal court, unrestrained in its eating and drinking. A study of inventories of the late thirteenth century backs him up: they tell how 'precious stones, textiles and goldsmith work accumulated in the treasuries of popes and cardinals'.[13]

There seems, for reasons that are not clear, to have been a falling off in the numbers of pilgrims entering Rome in the thirteenth century. There are reports of hostels closing and almost no surviving travellers' tales. By the fourteenth century, however, the lure of indulgences fostered a revival of pilgrimages. Indulgences for Rome were graded according to the provenance of the pilgrims. The veneration of the heads of Peter and Paul on the days that these were exposed gained an indulgence of four years and four Lenten seasons (each of forty days) for pilgrims who came from Rome or the neighbouring regions of Italy, but seven years and seven seasons if they had come to Rome by sea or over the Alps. When Pope Boniface VIII announced a Holy Year, for 1300 and every hundred years afterwards, he granted a plenary indulgence for those who came from outside Rome and attended the basilicas of the city for fifteen consecutive days, although this was raised to thirty if they were Romans. Then there were indulgences for specific shrines, with the popes increasing the days remitted from purgatory for those shrines they controlled themselves so that the great papal basilicas were always more attractive for seekers of indulgences than minor churches. Eventually almost every altar in St Peter's had its own indulgence and, in the early fourteenth century, a well-organised and very energetic pilgrim could make a full thousand years of remission in years when no plenary indulgence was available. Of course offerings were expected at every shrine. One account provides a nice vignette of two custodians at the altar of St Paul's continuously raking away the coins deposited there by the faithful.

The Holy Years were an important means of raising the status of Rome as a pilgrim city. The first, in 1300, had never been planned as a special occasion. Rumours swept northern Italy in the autumn of 1299 that anyone reaching Rome for 1 January would receive full remission of their sins and there would be lengthy periods of remission for visits during the rest of the year. No one knew where the rumour had originated. Some said it had always been the tradition for every centennial year, others that a document from God had been handed down from heaven. Inevitably, vast crowds began flocking to the city and headed towards St Peter's as midnight on New Year's Eve approached.

Pope Boniface and his cardinals were overwhelmed. They hurriedly consulted the archives but no evidence of any previous Holy Year could be found. Oral tradition was more helpful. Among their sources was a man of 107 who claimed that his father had told him of a Jubilee Year in 1200. French pilgrims quizzed by Boniface confirmed that there was a tradition in their country that told of centennial celebrations in Rome. This might have been a distant echo of the Secular Games that were indeed held in Rome once a century in pre-Christian times. By February Boniface had surrendered to the tumult. He issued a papal bull confirming that indulgences would be granted to all those who had confessed their sins and then visited the basilicas. 'This is the day of our salvation. . . . Think how near is the means of your salvation . . . of washing away the stains of sin from your souls, of exchanging the wretchedness of your earthly lives for everlasting glory'.

The crowds went on flocking into Rome throughout 1300, and reports from chroniclers suggest that the city had a major impact on visitors. The more literate even began to read the surviving classical authors. However, soon the taint of papal greed clouded the occasion. Boniface's own pretensions to claim total papal sovereignty over Church and State through a bull *Unam Sanctam* isolated him still further. In 1303 he was effectively overthrown and may even have committed suicide. The poet Dante Alighieri, who had placed his journey to the underworld in his *Inferno* in 1300, had Boniface already suffering in hell when he visited it. Rome depended on the presence of the popes. They provided spiritual authority for the city, of course, but they were also the impresarios who dramatised the attractions of pilgrimages and focused them on the papal basilicas and Holy Years. By 1309 the long Avignon exile had begun (see below p. 197) and, bereft of papal patronage, Rome fell further into decay. Warring aristocratic factions divided up the cities using ancient buildings, among them the surviving triumphal arches, as fortresses.

Although many pilgrims visited a shrine to gain their indulgence there, a visit could also be ordered as a penance for sins. The penances imposed by Hamo de Hethe, Bishop of Rochester in south-eastern England between 1319 and 1352, survive.[14] A man caught in adultery was ordered to provide a three-pound candle every year for six years to St Andrew of Rochester on the saint's feast day. However, in each of these years he was also required to make the journey to Canterbury to visit the shrine of Thomas Becket and then further afield, to Bury St Edmunds, where the martyred Anglo-Saxon king Edmund also had an opulent shrine, and then westwards to Chichester and Hereford to the tomb of Thomas de Cantilupe. The shrine of the Virgin Mary at Walsingham in Norfolk, where a vision of the Virgin in 1061 had led to the recreation of her house from Nazareth, was another destination. In the case of a second offence one sinner was sent off on the 'pilgrimage' naked except for his breeches.

The most serious case that Hamo encountered, the exotic sin of adultery with a godmother, merited something more substantial. The penitent was to travel to Santiago de Compostela in north-western Spain. In the ninth century the relics of the saint had been placed in a crypt for security – they are still there today. This shrine, like Jerusalem, had benefited from the opening up of new routes in the tenth century. The decline of the Umayyad

Caliphate in Spain allowed northern (Christian) Spain some peace, and the routes in from France had become safe despite a Muslim attack on the shrine as late as 997. As we have seen, the earliest recorded pilgrimage from France took place in 951. The shrine benefited from shrewd promotion and by the end of the tenth century there were already hospices along the road from France. The bridges were put in order by King Alfonso VI in the middle of the eleventh century, and Diego Gelmirez, the powerful archbishop of the shrine, began building the existing church as well as churches and more hospices along the route so that by the end of the eleventh century the road was said to be the busiest in Christendom. In the crucial battles against the Arabs, first at the battle of Clavijo in 844, James appeared as a warrior urging on the Catholics. In 1125, when Jerusalem was still held by the Christians, the Archbishop of Santiago proclaimed that 'just as the knights of Christ opened the way to Jerusalem . . . so we too should become knights of Christ and, after defeating his wicked enemies the Muslims, open the way to the Lord's Sepulchre through Spain'.

This all went against the scriptural record and there is a story that a Greek bishop living at Compostela was offended by the distortion. Surely the Gospels had made clear that James was an Apostle who had been a fisherman before his calling? That night a furious James appeared to the bishop in a dream. He was fully armed. 'I am appearing to you so that you will not doubt that God has made me a soldier and a contender and has set me to fight for the Christians against the Saracens [Arabs] and to gain the victory for them.' In the earliest account of his miracles, the twelfth-century *Codex Calixtinus*, James helps only men and the vast majority are soldiers. Some are delivered from Arab captivity and others given protection while in the Holy Land. They are expected to go on pilgrimage to Compostela to give their personal thanks to the saint.

Diego Gelmirez's vast church of St James as it exists today at Compostela is a showcase for this growth in pilgrimage. It is the largest Romanesque church in Spain and one of the largest in Europe. It was ready for consecration in 1128. Travellers were now seen in their multitudes. Already by this time a papal indulgence was being granted for those who arrived at the shrine in a Holy Year, a year when James's feast day of 25 July fell on a Sunday. So now Compostela had the same status as Rome and Jerusalem. One can see this from the scale of payments for those who wished to buy themselves out of a pilgrimage imposed by a priest as penance. Relief from a trip to Rome and Compostela 'cost' twelve livres, while the shrine of St Martin of Tours only required four livres.

The status of the shrine at Compostela was further enhanced by the readiness of St James himself to forgive the more heinous sins. Just as Hamo had insisted on his worst offenders travelling to the shrine, there are many other accounts of bishops being so appalled by a sin that only a visit to St James could secure forgiveness. This was a crucial step in making it one of the great pilgrim sites of Europe, and a whole network of roads spread back through Spain and northern Europe to serve it. The original crypt under the church was embellished with dramatic sculpture. A twelfth-century statue of James on the Portico de Gloria, a masterpiece of Romanesque sculpture, was, and still is, touched on the left foot by pilgrims when they have safely arrived. There was an enormous clamour especially when there was to be a special vigil at the shrine or the relic was due to be exposed. At Compostela, just before St James's feast day 'all sorts of noises and languages can be heard together, discordant shouts, barbarous singing in German, English, Greek and every other language under the sun'. There was increasing cynicism over the profits made by the locals. The citizens of Santiago are 'as fat as pigs and slothful at that, for they have no need to cultivate the soil when they can live off the pilgrims instead'.[15]

The experience of pilgrimage to Compostela was so powerful that many of the miracles attributed to James take place even before the pilgrim reaches the shrine.[16] One account relates how three knights are on pilgrimage to Compostela. They give help to sick and frail pilgrims they meet on the way. On arrival at the shrine one of the knights falls ill: it is said that this is because he has committed some unconfessed sin. In his delirium he sees demons coming towards him to seize his soul, but St James intervenes to save him in response to his acts of charity. He makes a full recovery. Another miracle story tells of a tanner who makes a pilgrimage to Compostela every year. One year he commits suicide while on the road. The devils claim him for this awful crime but the tanner's soul is conveyed to Rome, to the open space in front of St Peter's. Here the Virgin Mary and St James fight off the demons and restore him to life. He makes his way back to Compostela to be joyfully welcomed by his companions who never expected to see him alive. These miracles were widely reproduced throughout Europe, and one of the most beautiful windows in Chartres Cathedral shows Charlemagne following the Milky Way to Compostela and confronting the Saracens. These medieval legends portrayed Charlemagne as the discoverer of James's tomb, a new legend that supplanted the old.

Pilgrims to Compostela would bring back a cockle shell as a mark of their successful journey. Originally, it seems, they had continued on past the shrine to the coast to gather the shells but soon these were available in the market at Compostela itself. They were then cast in lead and it was the custom to fasten them on one's hat. They became magic charms in themselves – in 1120 a Coquille-Saint-Jacques was credited with healing a knight from Apulia from diphtheria.

Any arrival at a pilgrimage site must have been a profoundly emotional experience. The excitement on a saint's feast day was all the more intense. There would be a mass of disabled struggling to make their way to the shrine among the able-bodied. The custom of holding fairs in the streets around a shrine on the saint's feast day ensured that many clamouring to enter the shrine were drunk. Rather like fans gathering for a football match, national groups came together and began singing community songs. At Conques, the clergy, worried by the vulgarity of the proceedings, had to accept that they could not control each band of visitors expressing its enthusiasm in its own way. Every account of an exposition tells of the wailings and groaning of those who were convinced that their only chance of salvation lay in the help of the saint whom they had come so far to visit.

The turmoil at the shrines aroused the traditional fears of contamination by the experience. 'O how dangerous it is to lead attractive, nay beautiful young women (in whom levity and lust are inherent) into foreign parts in quest of indulgences, particularly inexperienced wives', wrote Pietro Azario, a mid-fourteenth-century chronicler of events in Lombardy, who tells of a nobleman who seduced women as they made their way south to Rome. Again, it was sensible to ask whether Christian duty lay rather in helping the poor than traipsing off overseas. An inveterate pilgrim from Piacenza, Raimondo Palmario (the 'palmario' a recognition that he had received a palm for visiting Jerusalem), lying asleep in the portico of St Peter's in Rome, contemplating another pilgrimage to Jerusalem, received a vision of Christ. In it Christ told him to return home to Piacenza where there was a desperate need for his charitable works. Other critics stressed that prayer alone was enough or that they could make do with the local relics. Archbishop Winchelsey of Canterbury forbade his monks to travel to other shrines as they had a 'greater abundance of the relics of saints than there is elsewhere'. So there was also a tension between those who were desperate for new experiences or who genuinely believed that a shrine would provide their salvation and those who distrusted the disruptions and temptations of travel so far afield.[17]

CHAPTER TWELVE

'The eyes are fed with gold-bedecked reliquaries'

T HE ARRIVAL of pilgrims meant that many of the stopping places along the way to the major shrines prospered. The important issue now for any ambitious abbot, bishop, or local city commune was how to display the relics of their favoured saints. They went for impact. 'The more grandly constructed a church is, the more likely it is to entice the dullest minds to prayer and to bend the most stubborn to supplication', noted the twelfth-century historian William of Malmesbury. In the larger churches, the resting place of the bodies of saints had usually been in a crypt below the high altar, as in the case of James at Compostela. These had become more elaborate so that, by the eleventh century, there were 'hall crypts' which covered a large area, not only the space beneath the chancel and apse but even the transepts. The crypt was supported by a forest of columns. It was a type especially popular in Germany and Italy, but the Normans added a major one under the new choir they built at Canterbury Cathedral between 1096 and 1130. The body of Thomas Becket was hurriedly brought here for safety after his murder in 1170.

The architectural style of the period from about 1030 is known as Romanesque, a sturdy expression of power through heavy piers, arched doorways and solid if rather monotonous arcades. All this was lightened by ornament along the piers, arcades and door mouldings. It symbolised the revival of craftsmanship and a growth in resources in eleventh-century Europe. So Edward the Confessor's church at Westminster, consecrated in 1065, represents a totally new departure from earlier Anglo-Saxon architecture, not least in the length of its nave, 87 metres. It draws on Norman examples from across the channel. Edward designed it as the site of his own burial and he was interred here in 1066, possibly in the apse close to the high altar. As his status grew as the most sacred of the Anglo-Saxon kings, sanctified for his chastity, the justice of his rule and his generosity to his poorer subjects, his body was given greater reverence, first in the twelfth century, then in the tomb behind the high altar which formed the centrepiece of Henry III's Westminster Abbey in the mid-thirteenth century.[1]

The rebuilding of most of the English cathedrals by the Normans after the Conquest of 1066 shows how the shrines of their saints were given special prominence.[2] Each cathedral had its own high altar with relics already encased within it. They would not be visible and only a limited number of pilgrims would be able to come close. So the shrine of a saint needed to be separate and in most of the examples of which there is record, including Canterbury, Ely, Winchester, Durham and Westminster, the shrine was placed in the nave but behind the altar, as Edward the Confessor's was to be. The chapels radiating behind it could be used for the relics of lesser saints. These English shrines disappeared during the Reformation (though Edward the Confessor's remains as a symbol of royal sainthood on which the coronation rituals were, and still are, based), but surviving instructions for clergy show that enough space was left for processions to move between them and the high altar. When the Archbishop of Canterbury made a visitation to the cathedral at Worcester in 1302, he was furious to find that a former bishop had arrogantly placed his tomb between the shrine and high altar blocking the light. Most cathedrals held more than one saint, and Winchester held the bodies of many kings. The custom was to space these out along the nave and transepts, as had been suggested by the earlier plan of St Gall, but the east end always had greater prestige and several bodies were often crammed in there. Ely was one example where the founding abbess, St Aethelthryth, was packed in behind the high altar beside three of the abbesses who had succeeded her.

Sometimes arrangements had to be ad hoc, a pragmatic solution to a sudden arrival sometimes through theft, such as that of the body of St Nicholas, the wonder-working fourth-century Bishop of Myra in Lycian Turkey, at Bari in southern Italy in 1087.[3] Bari's economy had been devastated in 1071 when it had been excluded from its once prosperous trade with the Byzantine empire after the city had been taken by the Normans. Its privileges had been transferred by the Byzantines to Venice and there was a desperate need to find a new source of income for the city. In 1087 a group of Bari merchants selling grain in Antioch heard that a band of Venetian merchants were on their way to Myra with iron tools to break open the tomb of St Nicholas and steal the body. The Barians rushed ahead and there was a frenzied search for the remains. The tomb proved recognisable through a flow of sacred oil. When it was opened, the body released a fragrance that reached the centre of the town and alerted the townspeople who gathered to try and stop the theft. The Barians managed to make good their escape and when they had got home the body brought miracles as if to confirm its pleasure at being moved.

So a shrine had to be hurriedly constructed and it was well under way by 1089. The traditional structure of a crypt was used. The new church was essentially a rectangular basilica with a tower on each corner of the eastern end. A screen of three elegant arches divided the nave from the chancel and under this there was a large crypt where the body was housed, as it still is. The Pope, Urban II, presided at the consecration of the relics in 1089. The coup proved an astonishing success and once Nicholas had been adopted as a patron of seafarers, commercial or otherwise, Bari became one of the most important shrines of the Middle Ages. In a wonderful early fifteenth-century painting by the Italian artist Gentile da Fabriano the shrine is crawling with pilgrims while others are being carried towards it in the hope of a cure.

The most dramatic and influential rebuilding of a shrine took place at the abbey of St Denis near Paris. It was already a hallowed spot. The Frankish king Dagobert had been buried there in 638, Charlemagne's grandson, Charles the Bald, had been an abbot and the Capetian kings had also chosen it as their resting place. It was certainly the most prestigious site in France. However, by the early eleventh century the building was in decay, there were cracks in the walls and the towers were crumbling. Supervision was so lax that relics were simply being lost or were mouldering away, while reports from the early twelfth century told of prostitutes lurking in the cloister.

The man who took this all in hand was Abbot Suger, appointed in 1122.[4] Suger was one of the most vivid personalities of his age. He was only ten when he was dedicated to the Benedictines at St Denis but he worked himself up through sheer energy and ambition. He tempered his extrovert personality with a wonderful ability to achieve his ambitions through reason, moderation and a readiness to compromise. As abbot he developed a close relationship with the French kings of the day, Louis VI and Louis VII, and on an international stage was instrumental in reconciling monarchy and pope at a time when each was suspicious of the other's pretensions.

In 1124 Louis VI had convened a great assembly at St Denis to try and unite the warring factions in his kingdom against the threat of invasion from Germany. Suger stage-managed it brilliantly. He was a master of ceremony and he had the relics of St Denis brought out from their crypt and set in front of the king where they were invoked to save France. A great banner of St Denis was placed in the king's hand and the saint was appropriated as the country's saviour. Amazingly, the German troops never invaded and Suger, always the opportunist, was able to claim the miraculous protection of his abbey for the kingdom of France. Louis lavished the shrine with precious stones and returned relics of the Passion of Christ that had originally been given to the church by Charles the Bald.

Soon the prestige of the shrine and the newly arrived relics, among them the 'Nail and the Crown of our Lord', led to serious overcrowding. On feast days the crush was such that late arrivals could not get into the church at all, while those who had forced their way in were often pushed out again as the crowds swarmed around the shrine:

No one, because of the congestion, could do anything but stand like a marble statue, stay benumbed or, as a last resort, scream. The distress of the women, however, was so intolerable that you could see with horror how they, squeezed in by the mass of strong men as in a winepress, exhibited bloodless faces as in imagined death, how they cried out horribly as though in labour . . .[5]

Suger's response was typical of the man. He would rebuild the church to allow its pilgrims proper access and glorify his monarch and the kingdom at the same time. His architect is not known. Suger was enough of a showman to link the rebuilding to himself so that the credit rested with him, rather than with the innovating craftsmen he employed. He was able to finance his rebuilding from the abbey's own resources; its lands, donations of pilgrims and income from the annual fair it held. There is no doubt that it was his enthusiasm and constant harassment of the workmen that brought the first phase of building to a triumphant conclusion in 1144 after only seven years of work. Five archbishops and thirteen bishops attended the grand ceremony of dedication alongside Louis VII, his queen and courtiers, and 'diverse counts and nobles from many regions'.[6]

What they saw was a transformed building. Despite their immense resources, the abbey officials had baulked at the cost of rebuilding the whole church – the nave was not to be reconstructed until the next century – but what had been achieved was certainly impressive. On the western facade there were now three great arched doorways, a symbol of the Trinity, although the *cognoscenti* might have recognised the influence of a Roman triumphal arch, such as that of the Christian emperor Constantine in Rome. (Suger knew of the ruins of Rome and had apparently hoped to get hold of classical columns from the baths of Diocletian for his abbey.) The doorways were flanked by figures of kings and prophets of the Old Testament, so linking the kings of France to these sanctified predecessors. Anyone approaching the abbey would have been awestruck.

Also transformed was the eastern end, where the relics were gathered. Here the vaults were lightened and the windows brought down almost to the level of the floor – the whole was now flooded with what Suger called 'a crown of light'. The radiating chapels remained but their walls were cut through so that when pilgrims reached the end of the church they could move one way through the ambulatory and then back through the chapels. Here was the birth of a new, if still tentative, style – Gothic – in which light and space was used for dramatic effect. A dramatisation of liturgy occurs at the same time. About 1200 the consecration is given a new theatrical impact when the priest is turned away from the congregation, shielding the host from its view, until, as the true body and blood of Christ, it can be raised triumphantly above his head to the sound of bells.

Suger was not content with mere building. His church was to be decorated in the most flamboyant way through the lavish use of precious stones 'in honour of the sacred bodies of the patron saints'. Most relics were disappointing in themselves and not easy to show to large crowds. Suger worked closely with his royal and aristocratic contacts to gather in treasures for his new decorative scheme. His donors provided a 'multifarious wealth of precious gems, hyacinths, rubies, sapphire, emeralds and topazes, and also an array of different large pearls for setting in shrines and altars'. Bishops and aristocrats alike would pull off their rings and ask that they be embedded in the reliquaries. Miracles played their part. Suger himself reported one. Just as the abbey was running out of money, a vast collection of gems, originally from the English royal collection, was brought in by some monks and offered to Suger for far less than their monetary value.

Long-forgotten relics were brought out from concealment. A treasure box buried alongside Charles the Bald was rumoured to contain an arm of the martyr Stephen and another of the Apostle James. Suger was advised to open the box in private in case it was empty, but this was not his way. A vast array of archbishops and bishops together with a great crowd of pilgrims were assembled for a grand procession to the designated altar. The box was brought out and opened by goldsmiths and it was declared that the documents inside next to the relics confirmed that the bones indeed belonged to Stephen and James. A ring of Charles the Bald found inside gave further proof of their authenticity as the gift of the royal abbot.

In his description of his work, Suger takes it for granted that creating an opulent shrine is one way of ensuring the protection of the saint. In an inscription over the tomb of St Denis, he describes the reworking of the chapel that houses the body and asks the saint in return to ensure access 'to the heavenly table'. He argued that as there were Old Testament precedents for the use of gold vessels in sacrifice, so the Eucharist, which was of so much greater status that these, deserved even more glorification.

Suger's new design was intimately related with ceremonial and the glorification of his shrine. The prestige of the abbey was such that it would be a model for others, and most of the archbishops who had attended his ceremonies began building Gothic cathedrals in the area around Paris. Work in many of the greatest – Sens, Senlis, the earlier cathedral at Chartres, Rheims and Notre Dame in Paris – were already in hand by 1160. 'The work at St-Denis seems to have initiated the Gothic-cathedral building movement that would continue for more than four hundred years.'[7] There was often immense popular enthusiasm, with the whole community joining in the bringing of stone (see below, p. 114).

Suger set the trend for the lavishing of gold and silver on shrines, and others followed. One of the most spectacular gifts of relics of his day were the bones of the Three Kings, the Wise Men of the Nativity, donated to the Archbishop of Cologne by the Holy Roman Emperor Frederick Barbarossa in 1164. They were to hold a particular attraction for pilgrims because their own journey from the east to the stable at Bethlehem was, of course, the first

Christian pilgrimage. They were treated in sumptuous style. The gilded silver reliquary of about 1200 that holds the three skulls is seven feet long and opulently decorated with the Old Testament prophets and the twelve Apostles. It is the largest reliquary in existence. In 1245 the Magi received papal approval when Pope Innocent IV was found granting forty days of remission from purgatory to pilgrims visiting them.

One of the bishops attending Suger's dedication was from the small town of Chartres. It was hardly a major pilgrim centre but it did have a prestigious relic, the shift or tunic of the Virgin. Tradition told how this had been at Chartres since the ninth century, brought to the town as a gift of Charles the Bald. He had inherited it through his grandfather Charlemagne who was said to have received it directly from the Byzantine emperor in Constantinople. It was claimed to be the very garment that Mary was wearing either at the Annunciation or at the time of Christ's birth. It is actually a length of faded cloth about five metres long. There was also a vase in the church containing drops of the milk of the Virgin. She had bathed the tongue of Fulbert, an eleventh-century Bishop of Chartres, with her breast milk when he was ill and these were three drops that had spilled onto his cheek and been preserved. From the eleventh century the cathedral had also boasted a 'Black Madonna' that had been placed in the crypt near the ancient well, which had given the spot its earliest sanctity.[8]

In the twelfth century Chartres, like all the towns of the Île de France, was prospering from the burgeoning wool trade; wool was processed into cloth there after being imported from England and Flanders and then sold on to southern France. Chartres was itself a centre of learning and its monks gained extra wealth from its large local estates that grew grain. The income from the estates is estimated at 6,000 livres a year at a time when a church tower could be built for 2,000. It was from these resources that the grand Romanesque towers of the early twelfth century were built.

Chartres provides us with an excellent example of how intense emotion and self-abasement could sweep a congregation. During the rebuilding of the cathedral in 1145, a mass of donors arrived at the cathedral with wagons full of offerings, corn, wine and oil to sustain the builders, but also stones (from a quarry five miles away), beams and lime for the mortar. Their wagons were drawn up around the church, relics were brought out in procession and the Lord's mercy and 'that of his blessed Mother' were called upon.

Haimon, an abbot who described the events, told what happened when cures did not take place. Men and women alike, and all the children who had come with them, stripped to the waist and entered the church on their knees. They then dragged themselves towards the high altar 'calling upon the Mother of Mercy in this new fashion of prayer' (compare the prayer I quoted earlier, p. 86). Next they called upon the priests to scourge them. 'Let these hands be smitten which have wrought iniquity, let these ears be lashed which have listened to vanity, these eyes which have seen it; this tongue and these lips which have uttered idle and lying words.' The priests obliged with suitable chastisement. This had its effect:

> Truly the Mother of Mercy is moved without delay to pious compassion on those who afflict themselves before her, and shows by the immediate efficacy of her healing hand how nearly she is touched and how truly she has heard their cries; for soon all the sick and infirm lead forth healed from wagon to wagon, casting away the staff on which they had hitherto leaned their crippled limbs, and hastening without support to render thanks at her altar.[9]

This was no less than cure through mass hysteria.

Disaster struck Chartres on 10 June 1194 when the eastern end of the cathedral went up in flames. Only the towers at the western facade were left standing. Worse still, the shift seemed to have perished in the flames. The word went about that the favour of the Virgin had been withdrawn in judgement for the community's sins. A gloom settled on the town. Then in a dramatic happening, now typical of the period, the papal legate to France, Cardinal Melior of Pisa, who had happened to be in Chartres at the time of the fire, summoned all the citizens to the main square. Here he harangued them on the importance of not abandoning the ruins of their shrine and claimed that the clergy had already agreed to cut back on their extravagant lifestyles so that the cathedral could be rebuilt. As the legate spoke the bishop, Renaud of Moucon, appeared at the head of a procession of monks. To the delight of all, the monks were carrying the sacred shift.

The story was soon told. As the flames had spread, two priests had rushed into the cathedral, seized the relic and taken it into the crypt where they were 'so preserved from mortal danger under the protection of the Virgin Mary that neither did the rain of burning timbers falling from above shatter the iron door covering the face of the crypt, nor did the drops of melted lead penetrate it, nor the heap of burning coals overhead injure it'.[10] A few years later the poet William the Breton told how the Virgin had considered the old cathedral inadequate and had allowed it to be consumed by fire so that one more worthy of her glory might be built.

So a vast empty space stretching eastwards from the surviving towers of the earlier cathedral was available for reconstruction. One objective of Romanesque architecture, with its thick walls, small windows and arched doors, was simply to create a building that would not collapse. Gothic architecture aimed to create impact even if there have to be buttresses on the walls outside to hold up the high walls, pointed arches (a major characteristic of Gothic) and lofty vaults. In Notre Dame in Paris and in Abbot Suger's royal church of St Denis, a few miles to the north of Paris, there had been already been intimations of the Gothic style – a long nave, a high vaulted roof and a preponderance of dim but glowing light through stained-glass windows – but nothing had yet been planned so harmoniously as this. What gives Chartres so much of its power is the comparative simplicity of the design – little is lost in unnecessary detail. The eastern end of the church ends in an ambulatory with several chapels set into the walls.

The facades and portals of Chartres had more to offer. If the display of a relic is to be important, then, as Suger had shown so well at St Denis, the facade of the church or abbey that houses it helps create the impact. The magnificent rose window in Chartres's western facade of 1215 is the boldest of its kind. There was a flourishing of sculpture. Figures of Christ or the Virgin Mary presided over the doorways and were surrounded by rows of accompanying saints on the piers and a mass of smaller figures on the archivolts that radiate out from each door. Chartres has its original twelfth-century portal on the west face but then two, even grander, three-door portals at the end of the north and south transepts added during the rebuilding in the thirteenth.

Many causes have been put forward for the Gothic revolution. It required massive resources, of course, but many wealthy abbeys and cathedrals were able to provide this, even if building programmes had to be extended over decades. It needed a wide variety of skills, especially in stone-working, although some aspects of a Gothic cathedral are easier to construct; the ribbed vault, for instance, in comparison to the Romanesque barrel vault. Above all the artistic revolution needed a vision, of a harmonious whole, in which light and space played on each other. What impelled this breathtaking sense of harmony has been endlessly debated. Complex theories have tried to link scholastic thought to the movement. Does it celebrate a triumph of reason, especially when one marks out the ordered divisions of space in a Gothic cathedral? It seems mundane to descend from the ethereal to the pragmatic use of light and space, to illuminate relics, to allow them to glitter, and to host the magnificent new liturgical processions that were increasingly a part of twelfth-century life. This seems to have been the impetus for Suger and it is a plausible explanation for the birth of Gothic. The earliest important Gothic building in England is, as already seen, the corona of Thomas Becket in Canterbury.

One of the most prestigious of the great stained-glass windows of Chartres is dedicated to Charlemagne.[11] The cult of Charlemagne had been revived in the year 1000 when the emperor Otto III had opened his tomb at Aachen and claimed to have found him sitting bolt upright as if he was still ruling. By the eleventh and twelfth century, Charlemagne had become a semi-mythical figure. The French kings used him as their spiritual forebear and they built up a series of legends to link him with pilgrimages and relics. These were now a mark of status, especially if coveted relics were given as gifts.

It was vital for the clergy of Chartres to anchor the authenticity of their relics and their provenance in glass. Two major pilgrimages were added to Charlemagne's biography and both are displayed in the scenes on the window. The first pilgrimage, which is no more than legendary, shows Charlemagne at Jerusalem from where he returns via Constantinople. It is a prestigious occasion and places the emperor as the equal of the Byzantines. In his capital the Byzantine emperor gives him the relic of the shift as well as part of the Crown of Thorns. (It was this 'Crown' that was venerated at St Denis where it had also been the gift of Charles the Bald.) However, many of the upper scenes build on the campaign that Charles did lead to Spain, in 778. Here the story of the pilgrimage is elaborated to create him as the finder of the tomb of James at Compostela, the championing of the saint as a Christian warrior, and the glorification of the tomb after what starts as a victorious campaign. The famous legend of the death of his nephew Roland is woven into the window. Roland had been given a sword by Charlemagne that was encrusted with relics, including a tooth of St Peter, hair of St Denis and part of the clothing of the Virgin Mary. When he attempted to destroy the sword to avoid it being taken by the Saracens, it proved indestructible, survived its master and ended up as a venerated relic at Rocamadour in south-western France.

With so much wealth and glitter displayed in the shrines it was hard for them to be venerated with appropriate solemnity. Yet there was little serious opposition to the new mass movements. The only attack on relics from this period comes from Guibert, the abbot of Nogent-sous-Coucy (1055–1124). Guibert was an austere, lonely and self-obsessed man who has, however, left a vivid picture of his age in his *Monodiae*, his autobiography. His *Treatise on Relics* may never have been circulated widely, as the only manuscript that survives is the one kept in his own monastery.[12] It is hard to gauge his purpose, partly because his argument is so tortuous, and it is possible that his opposition to specific cults is the result of rivalries with other shrines that are now forgotten.

Guibert's target in his *Treatise* is not the concept of relics themselves or even their power to bring miracles. He accepts that saints are 'worthy of our reverence and honour in exchange for their example and protection' and believes in the authenticity of the shift of the Virgin at Chartres, for instance. It is rather the uncritical enthusiasm of the laity that he deplores and one assumes he is distressed by the clamour and bustle of shrines, particularly those whose main aim seems to bring in money. For Guibert, corruption and credulity go hand in hand. He describes some monks from Beauvais who 'seduced by the gifts which the pilgrims frequently brought with them, allowed faked miracles to occur'. 'Vulgar common people are able to be duped in their greedy hearts by feigned deafness, affected madness, fingers pushed back into the palm on purpose, and feet twisted up under thighs', who were then, presumably, 'cured' by miracles. He berates the laity for accepting the authenticity of relics when there is no supporting evidence for them and points out the absurdity of there being more than one example of a particular relic. The two heads of John the Baptist is the example he gives. The digging up of saints and the division of their bodies revolted him. There could only be one resting place for each saint and he or she should remain there. Guibert detested the endless proliferation of cults, especially those involving the bodies of Christ and his mother. Both had been taken into heaven and so could hardly be around on earth. When the monks of St Medard claimed to have one of Jesus's teeth, Guibert retorted that this made nonsense of Christ's resurrection which must have been of the complete body. Guibert prefers the quiet adoration of relics under the supervision of the clergy, just as the host consecrated at the Eucharist might be venerated.

While Guibert's targets were the credulity of the masses and the corruption of the shrines, his near-contemporary, Bernard of Clairvaux (1090–1153), detested the opulence of the shrines although he too railed against their money grabbing. Bernard was a cold and polemical man, who was the leading inspiration for the Cistercian Order, founded in the first half of the twelfth century in the desire to return to a simpler rule based more strictly on that of Benedict of Nursia. The Order acted out its beliefs in bleak, if starkly beautiful, churches that ended in blank walls against which the altar stood. Bernard ridiculed the displays of sculpture that he saw around him in churches such as Suger's. In a letter to William, abbot of Saint Thierry, he blusters: 'What purpose is there in these ridiculous monsters, in this deformed comeliness and comely deformity . . . in these unclean apes . . . monstrous centaurs . . . this creature with many heads united to a single body'. As for the display of relics, he notes how 'ordinary people think them much more holy if they are plastered with precious stones. . . . The eyes are fed with gold-bedecked reliquaries, and the money boxes spring open. . . . People run to kiss it; they are invited to give; and they look more at the beauty than venerate the sacred.'[13] He went on to describe the mass hysteria of giving under which the more money a shrine accumulated, the more pilgrims gave. 'These are riches scooped through riches.' In the fourth century the ascetic scholar Jerome had decried the beautification of churches 'while Christ lies at the door, naked and dying'. He is echoed by Bernard who describes the churches as 'glistening with gold while the poor are starving and naked outside'. Although Bernard's anger had no immediate effect, such disgust at the diversion of resources into the shrines was to become a driving force of the Protestant reformers five centuries later.

CHAPTER THIRTEEN

Looting the East

THERE WERE many traditions that told of relics brought back to western Europe over the centuries from the eastern Mediterranean. One of the most spectacular caches was discovered in a chest found in Oviedo in northern Spain. The chest was credited with an itinerary that had taken it from Jerusalem, after the Persian capture of the city in 614, port by port along the coast of north Africa, then to Toledo, the first Christian capital of Spain, before it reached its final resting place in a cave near Oviedo. Such was the awe in which it was held that it took a further four hundred years for anyone to dare to open it. Eventually, in 1075, the chest was opened in the presence of Alfonso VI, the king who had done so much to set up the routes to Compostela. It was filled with a prestigious array of objects from the last days of Christ on earth; not only part of the Cross, but some of his blood, bread from the Last Supper, his shroud, a stone from his tomb, a robe of the Virgin Mary and some of her blood. Even the chest in which they were found qualified as a relic, having been made by disciples of the Apostles to house their precious treasures.

Twenty-five years later those on the First Crusade, launched in 1095, claimed to have found the lance that had pierced Christ's side in Antioch. It was revealed through a vision of the Apostle Andrew, and the crusaders credited it for their successful escape from the surrounding Muslim armies. Although its journey back to Europe is obscure, the Lance is believed to be the one still held in the Vatican in Rome. The capture of Jerusalem in 1099 saw the emergence of a piece of the Holy Cross, hidden, it was claimed, by Christians over the centuries. It was said to have been part of the Cross returned to the city by Heraclius and it was carried by the crusader armies in the Holy Land until Saladin captured it in 1187. Other slivers of the Cross arrived back in the west after the crusade, often accompanied by stones from the Holy Sepulchre. Archbishop Ubaldo Lanfranchi of Pisa brought back five shiploads of earth from the Holy Land to make the Campo Santo, 'the holy field', a burial ground next to the cathedral and baptistery of Pisa.

Legends emerging in these years also told of a much earlier haul of relics brought back by Charlemagne from Jerusalem (in a journey that he had never made). They included such an extraordinary array – the shroud from Jesus's head when he was buried, a nail from the Cross, most of the implements he used at the Last Supper, part of St Peter's beard, Mary's milk, some blood from the martyr Stephen, the arm of St Simon and the head of Lazarus – that the text, *The Voyage of Charlemagne to Constantinople and Jerusalem* (dated to the late twelfth century), may even have been a satire on relic worship.[1] Certainly a provenance from the east gave an added aura to any relic.

The winning of relics was seen as a sign of God's favour. He would make sure that they would be guided to the churches of those worthy to care for them, and any outburst of miracles from a newly arrived relic was simply confirmation of this. It went without saying that the previous owners, including Muslims, of course, and heretics, had no right to them.

In the middle of the eleventh century the Greek Orthodox Church of the Byzantine empire had been declared heretical by the popes in Rome. The schism was probably inevitable. Western Christianity had always been culturally and linguistically different from the Greek-speaking Church of the east, but so long as the papacy had kept some links with the Byzantine emperors the myth of a united Christendom could be preserved. It depended on the east paying lip service to the supremacy of the papacy and there being no major disputes over doctrine. However, the controversy over icons had angered the popes, and the Byzantines were affronted when Rome forged new alliances with the Franks. Intricate disputes over the nature of the Trinity, whether the Holy Spirit proceeded from God the Father alone, the Greek position, or both the Father and the Son as the ever-authoritative Augustine had argued, were magnified by the mutual suspicion. In 1054 the popes excommunicated the Greeks, a papal envoy throwing the bull of excommunication onto the altar of Santa Sophia. The two Churches were now in schism and thus to the 'Romans' all Greek Christians were henceforth officially heretics.[2] At a stroke their fabulous relic collections were now fair game for any 'Catholics' who could reach them.

In the aftermath of the schism there followed tortuous disputes between 'Catholic' Venetians and 'Orthodox' Byzantines over trade, both sides needing each other but each reluctant to grant too many favours. The Venetians showed little respect for the Greek shrines and soon set a precedent for looting their relics. In 1108 a monk from the monastery of San Giorgio Maggiore in Venice who had travelled to Constantinople to oversee one of their daughter houses, managed to get into a church where part of Stephen lay, broke into the tomb, confirmed the presence of the martyr by his fragrance, and spirited the relic out and eventually back to the monastery. The celebration of St Stephen's feast day at the church of San Giorgio on 26 December was an important event in Venice's calendar until the downfall of the Republic in 1797. Again, during a spat between the empire and Venetians in 1118, the Venetians had landed on the Aegean island of Chios where they had stolen another body, this time of the third-century martyr Isidore. It was later deposited in St Mark's, lost, refound and then glorified in a chapel that still glitters with fourteenth-century mosaics of the life of the saint.

Around the year 1119, after the capture of Jerusalem in the First Crusade, the bodies of the biblical patriarchs Abraham, Isaac and Jacob were 'discovered' in the Hebron Valley near Jerusalem and were absorbed into a new historical narrative that trumpeted the superior status of the Latin Christians. It was admitted that the Jews must have known the whereabouts of the bodies, but the Jews had been scattered at the time of the Roman conquest of Jerusalem and had never recovered them. Then relic seekers from Constantinople had come along but they had been struck blind as they approached the tombs, a sign that God recognised they were heretics. The successful discovery by the Latin Christians in the aftermath of the Crusade showed that they were truly the favoured of God and had been rewarded for having freed the Holy Land from the pollution of Islam.

The success of the crusaders proved all too short-lived. Further fighting in the Holy Land eroded their territory. The important city of Edessa was lost in 1144, and in his call for a new crusade Pope Eugenius III deplored the way the infidels had scattered Christian relics. The ensuing (Second) Crusade (1145–49) was a disaster. In 1187 Jerusalem itself was lost. There was horror when it was heard that the Cross had now been taken by the Muslims. 'Alas, this worthy thing was borne away unworthily by the unworthy', as one English source lamented. A Third Crusade (1189–92) disintegrated as the Christian leaders squabbled and lost the initiative they might have gained over the Muslim leader Saladin. Just as the success of the First Crusade had led to exuberant confidence in the support of God, so the subsequent two disasters were proclaimed to be a judgement for the wickedness of the age.

Yet, despite the humiliations and hardships of the campaigns, there were always restless young men eager for adventure and the eternal salvation that crusaders were promised. In 1198 the young and energetic Pope Innocent III launched yet another campaign to regain the Holy Land; what was to become the Fourth Crusade (1202–04).[3] A group of French aristocrats, led by the counts Thibaut of Champagne, Louis of Blois and Baldwin of Flanders, all men in their twenties, took up his challenge. They decided they would travel to the Holy Land by sea rather than by the tortuous route overland and they called upon the Venetians, the most accomplished shipbuilders of Europe, to provide them with a large fleet that, unwisely, they fixed a price for before they had begun to recruit men.

Far too few crusaders turned up in Venice. The deal had been a tough one, hammered out with the doge, Enrico Dandolo. Dandolo was now in his eighties and almost blind but he was acutely embarrassed at what he had committed his shipbuilders to, now that they were unlikely to be paid. The only way that Dandolo could save the situation was to ignore his age and infirmities and take charge of the crusade himself, but as part payment of their debts he forced the crusaders to agree to do Venice's business before they went on to the Holy Land. There was a rebellious city, Zara, on the Dalmatian coast, to subdue. So the Crusade set off in the autumn of 1202.

Zara was captured, to the immense displeasure of Innocent who now realised that he had lost control of his enterprise. (It was, of course, inevitable that any crusade took on a momentum of its own, free of any supervision from the Pope, as soon as it left western Europe.) Then there was another diversion. A contender to the Byzantine empire, one Alexius, the son of a deposed emperor, appeared and made some rash promises to the crusaders. If he was returned by them to Constantinople, he was sure he would be welcomed and placed on the throne. Then he would restore Byzantium to the Roman

Church, provide fresh supplies for the crusaders and pay them 200,000 silver marks, enough to settle their payments for the fleet. The Venetians could expect trading privileges within the Byzantine empire. Alexius would raise another 10,000 men for the crusaders to take with them on to the Holy Land. 'Wild promises of a witless youth', as a Byzantine chronicler of these events, Niketas Choniates, later put it. When Innocent heard of this plan, he recognised its infeasibility and refused to support it. This did not deter the crusaders and they set off towards the northern Aegean. They arrived at the walls of Constantinople in June 1203.

Even though he was too blind to see its massive fortifications, Dandolo must have realised the impact the glittering city would have on the French. The ten largest cities in western Europe would have fitted comfortably within its walls, and the domes which dotted the skyline, that of Santa Sophia dominating the rest, were truly exotic to those brought up in Europe. (It was only in these same years that Chartres was being built.) Ominously, however, the first approach to the walls was not met with joyous enthusiasm for the newly arrived Alexius that the pretender had promised. Instead, missiles and insults were hurled down on the crusaders.

It needed an attack and the breaching of the once sacred walls near the Blachernae in the north-west of the city before the ruling emperor, Alexius III, lost his resolve and left the city in search of fresh troops. Alexius was declared emperor (as Alexius IV) but once again promises could not be honoured. The money to pay for the fleet simply could not be found. Then, as news spread of the promise to reimpose the authority of Rome on the Greek Orthodox Church, outraged Greek mobs began sacking the homes of all Italian merchants and settlers in the city, whether they came from Venice or Venice's rivals, Genoa and Pisa. Many fled to the crusader camp and from here bands of Franks and Italians returned to the city, through the harbour of the Golden Horn and, in their turn, set the city ablaze. An inferno raged for three days across the most opulent part of Constantinople. Alexius's position was impossible. Accused by the crusaders of reneging on his promises and with little support from his Greek subjects, he in his turn was deposed by a senior court official who became Alexius V.

Alexius V, too, was in a hopelessly weak position. His city was ravaged and an enormous and restless army hovered around the suburbs with daily raids on his territory. It was now that Dandolo took the opportunity of pushing for impossible terms that Alexius would have to refuse and so open the way for the crusaders to launch a full assault on the city.

Dandolo's chance came in February 1204 when the new emperor had his unhappy predecessor strangled. The clergy in the crusading party then announced that Alexius V was a murderer, that his subjects had been complicit in the murder and that the schism between Greek and Latin Churches was still in force. It would now be a valid crusade to attack the Greek heretics. The remission of the sins of all those who died in the enterprise would be guaranteed as it was for other crusades. Venetians and Franks agreed that they would take the city, gather in some of its riches and settle all that was still owed to them. They would then appoint a new emperor, elected, as was the Venetian way of choosing their doges. The Church would come under Latin control. So the initial plan to win back the Holy Land had transformed itself into a very different kind of crusade. In April 1204 new attacks on Constantinople began and this time through a combination of supremacy in numbers and the daring of individual knights, the Byzantine forces were routed and the crusaders had full control of the once impregnable city. The Virgin Mary's protective power had failed, at least so far as the Greeks were concerned.

The gathering in of plunder was planned as an orderly process. The vast treasures of the city were to be brought into three churches and sold there to raise the money still needed to pay the Venetians. There would be enough left over for each of the crusaders to have his own share. The Byzantine empire was now to be replaced by a Latin one: Baldwin of Flanders was elected as its emperor and a Venetian, Thomas of Morosini, patriarch of the city. Trading bases were shared out, with Venice gaining several important ports. The Latin empire was to survive only until 1261 (when a Greek emperor was restored) and it presided over a city that had lost its spiritual and political purpose.

Now began the assault on the city's relics. One meticulous eleventh-century observer had counted the remains of some 476 saints represented by 3,600 individual relics. These were at the mercy of the crusaders. Gunther of Pairis, a monastery in Alsace, wrote his account of the crusade shortly after the events. His *Hystoria Constantinopolitana*,[4] is a biography of his abbot, Martin, who was one of the crusaders. Gunther mentioned that one reason why the crusaders agreed to go on to Constantinople in 1203 was that 'the Western church, illuminated by the inviolable relics of which these people had shown themselves unworthy, should rejoice for ever'. He may have been writing in hindsight, of course, but he establishes the ambition of the crusaders for the relics and their somewhat weak justification for the desecrations that followed.

Gunther goes on to describe how Abbot Martin visited the Monastery of the Pantocrator (Christ as 'ruler of all'). There he found other crusaders already inside stripping the church of its gold and silver. Martin primly considered it improper to commit such sacrilege 'except in a holy cause', but the acquisition of relics was certainly such a 'cause'. He bullied a priest to open up a chest full of relics for him which 'he judged more desirable to him than all the riches in Greece. . . . On seeing it, the abbot hurriedly and greedily thrust both hands into the chest, and, as he was girded for action, both he and the chaplains filled the folds of their habits with sacred sacrilege. He wisely concealed those relics which seemed to him the most powerful and left at once.' Martin secreted them in his sleeping quarters on the ship.

The final list of Martin's treasures was extensive and varied.[5] There was a trace of Christ's blood, a piece of the True Cross, the arm of the Apostle James, and parts of twenty-two martyrs including a tooth of St Lawrence and the foot of St Cosmas. Then there was an array of relics from holy places in the life of Jesus. These included part of the stone on which he was presented in the Temple, the stone on which John the Baptist stood when he baptised Jesus, and fragments of the place where Lazarus was raised and the site of the Ascension. There was even a relic from the rock that had been rolled away from the tomb and another from the table on which the Last Supper was eaten. Martin must also have grabbed some precious stones as, after his return home, he is recorded as giving some to Philip of Swabia, who was married to Alexius IV's sister. In the circumstances, it was a sensible goodwill offering.

In Constantinople the news that the private looting of relics was under way forced the senior cleric on the crusade, Nivelon, the Bishop of Soissons, to appoint his colleague, Garnier, Bishop of Troyes, to oversee the gathering of relics and their proper distribution to good homes in western Europe. Garnier made sure he did well for himself. He, too, got part of the True Cross, the chalice used at the Last Supper, an arm of the Apostle James the son of Zebedee and the head of the Apostle Philip. He also chose the body of the little-known St Helena of Athyra. This seems an odd choice as no one in the west seemed much interested in Greek saints, but apparently Helena was excellently preserved in a sumptuous silk-lined coffin and it is just possible that the names Helen and Troyes resonated with each other. Once in Troyes, Helena became the centre of a cult. She wore a ring that had the power to quench sexual passion and owned a handkerchief that did wonders for toothache.

These relics were on their way back to Troyes when Garnier died. The papal legate, Peter Capuano, took over responsibility for what was still stored in his lodgings. He authorised other clerics to take relics so long as no money changed hands but private enterprise continued. One Walon of Sarton tracked down two silver reliquaries with inscriptions on them, in Greek that he could not read. He went around other churches trying to decipher these and then, assured that he had the heads of both John the Baptist and St George, took them back to France. He gave the head of John to the cathedral in his native Amiens and was rewarded by being made a canon of the cathedral but, once the authorities heard that he had sold off the silver from the reliquaries, he was ordered to endow a chapel there with his proceeds.

All over Europe relics began to arrive as the crusaders straggled back or sent their plunder on ahead. Some relics found natural homes. The cathedral at Langres already had a shrine to St Mammes, a child martyr from the third-century persecutions who had died at Caesarea on the coast of Palestine. It was now delighted to have his head. Bishop Nivelon had a good haul and he distributed it around the different churches of Soissons. The cathedral was allocated the head of St Stephen, the finger of St Thomas, and part of the head of St Mark. Then there was a thorn from the Crown of Thorns and a swatch of the towel that Jesus had used at the Last Supper. The nunnery of Notre-Dame-de-Soissons was given the Virgin's girdle and the abbey of St John the Baptist their name saint's forearm. Some grants were more imaginative. Nivelon awarded the forearm of St Stephen to the cathedral of Châlons-sur-Marne on condition that part of the revenue the shrine gathered from pilgrims was spent on constructing a bridge over the Marne river. The recently completed cathedral at Chartres was already dedicated to the Virgin and held her shift. Now the count of Blois gave it the head of St Anne, the Virgin's mother. The sliver of the Cross that the emperor had borne into battle was taken by an English priest and it ended up at the small Cluniac monastery of Bromholm in Norfolk. Thirteen shrines claimed to have drops of the Holy Blood shed by Jesus on the Cross.

It was said that the Venetians tried to seize the famous *Hodegetria* from Constantinople, but the citizens successfully resisted the capture of their most famous icon. Instead Venice took other icons. The Blachernae seems to have been successfully raided and many of its icons, some on wood, some on stone, were taken to be placed in St Mark's or on its facade. As St Mark's was already modelled on the church of the Holy Apostles in Constantinople, the basilica was like a Byzantine pilgrimage centre. Unlike the rest of Europe where icons occupied only a modest role in cults, Venice prided itself on its Byzantine past, and after the Fourth Crusade many of the rituals surrounding the coronation of the doges echo those of the Byzantine emperors, as if Venice had taken on their mantle. The most famous of the icons looted by Venetians was the *Nicopeia*, 'the Bringer of Victory', an image of the Virgin that had traditionally been carried in their generals' chariots and then displayed in its own chariot during victory parades.

Venice's haul of relics was more modest. Perhaps it was its more mercantile spirit that led Venetians to concentrate instead on precious marbles, jewels, and silver and gold plate. The city's chief treasure from the conquest, the four copper horses, which had probably adorned a second-century AD triumphal arch in Constantinople, were put up on the *loggia* of St Mark's in the 1260s and became an important symbol of Venice's pride and independence. Nevertheless the Cross of Constantine, a phial of the Sacred Blood, an arm of St George and part of the head of John the Baptist were taken and were stored in the treasury of St Mark's. When a fire broke out there in 1231, they showed off their authenticity by surviving intact during the inferno and they still remain in the treasury.

The Venetians had proved the driving force behind the violence of the crusade and they had some difficulty in persuading Innocent III that the conquest of Constantinople was to be welcomed, especially when news of the looting and destruction of ecclesiastical property reached him. His initial reaction was that the looting was 'an example of wickedness and works of darkness'. However, the Pope was versatile enough to proclaim that the 'success' of the Crusade was part of an inevitable unfolding of events towards the unity of all under the see of Peter.[6] Whatever the hesitations he may have had, he could hardly ignore that once again events had shown that God was passing judgement on the Greeks for refusing to accept Roman primacy! An account of the Crusade written in Venice in 1222 declared that the unexpected outcome of the Crusade showed that 'God wanted more to punish the pride of the Greeks than vindicate the injury caused by the Saracens and barbarians'. Once again the dangerous belief that a victory, however nasty and brutal, confirmed the justness of a war in the eyes of God, had prevailed.

The rest of Christian Europe was naturally supportive. The newly arrived relics were soon causing enough miracles to show their pleasure in their new homes. Even the tiny community of Bromholm, consisting of eight monks when their relic of the Cross arrived, recorded thirty-nine resurrections from the dead and nineteen blind restored to sight. This helped assuage any guilt the looters might have had. As Gunther of Pairis put it, so far as the subject of his biography was concerned, 'none of the faithful ought, therefore, to believe or even imagine anything other that this was done under the shelter of divine grace, in order that so many important, deeply venerated relics would arrive at our church by the agency of a man [Martin] who retained his great modesty in the face of numerous obstacles'.

Meanwhile back in Constantinople, the newly elected emperor of Byzantium, Baldwin I (r. 1204–05), took up residence in the imperial palace and found the collection of relics from the Passion still safe within the church of the Pharos. Some visitors were allowed in to view the collection. The True Cross, the Crown of Thorns, the sandals of Jesus, a nail from the Cross, Jesus's winding sheet and even a gold container with the leftover leavened bread from the Last Supper were all on display. Yet Baldwin knew how vulnerable his position was within Latin Christendom. His election to the imperial throne had been conducted without any wider approval and he needed to gain it. So he used his relics collection to buy goodwill in Europe. The king of France, Philip Augustus, was sent back a large splinter of the True Cross, a thorn from the Crown of Thorns, part of the winding cloth and the scarlet robe that Jesus wore when he was being mocked.

Baldwin died in 1205 after he had been captured by the Bulgarians while on campaign. His energetic brother, Henry of Hainault, was elected emperor in his place and his agent, Ponce de Lyon, began raising money by the judicious sale of lesser relics. He returned to Constantinople with money and supplies. The remaining relics of the Passion remained intact, but in 1235 the emperor Baldwin II (r. 1228–61) was faced with new attacks from the Bulgarians and was desperate for money. A consortium headed by the senior magistrate of the Venetian community in Constantinople agreed to offer the emperor a loan, of 13,134 gold pieces, so long as the Crown of Thorns and the other relics of the Passion were handed over as surety. The Crown was deposited in the Monastery of the Pantocrator, with the Venetians in charge of it. When the emperor defaulted on the loan, the Crown was removed to Venice. Bargaining began and Baldwin II engineered the sale of the Crown to the French king Louis IX, a man of great piety. Louis set about acquiring the other relics that the emperors had pawned, another large piece of the True Cross, the Holy Lance, the Holy Reed, the Holy Sponge and the scarlet robe. They arrived in Paris in August 1242. Paris had become the New Jerusalem.

Constantinople, restored to Greek emperors in 1261, smarted at the loss of so many prestigious relics, and its rulers claimed that many had never left. The narrator of *Mandeville's Travels*, written in the middle of the fourteenth century, relates how he saw the Crown of Thorns in Santa Sophia, just as he had already seen it in the Sainte-Chapelle that Louis had built for it in Paris. Perhaps, he reflects, the Crown had actually been divided into two. There seems to have been such a miraculous reappearance of relics that, by the fourteenth century, Constantinople, although a shadow of what it had been as a city, appeared to be glittering with as many as it had started with.

CHAPTER FOURTEEN

Louis IX and the Sainte-Chapelle

ONE OF the most influential books of the Middle Ages, the *Golden Legend* compiled in the 1260s by the Dominican Jacobus de Voragine, told the stories of the saints.[1] Jacobus came from a village near Genoa where he first joined his Order, and he served mostly in northern Italy, finally becoming the Archbishop of Genoa. The *Golden Legend* was not an original work – in fact, Jacobus was assiduous in detailing his sources of which a hundred are known, including the early Church Fathers – but he had the knack of not overloading his readers and of rewriting many of his stories in a lively style. He began the liturgical year with St Andrew's Day, then as now on 30 November, and went on through the year giving the lives of each saint on his or her day. So the manuscript text could be followed through as the year progressed.

The scope of the *Golden Legend* was comprehensive. Jacobus began with an attempt to find the derivation of each saint's name and its spiritual significance. So Katherine (as in Katherine of Alexandria), feast day 25 November, meant 'total ruin', and this signified the 'total ruin' of the Devil's designs on her. Then there is an atmospheric description of each saint's exploits and confrontations with authority. Katherine's arguments confounding the philosophers are followed through in detail as the emperor, Maxentius, becomes increasingly frustrated with her intellectual triumphs. Next come graphic details of the four revolving wheels studded with nails and saws between which Katherine was to be mangled. Finally, after the wheels exploded, slaughtering the surrounding pagans, she was beheaded and taken by the angels to Sinai – a flight that, Jacobus informs us, took twenty days. He continues by talking of her relics and the special reasons why she is worthy of sainthood: her chastity, eloquence and wisdom. Jacobus concludes with some of the reservations he has about the historical details; whether in fact a scribe might have miscopied 'Maxentius' for 'Maximinus', an emperor who did indeed rule in the east at the right date.

The *Golden Legend* was designed as a handbook for preachers but it became an unexpected 'bestseller' making the transition from the monastery to the general reader so that, as one commentator has put it, 'barons in their *chateaux* and merchants in the backs of their shops could henceforth savour these fine stories at their leisure'.[2] More than seventy manuscripts of the text survive from the thirteenth century alone and a thousand overall – these can only be a tiny proportion of those originally in circulation – and it was translated into at least twelve European languages by the end of the Middle Ages. There are more editions of the *Legend* from the early years of printing than there are of the Bible (which could not, officially, be translated from Latin into other languages). Local communities, notably in England, added in their own saints to the flexible format. Although Jacobus shows a healthy scepticism about some of the stories he relates, pointing out inconsistencies between accounts and questioning whether some miracles happened, he gives accounts of a mass of miracles that he does accept as genuine and so the *Golden Legend* embedded the miraculous even more firmly in the medieval world. Monasteries were also busy compiling their own publicity materials in *Libri Miraculorum*, registers of miracles that acted as lures for pilgrims.

One of the stories already circulating but now collected in the *Golden Legend* tells the story of how the emperor Heraclius brought back the True Cross regained from the Persians into Jerusalem. As he rode in his full imperial regalia to the city gate, it suddenly closed before him with stones blocking the way. An angel appeared above the gate and told Heraclius that the 'king of heaven' had entered the city humbly on an ass. Heraclius knew what was expected of him. He took off his shoes and his hose and stripped down to his shirt. He then took up the Cross and the gate opened miraculously. 'Then the sweet odour that was felt that day when the Holy Cross was taken from the tower of Khusro and was brought again to Jerusalem from so far a country and so great a space of land, returned in to Jerusalem in that moment and replenished it with all sweetness.'[3]

No less a ceremony was required by which to receive the Crown of Thorns into Paris, the new 'second Jerusalem'. Louis IX had paid the sum of 135,000 livres for it, more than half his entire annual budget. Now, released from the treasury in Venice, it had arrived at Villeneuve-Archêveque near Sens and the king, his mother and his brothers assembled to meet it. In imitation of Heraclius, Louis stripped to the waist and took off his shoes before carrying the Crown into Sens. A week later, on 19 August 1239, after the Crown had travelled by river to Paris, Louis and his brother Robert carried the Crown into Notre-Dame where it was placed in the royal chapel. The arrival was greeted with shouts of 'Blessed is he who comes in the honour of the Lord, through whose agency the kingdom of France is exalted by so great a gift.' Gautier Cornut, the Archbishop of Sens, who had travelled with the reception party, rejoiced. 'Our Lord and Redeemer Himself has transferred the holy tokens of his most sacred passion from Byzantium to France. In this way, with their honours now equal, he has raised up one land to the level of the other. For he had thought it right to crown with much glory and manifold honour the kingdom of France.' Paris is the new Jerusalem.[4]

Louis had been only twelve when his father, Louis VIII, had died in 1226. His mother, Blanche of Castile, had become regent during her son's minority. Louis had been groomed for his role as king and followed it with an intensity that consolidated his position as the heir of his dynasty and, beyond that, of Charlemagne. With his commitment to the Church of which he saw France as 'the eldest daughter', his reform of justice and his sponsoring of the arts in a kingdom that was the wealthiest in Europe, Louis was seen as the quintessential Christian ruler. Other kings approached him for guidance and he made his court much more accessible to petitioners.

The growth of ceremonial royal courts such as Louis's and the possibility of intercession to secular rulers may have encouraged visions of the saints as intercessors at the heavenly court. This is certainly how Louis IX saw it, according to his biographer. 'It is the same, the king said, with the saints in Paradise as with the counsellors of kings . . . whoever has business with an earthly king seeks to know who he holds in high regard and who, having his ear, is able to approach him successfully. . . . It is the same with the saints in Paradise, who, being the friends of Our Lord, and his intimates, can invoke him in all confidence, since he cannot fail to listen to them.'[5] Now he also associated himself with the rulers of antiquity who had done most to preserve the relics of the True Cross, the Roman emperor Constantine through his mother Helena, the original finder of the Cross, and Heraclius, the most successful conqueror of the Byzantine empire.

The other relics of the Passion soon followed and Louis began a chapel to hold them. The Sainte-Chapelle in Paris was the most modern and sumptuous building in Europe, costing 40,000 livres, only a small faction of the total price Louis had paid for his relics but, at a sixth of one year's budget, a formidable act of extravagance. It was, in essence, a reliquary in its own right and proclaimed how relics had become entwined with political power and royal showmanship.

The chapel drew on earlier precedents and traditions. By this time, medieval kings had begun building magnificent palace chapels that acted as private places of worship as well as displays of the royal power and testimony of their patron's close relationship with God. In Constantinople there was the *Chrysotriklinos*, the audience chamber in the imperial palace. When the Norman king Roger II constructed his own resplendent *Cappella Palatina* in Palermo in Sicily in 1130, he may have used this as a model and he brought craftsmen from Constantinople to compose its mosaics. As in the *Chrysotriklinos*, there was a mosaic of an enthroned Christ above the throne. King and emperor were placing themselves under the direct care of the heavenly king in a sacred area that made no concessions to public display. The privacy of the chapel was confirmed by its lack of any western doorway, the normal place of entrance for the public. Roger was also looking towards France and the two most prominent French saints, St Denis and St Martin, were represented on his chapel's walls.[6]

The *Cappella Palatina* was well known in France and Louis would also have been aware of Charlemagne's palace chapel at Aachen. Having drawn materials from Rome and Ravenna, and certainly enthused by the church of San Vitale in Ravenna with its famous mosaics of the Byzantine emperor Justinian and his wife Theodora, Charlemagne had created a church on two levels. The upper church, dedicated to Christ, had private access from his palace; the lower space, more accessible in the sense that officials and courtiers could enter, was in honour of the Virgin. As has been seen, it was embellished with fine relics. In the thirteenth century the remains of Charlemagne himself were placed in a shrine in the chapel by the emperor Barbarossa who had forced the anti-pope Paschal II to canonise him.[7]

In Palermo and Aachen, there were also allusions to the ruler as the heir to Solomon, the builder of the original Temple in Jerusalem. In the Book of Kings (3 Kings:10) the throne of Solomon is described as being made of ivory, overlaid with gold, with six steps leading up to it. The royal thrones in both Palermo and Aachen have six steps leading up to them, and numerous references to Solomon confirm that this text must have been the inspiration. So the roots of the royal power were taken back to the dawn of biblical history. The Old Testament precedents of the wise king or a depiction of Christ as a ruler were both valid ways of expressing divine kingship.

The Sainte-Chapelle was to follow Aachen in being on two levels (the lower of the two reserved as the chapel of the palace staff) but it also drew on French models, notably the archbishop's chapel at Rheims of 1215–20, another chapel on two levels. The upper part of this chapel had four rectangular bays on each side with a polygonal apse at the east end. A similar design was taken further in a new chapel at the château at Saint-Germain-en-Laye, the royal hunting lodge, constructed in 1238. Here the buttresses, which had jutted into the floor space of the Rheims chapel, were moved outside the walls and much more space was given over to glass to allow the light to suffuse the interior.

So a number of forces and influences, both symbolic and architectural, came together to form Louis's vision of an appropriate grand setting for his prestigious relics. It was the combination of the beautifully light form of the Saint-Germain-en-Laye chapel with the opulent decoration of the Aachen and Palatine chapels that was to produce the dazzling interior of the Sainte-Chapelle. The name itself probably derives from the church of the Pharos in Constantinople, where the relics had originally been displayed. In the description brought back to France by Robert de Clari, one of the crusaders, the church is referred to as the *Sainte Capele*.

The Sainte-Chapelle has been much restored. In the surge of anti-Catholicism in the French Revolution, the relics were seized, the reliquaries melted down and any royal insignia defaced. The *Grande Chasse*, the opulent container at the eastern end of the chapel in which the relics were placed, vanished with them. However, a print of 1790, before the extremes of anti-clericalism of the Revolution had taken effect, shows how it looked.[8] It was composed as a porch made of silver and gilded copper enclosing an altar that could be concealed by curtains. The Crown itself was held in a gold chalice with the splinter of the True Cross and the Holy Lance both encased in crosses that stood either side of it on the altar. Other relics were placed in frames on the back wall of the porch or hung in containers from a rod that ran across the porch above the altar. They include everything from Christ's swaddling clothes, the towel with which he washed the feet of the disciples and a stone from the Sepulchre. There was even blood that had seeped out from an image of Christ when a pagan had struck it. The Virgin Mary was represented by drops of her milk, some of her hair and her veil. Although this was a private chapel to which the king had direct access from his own apartments, the relics were put on open display during Holy Week. Even as late as the eighteenth century, there was a bizarre ceremony at midnight on Maundy Thursday when epileptics and the insane were gathered from throughout Paris and taken or carried to kiss the reliquary of the True Cross in the chapel. By then journalists described the whole macabre event, which was watched by the fashionable elite, as 'a monstrosity'.[9]

The magic of the Sainte-Chapelle still emanates from its windows even though some of these were also lost when the chapel was looted during the French Revolution. Their theme is the glorification of Louis IX as the heir to the kings of the Old Testament and as the one gifted with the relics of the Passion. If one looks eastwards to the windows in the *chevet*, the polygonal apse, the main theme is the life of Christ with both the Passion and his childhood shown together with images of John the Baptist and John the Evangelist. Naturally the 'crowning' of Jesus with the Crown of Thorns is an important part of this display.

As often in these sequences the major Old Testament prophets, Isaiah, Daniel, Ezekiel and Jeremiah, are also woven in with narratives of their own. The integration of the Old and New Testaments, with the latter prophesying the arrival of Christ, was a common theme in this period. The main sequence of the windows, along most of the northern and the whole southern wall, follow Old Testament themes. The focus is on the kings of Israel, their coronations, their battles to save the Holy Land and their campaigns against idols. They are shown in the same court regalia as Louis would have worn and the soldiers are shown as contemporary French knights. Louis as King of France is now the heir of the kings of Israel with responsibility for the saving of Israel, the Holy Land. In the north-western panel, Louis, dressed identically to the kings of Israel, is shown receiving the relics. He has been integrated into the sequence.

In April 1248 the chapel was ready for dedication. One can imagine from what survives what an overwhelming experience it must have been when the interior was first opened to spectators. The response of Jean de Jandun, a fourteenth-century poet, was as follows:

> The refined colours of its paintings, the precious gilding of its images, the pure transparency of its windows which shimmer from all sides, the mystical power of its altars, the marvelous adornment of its shrines studded with precious stones, give to this house of prayer such a degree of beauty that on entering one would think oneself transported to heaven and one might with reason imagine oneself taken into one of the most beautiful rooms of paradise.[10]

The trajectory that Louis had set in motion through his buying of the relics and the creation of a reliquary for them was carried forward in his next endeavour, the leading of a crusade. The idea had matured when he was recovering from a serious illness in December 1244, but taking on such a burdensome and risky responsibility was intrinsic to the way he saw himself as Europe's leading Christian ruler.

Louis was to leave for his adventure just a few weeks after the dedication of the chapel. The auspices for a new crusade were not good. In 1244, just before Louis had made his decision, the Korezmian Turks had seized Jerusalem after it had been regained for a short period by the Christians. It may, in fact, have been the hope of an immediate reconquest that inspired him. Driven by religious fervour, Louis was hopelessly naïve in his belief that land could be held and Muslims converted to Christianity. The First Crusade (1095–99) had had its successes, the Second (1145–49) had been a complete disaster. The Third Crusade of 1189–92 had left Jerusalem under Muslim control and the Fourth (1202–04) had not even reached the Holy Land although it had given Louis his relics and his incentive to return to the east.

Yet Louis's crusade was well planned and there was an initial success when a disorganised Muslim army surrendered to the landing forces at Damietta in Egypt in June 1249. Louis would have done well to consolidate his victory. He was offered Jerusalem itself in return for Damietta but he refused. He somehow hoped he could persuade the sultan al-Malik as-Salih to glorify the Christian God. When negotiations broke down, the sultan took to the offensive, wore down the crusaders in a series of defeats, and by the end of 1249 Louis had been taken prisoner and led in chains into the city of Mansurah. Here the emir, Huam al-Din, mocked Louis for his foolhardiness. He told him that if a Muslim had been brought into a court of law having taken such risks with his own body and his property, the case would probably have been dismissed on the grounds of mental incapacity. It cost Louis another 400,000 livres to buy his release. In May 1250, he retreated to the port of Acre that the crusaders still held and stayed there without any success for another four and a half years. It was said that his total number of Muslim converts was no more than forty and the total cost of the crusade some six times his national income. Acre itself was lost in 1291. In 1270 Louis had returned to the eastern Mediterranean in another doomed crusade. He died soon after landing at Tunis of typhoid fever in the same year.

Despite this disastrous enterprise, Louis had earned his reward in heaven. From the moment of his death he was treated as a saint. His entrails were taken out and the rest of his body boiled in wine and water to remove the flesh. There was then an unseemly struggle for the remains. Louis's son, Philip, now Philip III of France, got the bones, while Louis's brother Charles d'Anjou, King of Sicily, had to make do with the entrails. Both sets of relics caused miracles as they were progressed across the Mediterranean to new homes, the bones being interred in the cathedral of St Denis, the traditional resting place of French kings. The cavalcade heading for France collected more corpses as it went. They included Louis's son-in-law, the King of Navarre, who had died on the way back from the crusade, and Philip III's own queen, Isabelle of Aragon, and their son who had died with her in childbirth in Calabria. In 1297 Louis was canonised by Pope Boniface VIII. The king's head was transferred into a golden reliquary and in May 1307 it was taken in a great procession from St Denis to be placed alongside the other relics in the Sainte-Chapelle.

CHAPTER FIFTEEN

Sacred Flesh Between Death and Resurrection

'He was like a grain of wheat that falls to the ground and is picked up by the hands of believers, and dying rises again in a fertile stalk. He was the grape that in the press gives forth much juice. He was the spice that, ground in the mortar by the pestle, gives forth a wondrous odour. He was the mustard seed that increases in strength when it is ground.'[1] The description of the body of the charismatic Dominican preacher Peter of Verona comes from the *Golden Legend* of Jacobus de Voragine. Peter Martyr, as he came to be known after his fateful end, was struck down by assassins near Milan in 1252. As his attackers were said to be heretical Cathars, his claim to martyrdom was impeccable.

In reality, the cut-about body of Peter must have been shocking to see, but such sights would not have been uncommon. Violent death, the exposed corpses of sliced-up traitors, disfigured lepers – all were part of everyday life. Anyone walking out through the west wall of a church, where traditionally the Last Judgement was painted, would have been used to seeing devils tearing apart the bodies of those condemned to hell. Yet Peter's body is experienced at a level that has nothing to do with empirical reality. It is fruitful and full of 'wondrous odour'. It has already achieved relic status and therefore its actual condition as a putrefying corpse is irrelevant. It will never be seen as such.

The belief in spiritually transformed bodies was as powerful in the medieval period as it had been in the early Christian world. There was unanimous agreement that every part of a human body survived at death, even if only as tiny particles, and God would reassemble it at the Last Judgement where it would continue to survive for eternity. The theologian Hugh of St Victor (*c*.1096–1141) assured his listeners that this was so because otherwise it would not be possible for sinners to be punished for ever. If the continuous mauling, burning and mangling effected by the devils in hell actually destroyed flesh and so brought the deserved suffering to an end, then the purpose of condemnation to hell would have been thwarted.[2]

Yet the status of the decayed or fragmented flesh of saints and martyrs was very different from their fellow mortals in that the former had already become the spiritual flesh that would shine in heaven with God. For the martyrs this transformation into spiritual flesh might only take place at the time of death, but for saints it was possible for the process to begin before then. One could prepare on earth the body as it would eventually shine in heaven. The issue came to the fore in the thirteenth century when a group of female mystics virtually gave up eating altogether. The result of their fasting fitted nicely with the medieval understanding of the nature of women. The letters of Paul assumed women's inferiority and this was consolidated by Aristotle's own views when these reappeared in western Europe in the twelfth century. Aristotle had argued that female inferiority could be seen in the unstable nature of women's bodies; they were softer, less rigid in form than those of men. Their labile nature was shown through features such as menstruation, an expulsion of blood over which women appeared to have no control. Yet it was soon discovered that extreme fasting would lead to the cessation of periods (a well-known consequence of anorexia). Here was 'proof', if any were needed, that the renunciation of food would help women towards achieving more stable bodies, closer to those of the ideal, men. Texts such as 'Until we reach the perfection of manhood, the stature of the full maturity of Christ' (Ephesians 4:13) had even suggested to many that women would reappear in heaven as men, 'the perfection of manhood'. Augustine had considered the matter but decided that women would retain their sexual features as, after all, in heaven their bodies would be in a state before the Fall where, as Genesis confirmed, there had been no lust and no shame about nakedness. Sexual desire would not be included among the joys of heaven and so women could look like women without fear of men being aroused by them.

Extreme asceticism brought another reward: the lighter a body the more easily it would arise upwards towards heaven. This might even happen before death. The model here was Mary Magdalen who was said to have lived entirely off heavenly food in her old age, not eating anything on earth for thirty-three years (see further below p. 184). She levitated seven times a day to receive heavenly nourishment. One of the stories accumulating around the mystic Catherine of Siena (1347–80) told how her body was also seen to rise from earth after the intense fasting she endured in emulation of Mary Magdalen. 'She was almost as if another Magdalen suspended on high from the earth', as one of her early biographers put it.[3] Catherine's death at thirty-three, the age of Jesus Christ at his Crucifixion and the same number of years that Mary Magdalen had fasted, confirmed the link with heaven. Later the sanctity of the Spanish saint Teresa of Ávila was affirmed by the lightness of her dead body, no more than that of a two-year-old child.

The transformed nature of the flesh, and hence saintliness, was shown not only by its lightness but by its lack of corruption. Theodore of Echternach, writing in the early twelfth century, told how, in the normal course of nature, worms consume the body. 'But the flesh is one thing from nature and another from the grace and merit [received from God]. From nature it is putrid and corruptible, but from [God's] grace and merits ... it repels the greedy worms. For he who puts away from himself worms (that is, nasty thoughts) will not be sweet to the worm.'[4] The bodies of those given God's 'grace and merits' will never putrefy and even their defects will disappear. While the main part of Catherine's body remained in Rome where she had died, the head was stolen and smuggled back to her native Siena with one of her thumbs. Both were uncorrupted and the head temporarily transformed itself into a rose as it passed by the Roman authorities.

Christ's own Resurrection had shown that a dead body could triumph over death and reappear in an apparently living state, and this left an ambivalence over whether there was an absolute barrier between life and death in the bodies of saints. The Resurrection was not given the unique status it has among Christians today (when an absolute barrier between life and death has been confirmed by science), and believers were much readier to accept that a body, especially one of a saint, could enjoy a form of life after death just as Jesus had.[5] With the resurrected Jesus able to move through closed doors, apparently appearing and disappearing at will, and finally ascending skywards into heaven, no one could argue that this was merely a human body. In the forty days before his Ascension, Christ hovered somewhere between the material and spiritual, making appearances both in and around Jerusalem and back in Galilee, a geographical reach virtually impossible for a human being on foot. Was this a space that the saints also occupied before the Last Judgement?

Many reports suggested that they did even if they did not achieve as many restored attributes as Jesus had. When Pope Nicholas V made a visit to Assisi in 1449, over two hundred years after St Francis's death, he ordered the tomb of the saint to be opened. The body apparently stood straight upon its feet and 'the eyes were open as if of a living man, and moderately lifted up to heaven. The *stigmata*, the wounds of Christ that had appeared on his body, were still bleeding.'[6] In many saints' lives, there are stories of the dead saint sitting up to revere a crucifix or the Eucharistic host. Bodies would bleed when those who had harmed them in life came near (as in the example of Thomas Cantilupe told in the next chapter); sacred oil, or in the case of female saints, milk, would be exuded. Doubters could be shown actual examples of hair and fingernails that continued to grow after death. A process of healing could take place. One remembers Queen Aethelthryth of Ely (see p. 64) whose ravages of cancer disappeared from her body after her death. There are, of course, many thousands of reported cases of medieval saints resurrecting 'dead' bodies. So relics may have a continuing life of their own.

Many saints wished to remain whole after their deaths. The thirteenth-century mystic Mary of Oignies cut off her hair while alive – and it was soon bringing miracles – but she ordered that the rest of her body remain unmolested. When a prior tried to take her teeth out after she had died, her jaw apparently clenched (yet another sign of continuing life). He begged her pardon, at which she relented, the jaw relaxed, and a few teeth were shaken out for reuse as relics. This was all that she would allow. Some cities felt that the power of their patron saints would be diluted if their bodies were divided, just as the popes had done in the first centuries of Christianity. Yet so far as reassembling them for the Last Judgement was concerned, it did not matter if bodies were broken up as all particles of flesh were believed to be indestructible.

In most situations, of course, the bodies of martyrs, whose reception into heaven could be assumed by virtue of their deaths, were not intact. The process of martyrdom itself had usually destroyed them. Peter the Venerable, one of the abbots of the great abbey at Cluny, explored the distinction between the soul in heaven and the remnants of the fleshly body left on earth when he welcomed the relics of the martyr St Marcellus to Cluny, in or about 1109. He described how God had divided Marcellus into soul and body – He

1 The news of Thomas Becket's death reverberated throughout Europe. This late twelfth-century enamelled casket, showing the murder and the subsequent burial of Thomas, is one of many produced in workshops in Limoges during this period. The murder scene is 'elevated' by showing Thomas attacked while celebrating Mass, something for which there is no evidence.

2 Ambrose still lies between his two saints, Gervasius and Protasius (one of them concealed beyond Ambrose) in the crypt below Sant'Ambrogio in Milan. The saint in the foreground is clothed in red vestments to signify that he is a martyr.

3 and 4 The 'discovery' of the bones of St Stephen, stoned to death by the Jews in Jerusalem, took place in 415 after a vision had alerted one Lucian to his presence. Stephen is shown here uncorrupted and the legend records that Nicodemus was found beside him. Bishop John of Jerusalem, shown on the right, played a prominent part in the discovery, so linking a relic cult directly to a bishop as happened often in early medieval Europe. (A wool and silk choir hanging made *c.*1500 in Brussels.)

The relics soon travelled and this ivory of *c.*420 shows an arm of Stephen being brought into Constantinople (in a casket) in a grand ceremony of welcome overseen by Emperor Theodosius II and his sister Pulcheria.

5 A bejewelled reliquary enclosing a piece of the True Cross, given as a gift by the Byzantine emperor Justin II to the city of Rome in the late sixth century. Reliquaries such as this may have inspired the writer of the Anglo-Saxon poem, *Dream of the Rood* (see p. 62).

6 and 7 These early saints' tombs were given holes into the space under the body and often sacred dust was collected from below and mixed with water to drink. The shrine of St Candida in the church of Whitchurch Canonicorum in Dorset survives (above). The medieval manuscript (below) shows pilgrims at the tomb of Edward the Confessor (died 1066) in Westminster. The coils in front of the tomb are candles left as thanksgivings by successful supplicants.

8 It was important for any community to create a foundation myth to justify their possession of a saint's body. This twelfth-century illumination shows the body of Martin of Tours (died 397), being smuggled out at night by the citizens of Tours through a window after he had died at Candes. The body was then taken up the river Loire to Tours.

9 A pagan by the name of Onalafbald had visited the shrine of Cuthbert at Durham and mocked the saint, saying he personally preferred the old gods. The saint had his revenge by fixing him to the door and letting him perish, to the amazement of more reverent pilgrims.

10 'When they saw it [the reliquary] for the first time, all in gold and sparkling with precious stones and looking like a human face, the majority of the peasants thought that the statue was really looking at them and answering their prayers with her eyes.' So wrote Bernard d'Angers of this reliquary of Sainte Foy in 1010. It is a rare survival from the tenth century. It is known to have been taken about to effect miracles in the countryside and, once, was even thrust in the faces of some rioters to quell them.

11 This medieval wall panel shows little William of Norwich found crucified. The story that he had been killed by the local Jews seems to have been concocted and elaborated by the monk Thomas of Monmouth in his *Life and Passion of St. William*. A servant who came forward as a 'witness' claims that a crown of thorns had been placed on William's head and that his side was pierced. This is what appears to be shown here. The image dates from the late fifteenth century.

12 and 13 Pilgrims waiting to enter the Church of the Holy Sepulchre in Jerusalem. After 1099 the church was extended to include the site of Calvary (the right hand corner of the courtyard) and pilgrims could ascend steps, presumably to get closer to spot where Christ actually hung above ground. The dome on the left is over the supposed place of the Resurrection and it was left open to symbolise the rising of Christ to heaven. Models of the church or parts of it were to be found scattered throughout Europe.

In Rome a circuit of seven pilgrimage churches was established. This sixteenth-century print shows the Vatican in the foreground with the other six across the Tiber. Three, Santa Maria Maggiore (left centre), Santa Croce in Gerusalemme (behind it) and St John Lateran (above the Vatican) are within the old third century walls, while St Lawrence, St Sebastian and St Paul were all honoured in basilicas outside the walls where they had been buried according to traditional custom. Note the processions of pilgrims passing from one to another.

14 Many of the miracles of St James took place on the road to Compostela. Here two pilgrims have been making their way there when one has died. The saint appears and then guides the survivor and the body of the dead man onwards to the shrine. The appearance of James as a living body shows the ambiguity surrounding the 'life' that might still be found in the flesh of a saint or martyr's body. Painting by Luca Signorelli, c.1508.

15 and 16 The Sainte-Chapelle in Paris was built by Louis IX as a reliquary for the Crown of Thorns and other relics he had bought from Constantinople. It was dedicated in 1248 and was typical of the Gothic churches of the period in which relics and the ceremonies surrounding them could be given light and grandeur. The insert from a medieval manuscript shows Louis with a cross and the Crown being displayed from a makeshift tower. Such displays of relics on feast days often aroused mass hysteria among onlookers.

17 and 18 By the fifteenth century, devils were given a heightened role and believed to be offering temptation to unwary sinners. This is brilliantly shown in *Death and the Miser* by the Netherlander Hieronymous Bosch of *c*.1500. The miser is first shown as a healthy man filling his strong box. A rosary hanging from his waist suggests hypocrisy. It is also possible that Bosch is showing a (paper) indulgence in the hands of the devil under the strongbox and so expressing the growing hostility to them at this time. Other devils are conspiring to ensnare the miser and he is shown a second time in bed, suddenly confronted by death entering the door. Only the ray of light coming through the crucifixion in the window offers hope.

Meanwhile, the miser can have no doubts about the fate that awaits him if he does not repent. Graphic descriptions of the horrors of hell were placed in most churches, here by Giotto in the Scrovegni Chapel in Padua (1305). The fear of eternal punishment explains much of the hysterical behaviour at shrines which offered the hope of salvation through the intercessions of favoured saints.

19 St Fina was a native of the Tuscan city of San Gimignano who died after a lifetime of resigned suffering in 1253. Her saintliness was confirmed at her death by the healing of the paralysed hand of her nurse, shown here in the centre of the scene, while the blindness of a small boy is cured when he kisses her feet. The church bells of the city were said to have been rung by angels. The magnificent fresco by Domenico Ghirlandaio (1470) is in the chapel dedicated to her in the cathedral in her home town.

20 St Nicholas of Bari, whose body had been stolen from Myra in Asia Minor, resided in a crypt under the church built for him on his arrival in Bari in 1087. It was a famous healing shrine and here pilgrims approach the tomb to be cured. One is even carried in, another limps in on crutches. Under the tomb another faints, possibly because a devil has been released from her. A healed man leaves the shrine with his crutches now over his shoulder. This image is from an altarpiece by Gentile da Fabriano, 1425.

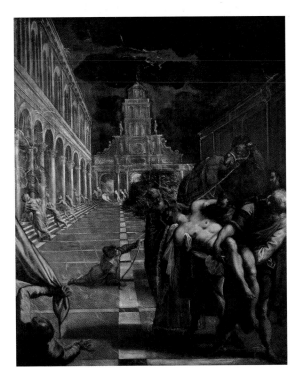

21 and 22 The legends surrounding the stealing of the body of St Mark, its loss in a fire and its miraculous reappearance in a crumbling column, were etched deep in the Venetian mind and reappear constantly in its art. The Venetian painter Tintoretto was commissioned to paint the stealing of the body of Mark by the Scuola of the saint in 1562 and he does so with typical drama. Note that the body, eight hundred years old by the time of its stealing, is uncorrupted. The wonderful altarpiece by Paolo Veneziano (1345) from the basilica of St Mark's shows the moment when the body is rediscovered, still uncorrupted, inside the column in 1095.

23 Relics were often the centrepiece of the ceremonial processions that were so much part of life in fifteenth-century Italy. Here the Scuola of St John the Evangelist carry their fragment of the True Cross across St Mark's Square. Venice, once under the rule of Constantinople, has incorporated many details of Byzantine ceremonial into the procession, notably the white-clad figures carrying candles. Behind the canopied relic, the kneeling figure is Jacopo de' Salis whose little son has just been cured through a miracle (see p. 161). Gentile Bellini's painting shows the procession on St Mark's Day, 25 April, 1496.

24 and 25 One day when the precious reliquary containing the Scuola's piece of the Cross was crossing a bridge, the crush of the crowds caused it to fall into the canal but it failed to sink. In this painting the young men strip off to rescue it but it is the Guardian of the Scuola, Andrea Vendramin, who jumps in and holds it above the water. The actual reliquary (below) survives among the treasures of the Scuola.

26 It was not only the Virgin Mary but the saints in general who acted as bulwarks against the threat of damnation. Their successful intercessions were vital. The wrath of God against a degraded humanity was a constant feature of medieval life. Here God fires arrows to earth (arrows are often a symbol of plague). The Virgin Mary, here, unusually, supported by Christ, has to protect her flock against them. Painting by Lucas Cranach the Elder (1516–18).

27 Mary's assumption into heaven meant that there were few relics of her at shrines so statues of her became venerated instead. This Black Madonna from Montserrat was believed to have been carved by Luke and tradition told how it had been brought to Spain by St Peter himself. The style is actually twelfth century. It became famous for refusing to move into Barcelona and had a special role as a bringer of fertility.

28 The Crucifixion at the back of the altar of the church of Saint-Maximin, attributed to Antonio Ronzen (c.1520) shows a bleeding Christ whose blood is being collected by angels. There were immense theological problems in deciding whether such blood could exist as a relic (see pp. 192–4). Meanwhile at the foot of the Cross, Mary Magdalen whose body lies in the church, kisses the feet of Christ. Her unbound flowing hair is seen as a mark of penitence for an alleged life of sexual excess.

29 This wonderfully crafted gold reliquary was made in the late 1460s for Charles the Bold, the wealthy Duke of Burgundy. It shows the kneeling Duke holding the relic while behind him stands St George. The reliquary is now in Liège Cathedral.

30 The Reformation in England. John Foxe's *Book of Martyrs*, first published in 1563 was a famous Protestant tract that gloried in the humiliation of the Catholic Church. Here it shows a church being cleared out of images and 'papists' carrying what they have saved to the departing 'Ship of the Romish Church'.

31 Prominent among the saints who were denigrated at the time of the Reformation was Thomas Becket. This panel, from the roodscreen of Burlingham St Andrew, Norfolk, is completely defaced.

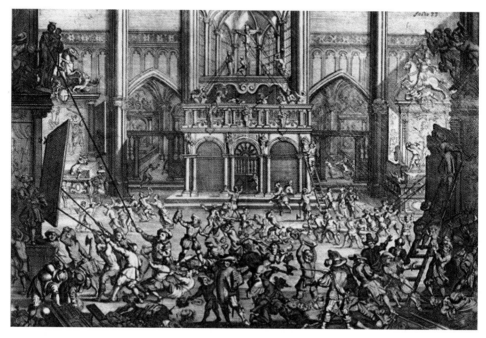

32 The drama and destruction of Protestant iconoclasm is vividly shown in this engraving of the dismantling of statues and images in Antwerp Cathedral in 1566. At that very moment the Catholic Church in Italy and Spain was reasserting the importance of opulently decorated shrines.

retained the soul for himself and gave, 'with marvellous largesse', the relics of Marcellus's sacred body, apparently only a few of his bones, to be venerated by the faithful on earth. 'We venerate them as temples of the Lord, revere them as palaces of divinity, hoard them as pearls suitable for the crown of the eternal king, and with the greatest devotion of which we are capable, preserve them as vessels of resurrection to be joined again to the blessed souls.' They must be offered due respect because, as the bones of a martyr, they will eventually spring to life at the Resurrection. 'Fresh flowers will be remade from dryness and youth reforms from old age. So you should honour them now full of life as if they were [already] in their future incorruption.' In case there are any doubters Peter goes on to say that God demonstrates he acknowledges the sanctity of the bones through innumerable miracles, 'which miracles are frequently experienced by those who come to venerate their sepulchres with devout minds'.[7] So it had to be accepted that, in this case, flesh would be found to clothe the bones of St Marcellus, and it would be his original flesh however far it had been scattered. His perfection would be shown in his beauty, strength and good health, and the ability to enjoy everlasting life.

As the case of Louis IX showed, it was now common to divide up the dead body of a putative saint, especially if it was far from home. However strong the belief in incorruption, in practice, entrails and the rest of the flesh were often left behind and the bones forwarded to the home shrine or for distribution to favoured recipients. If one was sure that all flesh would be reassembled at the Last Judgement, then there need be no inhibitions on dissections or the breaking up of a body into smaller pieces. One of the concerns of the Fourth Lateran Council of 1215 was that relics were being 'exposed for sale and exhibited promiscuously' (Canon 62). To counter this, sales of relics were forbidden (as they still are by the Catholic Church) and all relics had to be placed within a container.[8] In effect this meant that bodies had to be divided up, and so from the thirteenth century one finds a mass of reliquaries containing parts of bodies or even a whole collection of bones from different saints. In 1291 the Dominican theologian Oliver of Tréguier went so far as to argue that a division of relics allowed a greater accumulation of prayers when one added the totals at the shrines where they were honoured.

Another reason for cutting up a dead body was to see whether it had any marks of sainthood within it. This was a development of the fourteenth century. The nuns who were embalming the body of one of their number,

Clare of Montefalco, found an image of the crucified Christ on her heart. Margaret of Città di Castello, a little blind saint, had three precious stones inscribed with pictures of the Holy Family within her heart. By the fifteenth century, it was standard procedure at canonisation proceedings to ask for evidence from an autopsy of indications that a body might be uncorrupted or marked with a sign of sanctity.[9]

Peter Lombard, whose *Sentences* was the standard theological textbook of the period, tells how 'the bodies of saints will rise shining like the Sun, all deformities they had being cut off'. The iconography of the Last Judgement shows those who are blessed regaining their flesh as they emerge from the tombs and then rise in perfect bodies to be reunited with Christ in heaven. In Luca Signorelli's *Resurrection of the Flesh*, part of his Last Judgement in the Chapel of San Brizio in Orvieto (1499–1502), trumpets sound overhead and the physical remains of the blessed start getting themselves together. Those already whole help pull out those still stuck in the ground. Bones are joined up again, flesh put back on, and the end result is healthy muscular bodies ready for the ascent upwards. The French nun and mystic Marguerite of Oingt (died 1310) told of a vision of Christ in which she saw him in his risen body with the wounds of his Crucifixion shimmering in the light, as if they were the crystal glass of reliquaries. 'This body was so noble and transparent that one saw very clearly the soul inside of it. . . . so beautiful that one saw the angels and the saints as if they were painted on it . . . they [the saints] can never be sick, nor burdened, nor suffering, neither in soul nor in body'.[10] Those approaching the relics of saints and martyrs knew that they were in the presence of the sacred who prefigured the glories of heaven that they would enjoy in their reassembled state.

There were, of course, immense theological problems surrounding the reassembling of bodies. Augustine had tackled them in the closing chapters of his *City of God* and he writes with impressive prescience.[11] Every body, at whatever age it had died, would be advanced or brought back to the age of thirty-three, the age at which Christ had died. It would reappear in the prime of life. Discarded hair and fingernails would not keep their appearance but their particles would be redistributed within the reassembled body. This meant that even discarded fingernails could be venerated as relics. Signorelli, who is known to have consulted theologians before he began painting, shows all his blessed to be of equal age, presumably aged thirty-three as Augustine said they would be. Signorelli also portrays the destination of the majority, eternal torture in hell. Quite why the medieval mind became so preoccupied with such extreme punishment is hard to say, but the theologians from Augustine onwards did nothing to reassure the masses that they had any chance of salvation. It was this pervasive dread of suffering that accounts for so much of the emotional intensity driving supplicants to the shrines.

More problematic for the theologians were the bodily relics of Christ and the Virgin Mary who had already ascended into heaven. If every body part would rise at the Last Judgement, then surely those who had gone before, such as Christ and Mary, must have all their bodies with them. So there could be no relics of Christ's blood or the Virgin's milk. This is what Guibert of Nogent had argued when confronted by a tooth of Christ. Yet, the Vatican itself claimed to have relics of Christ, including one of several known examples of the Holy Foreskin. This small, but presumably uncorrupted, relic offered profound and unresolved theological challenges.

The flesh that remains uncorrupted, that exudes oil or blood, that is even able to give the appearance of life, could not represent any earthly reality. Here we are somewhere between heaven and earth where natural laws do not apply, where flesh is of a different quality altogether from that which ordinary human beings know. The idea is echoed in the medieval vision of the universe derived from the Greek scientist Ptolemy where a corrupted and unstable world is contrasted with the serenity and eternal stability of heaven. Relics are the portents of heaven shining in their glory among the dross of sinful humanity.

CHAPTER SIXTEEN

'Christ's recruits . . . fight back'

'IT IS enough that we have lived up to now in the peace of the church. Now, indeed, the harvest, long dried-out, should be watered, fittingly with the blood of the saints, so that Christ's fruit, weakened over length of years by old age, might return, moistened afresh, to its original beauty. We shall see the devil's war break out in open field. Now is the time for Christ's recruits to fight back.'[1] Pope Gregory VII (r. 1073–85) was taking the initiative in asserting papal supremacy against those who challenged it, here the emperor Henry IV whom Gregory was excommunicating.

Well might Gregory talk of fighting back. As the rulers of the emerging kingdoms of medieval Europe claimed themselves to be sacred, the popes were competing with them for spiritual authority. Their outreach from Rome was limited in an age when administration remained rudimentary and the average papal reign was short: sixteen out of twenty-four popes between 1047 and 1198 ruled for less than seven years. There was, of course, no dynastic succession, no royal lineage, and the popes had to rely on their descent from the apostle Peter and the status of Rome as the capital of Latin Christendom. This was hardly enough and was in any case diminished during the papal exile in Avignon between 1309 and 1377. The initiatives taken by popes over launching crusades, calling councils, eliminating heretics and extending control over clergy and laity have to be seen in the context of their desperation to make themselves heard.[2] It was force of personality exercised consistently over a number of years that proved the crucial factor, as seen in the reigns of the formidable Popes Gregory and also Innocent III (r. 1198–1216).

Other rivals of the popes for the spiritual loyalties of the Christian masses were the relic cults. So far the popes had played no role in the declaration of saints. Charlemagne had tried to bring the supervision of shrines under his own control but after his empire collapsed bishops and abbots returned to promoting their own men and women. It was increasingly common for an abbot to venerate the more holy of his monks after their death. Bishops saw it as one of their privileges to announce saints or control local cults but even their authority could be bypassed by the *vox populi*, when a saint's authenticity was proclaimed by mass adulation at his or her shrine. This was the case in Lucca, Italy, where an overworked and much-exploited servant, one Zita, aroused such fervour by her devotions that even her employers repented of their harshness. On her death in 1272, 150 miracles were claimed for her, but it was not until 1580 that her uncorrupted body was given a *translatio* into the church of San Frediano (where it still lies). It took a further century before Zita was canonised (1696) and she is now the patron saint of all domestic servants, including waiters and waitresses. There were many hundreds of such local saints, with their own cults and devotees, of which the institutional Church was hardly aware, although few sustained their appeal as successfully as Zita.

The popes had to assert their authority over such cults. Not surprisingly, it was the redoubtable Gregory VII who took the initiative.[3] Gregory declared that many of his predecessors were saints and that sainthood should be assumed for all popes unless proved otherwise. The quality of holiness was now assumed as intrinsic to the office. By the end of the eleventh century, texts talked of the popes as arbiters of sainthood in general, and with the growth of the papal law courts bishops began to ask the popes for formal recognition of favoured cults as one means of strengthening their own shrines against rivals. By the reign of Pope Alexander III (r. 1159–81) this was in the form of a proclamation that a dead man or woman had reached heaven without the indignity of enduring purgatory, and so was already in place to intercede 'face to face' with God for sinners on earth.

Innocent III was the next to take a stand. At the Lateran Council of 1215 it was formally decreed that no new cult would be recognised without papal approval. One theological commentator, writing in the second half of the thirteenth century, supported the initiative of the papacy on the grounds that the popes alone had the authority to decide on miracles and interpret the Scriptures if necessary. He went on to give more practical reasons, for example the *simplicitas* of bishops – they were too unsophisticated to make a sound judgement – and there was the danger that a plethora of saints would dilute the sanctity of each. It was better for the popes to concentrate on fewer favoured saints who would enhance papal authority. Certainly, a shrine that was given papal support, as that at Horsham St Faith in Norfolk or St Nicholas at Bari, might trump its rivals. On the other hand papal enthusiasm was not enough in itself. In 1208 the legate of Innocent III was murdered in the Languedoc in southern France, apparently at the command of the Count of Toulouse. The Pope was determined that his legate be proclaimed a martyr, but there was no evidence of any local devotion in the Languedoc for the outsider and Innocent had to back down. There was such shock throughout Italy on the assassination of Peter Martyr in 1252 that canonisation by Pope Innocent IV occurred very quickly – after a mere 337 days, the fastest papal canonisation in history.

There was little point in the popes proclaiming these powers unless they developed a process by which they could distinguish between 'good' and 'bad' candidates. Once again it was the energetic Innocent III who outlined the procedure.[4] In his definition of sainthood, Innocent insisted that the proposed saint must have lived a life of piety. A *Vita*, a life of the saint, had to be compiled and this was to be presented in such a way that it asserted the sanctity of the candidate while being edifying for those reading it. However, there must also have been miracles after his death to confirm that God was prepared to act through him as an intermediary. A good life in itself was not enough because Satan himself could change himself into the form of a saint, and some who are apparently saintly do good works only to earn glory from their fellow humans. God would have weeded these out before they reached heaven.

If official papal recognition of a saint's cult depended on miracles, a miracle had to be defined. The Greek intellectual elite had discounted the miraculous. They had concentrated on finding natural causes for events, gathering empirical evidence and trying to understand how this could be formed into laws from which predictions could be made (the essence of modern science). This approach had vanished in the fourth and fifth centuries AD, and the miraculous had been accepted without little further thought as to its definition. Peter Lombard distinguished between those causes which are intrinsic to the natural world, such that a horse can only give birth to a horse or a seed only grow into a certain kind of plant, and those events which go 'beyond nature', in that their causes belong to God alone. Thomas Aquinas brought the works of the empirical philosopher Aristotle back into the equation. He was aware from Aristotle's meticulous compilation of evidence and his reflections on the nature of scientific laws that many events considered by others to be miraculous had natural causes. It was recognised, too, that the 'natural' had to be extended to include the extraordinary freaks of nature, the extreme storm or the unexpected earthquake. Even so, everyone accepted that some events were so rare and inexplicable that they must be ascribed to God. Aquinas coined the word *supernaturalis*, 'supernatural', to define them.[5]

Yet everyone also believed that there were other supernatural forces, angels and demons, that could subvert the laws of nature. The classic scriptural example came from Chapter 7 of the Book of Exodus where Aaron and Moses appear before the Egyptian Pharaoh and, in order to show he has the support of God, Aaron throws down his staff and it turns into a serpent.[6] Pharaoh summons up his magicians and they, too, turn their staffs into serpents. Aaron's serpent, however, gobbles up the rest. The theologians had to distinguish between the act of Aaron and that of the magicians. Augustine had argued, in the fifth century, that it was good angels who had turned Aaron's rod into a serpent and bad angels who had succeeded with the rods of the magicians, a brilliant example of how these forces were imagined in continual competition with each other. Albertus Magnus, the teacher of Thomas Aquinas, argued that Aaron's 'miracle' was as a result of 'the command of God's will' and was 'an event raised above the cause of nature', but the distinction was not an easy one to make.

Despite all these conceptual problems, the matter of an authentic miracle could not be avoided and the best the Pope could do was to appoint the most experienced men he could to judge the issues. By 1200 the English Church had a well-defined hierarchy and was more receptive to papal influence than the Churches of Italy and France. It was here that the fullest accounts of the canonisation procedures are to be found. Among them is the case of Gilbert of Sempringham, founder of the only medieval monastic order to originate in England, who had died in 1198.[7] The English Church was eager to have him canonised but Innocent rejected the first set of petitions sent to Rome. Instead the Pope ordered a new inquiry and chose the commissioners himself, the Archbishop of Canterbury, the Bishop of Ely and two abbots. They had to interview witnesses to the claimed miracles and send their answers to Rome in their original form, not as a resumé. Accounts of the local reputation of the saint were to be included alongside any documents about him whose authenticity could be confirmed. Even when these were all sent in, some of the witnesses were summoned to appear at Rome for further questioning. Altogether a dossier of thirty healing miracles was compiled for Gilbert with between two and five witnesses for each. It all went well and in January 1202 he was proclaimed to be among the saints. This immediately gave his body and any other of his relics status.

Soon local pressure groups had grasped the new procedures. The interest of the Pope could be aroused by sending in a petition signed by as many churchmen as possible, the bishops, abbots and priors, as well as sympathetic royalty. The petitioners became increasingly sophisticated in the way they presented their case, adapting it to show their prospective saint in the guise that would most appeal to the Pope and approaching individual members of the papal court for further support. In Italy it was often the local commune that was influential. So it was the city government of Padua that petitioned the papacy in 1231 for the canonisation of St Antony. Antony had been known personally to the Pope, Gregory IX, so speed was crucial in case the Pope died before the petition had been considered. Antony was successfully canonised in 1231, the foundations of a new basilica to house his remains were laid the same year and the city was transformed by the mass of pilgrims coming to his shrine.

Less successful was the campaign for the canonisation of John Dalderby, Bishop of Lincoln between 1300 and 1320. A rush of letters from King Edward III, the archbishops of Canterbury and York (then bishops), the leading citizens of Lincoln and sixteen earls started the campaign. A special envoy was sent off to plead at Avignon. Then individual cardinals were targeted and a host of monasteries, nobles and Oxford University itself were involved. The Pope remained unimpressed and John Dalderby still lies in Lincoln Cathedral without saintly recognition.

Overall, in fact, the success rate remained low. Between 1199 and 1276 the popes were sufficiently convinced by petitions on behalf of individual would-be saints to order forty-eight inquiries.[8] Eighteen dossiers submitted in reply were not accepted as adequate and were sent back to be done again. Only twenty-three of the inquiries, fewer than a half, resulted in an actual canonisation. The number dropped off significantly in the fourteenth and fifteenth centuries, so that only twelve canonisations were pronounced between 1269 and 1431. One reason may have been a more critical approach to certain types of miracles. The commissioners became particularly suspicious of claimed cures from 'paralysis', although with time they became more receptive to 'resurrections from the dead'.

One of the relatively rare canonisations of the fourteenth century, officially promulgated in 1320, was of the English saint, Thomas de Cantilupe, Bishop of Hereford. It is worth exploring in detail.[9] Thomas had died in Italy in 1282. His flesh had been boiled off his bones and these had been returned to his native England. At Easter 1287 his successor as bishop, Richard Swinfield, moved the bones into a new tomb in Hereford Cathedral and the miracles began. One of the first took place as the bones entered the cathedral. The Earl of Gloucester, who had had many disputes with Thomas over land rights, approached the bones to claim redress and they began oozing blood. Gloucester was taken aback at this divine/saintly disapproval and withdrew his claims. By the early 1290s the shrine was accumulating £200 a year from pilgrims. Thomas was credited with sixty resurrections and numerous healings, and his shrine told the tale from the offerings left there when these were listed in 1307. Many must have involved the safe return from voyages as there were 170 silver ships and 41 wax ships. Also among the clutter were 129 silver and 1,424 wax images of people or limbs. There were 77 animal figures, 108 crutches and 3 wooden vehicles. In 1290 Bishop Swinfield felt confident enough to petition Pope Nicholas IV to enlist Thomas among the saints. He kept up the pressure for years, recruiting as allies his fellow bishops and the king, Edward I, who had known Thomas de Cantilupe personally.

It took sixteen years and a new Pope, Clement V, to get a favourable response. Eventually, in 1306, two French bishops and the Bishop of London, Ralph Baldock, were appointed by the Pope as commissioners of inquiry. They were all experienced and astute men, well trained in law and administration. The records of their inquiry survive. Meeting for the first time in London in July 1307, they swore in the notaries who would record their deliberations and interrogations in writing and then set out the twenty-five questions they wanted witnesses to answer. There were three areas they had to focus on. There was the 'faith, life and character' of the deceased bishop, his 'reputation, public report and opinion of him' and, not least, 'the

miracles'. The commissioners were especially interested in the public reputation of the proposed saint. Were the apparent miracles widely known
about and believed in, for instance? They were sufficiently versed in theological jargon to be able to ask whether a claimed miracle was 'above or contrary
to nature', although it must have been difficult for witnesses to make a satis-
factory response to this. Each witness would be taken through the list in the
language with which he or she was most happy, Latin for the clerics, French
for the upper class and English for the most local witnesses. One witness of
great importance testified in Welsh in 1307 through two Franciscan inter-
preters. The Franciscans prided themselves on the linguistic skills that
enabled them to reach minority audiences with their preaching, and these
two had been working in Wales.

This Welsh-speaking witness was one William Cragh, William 'the
Scabby', otherwise known as William ap Rhys. Cragh had been arrested by
one of the Anglo-Norman marcher lords, William de Briouze, who held
power along the boundaries between Wales and England. Accusing William
Cragh of several murders, de Briouze exercised his right to condemn him to
death by hanging in November 1290. Several witnesses had seen the hanging
take place and, afterwards, the body of William laid out in a house in Swansea
with all the signs that he was dead. Yet, here in November 1307, seventeen
years later, was William Cragh standing before the commissioners full of life.

William de Briouze had died in 1191 but his widow Mary was on hand to
testify, together with her son, William de Briouze the Younger, and the family
chaplain. They had given their evidence in London before the case had moved
to Hereford. William Cragh was himself able to provide a fairly coherent
account of events when he was interviewed in Hereford. He had been
sentenced to death together with another man (who had not survived execution) and the morning of his execution William had had a vision of the Virgin
Mary together with another saint called Thomas. He was sure that this was
Thomas de Cantilupe, not the recently martyred Thomas Becket, because he
had visited the shrine at Hereford and, while in prison awaiting execution, had
prayed to the saint for liberation. Of course when the hanging took place
William had lost consciousness, had come round expecting to be hanged again
but nothing more was done. He gradually recovered his full health over a
number of days or weeks (the witnesses disagreed). It was others who came
forward to say that he had actually died and that his body showed all the signs

of a hanged man, including eyes that had detached themselves from their sockets. (So this was not a case where a saint had appeared to hold his legs to save him from death.) On his 'recovery', William had heard that Mary de Briouze had interceded with Thomas de Cantilupe for him and, when he had revived, she had had the length of his body measured to fulfil the custom of leaving at the shrine concerned a candle the length of a person who had been cured. This 'measuring to the saint' was believed to bring continuing care.

The younger William de Briouze had seen the hanging from his castle walls, including a collapse of the gallows and the rehanging of William Cragh, and confirmed to the commissioners that his family would never have allowed Cragh to survive. The chaplain backed him up. De Briouze the younger also confirmed that his mother had uttered a prayer to Thomas de Cantilupe to revive William Cragh after his death. Mary herself assured the court that she had interceded with Thomas in the belief that William was dead and that the saint could help resurrect him. The commissioners were convinced. This truly was a resurrection brought about by Thomas and so it could be forwarded as such to the Pope.

In Hereford Cathedral documents still in the archive show that Mary de Briouze did indeed arrive at the shrine of Thomas on 2 December 1290 to give thanks for the miracle, and William Cragh was with her. It is unknown why Mary intervened with her prayer. By doing so she was going against the wishes of her husband and family, and it is hard to see what personal contact this well-born lady might ever have had with a Welsh brigand.

Eventually, the dossier was complete and the commissioners sent it off to Avignon where the popes were in exile. Even now it had to wait until 1313 before it was properly examined by a group of cardinals, and then in 1319 and 1320 all the evidence was looked at again by an independent but anonymous assessor whose meticulous report survives.[10] Essentially, the report is a critical assessment of twenty-six of the thirty-eight miracles submitted for the claim, probably drawn up for the cardinals who were conducting a review of the case before the final decision was to be made.

The assessor's report starts with a resumé of the miraculous in the Old and New Testaments. This not only confirms the miraculous as a part of God's work but provides the criteria by which claimed miracles can be judged. Then the writer deals with the miracles ascribed to Thomas de Cantilupe. There are the twelve that he rejects. Some did not appear to him to be miraculous at all;

the disappearance of a man's warts and the restoration to sanity of a 'mad' woman, for instance. Others were of so common a type that they may have been added in simply because they were miracles one would expect. The way in which Thomas's tombstone changed from being heavy to light was one (a similar property to that shown by the icon of the *Hodegetria* in Constantinople). Sadly, the case of William Cragh that had been so carefully assessed by the commissioners was among the twelve rejected. Perhaps the assessor had heard of too many cases where the death itself was not properly witnessed and the victim had revived naturally from unconsciousness. So the examination of William Cragh had been in vain. Other miracles were not selected because there were better examples of similar ones on the list.

The assessor did apply some empirical knowledge to the twenty-six selected miracles. He speculated how likely it was for a body to survive a fall from a height. He had to set out the criteria by which death could be assumed (and so the possibility of a genuine resurrection). The test was whether the soul had left the body as could be assessed from symptoms such as absence of movement or breath, or coldness or stiffness in the corpse. If a body revived after this, it might be a miraculous resurrection. It was crucial that any apparent cure was associated with some act of devotion or piety, a prayer to the saint, for instance. In the case of a woman whose paralysed legs became mobile again after a hot bath, it was the vision of Thomas de Cantilupe telling her to have the bath that was the clinching factor. Overall, the assessor seemed quite credulous. There was only one of the twenty-six miracles that he rejected completely with three others he considered to be dubious. He even accepted as authentic the case of little John of Burton who had been born without a tongue, made a pilgrimage to the tomb of Thomas at Hereford and miraculously acquired one. When the original inquiry was being conducted in Hereford, four Franciscans, who had come down from London to give evidence, declared this apparent miracle was, in fact, a hoax. The assessor overrode the doubts. Often the most important factor was that the miracle was the result of an invocation to God, through the saint, and that the resulting miracles strengthened faith and resounded to the glory of God.

Finally the assessor accepted ten miracles as authentic enough for them to be forwarded to the Pope and his cardinals for a final decision. This was more than the two that were needed, so the exclusions had had no effect. The Pope, now John XXII, consulted with several absent cardinals and then, from his court in Avignon, he declared in early 1320 'by apostolic authority that so many and so great things have been proven about the life and miracles of Saint Thomas of Cantilupe, bishop of Hereford, that they suffice for his canonisation'. On 17 April, the same year, the formal act of canonisation took place in the main church in Avignon.

There must have been great rejoicings in Hereford when the news reached the city, but it was all rather late. Studies of the offerings at Hereford had shown that the initial enthusiasm over the tomb of 1287 had already died down by 1300. While the first pilgrims had been ordinary villagers from the surrounding countryside, desperate to try out a new source of cures, by 1300 the visitors tend to be of higher class and many had come to give thanks for miracles that had occurred outside Hereford. By 1320 the heyday of the shrine had already passed and the feast day of St Thomas gradually became part of the normal run of annual events in the diocese with relatively few new miracles being reported.[11]

The papal canonisation process was much too bureaucratic to achieve its aim of asserting papal power over local cults. Many came and went before the Pope could respond to them, and the vast majority of cults probably only sought papal approval as a means of raising their status and to see off rivals. As the reputation of the papacy declined in the fifteenth century in many parts of Europe, official canonisation would have done nothing to enhance the prestige of a cult in any case. Many cults were so deeply embedded in their local communities that papal disapproval would never have dislodged them. This was certainly the case in the cities of northern Italy, as we shall see in the next chapter.

CHAPTER SEVENTEEN

Protectors of *il Popolo*

T HE MOST vigorous assertion of relic cults in the public arena was to be found in the Italian city states. The wealthiest of these by far was Venice, whose revenues from her ruthless exploitation of Mediterranean trade gave her an income, in the middle of the fifteenth century, greater than the whole of England. For cities such as this, owning the relic of a prestigious saint was an end in itself, a mark of the city's identity, not least against rival spiritual and political powers, including the established Church, and other cities.

For Venice this saint was St Mark the Evangelist. Mark would never have achieved this prestigious role if the Venetians had not stolen his body and provided some reason why he should be brought back to the lagoon. 'Mark' had been the name associated with the earliest of the synoptic Gospels since about AD 180 but was also the name given to the Apostle Peter's secretary. As with most early Christian figures a legendary past had been created for Mark. His travels had included a visit to the prosperous Roman city of Aquileia in northern Italy, where he had befriended a Christian called Hermagoras whom Mark took to Rome to be personally ordained by Peter as Aquileia's first bishop. It was said that Mark ended his life in Alexandria, another early thriving Christian community, and that his body was venerated there.

The earliest surviving account of the theft of Mark from Alexandria dates from about 1050, but it describes events placed over two hundred years earlier, traditionally in 828. In the early ninth century Venice's position as a newly founded city on the islands of the lagoon was still precarious. The settlement was officially part of the Byzantine empire but remote, of course, from Constantinople, the imperial capital, and so vulnerable to the ambitions of the powers on the Italian mainland. Ominously, the bishop of the ancient city of Aquileia on the mainland had been claiming ecclesiastical jurisdiction over the Venetian lagoon since the seventh century and Aquileia's claim had received the support of both Charlemagne, after his conquest of Lombardy, and the Pope. Aquileia had tried to boost its ecclesiastical importance further through its connection to Mark. In 827 the Pope and the local Carolingian bishops had issued a formal declaration of Aquileia's ecclesiastical primacy over Venice. Venice's independence was in danger of being strangled and the city needed a propaganda coup with which to proclaim its liberty.

It is hard to imagine a more imaginative and audacious response by the Venetians than to steal, or to create the story of stealing, the body of Mark.[1] The Venetian account of 1050 tells how two merchants from the Venetian lagoon, Tribunus of Malamocco and Rusticus of Torcello, were sailing in the eastern Mediterranean when their ship was driven off course and forced to land at Alexandria, by then under Islamic rule. Officially, the two were not allowed to trade with the Arabs but they heard a story that the Caliph was about to desecrate the tomb of Mark. They sought out the Christian custodians of the tomb and persuaded them that Mark officially 'belonged' to Aquileia (*sic*) and would be better protected there. When the tomb was opened, a wonderful fragrance emerged and local suspicions were immediately aroused. The merchants quickly crammed the intact body into a barrel and concealed it under a layer of pork. The Muslim customs officer fled in disgust when the barrel was passed before him and it was smuggled on board. Mark soon showed he was glad to be rescued. He awoke the crew just before they were shipwrecked, drove off a plague of devils who were gathering on the shore, and eventually arrived in Venice where the bishop of the city welcomed him with gratitude. The body was processed to the doge's palace and the doge agreed that a special *martyrium* would be constructed for it. This was the first basilica of St Mark, then, as now, next to the palace and so directly under ducal patronage. Mark seems happily to have ignored the promise that he really belonged to Aquileia.

In the history of Venice composed by Martino da Canal between 1267 and 1275, the story of Mark and Hermagoras originally written in support of Aquileia's claim is expanded to justify Venice's theft.[2] Mark and Hermagoras were indeed on their way to Rome as in the original story but they had to cross the lagoon. A storm sprang up. Mark took to the oars and rowed their boat up to the island of Rialto where the pair rested for the night. In a dream it was revealed to Mark that it was here that his final resting place would be. It was, of course, the exact place where the basilica still stands today.

The Bishop of Venice had his cathedral in San Pietro di Castello at the far eastern end of the city on the edge of the lagoon and the basilica of St Mark was always linked instead to the doge, the ceremonial ruler of the city, originally as his palace chapel. So this was always a 'political' relic. In 976 the first St Mark's burned down. A few officials were told where the relics had been hidden after the fire but over the following years the burial spot was forgotten. When a new church was being built in the mid-eleventh century, there were frenzied searches to find the body but all were in vain. Something more dramatic was needed to catch the saint's attention. In 1094 the doge, Vitale Falier, ordered a three-day fast in the city to be followed by a mass procession of citizens to St Mark's where there would be a High Mass. This did the trick. During Mass, on 25 June, a column began shifting, its plaster crumbled, and there was the body with a wonderful odour coming from it. A mosaic in the basilica records the moment as the doge and patriarch greeted the reappearance with joy. The Byzantine empire, to which Venice was still nominally subject at the time, was in crisis and it could be said that St Mark had reappeared just at the right moment for Venice to assert its independence. One eleventh-century preacher enthused that 'as the East, until very recently, was lit up by a golden radiance, now it is the West which glows in the rays of his [i.e. Mark's] presence'. Undoubtedly, Doge Falier had planned his event to this end.

St Mark is a fine example of a cult that was integrated into the political and ceremonial life of a city. The crucial moment in the development of the cult was the visit to Venice of Pope Alexander III in 1177. This was a thanksgiving by the Pope for Venetian support against the emperor Barbarossa who had invaded northern Italy. The Pope had come to the high altar of St Mark's and given the doge, Sebastiano Ziani, a gold ring and conferred perpetual dominion as 'lord of the sea' on him, in the hope that Venice would protect the Adriatic from any further imperial invasions. He also gave Ziani a white candle, a gesture that the Venetians interpreted as placing the cult of Mark under his direct authority. One can see the shift of the cult of Mark from church to city by comparing two mosaics of the Reception of the Relics in St Mark's. In the Capella di San Clemente, the sequence of twelfth-century mosaics displaying the stealing of Mark and his arrival in Venice show the body being received by a group of clergy. In a mosaic of 1265 above the Porta San Alipio, the body is being received instead by fifty lay figures, including the doge and dogaressa, nobles and, apparently, representatives of *il popolo*, the citizen body. The only clergy shown are those carrying in the relics. This is now a city cult.[3]

The doge's pre-eminence as patron of the cult was strengthened with further embellishments in 1341. During a fierce winter storm on the lagoon an elderly fisherman took on board three strangers in the hope that they would help him save his boat and tackle. They told him to row them to the mouth of the lagoon, and found there a ship full of demons that was causing the storm. Then the strangers revealed themselves as the saints Mark, George and Nicholas and they ordered the waters to calm. As the grateful fisherman dropped them back on dry land, St Mark handed him his ring and said that it must be delivered to the doge. Here again was proof that the doge should preside at the ceremonies, but St Mark's choice of go-between showed that he trusted the people to support his choice. From now on St Mark and the safety and prosperity of Venice went hand in hand. A fifteenth-century canon of the basilica, Gabriele Fiamma, told how he had been born a Venetian and lived 'in this happy homeland, protected by the prayers and guardianship of St. Mark, from whom that Most Serene Republic acknowledges its greatness, its victories and all its good fortune'.[4] Venice's presence overseas is still instantly recognisable by the lion of St Mark emblazoned on a city or castle wall.

There was a stunning setting for the cult's ceremonies, the Piazza San Marco, the square in front of the basilica. The model for the piazza may well have been the open courts of the Islamic east, the source of much of Venice's trade, and hence wealth. The huge courtyard of the Great Umayyad Mosque in Damascus has very much the same size and feel. The piazza was marked out and brought to completion with a fine herring-bone pavement, in the thirteenth century, in the decades after the Fourth Crusade (1202–04). Venice's most majestic possessions, the four copper horses looted from Constantinople, were placed as a symbol of triumph on the *loggia* in about 1260, during the reign of Doge Raniero Zeno (r. 1253–68).[5]

It was Zeno who brought the city's ritual to its zenith, not only in its opulence but in the display of himself in the form of a Byzantine-style

emperor. St Mark was incorporated in the elaborate annual round of ceremonies that consumed much of the subsequent doges' energies. Mark's feast
day was on 25 April and his relics would be displayed in the doge's procession. These included his ring, as delivered to the doge in 1341, and a book
that Mark was said to have written. The doge would light a white candle in
memory of the gift of the candle from Pope Alexander III and by doing so he
would reassert his relationship to St Mark and reinforce the saint's predom-
inant spiritual and political role in the city. The papal legate and the doge
would kneel together at the High Altar of the basilica, and to rule out any
squabbling over precedence they would make a confession of their sins
simultaneously to the officiating priest. The doge would then receive candles
from the Scuole, the religious confraternities that played such a major role in
the fabric of the city.

On 25 June the relics would again be out, this time to celebrate the
anniversary of the emergence of Mark's body from the column. On this occasion the clergy of the city would play a larger part in the ceremony, walking
in procession with the members of the Scuole and presenting their own
candles to the doge in recognition of his precedence over the Church. Then
there was a feast on 31 January to mark the first arrival of St Mark's body in
Venice, and another on 8 October, the anniversary of the dedication of his
tomb in the newly built basilica.

These rituals had the primary purpose of confirming the supremacy of the
doge over both Church and State, the whole under the auspices of St Mark.
They acted as a symbol of the independence and prosperity of a city whose
interests, by the thirteenth century, spread throughout the Mediterranean.
The Piazza San Marco was shown at its best with the long processions of
dignitaries, foreign ambassadors, clergy and the city's officials. The most
resplendent image of this is Gentile Bellini's *Procession of the True Cross in
San Marco*, which represents the occasion on St Mark's Day, 25 April 1496.
The gilded facade and domes of the basilica dominate the painting. While a
cross section of Venetian society displays itself in the open centre of the
piazza, along each side the vast procession wends it way from the Ducal
Palace at the far right corner.

In the centre foreground is a canopy carried by members of the Scuola
Grande di San Giovanni Evangelista (John the Evangelist) and flanked by
white-robed attendants carrying candles. The Scuola was one of the six

major charitable confraternities. There were many lesser ones and member-ship conveyed some social status in a city where only the nobility had the right to participate in government. Founded in 1261, the Scuola di San Giovanni still owns its fifteenth-century headquarters and meeting hall. In the upstairs Oratorio is kept its own most celebrated relic, of the True Cross.

The fragment of wood had been presented to the Scuola in 1379 by the Grand Chancellor of Cyprus who had received it from the Patriarch of Constantinople. The Grand Chancellor told how he had heard of the chari-table work of the Scuole but was drawn to San Giovanni Evangelista by his own devotion to St John and the high reputation of the guardian of the Scuola, Andrea Vendramin. The Scuola commissioned its own painting of the event by Lazzaro Bastiani (*c.*1430–1512), and he shows the moment when the Chancellor hands the relic to Vendramin in front of the altar in the Scuola. The view is through the courtyard outside the Scuola and here members of the Venetian nobility are assembled, giving added prestige to the occasion.

The fragment of the True Cross was the most prestigious relic in the city after those of St Mark. The wonderful gilded silver reliquary made for it is still in the Oratorio and it was here that the paintings of the procession and the presentation of the relic originally hung. (They are now in the Accademia picture gallery in Venice.) The scene in Bellini's *Procession of the True Cross in San Marco* focuses on the relic of the True Cross as the members of the Scuola proudly carry it on 25 April. This is not a mere portrayal of a typical proces-sion. Scarcely noticeable just behind the canopy is a man in red who is kneeling, the only person in the entire picture to be doing so. He is Jacopo de' Salis, a merchant visiting Venice from Brescia, a prosperous town in the centre of northern Italy. The day before he had received terrible news. His small son had suffered a fractured skull and was not expected to live. In desperation Jacopo knelt before the relic as it passed, 'praying piously to the almighty God that through that *sanctissima croce*, "that most sacred cross", he would deign to work a miracle for his son and free him from so much pain and peril'. Jacopo reached home and to his delight found that his son had indeed been cured. He sent back the good news to the Scuola, promising that he would bring the boy to offer due reverence to the Cross.[6]

Bellini has shown the miracle obliquely. Anyone unaware of the back-ground story would fail to recognise that any miracle was happening at all and perhaps would not even notice the kneeling merchant, so overpowering is the background to the procession. This painting was only one of several showing the miracles of the Scuola's relic that hung in the Oratorio. The picture's companions, by some of Venice's most celebrated painters, show other miracles. These are interesting paintings. Unlike the usual portraits of saints or the Madonna, a sacred object is put centre stage and depicted at the very moment of transformation, from disease to good health, from death to revival. Thus the vivid narrative painter Vittore Carpaccio shows a miracle of the Cross where a possessed man is looking up at it at the moment of being relieved of his demon. The bustling activity of Venetian canal and street life goes on below the *loggia* where the miracle is taking place, its participants apparently oblivious of its drama. In another painting by Gentile Bellini, *Miracle of the Cross at the Bridge of San Lorenzo*, the Cross has fallen into a canal after being upset by the crush of crowds on a bridge. It hovers above the water and young men strip off to go in and rescue it. However, it is Vendramin himself who saves it and is shown in his full robes, floating on the surface with the reliquary safely in his hand.[7]

Processions of the relics of the patron saint of a city were often the high point of the civic year. In Venice, in particular, they met the political needs of the doge and the city's elites. Relics brought status and the control of their display, by ruler or ruled, Church or State, reflected where power in the city lay. Venice was perhaps exceptional in integrating them so successfully in a system of government that was to prove to be the most stable of any city in Italy, but there are many other examples.[8]

The long-established patron saint of Modena, one of the most ancient of the northern Italian cities whose origins went back to the Etruscans, was St Germinianus, a fourth-century AD bishop. He was credited with famous miracles, notably one in which he had enveloped the city in fog as Attila the Hun was passing by and so had saved it from destruction. The saint's body remained in the city although nothing is heard of it until the eleventh century, when a freshly composed life of Germinianus, the *Vita Longior*, appeared.

The *Vita* was cleverly crafted. It told how, in the fourth century, Germinianus had been a popular local man who had refused election as bishop. He eventually gave way to the clamour of the citizens, recognising that the city would be better served by himself than by an outsider. When he died it was also through popular acclaim that a basilica was built over his remains to which the citizens

flocked – as at St Mark's, Venice. Whoever wrote the *Vita* used all the termi-
nology of his own day in describing *populus*, 'the people', and *cives*, 'citizens'. In
short, whatever the true background to Germinianus's elevation, the *Vita* was a
means through which he was championed as a man of the people, rather than of
the Church. The Palazzo Communale, the town hall, begun in 1046, was placed
next door to the original shrine of the saint.

The church that held the body in Modena was in ruins by 1099 and a decision was made to rebuild it. The city already had a strong communal government but it was one of many under the sovereignty of the Countess Matilda of
Tuscany who had inherited vast estates in central Italy. The citizens as well as
the clergy of the city supported the move, and building got under way on the
site of the original shrine. Eventually, the moment came to move the bones of
Germinianus into the new crypt of his cathedral. Here the local clergy asserted
their authority. They claimed the right to organise the ceremony of *translatio*
and announced that they wished to 'reveal' the body to the congregation. The
'knights' and the people of Modena gathered in protest. They sensed that the
clergy would grab the initiative and make capital out of it. Most of all they
feared that the clergy would divide the body and distribute it to other churches,
and so dilute its power. They appealed to Matilda and she wisely postponed
the ceremony until the Pope, Paschal II (r. 1099–1118), could carry it out
personally. There would be a six-month delay before Paschal, whose own reign
was riven with disputes over the extent of Church power, arrived, and meanwhile six knights and twelve citizens took over responsibility for the security
of their saint's body.[9] In October 1106 the Pope oversaw the *translatio*. The
cathedral, which was finished in 1184, remains one of the finest Romanesque
buildings in northern Italy, not least for its wonderful sculptures, and
Germinianus is still safely there in the crypt.

So, despite the intervention of the Pope in blessing his *translatio*,
St Germinianus had been absorbed by the people of Modena as their own.
By the thirteenth century, like many of the saints of the period, his body,
although still in the cathedral crypt, had been subdivided and his arm had its
own reliquary which could be displayed publicly to assert his presence.
However, in 1288 Modena lost its independence to the aggressive Este
family of Ferrara. Their rule was short-lived. In January 1306 the people
revolted and threw out their occupiers. In the heady days that followed,
St Germinianus came into his own.[10] In a proclamation of the city's liberty

the saint was invoked, after God and the Virgin Mary, as 'patron, protector and special defender of the city and people of Modena'. 'May he grant a health-giving state of peaceful liberty and the grace that Modena may be perpetually well governed by its rulers.' To protect the city from further attack, a company of a thousand foot soldiers, the Societa Sancti Geminiani, was formed with the insignia of the saint on its shields and banners. A platform was set up above the facade of the cathedral and on each anniversary of the liberation, the saint's arm was to be exhibited to the citizenry.

The arm soon had further duties. In future, members of the city's popular councils were to take their oaths in the cathedral over the reliquary. In early January 1307 it was ordered that the forthcoming feast day of St Germinianus, 31 January, the first since the city's liberation, was to be celebrated with three days of ceremonies. All would be welcome to the market that would be held at the same time, except 'criminals, exiles and all subjects of the evil tyrant, the marquis of Este'. Every householder had to attend the vigil of the saint with their own candles. Again the arm would be displayed.

Next provision was made to collect offerings by members of the city guilds to build a new altar to St Germinianus in the west end of the cathedral. This was the people's end of the church. The patrons of the altar were to be the guild officials and 'the defenders of the people'. They could appoint their own priest and although he had to be confirmed by the bishop, it was stressed that the bishop and chapter of the cathedral were to be allowed no rights over the chapel. There was one thing that the people could not do and that was to grant indulgences, but a document of 1307 records that the guilds planned to petition the bishop to grant the customary forty days to those visiting the chapel.

This is a striking example of how fully a saint could be integrated into the political life of a city and detached from the influence of the Church. Sadly, the independence of Modena was not to last. The Este dynasty regained control in 1336. There was nothing they could do to stop the feasting that had been instituted to commemorate their earlier expulsion. The official Este line was that the days of celebration in January now commemorated the ancient triumph of St Germinianus over Attila the Hun!

Lucca, towards the west coast of Tuscany, is another city with Etruscan origins and a Roman history.[11] The renewal of its wealth came in the twelfth century when it began to produce fine silks. In the same period, following the death of Matilda of Tuscany, who had made her court there, its communal government emerged. The founding bishop of the city was San Frediano and his body was held at a monastery dedicated to him. The cathedral clergy were deeply frustrated by this and their anger grew. Pope Eugenius II visited Lucca in 1147 and publicly venerated the relics of the saint in a *translatio* to a new altar in the monastery. The dispute degenerated. The cathedral forbade the monks to advertise that they had the body. The monks retaliated by waiting for the day of the dedication of the new cathedral and then announced they were launching their own feast day on the same day. This was to be of the patriarch Abraham! The Pope, now Alexander III, intervened, told the cathedral they could not prevent anyone visiting the shrine of San Frediano, and informed the monks that they must move the feast of Abraham to another day.

The citizens of Lucca simply sidestepped this unseemly squabble. They found a new relic that would trump all others! This was the *Volto Santo*, 'the Holy Face', a wooden statue of the crucified Christ that was said to have been carved by Nicodemus, the friend of Joseph of Arimathea, immediately after the Crucifixion. Nicodemus had fashioned the body and then fallen asleep. The face had been miraculously carved by the time he awoke. So here is a myth that echoes similar stories of the Virgin Mary being painted by the Evangelist Luke, in effect a wonder-working image rather than a relic as such. The *Volto Santo* provides a good example of how the boundaries can become blurred.

The Lucchesi developed a myth to explain the relic's arrival in Lucca. They claimed that the first *Volto* had been discovered in a cave in the east and then made its way to Tuscany in the eighth century. It had arrived in a boat without sails or oars (as the body of James had arrived in Spain), scorned a home at the port of Luni, an ancient rival of Lucca, where it landed and made its own way in a cart driven by oxen with the people of Lucca in support. It had chosen the monastery of San Frediano as its first home but then had miraculously transferred itself to the city's cathedral, which was dedicated to St Martin.

The *Volto* first appears in the cathedral records in the early twelfth century when the Bishop of Lucca, Rangerius, wrote an account of the city's festivities and made a reference to a 'cross' in the cathedral. His successor, Benedict, consecrated a chapel to the *Volto* in 1120. The Englishman Gervase of

Tilbury, who taught canon law at the university of Bologna, records the special prayers made to the *Volto Santo* in the later twelfth century. In 1181 there are references to a lay fraternity that was responsible for overseeing the carving, and its members were granted the rights to make their own collections for it, especially on 14 September, the feast day that was allocated to it. Eventually, the feast day became, and still is, the great civic festival of the Lucchese year, with a procession of the relic between San Frediano to the cathedral. Without overthrowing the power of the Church, the citizens of Lucca had successfully infiltrated their own relic into the religious calendar and made it the dominant cult of the city. Even as far away as England, William II is recorded as swearing by the *Volto Santo*. The papacy that had seen itself as the guardian of the original cult of San Frediano had simply been bypassed by Lucca's citizens.

The original *Volto Santo* has long been lost. It is said that it was destroyed by enthusiastic relic hunters who cut pieces off it. Illustrations of the relic survive that show it was typical of similar German statues of the eleventh century and this fits well with the first time that the cult is recorded at the beginning of the twelfth century. In its present form, it stands in its own shrine in Lucca Cathedral and opulent fittings are added to it on its feast day.

One of the most dramatic transfers of relics from church to community took place in the city of Prato, a prosperous neighbour of Florence.[12] In 1141 Prato had been bequeathed a Girdle of the Virgin by a merchant who had brought it back from the crusades. The Virgin must have had several girdles during her lifetime, but the story went that this was the one that had been thrown down to St Thomas by the Virgin herself as she was being assumed into heaven. It was placed in the choir of the Pieve (the term for a rural church with its own baptistery) of Santo Stefano. As the choir of a church was always the preserve of the clergy, it was, in short, under the direct care of the church. There is no record of its veneration until the end of the thirteenth century, but then it became a focus for a lucrative pilgrimage trade and may even have been bringing in as much income as the city's flourishing textile industry. In 1346 a magistrate, Donato di maestro Simone, marched into the Pieve with a gang of accomplices, entered the choir, seized the Girdle and took it to the west end of the church, the part normally seen as belonging to the community. This was a dramatic and apparently unscrupulous transfer of relic from Church to community. The clergy had nothing with which to retaliate and could only petition Pope Innocent VI, who had to intervene. The settlement he proposed was a compromise. The Girdle was to stay in the church, be shown to pilgrims by the clergy of the church, but the commune was to be entitled to two-thirds of the revenue as well as having their own key to the shrine. It was the commune that built the late fourteenth-century chapel that still houses the Girdle today. It is still displayed five times a year in the charming fifteenth-century pulpit on the facade of the Pieve.

The feast days of the patron saints grew more opulent in time, reaching a culmination of ceremonial splendour in the fifteenth century. So in Florence one can see the ever more elaborate celebrations of the feast of St John the Baptist on 24 June.[13] This was another cult that had gradually isolated itself from the local church hierarchy, with John appearing as the patron saint of the city on the prestigious florin first minted in 1252. The cult was based in the much-hallowed and ancient baptistery rather than in the cathedral. Unfortunately, the city had difficulty in finding relics of John the Baptist. In 1393 some unspecified relics that apparently were linked to John were bought by the commune from a merchant in Florence and some more from a widow in Venice, but it is not even recorded what they were. Then, in 1411 came news that the anti-pope John XXII had the head of John the Baptist for sale. The price was a massive 50,000 florins. Delegates from Florence were sent to negotiate. The talks broke down and the Florentines had to be content with one of the Baptist's fingers. Plotting went on. The Florentine architect Filarete was working in Rome in the 1440s and he was apparently instructed by the commune actually to steal the head they were after. This ambitious plot, too, came to nothing. The Florentines must have been furious when the Sienese Pope Pius II donated a whole arm of John to their ancient rivals Siena in 1463.

None of this marred the celebrations in Florence. The lack of relics of John the Baptist was more than made up for by the thousands of others that were on display. All groups in the city were under the direct orders of the *festaioli*, the officials designated to organise the festivities, and the extravagance was as much a flaunting of Florentine arrogance and wealth before citizens of rival communes as symbols of a united and prosperous city. On 23 June there was a grand procession of merchants who were ordered to dress as opulently as possible. After they had passed, the clergy followed. They were also ordered to dress in their finest vestments. 'And the number

of religious orders is great, with so many relics of saints as to be almost infi-
nite and moving.' The way in which these relics were taken around each
quarter of the city echoes similar processions in Constantinople (see earlier
p. 45). The clergy eventually came into the Piazza della Signoria, the seat of
the government, where they were reviewed by the city magistrates from the
ringhiera, the ceremonial rostrum, that had its own relics on upper shelves.
Included in the procession were the lay religious confraternities, marching
with the clergy of their own churches, and they, too, had their own set of
relics to display. These acted as the focus around which the procession was
grouped. The actual day of the feast, the 24th, involved all the major groups
of the city, including the Priors, the senior magistrates, who offered candles
to the altar of St John in the baptistery. This was the day on which the
commune itself asserted its authority over the city and it was in the venerated
baptistery, not in the cathedral as might have been expected, that the ceremony took place. The afternoon was made over to horse races.

Often the medieval Catholic Church is portrayed as an authoritarian insti-
tution that controlled, for good or ill, every aspect of life, but this is to deny
the vitality of local religious movements. Anti-clericalism and suspicions of
papal authority were rife in northern and central Italy. In the 1370s Florence
and other cities were actually at war with the papacy. Florence expelled its
own bishop and sold off Church property in the largest known expropriation
before the Reformation. The Florentine poet Dante in his *Divine Comedy*
places some of the more pretentious popes firmly in hell. The communes
saw no reason why they should not have a share in the protective powers of
their local relics and were prepared to uphold their allegiance to them when
they were challenged by the Church authorities. It was because relics could
act as symbols of prestige for so many different interest groups that diversity
in worship could be upheld against the power of the institutional Church.

CHAPTER EIGHTEEN

The Virgin Mary and the Penitent Whore

IN THE summer of 1113 a small group of clerics arrived at the little port of Wissant near the town of Calais.[1] Their leader, Boso, was accompanied by his nephew Robert, two canons from the cathedral of Laon in Picardy, and a number of other clergy. With them they had a precious feretory, a portable shrine, that carried the inscription: 'May I be consecrated by the sponge, the Cross of the Lord, with the cloth of thy face, also by the hairs of your Virgin Mother.' Inside, it was said, was part of the robe of the Virgin, the sponge lifted to Jesus's mouth while he was on the Cross, and part of the Cross itself. Some doubted whether there were hairs inside but it was said that a crusader, Ilger Bigod, had found a lock of hair in the Holy Sepulchre in Jerusalem where the lock had been placed after Mary had torn it out during her suffering at the foot of the Cross. Bigod had brought the lock back to France and it had been distributed to different shrines. Laon claimed to be one of them. In the travels that followed, it was the relics of the Virgin that appeared to have most impact, especially as the cathedral at Laon was dedicated to her.

This prominence given to Mary was a major development of the eleventh and twelfth centuries and it was to prosper in new forms throughout the Middle Ages and beyond.[2] In earlier centuries Mary had been seen as the stoical mother enduring the horrors of the Crucifixion. Now, just at the time when Christ's sufferings were being highlighted, Mary becomes the one who shares in his distress. She has borne many sorrows and so can understand those of others. 'The wounds of the dying Christ were the wounds of the mother; the pains of Christ were cruel torturers of the soul of the mother', as Ogier, abbot of the monastery of Locedio in Piedmont, put it in the early thirteenth century. There is a moving text from the Greek church that beautifully draws together her twin roles. Mary addresses Christ: 'Then I touched with my lips your lips as sweet as honey and as fresh as dew. Then you slept on my breast as a child, and now you sleep as a dead man in my arms. . . . Once I took care of your swaddling clothes and now of your shroud. . . . Once I lifted you up in my arms when you skipped and jumped like a child, and now you lie [motionless] in them like the dead.'[3] One of the most famous medieval hymns is the *Stabat Mater*, the mother standing close to Jesus as he dies on the Cross: 'through her heart, his sorrow sharing, all the bitter anguish bearing'.

Mary was the repository of the world's faith in the days between the Crucifixion and Resurrection and then, in other accounts, takes on responsibility for caring for the Apostles and nurturing the early Church after the Ascension. This new intimacy soon appears in art. In the wonderfully rich mosaic from 1140 of Mary's triumph as Queen of Heaven in the church of Santa Maria in Trastevere, Rome, she has become the beloved of Christ and he sits beside her with his arm around her shoulders. The earliest full sculptured facade of her Coronation alongside Christ is on the cathedral at Senlis in northern France. It dates from the 1170s.

The men of Laon had a clear objective. Their cathedral had been gutted in a riot just the year before in 1112, during which Bishop Gaudry had been killed. They did not much worry, however, about the death of their bishop. He had been a soldier rather than a cleric who had made his money as chancellor under the English king Henry I and bought the see of Laon. He had behaved so appallingly, in debasing the local coinage and threatening the ancient liberties of the townspeople, that he had provoked the rioting that killed him. In that robust attitude towards clergy that tells of the vitality of the medieval mind, all agreed that he was better off dead. A new bishop, Bartholomew, a nobleman with connections to royalty, appeared to have the energy and administrative expertise to get the rebuilding under way.

The Laon relics had already been paraded around northern France in the summer months of 1112 after the burning down of the cathedral. A ritual was well established for their display. The bearing party arrived and sought permission to enter a town. The feretory was placed on the high altar of the major church and here it could be venerated and offerings left for it. In some cases when a local lord was sympathetic, the relics would be displayed in a castle chapel. The bearers then put themselves at the service of the local community to provide any spiritual guidance asked of them. Those seeking a cure must first make a confession of their sins and could sleep at the shrine, and the relics would be dipped in water that the patient was given to drink. Nine cures had been reported from this first tour and one prisoner had been set free from prison. Enough money had been raised to carry the rebuilding of the cathedral on over the winter, but by the spring of 1113 the funds were exhausted. Something much more ambitious was needed.

England offered a much better opportunity and it was here that the little party was bound. Under the Norman king Henry I, England had been settled, well administered and was enjoying some prosperity. There were a growing number of towns exploiting the revival of trade and the currency was more stable. The real value of English currency may have been three to four times what it was in France. Moreover, the veneration of Mary was much better established than in France. The feast of the Conception of the Virgin had first appeared in Winchester in about 1030 after a monk had received a vision of the Virgin in which she had given exact details of the liturgy that was appropriate for her. The feast had spread across southern England and into East Anglia where it became part of the annual calendar at Bury St Edmunds, the shrine of the royal Anglo-Saxon martyr, Edmund. At the abbey of Ramsay, Mary had specifically requested the abbot to celebrate her Conception there after she had saved him from a shipwreck. There were relics in England too. Winchester had part of the Virgin's tunic and a stone from her sepulchre. Bath Abbey too had part of the sepulchre, a lock of her hair and some drops of her milk. Yet another lock of her hair was at Exeter along with part of her headdress. Among the new major shrines were Walsingham in East Anglia with its phial of her milk and a replica of her house at Nazareth, built after she had requested it in a vision in 1061.

The men of Laon had already made contacts with England. Anselm, the dean of Laon Cathedral, was a well-known teacher. The sons of the Chancellor of England, the Archdeacon of Exeter and two nephews of the Bishop of Salisbury had been among his students, and they must have been warned of the imminent arrival of the relics. The party also had especially good links with the trading community. Laon had a flourishing weaving industry and exported locally grown woad for dyeing. It was well placed on trade routes that ran northwards to Flanders, south to Paris and also west-wards to England. The relic carriers of Laon often recruited the local merchants of the English towns they visited as allies in their search for acceptance.

The earliest, short, account of these tours from Laon is by Guibert, abbot of nearby Nogent (*c*.1055–1124). It is to be found as part of his memoirs (*Monodiae*) but it is muddled because of his ambivalence about relics, especially when these were used primarily to raise money as here (see earlier p. 118). A much fuller chronicle of the tours was drawn up in the 1140s by Herman, the abbot of Tournai, who was present at the dedication of the rebuilt cathedral. From these accounts the tour can be reconstructed and its success in achieving its aims recognised. The passage across the Channel had its challenges. A pirate ship appeared and the feretory had to be produced to thwart it. The wind miraculously changed and the clerics escaped. At this a group of merchants on board who were coming to England to buy cloth promised an offering to the Virgin. When they arrived at Dover, they failed to honour their promise and the warehouse where their cloth was stored was burned to the ground. The Virgin expected to be given proper reverence and she would show her displeasure when slighted.

After Dover, the group made for Canterbury, the traditional centre of the English Church. Here a woman who had claimed that the Virgin had helped her through a difficult birth decided to send 'expensive priestly robes' back to Laon for the cathedral canons. After they had left the important Marian shrine of Winchester, the next obvious stop would have been the cathedral city of Salisbury. However, neighbouring Christchurch was due to hold a fair and they were encouraged by a group of merchants to travel with them there. Unfortunately, the local priory was attempting to launch a cult of its own saints and when a deluge of rain occurred as the feretory arrived at the priory it provided a divine warning that the visitors were unwelcome and could be turned away. A local woman took in the travellers instead, while the merchants boycotted the priory and took recourse to ringing bells to advertise the relics from Laon. In response to the ingratitude of the locals, lightning struck (or, as Herman of Tournai would have it, dragons appeared from the sea) and the houses of those who had not welcomed the relics were burned down. Pilgrimages thrived on such divine encouragement.

Then the men of Laon went on to the major cities of Salisbury and Exeter as well as Totnes, south of Exeter, a bustling market town with access to the sea. They stayed at Totnes priory and the city gave them a lucrative and varied haul, consisting of money, goblets, curtains and even a horse from the 'lord of Totnes'. At Bath Abbey a girl who had fallen into the hot springs was rushed to them. They appear to have administered first aid by warming her over a fire and keeping her mouth open with a wooden wedge. She revived and began vomiting water. As soon as she was given water that had been poured over the relics, she recovered.

A journey such as this could not be without its hazards. Even though it was summer, the weather was not always settled and despite the overall good order of the kingdom there were still rival lords at war with each other. Local clerics with their own shrines to advertise resented the intrusion of outsiders. Some locals questioned whether relics should be paraded so openly for money and when the men of Laon passed Exeter on their return route they avoided the centre in case they should be considered grasping. In Totnes, a group of youths ridiculed the relics and declared that 'miracles' were simply the result of trickery. One of the young men pretended to bend down to kiss the feretory but then gobbled up the coins that had already been left there. He went off with his friends on a drinking spree but his crime caught up with him. The account records that he was later found hanging in a local wood.

Altogether there were forty-five miracles on the English tour by the men of Laon. Most were cures. Water and wine were poured over the relics, then this was poured over a patient who was given some more of the liquid to drink. Other miracles protected the clerics from danger. Those who opposed them or who mistreated the relics were punished. The Virgin scrupulously respected diocesan boundaries. At Exeter a crippled man prayed before the relics for ten days without relief. It turned out that he was from the neighbouring diocese of Salisbury and he was cured only as the feretory crossed the boundary. One objective of the Laon men seems to have been to make an association between the community of each English city and their cathedral in France. On their return to Laon they announced: 'We bore many hardships on our journey, so that you might commend to God and his Holy Mother the souls of those who sent alms to you through us, and so that you might grant them to be participants in all the good things there are or henceforth will be in the church of Laon.'

The entire tour from Laon and back had covered some 1,200 miles, an extraordinary undertaking when roads were poor and conditions always unsettled, and a tribute to the power that relics exercised. Herman of

Tournai is meticulous in detailing every contribution with named donors, often prominent members of the host community. The haul was about £80 in the currency of the day while, in comparison, the first French tour of 1112 had only raised £4. Altogether it was a very successful tour. While it took a further hundred years to complete the rebuilding of Laon Cathedral, it remains one of the most magnificent Gothic cathedrals in France.

Relics of the Virgin Mary were rare. Mary's body, like that of Christ, had been assumed into heaven and this left it unclear whether any physical remains of her could remain back on earth. Nevertheless a variety of shifts, girdles, veils, her slipper (apparently completely without signs of wear) at a convent in Soissons, locks of hair and phials of her breast milk survived. They had been prominent in the shrines that Pulcheria had set up in Constantinople in the fifth century where Mary was the most prestigious protectress of the city. They achieve their own hierarchy so that, as has been seen, the Girdle of Prato claims to be the very one she discarded at the Assumption story, and threw to the Apostle Thomas as she left earth. Other lesser girdles were to be found elsewhere as were several of the Virgin's veils. Among the most treasured was one of fine, undyed silk from the Holy Land given by Tommaso Orsini to the Basilica of St Francis at Assisi as a votive offering after his recovery from an illness, a veil still venerated at Whitsuntide and Easter today. A less happy acquisition was the veil of Mary's mother, St Anne, to be found in the church dedicated to her at Apt in the Vaucluse, south-eastern France. The Lord of Apt and the town's bishop had both gone on the First Crusade of 1095–99 and so must have brought the veil back on their return a few years later. It was a strip of bleached linen woven with silk and gold. The purchasers could not decipher the Arabic woven into it and if they had they would have found that it came from the workshop of the Fatimid Caliph al-Musta'li and had been woven in Damietta, Egypt, shortly before, in 1096 or 1097![4]

The most substantial relic was Mary's house from Nazareth that had disappeared from there in 1291 and reappeared within a clump of laurels (*laureto*, hence Loreto) in 1294. Although it was said that angels had transported the relic to Loreto on Italy's Adriatic coast, it now seems that crusaders did bring stones from a house in Nazareth as far as Dalmatia with the help of a Byzantine family called Angeli. The stones crossed the Adriatic and were landed at the port of Recanati by the local bishop who re-erected them as a

house, the Santa Casa. The site became and remains one of the most important in Italy not least because, after the fall in 1291 of Acre, the last crusader
toehold, it recreated in Italy an authentic part of the Holy Land. In 1469 Pope
Paul II, who had himself received a cure at the house, granted a plenary indulgence to all who reached there. He proclaimed that there had indeed been a
miracle by which the house had been transferred by angels to Loreto, via
Dalmatia, and the Pope went on to embed the shrine within a surrounding
fortress at a time when raids by pirates were common. Inside the church that
protects it, the Santa Casa was encased in a sumptuous sculptured covering
designed by the architect Donato Bramante around which pilgrims made
(and still make) their way on their knees until they reached the entrance.
Loreto was revitalised by the Jesuits as the focus of new Marian devotions in
the Counter-Reformation. In one of his most moving paintings, Caravaggio
shows two pilgrims, their feet dusty from the journey, being greeted at the
door of the Santa Casa by Mary and the baby Jesus themselves.[5]

There were so few relics of Mary that instead her statues or images often
became the focus of spiritual potency. One of the most persistent legends is
that of the portrait of Mary and Child painted by the Evangelist Luke. The
earliest mention of such an icon, the *Hodegetria* in Pulcheria's church in the
Blachernae (see p. 40), dates from the sixth century, but an example is also
recorded in Rome in the early eighth century.[6] St Luke's Gospel, of course,
portrays the birth of Jesus with loving detail and it is perhaps for this reason
that Luke is linked to the image. Luke could not have been there, of course,
when Jesus was a child and this appears to have caused some hesitation in
accepting such images as authentic. What appears to have embedded them,
in the eastern tradition, was the need to find some form of physical presence
for the Virgin as she becomes more prominent there from the seventh
century onwards.

One result of the growing veneration of the Virgin was an explosion of
'discovered' Luke portraits of the Virgin, especially in Rome.[7] Two had been
known by 1200, the first in Mary's great church in Rome, Santa Maria
Maggiore. Here the Virgin was given the accolade 'Mother of Rome' and
shown without Christ, but this deficiency was remedied by the annual procession of an icon of Christ, also attributed to Luke, which 'met' the Virgin on the
feast of the Assumption. The other early icon was the Madonna of San Sisto,
in the ancient church of that name, that was attributed to Luke as early as

1100. It became famous when a Pope seized it for his private collection in the Lateran, and the icon showed its outrage by reappearing miraculously back in its rightful home the next morning. San Sisto became a Dominican convent in 1221 and the icon was made the pride of the order. In 1250 the Franciscans produced a virtually identical image of the Virgin in their church of the Aracoeli on the Capitoline Hill and claimed this, too, for Luke. An intense rivalry, 'the battle of the Madonnas', broke out between the two icons and their supporting Orders that lasted into the sixteenth century.

These icons were formal portraits and would have lost their claim to authenticity if they had not been. Another traditional portrayal of the Virgin saw her enthroned in majesty. These statues appear in the ninth century and are often found in crypts alongside reliquaries. The throne may be a deliberate attempt to give the Virgin Mary a royal status at a time when some were still doubting her role as *Theotokos*, 'Mother of God', the title accorded her by a Church council in 431. The throne of Solomon also provided a precedent and inscriptions on statues suggest a link to Mary or the baby Christ as founts of wisdom (a link strengthened by relating Mary to Solomon's Song of Songs, which was incorporated into the liturgy for the Feast of Assumption, 15 August). Then there are those statues in which two doors open from the body to reveal the Trinity within. Here the Virgin's role has been extended to make her protectress even of God, Son and Holy Spirit.

One powerful image of the Virgin in Florence was Santa Maria dell'Impruneta, the Virgin Mary of the Pines. It is a primitive but colourful icon in which the Virgin is shown enthroned with crown and jewels. Again it was said to have been painted by Luke and brought to Florence in the early centuries of the Church, and then hidden outside the city 'among the pines'. It was known as a miraculous rainmaker and as such echoed pagan cults that went back many centuries.

When drought persisted in Florence, it was assumed that God had been offended in some way and that the best recompense would be a ritualistic veneration of the icon. So the image was veiled and processed from its setting among the pines towards the city gates to reach them at sunrise. Its imminent arrival was announced by trumpeters and it would then be met with processions that had wended their way from different parts of the city, from the cathedral, the smaller churches and the headquarters of the confraternities, each carrying their own relics and perhaps an image sacred to them. The icon of

Santa Maria would be paraded for three days, the normal period of penitential mourning, with the climax in a vast open-air service in the Piazza della Signoria, the home of the city's republican government, where it would be unveiled. For the occasion the priors and magistrates would assemble on the lowest steps of *ringhiera*, the bishop of the city behind them and then above him, on several 'very ornate platforms . . . a multitude of relics, elevated so that everyone could see'. Following the correct rituals for the unveiling was crucial as it was the moment that the image became active and rain would fall. (The image was also versatile enough to bring rainfall to an end when flooding threatened.) Back in its shrine, the icon seemed unable to bring miracles.

Many early statues of the Virgin enclosed relics of their own as if the statues did not exude sacred power without them. From the 1160s the relics seem no longer to be needed and this goes hand in hand with the appearance of less formal statues that, unlike the austere icons and detached ruling Madonnas, interact on a personal level with the supplicant. This mirrors the shift towards a more human and approachable Mary.[8] So a mid-twelfth-century relief of the Virgin in the church of St Lawrence in Liège, Belgium, offers her bare breast to an eager Christ who stretches towards it. There is a wonderful sense of motherhood here and the statue soon gained a reputation for miracles. One of Mary's most devout adherents was the austere Cistercian, Bernard of Clairvaux. Once, when Bernard was before a statue of the Virgin imploring that she might be a mother to him, the statue became 'alive' and offered him her breasts to suck.

Within the next hundred years appear the exquisite Gothic statues of the Virgin, her face gentle, her body slender and curved to take the weight of her son. Then there are other forms such as Our Lady of Pity, the mother mourning the body of the dead Christ, first known in early fourteenth-century southern Germany and widespread in Europe by the end of that century. Michelangelo's *Pietà* of 1499, now in St Peter's Rome, is the supreme example. Another role, especially popular in northern Italy, is Mary as the protector of the community against plague. She is often shown with an outstretched cloak shielding citizens from plague arrows sent down from above by her own Son.[9] This is the most remarkable example of the intercession of a saint against the abiding anger of Christ.

This approachability is shown to perfection in the *Miracles of Notre Dame* by Gautier de Coincy (1177–1236), a light-hearted set of songs and stories in

which the Virgin Mary takes pity on a raffish collection of sinners, from pregnant nuns to idle students, so long as they respect her role in the Incarnation.
Among them is the charming tale of a tumbler who becomes a monk but is
totally unable to understand the prayers and is deeply depressed by the
gloominess of his fellows.[10] He finds a statue of the Virgin Mary in a crypt,
strips down to his tunic, something that seems impossibly insulting to the
Virgin Mary, and performs an array of somersaults and balancing acts day after
day before it. Inevitably, the abbot spots him missing from prayer and spies on
him. After a further energetic display of acrobatics the tumbler lies down
exhausted, but the Virgin appears from the rafters to fan him with a cloth, so
confounding the abbot's hostility. Gautier suggests that it is not only the set
order of prayers that brings divine approval. The tumbler is joyfully worshipping in the best way he knows how to and this is acceptable to the Virgin.

There is something of the same approachability in the story of the Virgin
Mary and the prison in Prato, the Italian city whose link to the Virgin had
already been established through the Holy Girdle. On 6 July 1484 an eight-
year-old boy called Jacopino was playing beside the ruins of the old prison of
Prato, a prosperous city north of Florence. Typically for his age he was
absorbed in chasing a cricket. Above the barred window of the prison wall
there was a fourteenth-century fresco of the Virgin Mary and Jesus with the
saints Leonard and Stephen. To Jacopino's amazement the figure of the
Virgin Mary came down from the fresco carrying Jesus with her. The baby
was set on the ground and the Virgin descended into the prison vaults. She
then set about a vigorous cleaning, scrubbing away with her hands, before
picking up Jesus and returning to her place in the fresco. The apparition
caused a sensation and soon crowds were flocking to venerate the image.
The excitement attracted the interest of Lorenzo de' Medici who appointed
the architect Giuliano da Sangallo to create the Greek-cross church, one
of the earliest in this style, that now houses a copy of the fresco. The power
of relics to define architectural magnificence and innovation passes from the
Gothic to the Renaissance.

The most pervasive and least explicable representation of the Virgin Mary
in medieval Europe is as 'a black Madonna'. Some 450 of these have been
recorded and nearly three hundred still remain, most of them in France.
They are usually full-length statues, in wood, with the flesh in black. Some
are made of ebony, others have been blackened with time or the fires that

destroyed so many churches in the medieval era. It is just possible that some were created black to reflect the verses of the Song of Songs in which the beloved is described as 'black and comely'. Others have argued that the Black Madonnas provide echoes of ancient earth cults. Almost all are associated with miracles and many have legends of origin that take them back to the first century AD. They acquired such individuality that in one, perhaps fictional, account of a shipwreck, all the passengers call on the Virgin but each specifies which specific Madonna he means.

One of the most spectacular, the (Black) Madonna of Rocamadour (in south-western France), is, like the *Volto Santo*, honoured as a carved statue from the time of Christ. Its creator, one Amadour, was believed to have been a tax collector mentioned in the Gospels, married to 'Veronica' of the veil of Christ's face. Amadour was a friend of St Martial and witness of the martyrdom of Peter and Paul. The lucky survival of a list of 126 miracles compiled in 1172 shows that this is a shrine for the most humble and afflicted. All forms of illness and disability, including depression and 'frenzy', are among those cured. Those with a reputation for violence were calmed. It is the detail of the miracles that has made the list a treasure trove of attitudes to medieval illness and disorders of the mind. Like Santiago de Compostela, Rocamadour was also the goal of those seeking penance, their humiliation exposed by the long climb up the steps to the shrine followed by an abject pleading for forgiveness from the image.

Another Black Madonna, of Montserrat near the city of Barcelona, had been sculpted by Luke and, in this case, given to St Peter, who had brought it to Spain. It had been hidden during the Arab invasions but rediscovered by some shepherds in 888. In fact, the statue dates from the twelfth century and shows the influence of Byzantine craftsmanship. It 'refused' to be moved into the city, so a shrine grew up around it. The bounty of the Madonna was shown by the fertility of the area. Here Mary is not so much associated with cures but with the bringing of fertility to women, and even today married couples can sleep at the shrine in hope of help in conceiving.

Mary represents absolute purity, so absolute in fact that it was an article of faith that she even gave birth to Jesus without physically losing her virginity. No such claim could be made for a much less prestigious saint whose potency came from her repentance and forgiveness by Christ himself: Mary Magdalen, Mary from the town of Magdala in ancient Israel.

A legend first recorded in the eleventh century told how, after the Crucifixion, Mary and her fellow Christians, including Lazarus and another of Jesus's disciples, one Maximin, had been persecuted in the Holy Land and then set adrift by their tormentors in a rudderless boat. They drifted the length of the Mediterranean and had been miraculously washed ashore at Marseilles in southern Gaul. Mary began a preaching campaign there to convert the pagan Gauls. Here the most famous of her miracles took place. She brought about the pregnancy of the wife of the pagan governor of Provence, saved their infant son and restored to life the mother who had died during childbirth. Promulgated through an extended version in Jacobus de Voragine's *The Golden Legend*, this miracle is often depicted in frescos of her life.[11] Maximin became the first bishop of the new congregation and it was in his church, St Maximin, that Mary's body was buried. The monks of the abbey at Vézelay in Provence claimed that they had found the body here and transferred it back to Vézelay.[12]

In the eleventh century the cult flourished. An energetic abbot, Geoffrey, secured papal recognition of the authenticity of Mary's body in 1058 and replaced the original dedication of the Romanesque church to the Virgin Mary with one to Mary Magdalen. The monastery was lucky enough to be on the pilgrimage route from Germany to Compostela and not far from St Foy at Conques and St Martin at Tours. It was soon part of the pilgrimage network and miracles were reported. Mary proved effective with problems of fertility and childbirth; she also liberated prisoners who prayed to her in jail and even raised the dead. Bernard of Clairvaux launched the Second, disastrous, Crusade from Vézelay in 1146 and, in 1267, Louis IX, now safely back from his own equally disastrous crusade, appeared at a special exposition of the relics and was given some fragments for his own impressive collection.

Then there was a shock. Just twelve years after the royal visit, on 9 December 1279, another body was discovered, this time at St Maximin by Charles of Salerno, an Angevin prince. The body was carefully examined and declared to be the genuine Mary Magdalen. She had never left St Maximin at all! Charles left a record of what happened, although this only survives in a much later, fifteenth-century, account. It tells how, during a popular uprising in Sicily against his father who had conquered the island (the so-called Sicilian Vespers), Charles had been thrown into prison. He had prayed to Mary Magdalen and he had been released. In a vision Mary declared to him that her body still lay at St Maximin. If he went down into the crypt and dug down he would soon find her wooden coffin helpfully labelled: 'Here lies the body of blessed Mary Magdalen'. When he opened it he would find that the flesh on her skull would still be intact on the spot where the risen Christ had touched her when he met her in the garden of Gethsemane. There would be an amphora full of earth soaked in blood that she had collected from the foot of the Cross and, as a final mark of identification, she would have a green shoot growing from her tongue. She then gave some instructions for the future. She needed a better church to be built for her and it should be placed in the care of the Dominicans, the Order of friars, as they were following in her footsteps as the new Apostles of Christ.

So it was on 9 December 1279 that Charles hurried to St Maximin, went down into the crypt and dug away with his own hands until 'the sweat poured in rivulets from his brow'. He found the coffin and it was as promised. By May the next year, everything was ready for a great display of the relics before the local crowds in a *translatio*. The relics were then broken up and placed in reliquaries, as required by the decree of the Lateran Council of 1215. The skin from Mary's forehead was preserved separately.

This dramatic discovery needs to be given a wider historical context. Charles had been feeling guilty. He was worried that the empire built by his father Charles of Anjou, which included Provence (an inheritance from his wife Beatrice) and other parts of southern France as well as, for a brief period, southern Italy and Sicily, had been unjustly won. He desperately needed to have some kind of recognition that the acquisitions had heavenly blessing. Who better than a saint close to Christ who had her own links to Provence? Mary Magdalen had come to Charles's rescue in time.

A miracle was always needed to confirm the authenticity of a saint's bones and his or her pleasure at being venerated. One soon materialised. A butcher had gone to the St Maximin shrine to offer his devotion. He was accosted on his way home by a friend who scoffed at his credulity. 'He had not kissed her [Mary's] shin bone, but the arm of some ass or pack animal which the clerics show to simple folk for the purpose of enrichening themselves.' The furious butcher engaged his friend in a duel and killed him. He was sentenced to be hanged, but Mary Magdalen appeared in a vision and promised he would be saved. Sure enough as he was being strung up, a white dove appeared from heaven, dissolved the noose and the butcher floated gently to the ground. Charles was impressed by the miracle and now had the head of Mary encased in a gold reliquary with a crystal mask through which the skull could be seen. On top of the reliquary was a gem-studded royal crown linking Charles even more closely to his saint. In 1295 Pope Boniface VIII confirmed that the St Maximin relics were indeed authentic and an indulgence would be granted to those pilgrims who visited the shrine on Mary's feast day, 22 July. The shrine at Vézelay had been outplayed and went into decline. Such was the cut-throat world of the relic shrines.

Mary Magdalen is one of six Marys who are mentioned in the Gospels, and is the most prominent of them after the Virgin Mary. The Gospels gave Mary Magdalen the honour of being the first to see Christ after his Resurrection and passing on the news to the other disciples. By the sixth century, her Gospel story had been fleshed out. She is the 'female sinner' described in Luke's Gospel who washes Jesus's feet with her tears. Pope Gregory the Great interpreted her sinfulness as sexual, so she becomes a prostitute who has repented. She is the same Mary who is the sister of the contemplative Martha at Bethany and so also sister of the Lazarus that Jesus raised from the dead. She is present at the Cross, the burial of Jesus, and is one of those bringing ointments to the tomb on the third day. Mary's earliest appearance in medieval literature comes in the ninth century among those disciples and Evangelists close to Jesus whose cults appear about this time.

One of Mary's roles was as *apostolorum apostola*, 'the apostle of the apostles', on account of her announcement of the Resurrection of Christ to the disciples, and legends went on to tell of her preaching to the pagans in Gaul.[13] 'It is no wonder that the lips which had pressed kisses so loving and so tender on our Lord's feet should preach the perfume of the word of God more copiously than any other,' writes the Dominican Jacobus de Voragine in his life of Mary in *The Golden Legend*. The green shoot coming from the tongue of her discovered body at St Maximin was the symbol of her role. Relics related to her preaching began to appear. She had lived during her preaching career in what was now the crypt at the church of St Victor and the table from which she ate had survived there. The church of St Lazarus housed the pagan altar from which she had launched her mission after arriving in Provence, as well as the head and body of Lazarus himself.

By the early thirteenth century Mary Magdalen had become the focus of the Dominicans, the Order of preaching friars which was formally constituted in 1220.[14] Their special devotion to her lies rooted in the values that they wished to highlight for their Order. She was the one who was utterly faithful to Jesus (unlike most of the male Apostles who had scattered at the Crucifixion). She showed intense compassion for Christ on the Cross, as the Dominicans did, and she was an active preacher. She even baptised converts – a font in the church of St Maurice in Angers in the Loire valley was shown as the one where she had baptised the ancient rulers of Provence. She had shown unswerving allegiance to the authority of Christ, and the Dominicans saw this echoing their own vow of obedience to the Pope.

Another feature of Mary Magdalen's cult now began to develop. If she was the sinner who had wept for forgiveness, she must have had a sinner's past from which she had repented. Her reputation as a whore dates from the late sixth century, but a more elaborate account was created after that Jacobus de Voragine told how Mary had come from a very wealthy background. Her family owned not only the whole town of Magdala but part of Jerusalem itself. 'Since Mary Magdalen was enormously wealthy, and pleasure is the boon companion of affluence, she was as notorious for her abandonment to fleshly pleasures as she was celebrated for her beauty and riches.' One result of overdressing and reeking with perfume was to repel men, and, as the Franciscan preacher Bernardino of Siena, who revelled in the denunciation of sexuality, imaginatively put it, to drive them to sodomy. Yet she repented and the most common representation of her is with her hair loose clinging to the foot of the Cross. Abundant hair always stood for sexuality and Bernardino even suggested that Mary had originally bleached her hair blonde in the hope of seducing Jesus. Instead, overcome by her encounter with Jesus, she had abandoned her plans and had, instead, bathed his feet and dried them with her hair. Her unbound hair as she grasped the Cross was a symbol of her penitence for her sexual excess. This was how she was depicted on the pilgrim badge that the Dominicans handed out to visitors at St Maximin in the fourteenth century.

Mary's role as penitent became even more important during the later Middle Ages. As a result of the tensions and disruptions of the age (see further p. 197) the desire to repent reached new levels of intensity. One early fifteenth-century *Instructions for a Devout and Literate Layman* tells the supplicant: 'With Mary Magdalen throw yourself at the feet of the most sweet Jesus, and wash them with your tears and anoint and kiss them.'[15] For women this was often linked to a self-abasement that reflected the status of their sex. Catherine of Siena always remained a virgin and so had no need of the repentance of a Magdalen, but Catherine still took her as a model (see earlier p. 141). She described to one of her correspondents how Mary despised herself 'for God's sake, for she saw that there is no other way to follow or to please him. She realised that she was the lowliest of all people. She was no more self-conscious than drunken women.'[16] So, too, should all women take this role. In this sense Mary Magdalen was used to define the subservience of women in medieval society.

Inevitably, Mary Magdalen's body at St Maximin was a bringer of miracles. The body was enclosed in a shrine in a basilica built by Charles with an adjoining royal convent for the Dominicans who oversaw the cult, just as Mary had demanded in her vision to Charles. In about 1305 Jean Gobi the Elder, prior of the convent from 1304 to 1328, drew up his register of miracles.[17] Many of these are linked to Mary Magdalen's specific concerns. So a blind woman comes to the shrine, she pours out tears just as Mary had poured hers out on the feet of the Lord and then asks that Mary 'who had obtained forgiveness for her sins from God, would seek grace for her so that her sight, lost perhaps on account of sin, would be restored because of Mary Magdalen's merits'. Here again, the woman's affliction is linked to her sinfulness; repentance to healing. Another man arrived at the shrine to offer thanks to Mary Magdalen for his release from prison. He had sinned badly and been imprisoned. One day he had heard the tolling of church bells, always a warning that an execution was due to take place the next day, and he became convinced that he would be the victim. He called on Mary as one forgiven by God through her penitence. He, too, was repentant and sure enough his chains split apart and he was able to make his escape.

Mary's life had already been extended beyond the Resurrection to a period of preaching and converting in Provence. Another legend gave her an extended old age. It told of how she renounced everything, even in some accounts discarding all her clothes, after she had successfully brought Christianity to Gaul. Her flowing hair miraculously covered her nakedness. She survived in a cave, 'La Sainte Beaume', in the wilderness for another thirty-three years, the same period of time as Jesus's own life. As we have seen, she even went without food although this was passed down to her from heaven and she apparently levitated to receive it. La Sainte Beaume became a centre for pilgrimage in its own right in the 1280s.

Alas for Vézelay and St Maximin, all too many parts of Mary Magdalen surfaced in later medieval Europe. Unlike the Virgin Mary, Mary remained fully on earth in her physical body. There were three more of her bodies, one at Senigallia near Ancona on the Adriatic coast, one in St John Lateran in Rome and one in the church of St Lazarus in Constantinople. Abbéville in northern France claimed to have her head while the Dominican nuns at Aix in the south insisted that Charles himself had given them her jawbone. One of her arms was in a reliquary in St Maximin but Cologne in Germany had two more. Five more were known but that at the abbey of Fécamp in northern France was damaged when St Hugh of Lincoln bent to kiss it and then took a bite out of it. When the monks protested, he riposted that if one could take the body and blood of Christ in one's lips at the Eucharist, there could be no objection in doing the same with Mary Magdalen.[18] Mary's fingers abounded and, hardly surprisingly, there were many locks of her abundant hair. Part of her hair shirt is still to be found in the treasury of St John Lateran in Rome, and the nearby church of Santa Croce in Gerusalemme had the stone slab on which Jesus was reclining as he forgave her sins. Her comb was in Bath Abbey in England. Jesus had wept when confronted by the dead body of Lazarus, but one of his tears had been caught by an angel, placed in a container and handed over to Mary Magdalen for safe keeping. It was now in the church of La Trinité de Vendôme in central France.

Mary Magdalen could never be as emotionally intimate with Jesus as his mother was, but she had scriptural support for her close relationship and so had a secure place as an effective intercessor. Her legendary life of excess followed by renunciation was a powerful model for those who were obsessed by their own sinfulness. She is even portrayed as a reconstituted Virgin, offering possibilities of forgiveness to those who had strayed from purity.[19] Vézelay and later St Maximin and La Sainte Beaume were important sites of pilgrimage, but the growth of other shrines shows just how powerful and universal the cult of Mary Magdalen had become. Relics, it appears, had been brought into being by the special appeal of a sinner whose penitence had earned her forgiveness. The Virgin Mary and the penitent whore provide for the profound needs of medieval women.

CHAPTER NINETEEN

The Wondrous Blood of Christ

I leap at Him [Christ on the Cross] swiftly as a greyhound at a hart, quite beside myself, in loving manner and fold in my arms the cross. . . . I suck the blood from his feet. . . . I embrace and kiss as if I was mad. I roll and suck I do not know how long. And when I am sated, I want yet more. Then I feel that blood in my imagination as it were bodily warm on my lips and the flesh on his feet in front and behind and so sweet to kiss.

This ecstatic outpouring comes from the fourteenth-century Middle English text *A Talking of the Love of God*.[1] It was a reflection of a more emotionally intense form of Christianity that appears in the fourteenth and fifteenth centuries, which brought veneration of the shedding of Christ's blood to the forefront of the medieval consciousness. At the heart of the many blood cults that grew up across Europe, but above all in northern Germany, was the belief that Christ's blood had been outpoured for the salvation of humankind. In fact, crucifixion was a largely bloodless form of death, although John's Gospel had recorded how a soldier had stabbed Jesus's side with a lance and there had been an outflow of blood and water. None of this deterred the adulation of sculptures and images of Christ on the Cross with blood also pouring out of the wounds on his hands and feet.

The most important sacrament of the Catholic Church, instituted by Jesus himself at the Last Supper, and celebrated from earliest times, was the Eucharist – a word rooted in the Greek for 'thanksgiving'. A piece of unleavened bread, normally in the form of a circular wafer (the host) and wine was changed into the real body and blood of Christ at a moment of consecration by a priest at Mass. By the thirteenth century the term 'transubstantiation' was being used to describe the change. After the consecration, the wafer and the wine were wholly the body and blood of Christ, even though they retained the 'accident', as it was termed, of still looking like the original wafer and liquid. Thomas Aquinas even managed to adapt the physics of Aristotle to support the idea. When a communicant chewed and swallowed the host, it was said that it was only the 'accidents' that were fragmented. The body and blood of Christ remained whole.

As both body and blood were wholly contained within the host, the custom of offering the consecrated wine in a chalice to the communicant was considered unnecessary and, from the middle of the thirteenth century, restricted to the priest alone. There were practical reasons for keeping the chalice from the shakey hands of communicants. All too often some wine would be spilt and then there would have to be a frenzied mopping up. So seriously was all this taken that a priest could be suspended from saying Mass if he spilt consecrated wine, while any cloth on which it fell had to be preserved as a relic. The restricted use of wine seems only to have enhanced its divine status and certainly many ordinary communicants continued to clamour for it. Their demands were met after 1414 by the radical John Hus, who reintroduced the chalice at Communion in his native Bohemia as a symbol of his opposition to traditional Church authority.

The sceptics could not see how a wafer that seemed completely unchanged after the consecration could have actually become something completely other. It made nonsense of any belief in the physical world as subject to natural laws. As the theologian Duns Scotus (1265–1308) put it: 'a philosopher, or anyone following natural reason, would see a greater contradiction in this negation of the bread than in all the articles of faith concerning the incarnation'. It is not surprising that miracles confirming the transformation had taken place were popular. One of the most famous had taken place in Bolsena, near Orvieto in Umbria, in 1263. A priest from Germany, Peter of Prague, was celebrating Mass at Bolsena on his way to Rome on a pilgrimage. He had his doubts that the host was truly the body and blood of Christ but, as he finished the words of consecration, the host he was holding above the altar began to drip blood over his vestments and down over the floor. The Pope, Urban IV, was present in Orvieto and when he heard of the apparent miracle and confirmed it, he ordered that the host and the stained vestments be brought to Orvieto Cathedral, where they still form its major relic. Meanwhile, red marks can still be seen on the floor of the chapel where the miracle took place. So the idea developed that a host could miraculously bleed, especially when its sacred quality was doubted.

The mystics of the period also reported flowing blood as they consumed the host at Communion. As she took the host in her mouth, Beatrice of Nazareth (died 1268) experienced 'all the blood that flowed from Christ's wounds poured into her soul and all the drops of that precious liquid so sprinkled on it that it was wholly washed by those drops and most perfectly cleansed from all the dust of sin'.[2] On a pilgrimage to Jerusalem, Margery Kempe had a vision of Christ on the Cross, his body 'completely rent and torn with scourges, more full of wounds than ever was a dove house of holes . . . the rivers of blood flowing out plenteously from every member, the grisly and grievous wound in his precious side shedding out blood and water for her love and her salvation'.[3]

Some shrines claimed to have drops of Christ's blood collected at the time of the Crucifixion. There may have been some thirty of these shrines in Europe by the thirteenth century, several having gained their blood from the return of the crusaders from Constantinople. More began to arrive. In 1247 a reliquary of Christ's blood was given by the Patriarch of Jerusalem to the English king Henry III.[4] The Patriarch sent an accompanying letter, that still survives in the Westminster Abbey archives, in which he confirms the authenticity of the blood and links his gift to a plea for help in the Holy Land against a resurgent Islam. Henry had his own motives for accepting the gift and making the most of it. He was all too aware of the marvellous cache of relics of the Passion that Louis IX was assembling in the Sainte-Chapelle in Paris. These might include relics that had been used during the Crucifixion, but the actual blood of Christ was surely more prestigious even than these. He could trump his French rival. Henry announced the arrival of the blood to his courtiers and insisted on carrying the vase containing it in procession for the two miles to Westminster Abbey, where he was already rebuilding the chapel of his own favourite saint, Edward the Confessor. In a sermon at the *translatio*, the Bishop of Norwich flaunted the superiority of the reliquary. 'Now it is true that the Cross is a very holy relic but it is holy only because it came into contact with the precious blood of Christ. The holiness of the Cross derives from the blood whereas the holiness of the blood in no way derives from the Cross. It therefore follows that England, which possesses the blood of Christ, rejoices in a greater treasure than France, which has no more than the Cross.'⁵

However, this was a cult that never prospered. There were simply too many rival Holy Bloods, including a number already known in England. The success of a competitor that arrived in England twenty years later, at the Cistercian abbey of Hailes in Gloucestershire, shows other reasons for the cult's failure. Henry's reliquary of Christ's blood had never been recorded in Jerusalem, and cynics noticed that the gift of the Patriarch was all too closely linked to his sudden need for help! Henry had none of the entrepreneurial flair shown by Louis IX and he never managed to supplant the traditional association of Westminster and Edward the Confessor with the new cult. The Holy Blood of Hailes came from Germany, with a history that took the relic back to Charlemagne and even to Roman emperors. It was this 'authenticity' that mattered. Hailes prospered as a major centre of pilgrimage while the offering books in Westminster Abbey show that Henry's relics attracted few visitors. Most humiliating of all, there is only one recorded miracle, the revival of a two-year-old boy who had been drowned.

Often an image of Christ or a Cross spurted blood when it was struck by an unbeliever. One of the most famous examples, from the eighth century, was a cross in Beirut that had been hit by a Jew. It bled copiously and phials of the blood were distributed around Europe. Louis IX had some of it, as had Worcester Cathedral in England. Another of these outpourings was recorded by the Milanese Santo Brasca when he visited Venice on his way to the Holy Land in Venice in 1480. A frustrated gambler had struck the breast of a figure of Christ on a Cross with a knife. Blood had gushed out and was displayed in St Mark's basilica every Ascension Day while the damaged crucifix was on permanent show there.

More common were the consecrated hosts that had bled when they were insulted. Tragically, these 'insults' became linked to anti-Semitism. The Jews already carried the burden of deicide, responsibility for killing the Son of God, and it was assumed that they would desecrate a consecrated host if they could get hold of one. From the 1290s, stories were passed around that the Jews knew that the host was the consecrated body of Christ and they set out to damage it so as to inflict further torture on Christ deliberately. A much-repeated legend involves a Christian woman selling or pawning a host to a Jewish merchant. He then attempts to burn the host. It spurts out blood that quenches the fire. The host is rescued and there is a ceremonial reparation in which it is restored by the entire Christian community to the church. The Jew is then burned to death and the seller of the host is also executed.[6]

These stories were then acted out in horrific reality. This was a period of tension and growing fears that God was punishing mankind through plague and famine. Scapegoating the Jews was one response. Already in Germany from the 1290s onwards, there had been massacres of Jews: 3,441 Jews are recorded as dying in 1298 and as many as 6,000 between 1335 and 1338. It is perhaps not surprising that 'the greatest persecution of a single group in the Middle Ages was the massacres of Jews between 1348 and 1350', the period of the Black Death.[7]

The stories continued and one is worth recounting in detail. In the parish church of the little town of Sternberg in the duchy of Mecklenburg, northern Germany, there were relics of consecrated hosts.[8] They had been placed there after being dug up in 1492 by local clergy when they had been alerted to them by a dream. The relics were bloodstained and soon began bringing miracles. A search was then made for the thief who had buried them. Witnesses were tortured and eventually a priest, Peter Dane, was arrested. He confessed that he had pawned a pot to a Jew and redeemed it with a consecrated host. The Jews had stuck the hosts with knives and they bled. When they tried to destroy the evidence by throwing the hosts into water, these refused to sink and so it was that they were eventually buried.

Sixty-five local Jews were rounded up and tortured. The act of desecrating a host was in itself a capital offence. Twenty-seven were burned to death. So was the priest. The rest of the Jewish community of Mecklenburg was expelled. It was a vicious act of anti-Semitism, but the parish church revelled in the events and used the relic cult as a medium for its prejudice. The nails that had pierced the hosts and the iron pot the priest had tried to redeem were placed in the church. Two 'relics' are still in the chapel built alongside the church today. One is a stone with two footprints embedded in it. They were left by the feet of one of the Jews who had unsuccessfully tried to drown the hosts. Then there is a large tabletop heavily scarred with knife marks that purports to be the surface on which the hosts were desecrated. The Sternberg story was one of the first to benefit from the invention of printing – an anti-Semitic pamphlet was soon being circulated that also acted as an advertisement for the shrine itself. Sternberg soon became a major pilgrimage site. Offerings were made to build a chapel and once this was completed they were divided between the local bishopric and the site itself. The influx of offerings bound the local community tenaciously to its shrine but consolidated the anti-Semitism that had given rise to it.

The most famous shrine to honour the blood of Christ was at Wilsnack, also in northern Germany. In August 1383 a knight had set fire to the church of the small town of Wilsnack.[9] Several days later, the parish priest was sifting through the burnt ruins that had already been soaked by rain. A dream alerted him to search further and eventually he found three white hosts completely intact despite the fire and rain, each with a drop of blood in the centre. Miracles began almost at once. Three of the first five involved resurrections from the dead, including a woman revived from drowning.

The bishop of the diocese, Havelberg, then arrived to investigate. He feared that the local population were making fools of themselves through worshipping a host that had never been consecrated and he went through the rite of consecration over the discovered hosts. One of them then became totally suffused with blood to show that it was already fully the body and blood of Christ. By now the news had reached Pope Urban VI and he was quick to offer an indulgence for those visiting the hosts, the proceeds from which would go towards rebuilding the church, with the remainder going to the bishopric. By 1400 the shrine was flourishing.

There were many other blood relics in northern Germany. This part of Europe was remote from the Mediterranean and its conversion to Christianity had been much later. It was hard to acquire relics with any authentic background, but bleeding hosts were relics that had appeared spontaneously. They did not even have to be paid for. The market in northern Germany was soon sated with blood relics and so battle broke out between rivals. Wilsnack's extraordinary success meant that it had many enemies. The story was soon going around that the priest had later confessed that it had all been a fraud. Officials were sent to inspect the hosts and said that they were only spiders' webs and there was no trace of anything red on them. 'The people venerate a blood relic there but we have no idea of what it is: since there is in fact nothing there and nothing similar to blood', ran one report. Heinrich Tocke, a canon of Magdeburg Cathedral, became almost obsessional in his opposition. He claimed that he had visited the shrine a hundred times and had never seen anything red on the hosts. The theological faculty of the university of Erfurt gave a learned judgement condemning the shrine. Those who visited Wilsnack were said to be heretics, using the hosts for veneration instead of taking the Eucharist like true Catholics. There were cases where pilgrims returning from the site had their pilgrim badges ripped off them by outraged clergy. Tocke eventually persuaded the papal legate, Nicholas of Cusa, to issue a decree throughout Germany in which blood cults were condemned as all too often originating from the greed of clergy who falsely publicised their shrines to deceive the simple. Nicholas ordered that all such hosts should be consumed by the priests.

Nothing stopped the flow of pilgrims to Wilsnack. The bishops of Havelberg stood firm, as well they might when so much revenue was coming their way. The arrangements for the shrine had incorporated it under the local bishop's direct control and two-thirds of all offerings came to his see. The vast church of St Nicholas rose to house the hosts. In 1447 Pope Eugenius IV, an enthusiast of host miracles, gave the shrine his blessing. He insisted, however, that a fully consecrated host be placed beside the relics to minimise the risk that they were being adulated at the expense of the Eucharist. In 1475 pilgrims were recorded from Hungary, Austria and France as well as Germany, and pilgrim badges from Wilsnack have been found throughout northern Europe, even across the Channel in England. The English visionary Margery Kempe attended the shrine in the company of her German daughter-in-law. The shrine had a special attraction for children and gangs gathered, children's crusades in effect, to visit the shrine. One estimate is that 100,000 pilgrims a year were visiting the shrine in the 1470s, making it the fourth most popular pilgrimage destination after Rome, Jerusalem and Compostela.

However, there were also complex theological issues raised by these cults, some of which fed into the rivalries.[10] As early as the twelfth century, Guibert of Nogent (see earlier p. 118) had argued that as Christ had been resurrected, it was impossible for any of his body, including his blood, of course, to have been left behind. A century later, Thomas Aquinas, the sharpest mind on the matter, agreed that the core blood of Jesus must have been resurrected. His body was perfect at the time of his death and there was nothing superfluous to it that could be left behind. Thomas argued that the blood that spurted out of crosses when these were struck was a completely different kind of blood, simply a symbol of the sacrilege that had taken place.

An ingenious argument against Guibert's view had been put forward by the English scholastic philosopher and Bishop of Lincoln, Robert Grosseteste (1175–1253), a supporter of Henry III's blood relic. Grosseteste divided blood into two types, 'the necessary blood of life' that runs deeper in the human body and 'surplus' blood that is produced as the result of nutrition and expelled if there is too much of it, as in a nosebleed. Christ had taken his 'necessary' blood with him at the Resurrection, but the 'surplus' blood could be left behind. The Franciscans (always ready to challenge a Dominican such as Thomas Aquinas) offered similar arguments specifically in support of the Wilsnack shrine. The survival of Jesus's foreskin showed he could leave things behind and then, with extraordinary theological ingenuity, they put forward the argument that the glorified body of Christ (and, in fact, any glorified body) needed less blood in its resurrected state than when it was on earth, and so some could be safely left behind to be honoured as a relic. This was superfluous blood but it could be venerated, here as a symbol of the humiliation that Christ went through for humankind. In a text of 1455 one Franciscan, Johannes Bremer, suggested a hierarchy. At the lowest level there were the relics associated with Christ's Crucifixion – the Cross, his garments, nails and so on. Then there were relics of his body left on earth before the Resurrection – the foreskin and the blood shed from the Cross. Finally, there was the consecrated host that was superior to the foreskin and the blood shed on earth, in that it had gone through the divine process of consecration. The hosts that bled did so to confound heretics and convince doubters (like Peter of Prague).

Another debate raged over what the redness that appeared on a bleeding host actually represented. Was it truly the blood of Christ, created through the act of transubstantiation and making itself known, or was it a form of symbolic blood, perhaps a miraculous red stain just to make the point that this was a host? If it was truly the blood of Christ then it could surely never dry up. For some shrines, this became crucial. In a world of intense competition, a relic of blood that did not dry up was clearly more prestigious than a mere stain on a cloth that may, as Aquinas had argued, merely have come from blood from an image that had been struck. So the shrine at Weingarten, the richest monastery in Swabia in southern Germany, placed great emphasis on its liquid blood. It was none other than that which had flowed out when the Roman soldier, traditionally known as Longinus, had pierced the side of Christ as recorded in John's Gospel. Longinus had preserved it in a leaden box that he had buried at Mantua in Italy. It was lost and rediscovered twice and finally a sample of it had descended through the family of the emperor Henry III until it had been presented to the monastery at Weingarten in 1090. The monks of Weingarten were having nothing of superfluous, second-rank blood. Whatever the theological difficulties this was the real thing and showed its authenticity through being always liquid. When Bishop Rudolph of Constance awarded an indulgence for those who visited the relic at Weingarten, he emphasised that the blood was still miraculously preserved from corruption. The monks composed their own liturgy for their relic, which talked of the blood as if it was still coming from a living spring and cleansing them, 'making us fruitful for the good'. Wine was poured over the container holding the blood and then drunk.

At La Rochelle, in south-western France, the Franciscans also claimed to have the true blood of Christ, in their case gathered by Nicodemus who assisted Joseph of Arimathea in preparing the body of Jesus for burial. In 1448 a fierce debate broke out between those who claimed that Christ could have left blood behind and those who insisted that it was theologically impossible. Matters became so heated that the university of Paris appointed five professors of theology to make a definitive judgement. They sided with the Franciscans even if their statement that 'it is not repugnant to the piety of the faithful to believe that something of Christ's blood poured out at the time of the passion remained on earth' seems rather half-hearted. The local bishop disagreed and forbade the friars to venerate their blood. The friars appealed to the Pope, Nicholas V, who issued a somewhat lukewarm statement in their support. The shrine had a long tradition, he said, there was nothing in the devotion of the masses to the relic that was 'contrary to the truth of the faith' and he saw no reason to disrupt their piety. However, he seemed to imply that the blood was similar to that from the Cross at Beirut – it had been produced in response to an insult. This was not good enough for the Franciscans who in 1461 approached a later Pope, Pius II, to get him to support the original judgement of the Paris theologians. A report from the sixteenth century makes it clear that visitors to the shrine were firmly told that it was indeed the blood collected by Nicodemus!

These debates reflect the growing tensions within the Church in the fifteenth century. There was a continuing proliferation of cults that not only strained the credulity of those with some education but which threatened to take popular worship beyond the control of the clergy. The response of the clergy was to isolate the consecration of the host from the faithful. The rituals of consecration were elaborated. The correct words were spoken in Latin and thus were incomprehensible to the mass of the congregation; the priest stood with his back to the congregation so that his consecration of the host could not be seen; the host was given an *elevatio* by being raised above the head of the priest; the consecrated host could not be touched by the communicants but only placed on their lips. (Well into the twentieth century, Catholic children were instructed not to touch the host with their teeth.) Intricate theological debates were held about the exact moment in the ritual when the host and wine became fully body and blood.

So the host became another species of relic in that the original bread and wine had no sacred power at all but it had been transformed into the most sacred relic of all, the actual body and blood of Jesus, through the act of consecration. This safeguarded the status of the clergy who alone could effect the consecration. Francis of Assisi went so far as to compare the priest who actually handles Christ with the Virgin Mary who bore him and John the Baptist who baptised him.[11] By widening the gap between priest and laity this was one of the developments that fragmented medieval Christianity.

The ubiquity of the host as relic meant that it was consumable. More could always be consecrated, and this added another level of emotion to the experience of receiving Communion. It went without saying that anyone who was unable to swallow the host was believed to be harbouring uncon-fessed guilt but, for those worthy of it, the experience was intense. The thirteenth-century mystic Hadewijch from the duchy of Brabant revelled in the ecstatic communion she found with Christ after ingesting his body. 'Then he gave himself to me in the shape of the Sacrament . . . and then he gave me to drink from the chalice. After that he came to me, took me entirely in his arms, and pressed me to him; and all of my members felt his in his full felicity, in accordance with the desire of my heart and my humanity. So that I was outwardly satisfied and fully transported.'[12] Here the 'relic' suffuses the recipient to give an erotic intensity to her experience, yet it also serves to isolate her from what had been, in the early Church, a communal experience.

What was distinct about this 'relic' was that it could, of course, be created at will, so long as the correct ritual was followed, and then distributed to all those considered worthy of it. Yet so long as it was unconsumed, the relic retained its power. By the thirteenth century the host is treated as if it were a 'normal' relic. When the feast of Corpus Christi, of the body of Christ, was instituted by Pope Urban IV in 1264, the earliest accounts show that the host was carried in the same procession as relics as if it had simply been added in as an extra.[13] Then it is given its own elevated place, raised on a special litter, accompanied by its own priests. One sixteenth-century account describes such a procession as one of Christ (the host) surrounded by his disciples (the lesser relics). In England these Corpus Christi processions became major civic events, tied to the performance of mystery plays, a cycle of plays that covered the world's history from the Creation to the Last Judgement. Again, the veneration of the host displayed on the high altar of a church in a monstrance took place on certain feast days, such as Maundy Thursday, the day on which Christ had instituted the Eucharist, just as a saint's relics were exposed on his or her feast day.

It is also fascinating to see the way in which the host accumulated many of the powers of relics. Lost hosts emerged some time later as uncorrupted as the body of any saint. Hosts could also ooze blood just as relics did, they could put out fires and heal. In some areas they were taken out to the countryside as relics had been on Rogation days (see earlier p. 82) and used to ward off lightning and hailstones. When the priest had washed out the chalice, the water was said to cure cripples and the blind. Bernard of Clairvaux expelled demons from a woman by placing the paten, the dish on which the host lay before consecration, on her head. So the concentration on the Eucharistic host can be seen as one way in which the clergy could divert attention from popular relic cults that were threatening to the established Church. Yet at the same time the development marks a new phase in the process by which the clergy isolate themselves from the laity. This was certainly to be one of the factors that led to the readiness with which many were to abandon the Church at the Reformation.

CHAPTER TWENTY

Rescuers and Devils

In the fourteenth century relics became caught up in the shifting mentalities of a very troubled age. It was already a time when spirits were low. The fall of Acre, the last crusader toehold in the Holy Land in 1291, had spread gloom throughout Europe. Such an abject failure could only be seen as the judgement of God on a sinful Christian humanity. Lack of effective leadership did not help. For much of the century (1309–78) the papacy was in exile from Rome in Avignon, an enclave in southern France.[1] Even though the Avignon popes were relatively able and their administration more efficient than it had been in Rome, their authority depended on their status as bishops of Rome and successors of St Peter. They were now remote from their spiritual home and were all too easily ridiculed as puppets of the French king. Eventually, Pope Gregory XI made his way back to Rome, not without difficulty as he was at war with the cities of northern Italy. On his death in the city in 1378, the election of the austere and provocative Urban VI impelled some of the cardinals to elect an 'anti-pope', Clement VII. Europe split into two as rival secular rulers backed one or other of the popes. Two distinct papacies lasted until the early fifteenth century. The Great Schism shattered the aura of a single religious leader and papal administration faltered. 'Not even a hardened heart can be unmoved at the sight of Holy Mother the Church in such agony', as one Paris theologian put it.

The collapse of Church authority took place against a background of almost complete social breakdown. Between 5 and 10 per cent of the population may have died in a major famine that struck northern Europe in 1315. From the end of 1347 the Black Death made its inexorable way through Europe, killing perhaps a third of Europe's population, and recurring unexpectedly and dreadfully at frequent intervals, typically between six and thirteen years. The Black Death consolidated the idea, already preached by the Church, that humankind was vulnerable to the unforgiving interventions of God. 'Since people knew of no remedy for the event, many thought it was a miracle and God's vengeance', wrote one contemporary chronicler.[2] It led to profound personal anxieties: *Timor mortis conturbat me*, 'The fear of death throws me into confusion', as a response from the Church's Office of the Dead put it. Grotesquely emaciated bodies and groups of dancing skeletons pervade popular art of the period. 'Every man must know that the world is but a temporary habitation and that death, harsh and unpitying, is imminent', was the bleak but entirely typical reflection of the knight Nompar de Caumont.

Inevitably, the fourteenth century also recorded much higher levels of social violence. There were peasant revolts, in Flanders between 1323 and 1328, in the Seine valley in 1358, in England in 1381, and workers' uprisings such as that of the *Ciompi*, the wool carders, in Florence in 1378. In their turn the authorities became more brutalised and torture appears commonplace. The increasing use of mercenaries in war led to a breakdown of traditional conventions. The Provençal Honoré Bonet (*c.*1340–1410) lamented that warfare no longer followed 'the ordinances of chivalry of the ancient custom of noble warriors, who uphold justice, the widow, the orphan and the poor'.[3] One of the most horrific events of the period, recorded by the French chronicler Froissart, was the sack of the city of Limoges by the English after its surrender by the French in 1370. The English are said to have murdered three thousand of its citizens.

One important response was the appearance of 'rescuer' saints, some well established, others new. The cult of St Martial at Limoges had already been important in the ninth century and again in the late tenth during the Peace of God movement. It was now as if the horror of the sack of his city revived Martial's miraculous powers.[4] When a truce between England and France was signed in 1388, his head was displayed in the city cathedral and 'the sweetness of the peace' was attributed to his 'prayers and merits'. It was even hoped that his virtues would help bring to an end the Great Schism. This account was followed by a list of seventy-three miracles effected by Martial between 1378 and 1389.

The list provides an insight into the tribulations of a war-torn age. Martial's reach extended to a sixty-mile radius around Limoges and included many captured French soldiers festering in English-held castles. Among those who credited their rescue to Martial were soldiers and non-combatants threatened with death when they could not pay ransoms, pilgrims whose safe conducts were not honoured, and villagers whose homes and fields had been ravaged. Pierre Poyaudi, a wine merchant, was nearing Limoges when he was taken by the English, trussed up and put in prison. After he had called on St Martial for rescue, the French launched a counter-attack, released him and he was able to regain his goods and enter Limoges to give thanks at the shrine. This most French of saints extended his care even to Englishmen. An English squire rode into a raging stream, his horse's reins broke, and both squire and beast were plunged into the water. The Englishman had heard of Martial and called upon him. When he had promised that he would bring wax to the shrine and never again take up arms against any Christian, both he and his horse managed to scramble to safety. Martial dealt with forged coins, confronted thieves and murderers roaming in the forests, and intervened to save travellers from the dangers of life on the open road.

There were other important saints who 'rescued' those affected by the breakdown. One effect of the massive depopulations brought by the Black Death was the encroachment of nature on once cultivated lands. Woodland regenerated, tracks became abandoned, bridges decayed. Packs of wolves even raided into villages to take off children. Stories of demons, devils and werewolves lurking in forests become commonplace. Bands of displaced men roamed the wastelands and some even achieved heroic status. The legends of Robin Hood in Sherwood Forest date from just this period, the late fourteenth century.

One famously austere figure was Pietro da Marrone, who served for a brief period in his eighties as Pope Celestine V (r. 1294) and was later canonised. The miracles accorded to him in the remote mountain areas of the Abruzzi, east of Rome, involve victory over forest fires, drought, wild beasts, snakes, hunger and cold. On his death, he too was fought over by three different mountain towns and the monks protecting his body had to conceal it. He was eventually buried at L'Aquila and it was acclaimed yet another of his miracles when his body survived the earthquake of 2009 intact despite there being so much destruction of life and property around him.

Perhaps the most successful of these 'rescuing' saints was the Augustinian monk Nicholas of Tolentino (c.1236–1304). Tolentino was a small town in the Italian Marche close to Nicholas's birthplace, and when he moved back there he proved a resourceful mediator in the conflicts between factions in the city. Already in his lifetime Nicholas had the reputation of resuscitating those who had drowned, especially children, and he was immediately venerated on his death. His tomb became a centre of pilgrimage. In 1345 a visiting German pilgrim broke into it and made off with the arms from his body but was soon spotted when blood poured from them.[5] Nicholas's body was hidden (and only rediscovered in 1926), but the arms flourished and had their own reliquaries that could be processed through the streets of Tolentino. They warned of impending crises by bleeding.

Whereas pilgrims normally visited a shrine in the hope of a cure, 'rescuer' saints had to effect their miracles on the spot wherever they were needed. It was afterwards that a saved person was expected to go to the shrine to offer thanks and gifts and the miracle would be recorded. Nicholas's rescuings from drowning continued. Many bridges must have rotted away through neglect in this period and Nicholas's book of miracles tells of those that collapsed during floods, with children swept away only to be saved by prayers to the saint. One Bernard Nuctii, sentenced to death for a murder of which he claimed to be innocent, prayed to Nicholas and managed to escape, evading a band of two hundred sent to track him down and crossing an impassable river. Another famous miracle involved the rescue of nine men in a storm when Nicholas appeared in the sky before them with a lily in his hand. Several of them came along to the canonisation inquiry to testify to their rescue. Nicholas's most spectacular 'rescue' was of the Doge's Palace in Venice. It had caught fire but Nicholas appeared above it, threw down some holy bread and extinguished the flames. When he was eventually canonised in 1446, more than three hundred new miracles followed.

Inevitably, relic cults became caught up in the shifting mentalities of the age. Sudden outbursts of religious fervour were aroused by the rumour of a statue that had wept or spoken. Vast crowds flocked to them. In some cases these movements rose and fell in a few weeks, and it is often chance reports that tell us of them. Most were localised, meetings of 'the simple people of Christ' at shrines close to their homes. Often sheer desperation drove crowds of the dispossessed to flock together in search of both material and spiritual relief. So one observer of the children's pilgrimage of 1475 that ended up at Wilsnack noted how the children were driven to pilgrimage for lack of bread to eat and fear of begging locally among those who knew them. When questioned, they could not say what drove them other than 'an irresistible impulse'.[6] For this pilgrimage Wilsnack was the destination, for other children's pilgrimages it was the great Norman abbey of Mont-St-Michel in Normandy.

Mont-St-Michel seems to have been publicised after there were stories of a glow on the spire of the abbey at Pentecost in 1333, almost certainly the result of an electrical storm. The children who gathered at the site soon afterwards were said to be from poor peasant families, lured in by the phenomenon. They dubbed themselves the *pastoureaux*, linking themselves by this name to an agrarian revolt of a few years before which had claimed that the Virgin Mary had ordered the extermination of the Jews. What was extraordinary about this movement was that it spread among the poor of the French countryside, and later those of German towns, with pilgrims as young as nine making their way to Mont-St-Michel. The children had widespread popular support and were often fed and sheltered along the way.

These mass popular movements of the poor were deeply unsettling to the authorities. The Church understood that many cults were now out of their control. The response was to condemn the young for their inability to work or to accept the poverty that was their lot and even to threaten excommunication of those who took to the road. So far as Mont-St-Michel was concerned, it had no effect: pilgrimages were still arriving from Germany a hundred years later. It was inevitable that there would eventually be a major confrontation and it took place in 1476, a year after the children's pilgrimage to Wilsnack, in the small village of Niklashausen in Wurzburg, southern Germany.[7]

Once again it was a statue of the Virgin whose miraculous powers were extolled, here by a local shepherd, Hans Böhm. Böhm emerged as a gifted and charismatic speaker who called for the repentance of sinners. He usurped the power of the authorities by proclaiming that a visit to the statue would earn a plenary indulgence. Times were dire. Harvests in southern Germany had been poor in 1475 and by the time Böhm began preaching in the following Lent supplies were at their lowest. The prince-bishops of Wurzburg had increased taxes. Böhm told of apparitions of the Virgin Mary in which he was told that all these afflictions were a deliberate punishment inflicted by her and her Son for the wickedness of mankind. The despair brought an extraordinary rush of pilgrims to Niklashausen, many from further afield, from areas where famine had also struck. There are estimates of between 40,000 and 70,000 camped in the fields around the village.

Böhm had started conventionally enough with demands that his flock dress soberly, devote themselves to God, and renounce loose living. No one in the Church could object to that, especially as there was some sympathy for reform within the Church as a whole. However, his very presence as a free-speaking preacher outside the confines of the established Church was disturbing. Soon he became buoyed up by adulation of the crowds and their deep distress. He began preaching more radically. 'Bishops, princes, counts and knights should be allowed to possess as much as ordinary men and no more. There will come a time when even they will have to work for their living.' He called for his followers to refuse to pay taxes and then called for a mass meeting at Niklashausen that would launch an attack on both civil and religious authority.

The counter-attack was inevitable. On the day of the planned uprising in July, Böhm was seized by a group of horsemen and rushed off to prison. Cannon was used to disperse his followers and Böhm was later burned for heresy. His church was razed to the ground. Without leadership the movement collapsed. The cults that had so often promoted harmony were beginning to provide a focus for social disharmony. The Virgin Mary who had played such a powerful role as the compassionate and stable mother who would plead against the anger of her Son had become, among the poor, an instigator of social revolution.

Although Böhm's movement was crushed, as would be other peasant revolts in the years to come, these popular movements had to be given some explanation by those in authority. It was now that the Devil emerged as the manipulator of evil things. Devils, fallen angels doing the bidding of Satan himself, had always been believed to be around, of course, lurking in the airwaves or remote places, but in the fourteenth and fifteenth centuries they were given an expanded role. Saint Bernardino of Siena (1380–1444) revelled in sermons in which he claimed he could actually see the devils before him, outnumbering his congregation. When he ordered vast bonfires of 'vanities', the climax was invariably a devil 'seen' rising in anger through the flames.[8] Devils were said to know the human mind, to foretell the future and use human beings for subversion.[9] By the early fifteenth century there are the first witch hunts, predominantly of 'credulous' women whom the Devil had infiltrated for evil ends. There were stories of devils stealing human semen and impregnating women. Pale-faced children of uncertain origin, 'changelings' in medieval folklore, many of whom must have been homeless, starving or disabled, were seen as the offspring of such sex and if they died early it was merely a confirmation of their status.

Relic cults and devils became entwined in two ways. It is in the fourteenth century that sophisticated churchmen begin to become suspicious about activities at the shrines. Jean Gerson (1363–1429), chancellor of the university of Paris and the most accomplished theologian of his generation, was worried that supplicants at shrines were saying meaningless words or simply engaging in magic and claiming that was acceptable 'Catholic' behaviour. They expected results simply by going through the correct ritual. This was an insult to God who retained an absolute right to grant or withhold a miracle. Such superstitious practices encouraged the Devil. 'The superstition is all the worse, the more good things are mingled in with it, since by that means by which God ought to be honoured, the devil is honoured.' So superstition is the activity of the Devil.[10]

The word 'superstition' is notoriously flexible. One man's superstition is another man's legitimate act of devotion. Heinrich von Gorkum (1378–1431) considered the problem at length in his *On Certain Cases of Conscience Relating to Superstition* in which he examined cases of apparent superstition such as the custom of placing joints of meat inside the altar during Holy Week, fashioning the bones into crosses and then using these as protection against shipwreck, robbery and other dangers. His argument was that no object had magic power unless God himself had infused it. An axe had no potency in itself but only cut wood when an artisan actually used it. So also with the sacraments, relics and the sign of the cross, there was no actual potency 'unless the motion of the supreme artisan [i.e. God] specifically cooperates towards achieving those effects for which they are destined'.[11]

So it follows that anyone who believes that a relic has potency in itself makes 'a tacit contract with the ancient adversary [i.e. the Devil], with whom we are committed to eternal warfare'. Pastors were advised to warn their congregations that such practices were 'invented by evil spirits who try to cover their deviousness under the cover of goodness'.[12] John Grandison, Bishop of Exeter, was infuriated by the number of cults that were springing up spontaneously in his diocese in the 1340s. They even included one to a priest who had committed suicide. He sent a commission to go around the villages stamping them out. 'I fear these miracles hard to believe and impossible to prove. I fear that the people have given themselves over to idolatry and strayed from the path of the true Catholic faith . . . deluded by insane and untrue visions inspired by the Devil and his agents.'[13]

If these were practices and shrines that the Devil had infiltrated, it was also through shrines that devils could be thwarted. The saint who was the model here was St Antony, a fourth-century ascetic who lived for decades in the Egyptian desert and is often seen as the father of monasticism. His relics had travelled from Constantinople to the French abbey of St Antoine in southern France sometime in the eleventh century. Medieval legends told of the mass of devils, some of them horrific animals, others naked women, who assailed him in his loneliness and these were often dramatically shown in late medieval art.

The Devil could only be successfully confronted if the supplicant focused veneration directly on God or the saints. This did not mean that relics did not have a purpose but it was rather as catalysts that connected the worshipper to God. Martin Plantsch, a theologian from the university city of Tübingen, described in his *A Short Work on Witches* (1505) how certain relics appeared particularly useful in invoking God for help against specific misfortunes. He notes that 'St Antony's water' worked for ergotism while St Blaise's candles were useful if placed on the neck and a paten, the dish on which the host was placed, could be waved in front of the face to ward off blindness. 'All these things can be used with pious intention . . . to cure ailments and drive away demons, so long as the hope is not placed in them, but the effect is looked at from God, because of the devotion of the person using them, or because of the intercessions of the saints whose names are invoked in the blessings and in whose reverence these things are used.'[14] Quite how one found the right balance, between using a relic but not letting it have any potency, was unclear.

It was obvious, in short, that the rise of the Devil in late medieval Europe brought a great deal of confusion. Boundaries between good and evil, between superstition and divinely approval rituals, had become arbitrary. The confusion was deepened by a theological impasse. If the Devil is able to exercise his powers quite so easily, then God must either be impotent to stop him or he must actively will his activities. The first was impossible so it was accepted that the Devil had God's permission to act. Plantsch was forced to argue that there was 'a most righteous [sic] and hidden cause of evil within God' that was beyond human investigation. This echoed an earlier belief, put forward by the Franciscan Bonaventure (1221–74), that God had the power to save the damned at any time but chose never to do so.

These theological conundrums were symptomatic of a wider malaise. Medieval Christianity had never been as monolithic or authoritarian as it seemed but now there were the beginnings of serious fragmentation. The sudden rise and fall of relic cults was fuelled by a volatile population who were convinced more than ever by a series of disasters that God had judged them unworthy. Although the scepticism of the theologians such as Gerson may not have had much impact on ordinary believers, worshippers must have been aware that the Church was beginning to divide shrines and practices into 'good', inspired by God, or 'evil', inspired by the Devil. 'Good' and 'evil' had become cosmic forces with no space in between. How anyone could possibly work out what they should be doing to ensure salvation was impossible to say. It is no surprise that this is an age of withdrawal, into the private chamber with Books of Hours for the literate. Thomas à Kempis's *The Imitation of Christ* was just one manual that catered for agonised introspection and that inspired self-punishment. Within the Italian cities, public worship was increasingly transferred to the confraternities who had their own collections of relics and the priests to care for them. When more determined assaults began on the shrines, they would have surprisingly few active supporters.

'Of far-off saints, hallowed in sundry lands'

'T HE FIFTEENTH century was the last century of mass pilgrimages. While the poor seem to have kept closer to home and rushed in crowds to local shrines at the news of a fresh miracle, other groups were treading the ancient routes. So it was with the cheery characters who assembled to walk to Canterbury in Geoffrey Chaucer's *Canterbury Tales*. Chaucer, writing at the end of the four-teenth century, brilliantly catches the atmosphere of the burgeoning spring enthusing the pilgrims with the desire to seek new spiritual adventures. Several of them have already travelled far in their lives as knights, merchants, sailors or pilgrims. The worldly-wise Wife of Bath has clocked up Jerusalem, Rome, Bologna (presumably the shrine of St Dominic who died there), Compostela and Cologne (the bones of the Three Magi). These feisty individuals would have made their way alongside the genuinely disfigured, crippled and suffering men and women who dragged themselves to Canterbury or other shrines, as well as those heavy with sin sent there as a penance.

The most important setting-out point for pilgrimage in the fifteenth century was not the Tabard Inn in Southwark where Chaucer's characters assembled, but Venice.[1] The city prided itself on the safe passages it offered to the Holy Land and regaled with stories of Catalan and Sicilian boats that had never made it and were lying on the seabed. When they arrived in the city prospective pilgrims would make their way to the flagstaffs in front of St Mark's basilica where travel agents would tout their package tours, their galleys moored for inspection in front of the Ducal Palace, not far from the Piazza San Marco. However, they would now face a delay. Venice resorted to keeping pilgrims spending money in the city as long as possible. One ploy was to hold back the departure of the pilgrim ships until after the great feast of the Ascension when there was the opulent ritual in which Venice was symbolically 'married' to the sea. The feast took place at the same time as a merchant's fair in Piazza San Marco and those who attended gained their plenary indulgence. Cynics said that the city authorities deliberately delayed granting certificates of seaworthiness to the pilgrim ships and so the pilgrims had to hang about, sometimes for weeks, until the bureaucrats relented.

There are vivid accounts by William Wey, a Fellow of Eton College, of his two pilgrimages to the Holy Land in 1458 and 1462 which make it seem a whirlwind of visits from one shrine to another.[2] William Wey had his own experience of a delayed departure as he waited to set out on his journey. He had arrived in Venice on 22 April 1462 and so was in time for the festivities of St Mark's Day on the 25th. Unexpectedly, a few days later the doge died and Wey saw the opulent funeral the city arranged. It was not until 26 May that his ship left. He had been strongly advised to pay for a berth on the higher levels of the galley as the hold was 'ryght smolderyng hote and stynking'. He had to buy his own feather bed, mattress, pillows and sheets, but the shop promised him they would pay him back half of the cost if he returned them. He then bought up red wine (as more reliable to drink than water) and dried fruits such as raisins and figs, with saffron and cloves as spices and medical supplies for stomach upsets (*medicinas laxativas et restrictavis*, as his Latin account engagingly records). Not the least of the delights of his account is his list of useful Greek phrases that he recommended to other pilgrims. 'Man (woman), have you good wine?', 'I understand thee not' and 'Where is the taverne?' are among them.

While he was gathering his supplies, Wey was taken on an exhausting tour of Venice's saints. Venice had become, after Rome, the city with the largest collection in Europe. Despite its modest haul immediately after the Fourth Crusade (1202–04), the city had had many other opportunities to bring in relics from the east and its wealth allowed it to build elaborate shrines for them. Wey started his itinerary of those on show in St Mark's. Although the relics of St Mark's body were not on display, he could see St Isidore and the cross that had been struck by a Jew and spurted blood. Off he went around the canals to see the bodies of almost fifty saints. Finally, the order must have been given for the pilgrimage to set out. It took a month to reach Jaffa, the port where pilgrims disembarked, but there were lots of stops on the route and Wey recorded even more relics in each church as he progressed from port to port.

In Jaffa the group paid their visit to the places associated with St Peter's resurrection of Tabitha (Acts of the Apostles: 9–10) and earn a plenary indulgence for their trouble. They were met by Franciscans from a monastery that had been set up in the ruins on Mount Sion, within the biblical walls of Jerusalem, in 1335. This was one of the most sacred sites in the city. David and Solomon were supposed to have been born here. There was an 'Upper Room' that had seen the Last Supper, the appearance of the risen Lord to the Apostle Thomas and the descent of the Holy Spirit on the Apostles at Pentecost.

The more committed of the pilgrims would hire donkeys for the journey to Jerusalem and so would enter the city as Jesus himself had done. Wey advised his readers to book ahead early as the best ones were soon taken. It would have been an extraordinary moment as the city came into view from Mount Joy. The Gospel stories were so deeply embedded in the imagination that it must have been like an entry into another world and overpowering emotionally. The earliest autobiography in English, *The Book of Margery Kempe*, a merchant's wife from King's Lynn, written in the 1420s, details the experiences of a highly impressionable and emotionally volatile woman whose desire to gain spiritual peace drove her to almost every major shrine in Europe. When Margery arrived in Jerusalem she was so overcome by the experience that she believed that Christ had come before her. 'She did see Him standing there before her in her soul. . . . And when she went up Mount Calvary she fell to the ground, unable either to kneel or stand, and she rolled and writhed her body, spreading her arms out and crying loudly as though her heart had burst open; for in the city of her soul she truly saw Our Lord's crucifixion. Before her very face she saw and heard, in mystical sight, the mourning of Our Lady, of Saint John, Mary Magdalene, and of countless others who loved Our Lord.'[3]

Two rather different destinations awaited the pilgrims. Whatever the spiritual resonances of Mount Sion, the comfort and good wines offered by the friars were renowned and this was the aristocratic destination. This period saw a mass of noblemen and their retinues making their way to Jerusalem. So the Earl of Derby stocking up in Venice before his departure in 1392 accumulated a warehouse full of provisions, including oxen, eggs, dates and almonds, to load aboard ship. He spent some forty times the normal fare of passage. In 1413 Niccolo d'Este had a large contingent of orderlies, chamberlains, his own chefs and even a pair of trumpeters. Another nobleman, setting out from Crete, chartered a separate ship for his horses and falcons. Even though it was the custom for everyone to put on ragged clothes when they arrived in the Holy Land, these were the class of guests the friars preferred. A group of Italian aristocrats who arrived at the same time as Wey were welcomed there.

The mass of pilgrims were taken into the Hospital of St John run by the Order of Hospitallers and there was some resentment over those who lived it up at Mount Sion. A preacher complained: 'If the Lord chose to enter Jerusalem on a mule rather than a horse, what are we to think of those who parade up and down on horseback. . . . Truly', he went on with some severity, 'these are not real pilgrims at all, but thieves and robbers who have abandoned the way of specific apostolic poverty and chosen instead the path of damnation. . . .'[4]

The Muslims were tolerant of visitors despite the appalling bloodshed of the conquests and reconquests of the city. Two Muslim families held the keys of the church of the Holy Sepulchre and allowed visitors in through a side door. Again monks from the friary presided over the tours that followed, warning their group that they must not break off stones or engrave their coats of arms on the walls. (Their requests were disregarded, a mass of small medieval crosses carved on the stone still survives in the sanctuary.) Pilgrims entered through an atrium into the basilica itself and beyond this was a courtyard and then the site of Christ's tomb where the rock had been cleared away to reveal the actual spot of the Resurrection. The focus of the visit was the circular shrine set within the twelfth-century sanctuary built after the success of the First Crusade (1095–99). This extended to enclose Calvary where the Crucifixion had taken place. Visitors were shown traces of Jesus's blood that could be seen staining the rock. One of the most extraordinary finds here had been the head of Adam. The legend went that the head had been recovered by Noah before the Flood, stowed in the Ark and then buried on Calvary when the waters receded. The *Golden Legend* went on to tell how the seeds of the tree from which the Cross was made were placed in Adam's mouth when he was buried and they sprouted from there. The head had been penetrated by the blood of Jesus as it seeped downwards. The stone where Joseph of Arimathea had washed the body of Jesus after the Crucifixion was in the Church. Other sacred sites, where the risen Christ had appeared to Mary Magdalen in the garden, where the Cross had been buried, where the soldiers had drawn lots for Jesus's clothes, were also enclosed within the sanctuary of the church.

Outside the sanctuary of the Holy Sepulchre pilgrims recreated the *Via Dolorosa*, the road that traced Jesus's last hours. According to the Gospels, it led from the Garden of Gethsemane to the house of Caiaphas, the high priest; from there to Pilate's palace and then on to Calvary. It had several 'stations', moments on the route where significant moments in Jesus's passage were commemorated. There were originally eight of these but in Europe 'The Stations of the Cross' had fourteen and these were eventually imposed by western pilgrims into the Jerusalem route, as Wey himself recorded. There is no archaeological backing for the authenticity of the *Via Dolorosa* as it runs at present, but it became an indelible part of the Jerusalem experience for those who had travelled from the western Mediterranean.

Hardly had William Wey completed his own round of visits in Jerusalem than he was off on a hectic excursion into the countryside. The place where the Virgin Mary and her cousin Elizabeth had met, where John the Baptist had been circumcised, the tomb of Lazarus in Bethany, the stone on which Martha had sat while she listened to Jesus, the cave where the Apostles had hidden after the Crucifixion – all had to be covered. In Bethlehem there was the sepulchre of the Holy Innocents, the spot where the Magi had handed over their gifts, the stone on which Jesus lay when he was being circumcised and the chapel where Jerome had made his translation of the Bible. The River Jordan had to be inspected, although there were warnings that drinking its water could bring on fevers and fluxes. Wey must have been exhausted when he finally arrived back in Jaffa for the boat home.

Rome continued to be a major focus for pilgrims.[5] It had, of course, its distinct identity as the capital of Catholicism and the traditional home of the popes. Although the route to Rome from northern Europe was a demanding one, the pilgrim had the advantage of being among fellow Christians when he arrived. It has been estimated that a million pilgrims visited the city in the first Holy Year of 1300. Even though the popes were in exile in Avignon, it was announced that another Holy Year would be held in 1350. The original plan was to hold them every hundred years but the chance to reap in more revenue by halving the period between Holy Years was also one not to be missed. Meanwhile Pope Clement VI found a new source for indulgences.

Christ, the Virgin Mary and saints and martyrs had, of course, accumulated merit during their lives well above that needed to enter heaven and this, he announced, lay saved in a 'treasury' from which it could be released, through the personal dispensation of the papacy, to pilgrims during the Holy Year to help offset their own time in purgatory.

As it turned out, the auspices for 1350 could hardly have been more ominous. The Black Death had devastated Europe, wars between the European nations ravaged the countryside even further and looked like endangering the routes towards Rome. In Rome itself an earthquake brought down the roof of Santa Maria Maggiore and the campanile of St Peter's. The rubble lay there for years. The poet and humanist Petrarch, by now increasingly captivated by the classical past of Rome, believed that no worse disaster had befallen the city in the two thousand years since Rome's foundation. Yet the pilgrims still set out. The people of Florence, themselves coming to terms with the loss of a third of their population through plague, were astonished to find so many passing through 'despite all the hardships of the time, unbelievable cold, ice, snow and floods'. Accommodation in the shattered core of Rome was scarce and food had to be imported from northern Italy at great expense to meet demand. Still, enormous crowds, as many as five thousand new pilgrims a day, were reported right up to the last day of the year. The crush around the veil of Veronica was so great on each Sunday afternoon when it was exposed that three or four pilgrims, on one occasion even twelve, were crushed or suffocated to death. Even the sophisticated classical scholar Petrarch, who visited most of the sacred sites in the city, recorded his overpowering need to see the face of Christ on the veil. The ardent pilgrim would then set out on a tour of the seven main basilicas, a circuit of eleven miles in total. Eventually, the number of required visits for an indulgence was reduced simply so that pilgrims could be moved out of the city more quickly.

Yet, with the Pope absent in Avignon and the city so shattered (reports suggest pilgrims falling into unfilled crevices), there was a sense of spiritual doom. The rapacity and lack of Christian virtue shown by the Romans shocked many of the visitors. Although Clement went on insisting that only a visit to Rome could earn an indulgence, the very next year he was granting post-dated indulgences for anyone who paid for them. In May 1351 the King of England, Edward II, his queen and the Prince of Wales all handed over the cost of a trip to Rome in return for the indulgence. A special deal was done with the people of Mallorca. In return for a single payment of 30,000 gold florins to the papal treasury, they could gain the indulgence simply by visits to their cathedral and every parish church in the city.

Like the great monetary inflations of later history, devaluation simply brought greater devaluation. It was as if the decay of the city during the papal exile, and later the Great Schism, could only be compensated for by massive rewards for pilgrims.[6] The Roman indulgences, remarked a papal secretary, 'exceed in indulgences all the other churches in the world combined, which is why every year an unending throng of pilgrims come to the city of the apostles to pray, to gain the indulgences, and to venerate the holy relics of its churches'. A walk across Rome, from the Lateran to the Vatican, would earn more indulgences than an entire pilgrimage to Jerusalem. Just how spectacular the inflation had been can be seen on the *Liber Indulgentiarum*, 'Book of Indulgences', from the 1370s, that claimed to contain the indulgences proclaimed by Pope Sylvester, the Pope at the time of Constantine's conversion to Christianity in the fourth century. There were twenty-nine steps up the front of St Peter's. Now a pilgrim could earn seven years' remission from purgatory from ascending each one. The eighty altars inside St Peter's were assessed at twenty-eight years remission for each. The veil of Veronica was the most lucrative. Gazing on it for an hour gained an indulgence of three thousand years for local Romans, nine thousand years for Italians and twelve thousand for those from further afield. A Viennese prior visiting Rome in 1377 was not going to miss his chance. He spent twenty-seven hours of prayer in front of the veil and so accumulated an impressive 324,000 years off his period of suffering in purgatory. Yet this was hardly worth it when a plenary indulgence could be gained simply by visiting the high altar of St Peter's a few yards away.

The Vatican archives hold thousands of petitions from sanctuaries destroyed in the Hundred Years War which pleaded for the granting of a papal indulgence as the only way to rebuild and lure back visitors. Many shrines gained the right to commute vowed pilgrimages to distant shrines. So in 1470 Canterbury Cathedral could grant, for a sum, the release of a vow to go to Rome or Santiago. This became sophisticated business. By 1500, the cost of release was graded according to the income of the supplicant. There was also the practice of transferring an indulgence granted at one church to another. The little chapel of the Portiuncula, close to Assisi, where St Francis received his vocation and had later died, had been granted a plenary indulgence. This was now extended to the church of La Verna where he had received his *stigmata* and then to many other Franciscan churches throughout Europe, including forty in England. The indulgences of St Mark were also scattered far and wide by profligate popes, especially Boniface IX (r. 1389–1404). The process aroused great resentment from shrines with well-established indulgences who saw themselves being upstaged by the newcomers. In 1402 Boniface, weakened by his position as one of two schismatic popes, was forced into a humiliating climbdown and many of his grants were withdrawn.

It was only in 1420, after the arrival in Rome of Pope Martin V of the ancient Roman family of Colonna, that stability returned and a single Pope now represented the Church from the see of St Peter.[7] This was the age of humanism in Italy. Humanism challenged the stress on spiritual withdrawal that had isolated the religious from society, and it restored the ancient classical ideal of active involvement in city life. Even the popes responded to the new mood. Rome was to become the only shrine that consciously transformed itself in line with the spirit of a new learning. Part of the immense revenues generated by the Holy Year of 1450 were spent by Pope Nicholas V on Greek and Latin manuscripts that made the Vatican Library one of the finest in Europe.

The incentive for a dramatic rebuilding of Rome in the fifteenth century sprung from the belief that pilgrims would be impressed by grandeur. Martin had set the tone by commissioning his new tiara from Lorenzo Ghiberti, the top goldsmith of the day. On his deathbed in 1455, Nicholas told how 'buildings, which are perpetual monuments and eternal testimonies seemingly made by the hand of God, show that the authority of the Roman church is the greatest and highest'. Pilgrims, he believed, would be strengthened in their faith if they saw 'great buildings seemingly made by the hand of God'. An efficient and prosperous city went hand in hand with a harmonious Christianity.

It was Nicholas V who presided over the Holy Year of 1450. In terms of numbers of pilgrims, it was an astonishing success. There may have been as many as forty thousand a day entering the city. The crowds were so great that the porticos of the great basilicas were crowded with those bedding down there, while others were forced to sleep under the vines in the surrounding countryside. Nicholas had to keep reducing the number of days needed to earn a full indulgence so as to keep numbers moving. Pilgrims were now aware that this was a city that was reviving through papal patronage, but the interest in relics remained intense. Pilgrims reported that a piece of St Lawrence was still fused together with the coals that burned him, the head of St Peter sported a beard that was somewhere between black and grey, while the Apostle Paul still had his red hair and beard intact.

Alas, the protective power of these saints proved limited. In the heat of the summer plague broke out in Rome and it was spread up the pilgrimage routes to the north as those infected left the city. Another disaster took place in the final week of the Holy Year in December. It was a Saturday and the veil of Veronica was due to be put on display. Crowds were massing on the ancient bridge that led from the eastern bank of the Tiber towards the Castel Sant'Angelo, and thence to the Vatican, when news came that the exposition had been cancelled. The disappointed pilgrims turned around only to face those still incoming. The crush on the bridge was intense and when the bridge was finally cleared 178 bodies were found. Many pilgrims had jumped into the Tiber and another seventeen bodies were later recovered from the river.

None of this lessened the ardour for the veil of Veronica. A 'vernicle', a badge with an image of Christ's face from the veil, became the symbol of pilgrimage to Rome and was pinned on each pilgrim's hat. When the lawyer Francesco Ariosto visited Rome in 1471 he attended an exposition of the veil and recorded how the crowd prostrated itself before the cloth and then burst into howls of repentance. 'They beat themselves repeatedly, causing themselves great pain, for they felt that by their sins, they had inflicted on Christ those wounds whose marks they saw before them: and now they hoped to wash away their guilt with tears, to purge the stains of sin with groans of pain.' This enthusiasm took place against a cavalcade of new relics. The bones of St Monica, the mother of St Augustine, were brought in from Ostia where she had died. Others arrived as the Ottoman Turks spread across the Byzantine empire after the fall of Constantinople in 1453. In 1460 the governor of the Greek Peloponnese (then known as the Morea) arrived in Rome with the head of St Andrew and this was given a flamboyant *translatio* to St Peter's that drew vast crowds. Ceremonial processions now became a major part of Roman life, as they did in many other Italian cities. The most important was the *possesso* when a newly elected Pope made his way from his cathedral, St John Lateran, across the ancient centre of Rome, even passing through Roman triumphal arches on the way, to take up residence in the Vatican. Outside the city itself the catacombs on the Via Appia, accessible from the church of San Sebastian, were now open to pilgrims and descent into their narrow passageways was believed to wipe the soul of the visitor clean.

This was the setting for the great renovations. Sixtus IV (r. 1471–84) was the first pope to redesign the city intelligently. He built a new bridge, the Ponte Sisto, so that there was an alternative route across the Tiber for pilgrims, he restored many decayed churches and created a new wing for the Hospital of Santo Spirito, the city's largest hospital. A gift of ancient bronzes to the city in 1471 saw the foundation of the Capitoline Museum, the oldest public museum in the world. Sixtus is best remembered for the Sistine Chapel within the Vatican Palace. Its measurements, based on those of the Temple as recorded in the Old Testament, appear to have been another deliberate attempt to recreate some of the spirit of Jerusalem in the papal capital. New streets were created between shrines, part of a programme that extended over the next sixty years.

These ambitious projects and the substantial funds they required may have dazzled some but they did nothing to raise the spiritual authority of the papacy, especially when money was demanded from across Europe through the sale of indulgences to finance them. Those seeking indulgences were always expected to make offerings to shrines they visited, but the practice of buying indulgences directly became more blatant. By the early fifteenth century the papal legates throughout Europe were selling dispensations from pilgrimages. The Council of Constance, meeting in 1418 with the hope of reforming the Church, did attempt to restrict the process but by now the pressures on the popes to give each shrine its own privileges were irresistible.

There was a major development in the late fifteenth century. In 1476 Sixtus confirmed a practice, first attested in the thirteenth century, that an indulgence could be transferred to the other world to shorten the agonies of one of the deceased who was already suffering in purgatory. So, in a surviving 'testimonial letter' of 1488, a named pilgrim is acknowledged as giving a twentieth of a ducat for a named soul in purgatory. It is sealed with a woodcut of a pilgrim and his staff and the pilgrim badge of St James, a cockle shell, on his hat. Stories circulated that each indulgence would allow a soul to fly to heaven. One of

St Bridget of Sweden's revelations when she was in Jerusalem was a vision of the many souls her devotions had released. Another account tells of a man reaching purgatory who finds his father still there, furious at the failure of his family on earth to release him. The ethos of personal responsibility was corroded by these developments. The chancellor of Oxford University, Thomas Gascoigne (1401–58), was brazen enough to declare, 'I do not care how many sins I commit for I can easily and speedily have a plenary remission of guilt and punishment, by acquiring a papal indulgence.'[8]

While it is natural to applaud the humanist popes for their openness to new learning, none of them applied their invigorated minds to the successful reform of the Church. Even before the Reformation had begun, the radical preacher Girolano Savonarola (1452–98) preaching in Florence lambasted the papacy for its isolation from the mass of the laity. 'There [in Rome], thou seest the great prelates with splendid mitres of gold and precious stones on their heads and silver crosiers in hand; there they stand at the altar, decked with fine copes and stoles of brocades, chanting those beautiful vespers and masses very slowly.' He suggests that the beauty of ritual has transcended concern for the needs of the poor. In a dig at the new learning, he accuses the Roman prelates of having no concern with anything but poetry and rhetoric and even using the classical authors as guides to the salvation of souls.[9]

While Rome may have dazzled or shocked the visiting pilgrim, the numbers still poured in. Other traditional sites of pilgrimage, in contrast, seem to have been in decay. The evidence from England in the fifteenth century is of falling offerings, fewer miracles and growing scepticism about cults.[10] Although cathedral incomes rose in the second half of the fourteenth century, perhaps as a result of pilgrimages infused by fear of the plague, they then drop off. Westminster Abbey had gathered in £120 in the year 1372–73, but only £10 a year under Henry VI a century later. At St Cuthbert's shrine in Durham Cathedral, £35 a year was being collected in the 1380s, but only £16 in the 1450s. A minor saint in the same cathedral attracted the pitiful figure of a single shilling in the early sixteenth century. By the sixteenth century ancient popular shrines such as Thomas of Cantilupe at Hereford, Cuthbert at Durham and Aethelthryth's at Ely had almost no offerings at all. The statutes of Lincoln Cathedral talk of 'a chilling of devotion'.

At Canterbury, where Thomas Becket's shrine had international appeal, there was more success. Throughout the fourteenth century offerings remained high. The shrine appears to have attracted those who had survived the Black Death or who feared they might catch it. Even as late as 1471 an outbreak of plague brought anxious pilgrims to the shrine from as far as the West Country. However, from about 1420, income had begun to fall and only £36 was recorded in 1535 on the eve of the Reformation (compare the £1,142 received in 1220, the year of Thomas's *translatio*). Canterbury was, of course, the destination of Chaucer's pilgrims, but miracles were so few and far between that in 1445 the monks of Canterbury, who had listed some seven hundred miracles early in the shrine's history, went so far as to make a public declaration of a single one. The last recorded cure by Becket, in 1474, was recorded in Coventry, a long way from Canterbury! The shift in allegiances is well shown in the touching story of one Miles Freebridge, aged nine months, who swallowed a pilgrimage badge from Canterbury. He was choking to death but it was not Thomas who saved him but King Henry VI, now revered by his people as a saint. After appropriate prayers had been said to Henry, Miles coughed up the badge. The relieved parents made for Windsor to hang the badge on Henry's shrine.

Henry VI, the pious founder of Eton College and King's College, Cambridge, who was buried at Windsor after his death in 1471, was credited with three hundred miracles by the end of the century. He had always presented himself as a gentle and humane ruler, ready to forgive his enemies and enduring in the face of hardship, 'the most speedy succour of the oppressed, as the fame of his miracles showed'. His cult tapped into memories of the saintly Anglo-Saxon kings of East Anglia. On display was his simple hat that pilgrims found useful to put on as a cure for headaches, but many of Henry's miracles were more spectacular. A little girl, Alice Newnett, had died of the plague and was being sewn into her shroud. Henry appeared in a vision and brought her back to life, insisting that she stay in her shroud for the time being so that everyone would recognise she had genuinely been given up for dead. The body of a drowned boy was retrieved from a mere and brought back to life when Henry was invoked. Many pilgrim badges survive from the fifty years that his cult was popular. Henry VII completed a magnificent chapel for his relics in Westminster Abbey. His royal successors backed a campaign to get him formally canonised, but this foundered when Henry VIII's relationship with the papacy disintegrated in the 1530s.

By the later fifteenth century veneration in English churches appears to have been focused on paintings of favoured saints.[11] One reason for the proliferation of images in English parish churches was that an image of a saint could be easily commissioned at a time when new relics were difficult to obtain. So Alice Chester of Bristol ordered a set of twenty-two images in 1483 for a great screen that would focus on a crucified Christ. Typically, the images of saints were placed so that they were clustered around, but subservient to, the figure of Christ on the Cross, the Rood, that was set on a central screen. The saints were given a visual role as intercessors. This made the concept of intercession more accessible and, of course, the image itself was a more vivid reminder of the saint than a piece of rag or bone. So the early fifteenth-century tract *Dives and Pauper* provides a traditional defence of images. They concentrate the mind on Christ, his Incarnation and his Passion and the lives of the saints. They stir the minds to devotion more than mere hearing or reading and they provide images for the unlettered that the literate are able to find in their texts.

Most perceptive observers of the period accepted the ambiguity of the devotions shown to images. While the conservative Catholic Thomas More might argue that 'the simplest fool will tell you that our Lady herself is in heaven' (and therefore not in the image), others who observed the obsessive behaviour of supplicants when relics and images were exposed were not so sure. In the late fourteenth-century treatise *De Adoracione Ymaninum* the author talks of the illiterate layman who is easily seduced by the material image 'as simple people are wont to do when they see a beautiful image artfully depicted and preciously adorned – straightway their mind is moved by carnal reverence to the adoration . . . and their intellect and devotion are wrapped up more in the outward appearance than spiritually to God'.[12]

So behind the apparent flourishing of some shrines and the decay of others, there were more deep-rooted tensions. Many shrines prospered outside the auspices of the Church, while others simply lost their appeal. There was a growing sense of alienation from the opulence of Rome. Above all the fundamental criticisms – that objects were worshipped at the expense of God, that superstitious practices were widespread, that the Church was distancing itself from the laity – were now coalescing to create the first major challenges to the concept of the shrine itself.

'dead images that ... may not ... help any man of any disease'

ONE OF Chaucer's exuberant band of pilgrims in *The Canterbury Tales* is a pardoner. He carries a pillowcase of relics around with him that includes a veil of the Virgin and part of the sail of the boat from which Peter walked towards Jesus on the waves (Matthew 14:22–33). Among his collection is 'a rubble of pigs' bones'. He is adept at coaxing money out of credulous folk who will willingly pay to kiss the relics and believe that their sins are absolved. The pardoner pleads his case to his fellow pilgrims but is soon rebuffed by the Host, who threatens to castrate him and enshrine his balls in a hog's turd as yet one more absurd relic.

Many of the more impressive theologians of the early fifteenth century, for example Jean Gerson or Pierre d'Ailly, both gifted theologians from the university of Paris, were determined to work for reform within the Church by boosting the status and frequency of Church councils. Others remained 'Catholics' but carried out their devotions within confraternities or their private rooms. It was also inevitable, nevertheless, that some individuals would dare to reject the Church completely.

In England, the growing anti-clericalism crystallised in the work of John Wyclif (*c.*1324–84), a philosopher at Oxford University, and his followers in the next decades, the Lollards.[1] Wyclif was coherent and articulate in his beliefs that were rooted not only in popular anti-clericalism but in the unresolved debates of the theologians from the thirteenth century.[2] His theology was, for its day, radical. He challenged the institutional hierarchy of the Church, the power of the Pope, the wealth of the Church and the widening division between clergy and laymen. His rejection was only deepened by the trauma of the Great Schism. As those who were to be saved must already be known to God, mediators on earth were superfluous. Christ was the true authority and his teachings could be found in the Scriptures which should be available equally for all, so English translations of the Bible were essential. Wyclif aimed to show how the ceremony of the Eucharist had developed well beyond anything instituted by Christ in the Bible: in fact, he disputed the very idea of sacraments. He denied transubstantiation in the sense that he believed the bread and wine must continue to exist alongside the body and blood of Christ and not be subsumed within it.

Wyclif stirred up dissensions in Oxford and was expelled from the university in 1381 but he survived and eventually died, of natural causes, in 1384. (His bones were dug up and scattered later as befitted a heretic.) Directly or indirectly, his ideas circulated among the wider English community. The Lollards, 'those who mumbled', were never a cohesive group, and certainly never founded an alternative Church, but they spread Wyclif's ideas through personal networks and the constant re-reading of the early Lollard tracts, almost as if they were a form of Scripture in themselves. It was perhaps inevitable that the Lollards would challenge the popular enthusiasm for relics. One Lollard tract of 1394 suggests that the pilgrim should ask himself whether a visit to the shrine is really for the joy of the saint rather than for the profit of the almshouse that is already well endowed. If the lance and nails of the Cross, both used to wound Jesus, are to be venerated, why not the lips of Judas, the traitor? The Lollard response to the spread of images in the English churches was to condemn them as idolatrous. One anonymous Lollard pamphlet told of 'dead images that neither thirsteth nor hungered nor feeleth any coldness neither suffered disease, for they may not feel nor see nor hear nor speak nor look nor help any man of any disease, as the holy prophets witnesseth'. As the reference to the 'prophets' makes clear, the Lollards looked back to the Scriptures that, they felt, the Church had ignored or made inaccessible to the laity.

This was a major challenge to the network of shrines, pilgrimages and the many rituals that surrounded them. In response, the English hierarchy was determined to destroy the Lollards. In 1401 the statute *De Haeretico Comburendo*, 'Regarding the Burning of Heretics', authorised the burning of all heretics who preached or even held beliefs contrary to the Catholic faith. It was aimed specifically at the Lollards. In 1407 all English translations of the Bible were banned. In 1413 a council in Rome ordered all Wyclif's works to be burned. The tenets of orthodox faith were reasserted by the Archbishop of Canterbury, Thomas Arundel, in his *Constitutions* of 1409. On shrines he ordered that 'it be commonly taught and preached, that the cross and image of the crucifix, and other images of the saints . . . are to be worshipped with processions, bowing of knees, offering of frankincense, kissings, oblations, lighting of candles and pilgrimages, and with all other kind of ceremonies and manners that have been used since the time of our predecessors'.[3] However, the movement was too diffuse and drew on too many grievances to be easily suppressed. 'Heretic' was a polemical term that was impossible to define with any theological clarity. Lollard ideas persisted in England through to the Reformation, as the tattered remains of constantly re-read tracts attest. Eventually, the Lollards were absorbed into the wider stream of Protestantism.

One unexpected offshoot of Wyclif's preaching flourished in Bohemia. A link had been provided by the marriage of the English king Richard II to Anne of Bohemia, the daughter of the Holy Roman emperor, in January 1382. When the couple returned to Bohemia, Wyclif's ideas appear to have travelled with them. The Czech nobility were as restless with traditional Catholicism as were the followers of Wyclif. Prague was open to new ideas, not least those of Renaissance Italy, which had influenced its architecture as early as the fourteenth century. Jan Hus (*c.*1370–1415), a priest in the university of Prague's faculty of philosophy and later rector of the university, warmed to Wyclif's concerns.[4] In an attempt to create a distinctive movement that responded to popular belief, Hus reintroduced the chalice to the Eucharist and so gave new purpose to the sacrament in a way that Wyclif would not have approved. On other issues Hus followed Wyclif. His *De Sanguine Christi*, 'On the Blood of Christ', written in about 1405, is a major attack on blood relics, especially the shrine at Wilsnack that Hus had examined in person. His reports, as a commissioner sent by the Bishop of Prague, had resulted in members of the diocese being forbidden to go there.

Hus develops his argument to go beyond blood relics. His attacks were rooted in the desire to return to a purer Church, centred on direct devotion to Christ, and free of the many corruptions that had crept in. Faith needed to be directed towards God and should not be distorted or disrupted by the medium of relics. He quoted John 20:29: 'Blessed are they that have not seen, and yet have believed.' Relics were often fakes or even works of the

Devil and diverted worship from the sacraments such as the Eucharist. Wilsnack was a good example as the bloodstained hosts there were given greater reverence than the consecrated host itself. The lure of offerings encouraged unscrupulous priests to create relics for profit.

Hus follows Guibert of Nogent (see p. 118) in refusing to accept that Christ could have left any of his body on earth. To venerate pieces of Christ was a denial of everything that the Saviour had offered of himself by ascending in perfection to heaven. Hus focused on stories he had heard where blood relics had been seen to be fraudulent: a host had been smeared with blood from a priest's bleeding finger; a miracle of the healing of a withered hand had been proclaimed from the pulpit when the supposed recipient was able to hold up a hand to show it was as withered as ever.

This was only one aspect of Hus's teachings. He challenged the hierarchy of the Church, its persistent superstitions and the corruption of the popes. With the Great Schism under way, Hus exploited the disillusionment of the faithful and he had widespread public support. However, opposition coalesced against him from conservative churchmen and Wenceslas, the king of Bohemia, who was worried at growing popular unrest. The popes granted secular rulers a percentage of money raised from their territories through the sale of indulgences, and so Wenceslas stood to lose if indulgences were abolished as Hus demanded. Hus was taken to questioning at the Council of Constance and here, refusing to recant his opposition to the structure of the Church, he was condemned to be burned in July 1415. This is a reminder that conciliar government in the Church would not necessarily have led to greater tolerance of dissent. Hus's death caused fury in Bohemia and concerted assaults on shrines took place at the hands of his followers. This was the first major outburst of iconoclasm in western Christendom.

Hus's followers retained Communion in both kinds, host and chalice, body and blood, as the symbol of their commitment to his memory. The movement was widespread enough to support an independent 'national' Church rejoicing in the use of Czech for its worship. The Catholic Church retaliated through a series of crusades against 'Wyclifites and Hussites, and other heretics and unbelievers infesting the whole of the Kingdom of Bohemia and its adjacent regions and striving to wipe out the Catholic faith'. Both sides claimed that theirs was a holy war and each victory was treated as evidence that God was on their side (the normal pragmatic justification of a legitimate holy war). Despite the hostility of the papacy, the Hussite Church survived as the most visible example of the decentralisation of fifteenth-century Christianity.[5]

The followers of Wyclif and Hus drew on deeper popular resentments. The next attack was more elitist and deliberately satirical, from one of the finest minds of the sixteenth century, Desiderius Erasmus (c.1466–1536). Erasmus was born, probably in Rotterdam, the illegitimate son of a priest.[6] He had a solid monastic education and was himself ordained a priest before taking vows as an Augustinian canon. However, the monastic life was never attractive to him and he became the model of the wandering scholar, visiting French and Italian universities as well as Cambridge where he taught between 1511 and 1514. His correspondence was vast, his curiosity intense and his mastery of Greek enabled him to penetrate beyond the crude translations of the New Testament made by Jerome in the fourth century to search for the deeper original meanings of, for instance, the letters of Paul, which had never been read in the original in the west. Erasmus had the sensitive, well-trained and searching mind of the humanist (see further p. 247 below) and a natural antipathy to the pretensions of the popes, their wealth and the superstitions they condoned. Julius II (r. 1503–13) was a target of his satire. Erasmus imagines how Julius arrives at the gates of heaven puffed up with his 'achievements', only to be refused admission by St Peter.

Erasmus's work on the Scriptures had shown him that the cult of the Virgin Mary was based on later legend and so he was unenthusiastic about the shrines in her honour (although he retained a belief in her perpetual virginity). He wished to cut down the foliage of her titles and see her instead as a woman of great but simple faith, free of the richness of clothing and bejewelled thrones that traditional Catholic iconography had made obligatory. Here he would be at one with the Protestant reformers. One of Erasmus's most biting satires has Ogygius, a traditional Catholic of some credulity, visiting the shrine of Mary at Walsingham and, on his return, regaling his sceptical friend Menedemus with an account of his experiences. Erasmus had visited the shrine himself twice as well as that of Thomas Becket in Canterbury, also included in the satire.

In the *Pilgrimage for Religion's Sake*, published for the first time in 1526, and so when the Reformation's assaults on the shrines (described in the next chapter) had already begun, Ogygius begins by telling of a 'relic' of a letter the Virgin has written through the hand of an angel.[7] It is addressed to a Protestant preacher and thanks him for telling his congregation that intercession through the saints is worthless. The Virgin explains that she has been overwhelmed by petitions. Many of these are hopelessly inappropriate. There are philosophers asking for help in solving problems, a priest in search of a better benefice, old men who want a return to youth, young girls demanding a rich husband and soldiers praying for more loot from war. Now she is relieved of all this importuning. She may be left with nothing more than a mouse-eaten cloak in comparison to the gold and jewels she used to be clothed in, but she can endure this. However, she now hears that everything belonging to the saints is to be removed from the churches. This is hardly fair so far as she is concerned as, unlike saints like George with his spear and the Apostle Peter with his power to shut the gates of heaven, she has no weapons for a counter-attack against the despoilers. She does warn the preacher, however, that if he expels her from the Church, she will take her Son with her.

Here Erasmus seems to be referring to the sweep-out of the cults that followed the Reformation in Protestant areas (see Chapter 23) and he suggests it might have gone too far. Even Christ risks being thrown out of the Church. Erasmus was at one with his friend, the devout Catholic and future English martyr Thomas More, who freely accepted that many relics were fraudulent but the principle of intercession of the saints through their shrines remained valid. However, when Ogygius arrives at Walsingham (which the English Reformers did not dismantle until the late 1530s), Erasmus uses him to gently ridicule the shrine. There is a box for offerings but one of the monks is always beside it and so it is difficult to avoid giving. There is some embarrassment when one of Ogygius's companions is shown a large thighbone which is apparently that of the Apostle Peter. When he mocks the claim, the custodian becomes angry and they have to pay more money before they can be shown the shrine's other relics. The copy of the Virgin's house at Nazareth that houses the her statue seems suspiciously new, but they are shown an old bearskin nailed to the door as 'evidence' of its antiquity. The famous phial of the Virgin's milk is picked up by a monk who has clad himself in a special stole before he proffers it to the visitors. When Ogygius innocently asks how they know it is the real milk, they are shown a board with all the details of the long journey through many hands that the phial had made from Constantinople. The custodian assures them that while most other relics of the Virgin's milk have been scraped off rocks, this one was gathered straight from her breasts.

Then Ogygius is asked to help decipher some old script and he is able to translate a few words from the Latin. In return he is offered a piece of wood from a beam on which the Virgin Mary had once stood. The fragrance of the wood confirms its sanctity. Ogygius is so delighted with his gift that the custodians decide to show him the more precious relics. One of these is a jewel placed at the foot of the Virgin's statue that has the image of a toad in it which seems alive. When Menedemus refuses to believe this, Ogygius replies that he has actually seen it and just as no one would believe a magnet could attract or repel steel unless they had seen it happen, his word must be taken on trust. The jewel had been placed before the Virgin as a symbol of her power to overcome impurity and avarice and all worldly passions.

Then Ogygius moves south to Canterbury. Here the shrine of Thomas Becket is altogether more opulent. It is housed in a massive church complete with two towers. On the altar inside is the rusty sword that killed Thomas, and the pilgrims reverently kiss it. Thomas's skull, encased in silver with an exposed patch at the top for kissing, is in the crypt together with the hair shirt, girdle and drawers he was wearing when martyred. A jumble of other relics are kept in the choir. As they wander around with the guide, one Gratian, an Englishman, joins the group. (Gratian was modelled on Erasmus's friend John Colet, the scholar and Dean of St Paul's.) Gratian is less happy than Ogygius with all these bones and the gold, silver and rich vestments they are shown and he begins asking pointed questions. 'Was Thomas kind to the poor when he was alive?' 'Yes, he certainly was', replies the guide. 'Then surely he would have wanted all this opulence to have been distributed to the poor', Gratian ripostes. The guide is furious at the suggestion and would have thrown them out if Ogygius had not made a further offering and claimed the friendship of the archbishop. Among other relics, they are shown Thomas's used handkerchiefs and other rags, and the guide is most offended when Gratian refuses to accept one as a gift.

Menedemus supports Gratian's point but, in reply, Ogygius does his best to justify the wealth of the shrines. The money is better spent here than on gambling and war. If the gold and silver were sold off, no one would give more offerings. The dismemberment of the shrines would encourage theft and sacrilege. 'I'd rather see a church abounding in sacred furnishings than bare and dirty as some are, and more like stables than churches.' When the pilgrims leave Canterbury for London, they are accosted by an old beggar who thrusts a shoe under their noses. He claims that it is Thomas's shoe and he has a crowd of dependants to support. Gratian again is offended but Ogygius gives the old man a tip. He concludes by reflecting that Thomas is almost more use dead than alive. He caused a great Cathedral to be built, won more power for the English clergy through the manner of his death and a worn shoe of his seems able to support a whole household of beggars.

Erasmus had hoped against hope that the Catholic Church might reform itself, cutting out superstitions and indulgences and quelling the arrogant behaviour of the papacy. He also wished to restore the optimism about the human condition that had been so badly eroded by the doctrines of Augustine. Here Erasmus championed Origen, the third-century AD Church Father from Alexandria. Origen was a man of enormous learning, tolerance and humanity, an understandable role model for Erasmus himself. He believed in the power of human beings to earn salvation through their own efforts and had even suggested that there was no place for a hell of eternal punishment. Origen argued that eternal damnation made nonsense of the idea of a forgiving God. Could God really be so easily thwarted by mere human beings that he could only respond by throwing them into the flames? Decrying Augustine's views on the burden of original sin, Erasmus argued instead that 'the greatest part of the tendency to evil comes not from nature [e.g. the state of original sin] but from corrupted educational method, poor nourishment, the habit of sinning and an evil will'.[8] Human beings have some control over their destinies and can, surely, rely on some support from God in doing right. If this was the case, they would not, of course, need to rely on the intercession of saints, still less on indulgences.

As Erasmus was composing his satires on the worldliness and superstition of the Church, in 1517 in the small university town of Wittenberg, Martin Luther (1483–1546), an Augustinian monk, challenged the new wave of indulgences that the Pope had launched to raise money for his building programmes in Rome, notably the completion of the new St Peter's, and to launch a crusade against the Turks. A single monk was an unlikely protagonist for an assault on the Church, but anti-papal feeling ran so high in Germany that his campaign had massive popular support that extended to many of the German secular rulers. Luther was handled clumsily by the Church authorities sent to confront him, and between 1517 and 1520 he matured as the instigator of a complete break with Catholicism. 'Here I stand, I can do no other,' was his famous riposte to the Habsburg emperor, Charles V, at Worms in 1521, when summoned to the Diet there to explain himself. The Protestant Reformation had truly begun.[9]

Protestantism and the New Iconoclasm

İn 1516, while Martin Luther was still formulating the theology that would lead him to break so decisively with the Catholic Church, he delivered a series of sermons that condemned idolatry.[1] As one element of 'idolatry' he included the superstitions to be found at the shrines. He noted how Christians had made the saints their slaves and returned to polytheism. 'It still causes us Christians no shame to share out the business of worldly things among the saints, as if they had now become servants and bonded labourers: things have nearly gone back to that morass of superstitions, such that we have once again created the confusion of gods among the Romans, and made a new pantheon.'[2] Here Luther was going no further than many other clerics and critics of his day.

This was, however, only the beginning. As Luther developed a more coherent theology he reiterated, to Erasmus's intense disappointment, a belief in the abject nature of humanity. There would have been no point in the death on the Cross if humanity had not been in desperate need of salvation. 'If we believe that Christ redeemed men by his blood, we are forced to confess that all of man was lost; otherwise we make Christ superfluous which is blasphemy and sacrilege', as he put it in his *On the Slavery of the Will* of 1525. Here Luther proved himself a champion of Augustine (and, through Augustine, the Apostle Paul) rather than Origen. It was an allegiance of immense importance for the history of western thought as it left the majority of humankind still destined for hellfire. Luther went on to claim that it was faith and faith alone that might win salvation. Good works or any other way of manipulating God into forgiveness meant nothing. Nor was there anything about purgatory in Scripture: it was heaven or hell with nothing in between.

In his *Open Letter to the Christian Nobles of Germany* of 1520,[3] a rallying cry for opposition to the papacy and all its evils as he saw them, Luther went on to lambast the whole set-up of indulgences, pilgrimages and shrines. Pilgrimages are a misuse of money. 'It often happens that one goes on a pilgrimage to Rome, spends fifty or one hundred guilders more or less, which no one has commanded him, while his wife and children are left at home in want and misery.' There is enormous competition between shrines to encourage pilgrims even though the aim is solely to get more money. 'Where pilgrimages are a failure, they begin to glorify their saints, not to honour the saints, who are sufficiently honoured without them, but to cause a concourse, and to bring in money. Herein pope and bishops help them; it rains indulgences. I wish one would leave the good saints alone, and not lead the poor people astray.' Instead, Luther argues, every man should keep to his own parish, 'where he will profit more than in all these shrines, even if they were all put together into one shrine. Here a man finds baptism, the Sacrament, preaching, and his neighbour, and these are more than all the saints in heaven.' Luther does not deny miracles can occur but he deplores the way they are presented and used by those who will get monetary advantage from them.

Luther goes on to develop the theme of his *Open Letter* to argue that intercession through the saints is meaningless:

> For the Word of God is the sanctuary above all sanctuaries, yea, the only one which we Christians know and have. For though we had the bones of all the saints or all holy and consecrated garments upon a heap, still that would help us nothing; for all that is a dead thing which can sanctify nobody. But God's Word is the treasure which sanctifies everything, and by which even all the saints themselves were sanctified.

This was a critical shift of focus towards Christianity as a meticulously examined body of sacred texts that had been screened too long from the faithful by the glamour of relic cults.

By destroying any justification for the shrines, Luther was creating a void. One might hope that in an age when breadth was returning to learning through the humanists, he would attack all forms of superstition and thus open the way for a more rational approach to religious belief. Far from it.

Luther had removed purgatory, indulgences and the shrines, all the traditional methods of avoiding eternal suffering, but he had left the prospect of that suffering intact. Not even good works would help to avoid it. The only hope he left was that God might look benevolently and directly on His creation. This hope was shattered by Luther's adoption of the fifteenth-century view of the Devil as a constant and God-permitted presence in the material world:

> For it is undeniable that the devil lives, yes, rules, in all the world. Therefore witchcraft and sorcery are works of the devil, by which he not only injures people but sometimes, with God's permission [*sic*], destroys them. We are guests in the world, of which he is the ruler and the god. Therefore the bread we eat, the drinks we drink, the clothes we wear – in fact, the air and everything we live on in the flesh – are under his reign.[4]

So, Luther goes on, it is the Devil that is responsible for corrupting the pure Scriptures and replacing them with the power of the Catholic Church. This elevates the whole debate to a level of cosmic drama far beyond anything that the fifteenth-century demonologists had envisaged. It was Luther and the Scriptures on one side; the Devil and the Catholic Church on the other. *On the Papacy at Rome, Founded by the Devil* is one tract of 1544. So this was still a world in the grip of supernatural forces, but the evil ones appeared to be dominant. The only consolation Luther could offer was that eventually Christ would triumph. In a passage from a commentary on Galatians, Luther argues that the Devil attacks humans precisely because they do have faith, yet ultimately 'Christ has always led us in triumph, and he is still triumphing through us. From this we gain the firm hope that through Christ we shall eventually emerge as victors over the devil . . .'.

Faced with demands for the actual destruction of shrines, Luther proved cautious. He was a natural conservative, quick, for instance, to support the authorities and their repression of a major peasants' revolt in 1524–25. Lutheranism would never have survived in the long run without the support of princes. He accepted that altars, pulpits, fonts and vestments played a legitimate role in worship even though they could not, of course, hold any sacred power in themselves. So he did not urge stripping out the churches.

However other, more radical, Protestant preachers were not so restrained. They were encouraged by an important shift in the presentation of Scripture. The Old and New Testaments had been known only in the west in Jerome's Vulgate (Latin) translation of the fourth century, but now original Hebrew and Greek versions became available for scholars to translate into vernacular languages and so make available for all. It was quite startling for many to read St Paul's letters in the original Greek for the first time, nearly fifteen hundred years after they had been written. They opened up fresh challenges of interpretation.

With no one in the west able to read the originals until now, Augustine's personal interpretations of the Scriptures had remained enormously influential. One of his readings had involved conflating the first two Commandments as if they were one so that the First Commandment, 'I am the Lord your God, who brought you out of the land of Egypt, out of the house of slavery; you shall have no other gods before me', was joined to the words 'You shall not make to yourself a graven image, or any likeness of anything . . . you shall not bow down to them or serve them'. In 1523, for the first time in the west, a distinguished Protestant and a Hebrew scholar, Leo Jud (1482–1542), pointed out that in the eastern Church these had always been two commandments. With the second standing on its own, it gained a new resonance. The vast displays of imagery, including statues, shrines and relics, were all vulnerable to scriptural assault, and so it proved.[5] In the 1520s a number of cities began the destruction of images, shrines and relics.[6]

It is extraordinarily difficult to assess the various forces, social, economic, political and, not least, theological, that coalesced to allow the systematic destruction of the shrines. There was, of course, educated opposition to many of their rituals even within the Catholic Church itself. There was a deeper sense of alienation created by the wealth of the Church and, in northern Europe in particular, the Roman papacy must have seemed irrelevant to everyday religious life. This fuelled ever greater resentment towards its fundraising campaigns. The clergy had become an elite whose sanctified position as creators of the 'body of Christ' had distanced them from the laity. In contrast, the reformers were often excellent preachers, able to restore rapport with the masses. They appealed, too, to the urban middle classes, hard-working thrifty citizens, many of whom had already found alternative forms of religious expression in the years before the Reformation. These men were to be found on the town councils that were now to take the opportunity to make laws of religion. Even though the mass of the population, and some artisan classes who benefited from the demands for craftsmanship, might have been happy to acquiesce in sustaining Catholicism, they were outflanked by new sources of spiritual energy.[7] The focus on the destruction of the shrines suggests that they had become the most obvious and visible symbol of the old Church and the easiest to dislodge without retaliation.

Leo Jud preached in the Swiss town of Zurich. Among his colleagues there was Huldrych Zwingli (1484–1531), a charismatic preacher who had broken with the Catholic Church in 1520 and begun pushing for reform. Zwingli found a ready audience in Zurich, especially as the papacy had recently allied with the Catholic Habsburgs, traditional enemies of the Swiss, and there was growing fear that the undercurrents of reform in the city would be extinguished by these powers.

Yet, nominally, Zurich was still a Catholic city and, despite growing popular support, the reformers were no more than an uncoordinated movement of enthusiasts. Tensions ran high. In January 1523 the town council called a meeting to discuss the religious future of the city. The council represented the craftsmen and artisans and while there was some sympathy for reform there was none at all for disorder. The first, hesitant, decision of the council was to agree to base future laws solely on the authority of Scripture. The Protestant preachers insisted that this would mean the removal of images and relics.

The process was not smooth because the town council feared that a free-for-all would result in destruction and theft. They used some clever semantics. Normally, an assault on a sacred object would have been classed as 'blasphemy'; now it was recast as mere 'vandalism'. When a crucifix with the body of Christ on it was pulled down by a reformer, the perpetrator was punished only for 'riotousness'. One 'defence' to such charges was that the money tied up in the wood of the statues and images might be better used to make fires to keep the poor warm, and so the destroyer of the image was acting with benevolent intentions.

The reformers saw their chance. In October 1523 a second meeting of the town council to discuss the issue was dominated by passionate arguments in favour of removing all images. Still the council wavered. It agreed that anyone who had contributed an image or statue themselves to a church could remove it. Otherwise, images that had been provided by a parish could only be cleared out if the parish agreed to it. This seems to have held in check the movement in the town, but there were now reports coming in from rural communities, where the authority of the council was weaker, of individuals attacking images and removing them.

It was during 1524 that the council of Zurich gradually came to accept that popular feeling was in favour of removing images and that it must act to keep the initiative. Its members articulated their new policy in theological terms. A law of June 1524 ordered that all should 'turn themselves from the idols entirely to the living true God'. The wealth of the dismantled shrines and images should be turned over to the poor 'who are a true image of God'. The council attempted to make the process as orderly as possible, urging preachers to oversee the removals, but only a month later it accepted that the only way to avoid chaos was to take charge of the dismantling of images itself. So it was the council that closed off each church and sent in craftsmen to destroy the sculptures, altarpieces and wooden panels. The sculptures were turned into cobblestones, the metals melted down for the poor and the vestments handed to them to wear. The relics of the patron saints of Zurich, Felix and Regula, disappeared; they may have been secretly buried.

So, in Zurich, the Reformation and the destruction of shrines and images was a fairly well-controlled process. In other cities there was a different balance of forces. Strasbourg with a population of some 20,000 was four times as large as Zurich and an important commercial centre on the borders between Catholic (Habsburg) territories and newly Protestant ones. Its government was stable and was to prove more resistant to the importuning of radical preachers for the removal of images. There were conservative forces, some religious, notably in the great cathedral that dominated the city, and they remained solidly Catholic. Other forces were commercial, notably among craftsmen whose livelihood depended on commissions from the many churches and monasteries. The Reformers were led by Martin Bucer, one of the most effective preachers of the period.

On 2 February 1524, the Feast of the Purification of the Virgin, there were signs of unrest. Normally on this feast day a procession set out from Strasbourg Cathedral carrying the city's relics, among them those of St Agnes, a Roman martyr. When these relics were returned to St Agnes's chapel in the cathedral, a group broke in, grabbed the offerings made to the shrine and stuffed them into the poor box. The attending priest was told to clear out and take his idols with him. In March, during Holy Week, the week of the Passion that led to Easter, a similar attack took place in Young St Peter's church that had been given special rights by the Pope to award indulgences during Holy Week. Here again, collection boxes were grabbed, lamps extinguished and the money put into the poor boxes.

Throughout 1524 these disruptions continued in Strasbourg. As with Zurich, it was the sheer cost of all the ornaments, cloths, processions and candles that were the subject of attack. Lamps set before images and shrines were always unpopular, not only as a symbol of the reverence shown to images, but because the cost of their oil was a constant one that came from the tithes contributed by the faithful. In November, probably as a direct response to the traditional Feast of All Saints, Martin Bucer was responsible for organizing a raid on the church of St Aurelia, digging up its patron saint's grave and throwing bones found in the coffin into the charnel house.

The town council of Strasbourg prevaricated. It announced that it was considering the question of images but until it had come to a decision they must be respected and left in place. It called for responses and one survives from six burghers. They listed a number of images that they saw as 'a grave affront to the Word of God'. 'All idols are aggravating, in all churches, not to the perfected Christians, but to the weak, and to those who have not yet taken on the Word of God, whence the great uproar. For all idols are against the Word of God and therefore risen from the Devil. They can bring no good fruit.' The burghers represented a swell of public support. By 1526 even the guilds were petitioning the town council to allow them to sell the ornaments and gems they used in religious processions and distribute the proceeds to the poor and the smallpox hospital. The council agreed and the city seems to have become calmer for the next three years.

In 1529 a much more aggressive campaign began in Strasbourg against all images and superstition. It was led by the preachers. By now they seem to have built up widespread support and the town council gave in. In a law of February 1530 they decreed that 'images are completely against God and his order'. The alms officers were to supervise their removal. It was a vain hope that order would be kept. Even when the officers were actually at work, gangs broke in to churches and began breaking up images. Those at Young

St Peter's were 'mischievously thrown out, smashed and handled to great offense'. The more ardent reformers insisted that the churches should be cleared so thoroughly that it would not even be obvious where the altars had originally stood. Even so, some images survived in the city and when, in 1681, Strasbourg was annexed to France and the city 'recatholicised', the churches were once more filled with decoration.

Just a year before, on 9 February 1529, a crowd of some two hundred had moved through the Swiss city of Basel, entering each church and smashing all its statues, crucifixes, reliquaries and chalices. The next day the town council oversaw the completion of the destruction, piling up the wooden statues before the churches and burning them. The violence was all the more surprising for Basel had a reputation as a civilised and peaceful city that had been a haven for erudite humanists, including Erasmus. However, it was also noted for the division between the clergy, ensconced in the city's cathedral almost as if in a fortress, and the laity. The cathedral chapter drew its members only from the nobility and these did not even have to be natives of the area.

The town council of Basel had been aware of increasing tension among the more extreme preachers and lay people of the city, but many of its members remained Catholic and reluctant to sanction any moves to abolish the traditional Mass. There was soon an impasse, with the reformers insisting that there could only be one true Church of God and the council refusing to go further than to limit the traditional powers of the city's Catholic bishop. It was this frustration that led to crowds gathering on 9 February, targeting the cathedral that had locked its doors against them and then destroying whatever they could get hold of. The town council capitulated completely. When more violence broke out the next day in squabbles over how the wood from the statues should be distributed, the council took the initiative of ordering the burning of the statues.

All the famous relics the city had accumulated were thrown out with the statues. They were an impressive array, parts of the Apostles Peter and Paul and Andrew, the martyr Lawrence, the monk St Benedict, Henry II the founder of the cathedral, milk of the Virgin and a finger of John the Baptist. There were three heads: of St Panthal, the founding bishop of the city, of St Ursula and St Eustace. The transformation that had taken place in Basel was not simply the destruction of superstition, it was also about who actually controlled religious belief. The rioting was the symbolic moment when the people took possession of the city's religious life from the isolated Catholic hierarchy who had dominated it until then. There was a political edge to what seemed an outburst of religious fervour.

A much more sweeping written denunciation and dismissal of the cults came from John Calvin (1509–64), who presided over the Protestant community in the Swiss city of Geneva.[8] Calvin was well educated, a lawyer rather than a theologian by training, a vivid writer, and his published works sold widely in Protestant Europe, even though the Lutherans found him too radical. While his position in Geneva was always precarious, he was consistent in his opposition to any form of religious practice or behaviour that seemed to come from man rather than from God and this is what impelled his famous critique of relic cults, the *Treatise on Relics* (1543). It is a brilliant piece of propaganda.

Calvin begins the *Treatise* by going back to Augustine's own (early) suspicion of cults and stating that ever since the fourth century greater corruption has crept into the practice. It had distracted from the worship of God. 'Instead of discerning Jesus Christ in his Word, his Sacraments, and his Spiritual Graces, the world has, according to its custom, amused itself with his clothes, shirts, and sheets . . .'. It was much the same with the Apostles, martyrs, and other saints:

> Instead of observing their lives in order to imitate their examples, it directed all its attention to the preservation and admiration of their bones, shirts, sashes, caps, and other similar trash. . . . It will thus be found that, to have relics is a useless and frivolous thing, which will most probably gradually lead towards idolatry, because they cannot be handled and looked upon without being honored, and in doing this men will very soon render them the honor which is due to Jesus Christ. . . . In short, the desire for relics is never without superstition, and what is worse, it is usually the parent of idolatry.

Calvin also denies any idea that bodies can be preserved in a state fit for resurrection. 'All flesh is dust and to dust it must return.' Only at the Last Judgement will the 'dust' be reassembled into the bodies of the deceased and until then they must be left unmolested in the grave.

Once he has established his theme, Calvin embarks on a survey of many of the shrines he has visited. Virtually every event, whether recorded in the Gospels or not, has its relics, and often the relic of the same object is in several places. So the water pots that held the water changed into wine at Cana are to be found in Pisa and Ravenna in Italy, Cluny in France and Antwerp. At Orléans the cathedral goes one better as it has the actual wine itself and once a year the priests give it out in spoonfuls, with the residue always being replenished from year to year. As for the Crown of Thorns, Calvin suggests that the thorns must have sprouted. In addition to the Crown in the Saint-Chapelle in Paris, there are two more churches in Paris with individual thorns from the Crown. Then there are 'a good many at Siena, one at Vicenza, four at Bourges, three at Besançon, three at Port Royal, and I do not know how many at Salvatierra in Spain, two at St. James of Compostela, three at Albi, and one at least in the following places – Toulouse, Macon, Charroux in Poitiers, Cleri, St. Flour, St. Maximira in Provence, in the abbey of La Salle at St. Martin of Noyon'. There are so many pieces of the True Cross that they would fill the hold of a cargo ship.

Calvin also criticises a shroud in which it is claimed that the body of Christ was wrapped while he was in the sepulchre. (It seems similar to the shroud then in Chambéry, now in Turin, but there were many such shrouds by the sixteenth century).[9] However, as Jewish burial custom requires the head to be wrapped separately and John's Gospel specifically states that 'a napkin which had been over his head' is described as lying apart from the other wrappings in the tomb (20:6), then that in itself is enough to destroy the authenticity of the shroud. 'With regard to the milk [of Mary], there is not perhaps a town, a convent, or nunnery, where it is not shown in large or small quantities. . . . Indeed, had the Virgin been a wet-nurse her whole life, or a dairy, she could not have produced more than is shown as hers in various parts.' Calvin is particularly scathing about relics that appear to have done harm, such as the nails of the Cross or a knife that pierced a host, which still receive veneration in their own right. Then there are relics that are supposed to have been used by angels, such as the sword with which the archangel Michael took on Satan, preserved at Carcassonne. Calvin remarks that it is so small it is hard to see how it could have succeeded in its task.

So Calvin works his way through the saints. John the Baptist is represented by several heads and the finger with which he pointed out Christ. At

St John Lateran in Rome, they claim to have the camel skin that he wore in the desert, but it turns out to be made of horsehair. The Apostle Paul apparently wore slippers of satin embroidered with gold, as preserved at Poitiers in central France. Six of the Apostles have two bodies while Bartholomew has his skin preserved at Pisa in northern Italy. St Stephen is scattered among three hundred shrines and several of them also have some of the stones that killed him. So the litany goes on. Calvin concludes:

> I repeat what I said at the commencement of this treatise, that it would be most important to abolish from amongst us Christians this pagan superstition of canonizing relics, either of Christ or of his saints, in order to make idols of them; for this is a defilement and an impurity which should never be suffered in the Church. We have already proved that it is so by arguments, and also from the evidence of Scripture. Let those who are not yet satisfied look to the practices of the ancient fathers, and conform to their examples.

The process of Reformation in England was similar in its eradication of the shrines, yet different in that the riches of the shrines were not diverted to the poor but to the coffers of the wealthiest man in the kingdom, King Henry VIII. There were deep-rooted tensions within English religious life well before the 1530s, as the persistence of Lollard activity makes clear. However, they would never have coalesced into a reform movement without the impetus given by the king. By 1525 the energetic and brilliant youth who had succeeded his father, Henry VII, in 1509, had become preoccupied by the failure of his wife, the devoutly Catholic Catherine of Aragon, to provide him with a male heir (she had only produced a daughter, the future Queen Mary). Obsessed with his predicament, which he ascribed to the wrath of God, Henry began importuning the Pope, now Clement VII, to annul the marriage.

The Pope stood firm and Henry now claimed that ancient precedents allowed him to assert himself as head of the English Church. The marriage with Catherine was declared invalid. In 1533 Henry married his pregnant mistress Anne Boleyn and she presented him with another daughter, Elizabeth, like her elder half-sister, Mary, a future Queen of England. The Act of Supremacy of 1534 was the formal recognition of a new regime that had eliminated papal authority in England. Thomas More, formerly the king's Chancellor and friend of Erasmus, was executed when his conscience refused to allow him to acquiesce in the coup. Anne followed him in 1536 after her own failure to produce a male heir grated on the king. Only in October 1537 did the third of Henry's wives, Jane Seymour, produce the hoped-for male heir, the future Edward VI, before herself dying of the complications of the birth a few days later.

The Act of Supremacy gave Henry the right to 'visit, repress, redress, reform, order, correct, restrain and amend all such errors, heresies and enormities which by any manner of spiritual authority or jurisdiction ought or may lawfully be reformed. . . .' No one could be sure in 1534 what this would mean in practice. The king prided himself on his theological expertise but there were other able men ready to give a spiritual cloak to the king's ambitions to make himself Supreme Head of the Church of England. These men had their own links to the continent. The Archbishop of Canterbury, Thomas Cranmer, was a reformer, a close friend of Martin Bucer of Strasbourg. The most powerful and efficient of the king's ministers, Thomas Cromwell, was more pragmatic and opportunist but he was able to divert the theological currents in such a way as to secure the resources of the Church for the Crown. While the shape of the future Anglican Church was still unresolved, the demands of Cromwell and the reformers were to see the dismantling of the rich panoply of English parish life.

From 1535 onwards the ever efficient and ruthless Thomas Cromwell began organising visitations to the monasteries that still dotted the English landscape.[10] By 1536 it was clear that this was not merely a traditional visitation, to ensure that there were no abuses, but a campaign to close the smaller monasteries down and to transfer their wealth to the Crown. They were accused of harbouring 'manifest sin, vicious, carnal and abominable living', and in the next four years all monasteries and friaries were dissolved. A smear campaign produced such texts as *A Declaration that the Prior of the Crochet Friars in London was found in Bed with a Whore*. A growing number of references to superstition crept into the legislation that dealt with the monastic houses. At first, the only restriction placed on relics was that they should not be displayed openly, but the commissioners began ridiculing those that they found. Bath Abbey had a comb used by Mary Magdalen and the chains of St Peter that women wrapped around them when about to give birth. Several other shrines had girdles of the Virgin that their women used for the same purpose. Bury St Edmunds had some coals from the fire over which Lawrence was roasted and St Edmund's pared fingernails. The commissioners warmed to their task, competing with each other to express their disdain at what they had found.

The most sweeping denunciation of relics came from the Bishop of Worcester, the reformer Hugh Latimer, in June 1536. He must have had official backing for such an outspoken attack, but he was able to add in his own contempt for what he saw as the superstitions of Catholic life. The gold and silver that clothed so many statues could be better used to relieve distress. The vast numbers of saints' days broke up the working year and made it hard for the poor to earn a sustained living. Far too many of these feasts ended in drunkenness and dissolution. Pilgrimages had degenerated so that they were no more than a means of traipsing from one image to another. As for relics, they were often pigs' bones that deluded the credulous minds of the faithful. The 'deceitful and juggling images' must all be swept away.

This was too radical for many of the clergy, most of whom wished to get rid of obvious abuses without destroying the fabric of Church life. Cromwell was too determined for them. Claiming that the feast days were disrupting the bringing in of harvest, he issued an Act in June 1536 that abolished most of the feasts held between 1 July and 29 September. As grumbling spread among some bishops and within many of the parishes, Cromwell issued a series of Injunctions to ensure conformity. Some of these involved the provision of English Bibles and instruction of the faithful in the Creed, the Ten Commandments and the Lord's Prayer, but they also included the first direct attack on parish relics. Clergy were ordered not 'to set forth or extol any images, relics or miracles for any superstitious lucre, nor allure the people by any enticements to the pilgrimage of any saint'. The money spent on pilgrimage should be diverted to alms for the poor and God should be appealed to directly rather than through the saints.

This was the first shot in the battle between old and new. Many resented the changes. In the north of England a 'Pilgrimage of Grace' in defence of traditional religion sputtered into life in protest, but it was easily suppressed. There were conflicts within parishes as clergy and congregations disagreed on how images and relics should be dealt with. Cromwell replied with skilful propaganda. The Rood of Boxley, a wooden statue, was found to have a mechanism inside that allowed its eyes to move. Cromwell used this as an example of how the monks had deliberately deceived visiting pilgrims. The famous blood of Hailes was shown to be a yellowish gum stained to make it appear red, although other reports said it was duck's blood that had been secretly renewed every week. A collection of wooden statues from the shrines were brought to Cromwell's house and the statues were burned in July 1538. They included the statue of the Virgin Mary from Walsingham that had been venerated by Henry only a few months earlier when he had visited the shrine and offered a candle there.

In September 1538 a harsher set of Injunctions were issued. The people were ordered not to 'repose their trust and affiance in any other works devised by men's phantasies beside Scripture; as in wandering to pilgrimages, offering of money, candles or tapers to images or relics, or kissing or licking the same, saying over a number of beads, not understood or minded on'. No longer could candles be placed before images or relics, and any clergy who had continued to preach the value of pilgrimages, relics or images must publicly recant. The bells that had traditionally been rung on the feast days of the Virgin Mary must be silenced.

The bishops responsible for enforcing the Injunctions varied in their zeal for reform. Archbishop Lee of York dutifully recited the demands of the king to his diocese and reiterated that images were no more than a means of learning from the examples of the saints portrayed. There must be no pilgrimages to an image and no offerings to any saint. Yet the pilgrimage shrines are the only ones he orders to be removed. Lee says nothing about banning the litanies of the saints or invocations to them. His language is moderate and he shows no enthusiasm for any abolition of the old ways of worship.

Contrast this with the fervour of Bishop Shaxton of Salisbury. In a document full of 'the perils of idolatry', the ignorance of lay people, the decrying of superstitious observances and the denouncing of 'old foolish customs', he is especially incensed by the relics that he has come across in his diocese, instruments of 'abominable idolatry'. They included 'stinking boots, mucky combs, ragged rochets, rotten girdles, pyld purses, great bullocks' horns, locks of hair, and filthy rags, gobbets of wood, under the name of parcels of the holy cross and such pelfry beyond estimation'. The Bishop of St David's was infuriated by the 'clatteringe conventycles of barbarous rurall persons' in his diocese who persisted in worshipping relics. For centuries pilgrims had made no mention of the actual state of the myriad of bones and fragments of flesh that they had seen displayed. Suddenly the reality of such relics was exposed. The emperor had no clothes.

Henry seems to have been taken aback by his minister's Injunctions and the radical way that some bishops such as Shaxton interpreted then. Later in 1538 the king issued a Proclamation that urged caution. One should not venerate images but this did not mean that they should be actively destroyed. This Proclamation is remarkable for shifting the propaganda away from the parishes to the memory of England's most celebrated saint, Thomas Becket. The enthusiastic canonisation of Thomas by Pope Alexander III in 1173 had been grounded in the determination of the Pope to humiliate an English king, Henry II. Henry VIII could not resist hitting back by rubbishing the cult of Thomas. There had always been doubt over Thomas's saintliness and the Lollards had questioned his immense wealth and worldliness, so there was some popular support for what was, in effect, as much a political as a religious campaign. Henry's propaganda insisted that Thomas had really been a rebel who had betrayed his country by fleeing to France and then fawning to the Bishop of Rome in the hope of overthrowing the legitimate laws of England.[11] Thomas was never worthy of being a saint. All images of him should be taken down, his feast day abolished and his name mentioned in no services. He was no martyr, wrote John Foxe in his celebrated *Book of Martyrs*, 'but a stubborn man against the king. . . . So superstitious he was to the Obedience of the Pope, that he forgot his Obedience to his natural and most beneficial king.' Foxe drew on ancient gossip that his miracles had not been true miracles but 'feigned and forged by idle monks, and religious bellies, for the exaltation of their churches and the profit of their pouches'. In a bizarre ritual Thomas was 'tried' at his tomb as a traitor.[12] He was given thirty days to 'defend himself' by miracles and when none were forthcoming, he was found guilty, his bones were to be burned and his personal property forfeited to the Crown. This was held to include the gold and stones on his shrine. It was duly dismantled in September 1538, the bones were dispersed and the treasures sent off to the king, who made a ring for himself out of the finest ruby.

Cromwell was executed in 1540 after the fiasco of the king's fourth marriage to Anne of Cleves, which had been arranged by Cromwell but was deeply distasteful to Henry as soon as he saw his new bride. Henry may also have been disturbed by the speed of change. There followed a difficult time as the ageing king's moods became increasingly irascible and unpredictable. The English Bible was now being read by the laity but as soon as Henry heard of quarrels going on over its interpretation, he reined in debate. However, when, on progress in the north of England, he passed through conservative areas where the shrines were still standing, he railed against them as a means 'to allure our subjects to their former hypocrisy and superstition'. The cathedrals must start clearing their shrines and the practice must then spread to the parish churches. *The King's Book* of 1543, a manual setting out details of acceptable worship, supported the dissolution of shrines and their relics but still allowed images of Christ and the saints so long as they were not given 'godly honour'. The *Book* denounced the abuses that belief in purgatory had given rise to but accepted that masses could be said for the dead. No wonder Archbishop Cranmer, himself intent on much more sweeping reform of traditional worship, was increasingly frustrated, but his influence over the king reasserted itself towards the end of Henry's reign when the *King's Primer* of May 1545 acquiesced in the disappearance of most saints' days and the traditional references to the Virgin Mary.

The death of Henry in January 1547 saw the accession of his nine-year-old son Edward, an intelligent but always sickly boy. As Edward grew into adolescence he was sympathetic to reform and Cranmer could now at last move to a more radical programme. A new set of Injunctions in 1547 launched an aggressive attack on the remaining shrines. Images might still remain but only as a remembrance of the saints portrayed on them. There must be no acts of reverence towards them, no candles or incensing. Injunction Twenty-Eight ordered the destruction of all 'monuments of feigned miracles, pilgrimage, idolatry and superstition'. All processions, including those always held before Sunday Mass, were to be banned. The traditional ceremonies of healing that involved the sprinkling of holy water were to be abolished as well as any 'superstitious' practice of ringing bells or blessing candles to discharge sin or drive away demons. Thirty commissioners were appointed to oversee the campaign and England was divided up so that between them all parishes would be covered. There was chaos as some enthusiasts broke up images and smashed stained-glass windows. Others bitterly resisted. The government wavered by insisting that images should only be painted over, not destroyed completely.

Whatever the attempt to avoid overt destruction, the Injunctions went to the heart of the life of the laity. An Act of January 1550 'for the defacing of images and the bringing in of books of old Service in the Church' took the process even further. The Mass was now recast as a ceremony of remembrance with every reference to sacrifice or consecration removed. Altars were to be replaced by an unadorned table and the clergy could wear only a simple surplice. The rich vestments of traditional worship were to be discarded. This was all enshrined in the Prayer Book of 1552, the most radical expression of the new Church. Even prayers for the dead disappeared as those deceased drifted into some ethereal world where they could no longer be reached by the intercessions of those left behind. The chantry chapels where their souls had been prayed for were closed as 'phantasising vain opinions of purgatory'. With them went their clergy who must have contributed in many ways to parish life as auxiliaries to the parish priest. Just before his early death in 1553 from tuberculosis, Edward assented to the Forty-Two Articles where it was declared that the worship and adoration of 'images, as of reliques, and also invocation of saints, is a fond thing vainlie feigned, and grounded upon no warraunt of scripture'.

After Edward's death, his half-sister Mary succeeded in 1553. She brought a return to the Catholicism of her devout mother Catherine of Aragon. Cranmer and other reformers were burned at the stake and the restoration of the traditional religion was put in hand. Vestments and images reappeared. The host was once again consecrated and even encased in a tabernacle in the centre of the altar. (This custom spread to the continent where tabernacles vied with each other in splendour and opulence.) Some relics emerged from hiding. Those of Edward the Confessor in Westminster Abbey had been hidden in 1540, were replaced in 1556, and are still there in their medieval shrine today.

Catholicism vanished again on Mary's death in 1558 when Anne Boleyn's daughter, the redoubtable and canny Elizabeth, succeeded. Elizabeth recognised the impossibility of enforcing religious attitudes on her people but she had to draw boundaries. Catholicism remained proscribed and there was another toll of martyrs, many of them priests secretly working for the restoration of the Catholic Church. The images and statues restored under Mary were stripped away again. Otherwise Elizabeth shrewdly fostered a moderate Anglican Church. Her Prayer Book of 1559 was a more restrained version of that of 1552. The prayers for the deliverance of the state from the tyranny of the Pope were dropped. The rubrics on the Eucharist suggested that the body of Christ might nourish after all. Priests could wear copes. Prayers could once again be said for the dead. The settlement was given vigour and status by fears that the Catholic states of Europe, above all that of Philip II in Spain, would try to reconquer England for their Church if she was more overtly radical.

The monasteries and friaries never again became an important part of English life. The new owners of their estates clung to them and the buildings fell in or were converted into mansions. There was no incentive to find the resources to endow new foundations. The shrines had disappeared. Their gold and silver was gathered for the king, hidden away or stolen. Remarkably little has survived. The medieval churches of England today still have the stone work or wooden screens on which their rood stood – the stone staircase up to them is a telltale sign – there are niches without statues, disused holy-water stoups and, in some lucky cases, wall paintings uncovered from the whitewashing of the reformers. The great windows of King's College Chapel, Cambridge, the commission of Henry VIII himself, and still dazzling in their depth of colour and sophistication, are a vivid reminder of how much has been lost. It was only below the surface that many ancient feast days survived, recast into the rhythm of the agricultural year that may have been their original inspiration, whatever the saint allocated to them. Sacred wells re-emerge as healing spas. The healing waters of Bath Abbey found a new life as the most fashionable watering place in England.

The ebb and flow of theological change between 1530 and 1570 was perplexing for most worshippers. Doubtless, if left to itself, English Catholicism would have survived. The English never had the obsession with doctrinal purity that could be found in Spain and so it is unlikely that there would ever have been a repressive Inquisition to arouse resentment. With England's growing wealth and openness to the world of Atlantic trade, commercial classes might have shown little respect for the more arcane practices of Catholicism, but it is hard to see them setting up a rival Church. The shrines might simply have faded away, curiosities from an earlier period. This is what the evidence of decline in the fifteenth century suggests. In the countryside things were more conservative and the changes felt more keenly. As Eamon Duffy has shown, in a number of sensitive studies of religious practice in English parish churches, much of comfort had been obtained from the annual round of rituals and feasts that gave structure to the rigours of agricultural life. This was now lost.[13]

As the potency of the images and relics disappeared and most vanished for ever, there was no appreciation that they might have an aesthetic value. The idea that the colour and exuberance of the churches added something to devotion or piety faded. The iconoclasm, which was to be renewed in the seventeenth century by the visitations of Cromwell's Puritans, in a campaign that saw the end of much medieval stained glass, was to have a further devastating effect. It is often forgotten how much of the rural economy was tied up in the maintenance of shrines and images in a period when foreign craftsmen had been attracted to England and were bringing new styles with them. Carvers, painters, glass-painters, embroiderers, goldsmiths and masons all had their skills enriched by Church patronage and these now atrophied. A satirical comment can be found in a book of 1590: 'Whereupon, the painters that lived with such trash, as trimming of shrines and roods, altars and saints, and the carvers, that made such images, were fain to cry out against [the apostle] Paul and his doctrine; having so little work, that they almost forgot their occupation.'[14] The shrines had played a major role in the medieval economy, and in Protestant areas this had now vanished. It was not until the eighteenth century that accomplished sculpture reappeared in England.

Intimations of Reality

W<small>HEN AN</small> earthquake hit Venice in 1511, the Patriarch interpreted it as a sign from God in response to the increase of sodomy in the city. The Doge agreed with him. After all, the city's prostitutes had been complaining that their own business was suffering as a consequence of this diversion in sexual behaviour. The diarist Marino Sanudo, who recorded the earthquake with his customary detachment, noted that all the ensuing days of fasting, procession and preaching that followed might have helped improve piety, 'but as a remedy for earthquakes, which are a natural phenomenon, this was no good at all'.[1] The 'heresy' of Philastrius of Brescia (p. 12 above) had been reasserted. Sanudo is reflecting a growing understanding of the natural world as subject to its own laws. This was just the period when the educated elites were returning to ideas that had been in abeyance for a thousand years, that the miraculous interventions of God were perhaps overplayed and that reasoned thought could be applied to most, perhaps all, natural phenomena. Symbolically, the moment of transition is Nicolaus Copernicus's recognition in *On the Revolutions of the Celestial Spheres*, published just before his death in 1543, that the earth and other planets revolved around the sun, 'one of the greatest of the intellectual leaps known to mankind'.[2]

The cults were as vulnerable to these intellectual developments as they were to the ridicule of the reformers, and this is why it is important to trace the revival of ideas that were independent of medieval theology. The cults relied on the pessimistic view of humanity passed down to the medieval Church from the works of the late Augustine on original sin. As so many medieval texts make clear, this view had placed an enormous psychological burden on the 'faithful' and helps explain the intense emotional relief that the relic cults offered. There had been some challenge to this pessimism from theologians such as Albertus Magnus and Thomas Aquinas who, through their studies of Aristotle, revived the idea that human beings could use reasoned thought for themselves. The Church now accepted that God's grace was not given arbitrarily but might be gained through the sacraments, good works and almsgiving. Even so, the use of reason was acceptable only so long as it did not conflict with the faith and authority of the Church.[3]

The Protestant reformers did not challenge the belief that human beings were unworthy and abject before the might of God. In fact, Luther was as accepting of Augustine's pessimism as the Catholic Church had been. Yet the destruction of the shrines by the Protestant reformers saw the disappearance of the saints in their role of 'servants and bonded labourers'. This meant that sinners had no one left to intercede for their salvation. The Protestants also rejected purgatory, so there was no longer the possibility of making one's journey to heaven through a process of purification. It was heaven or hell with nothing in between. Although the return to Scripture made good theological sense, it soon became clear that there was no consensus on the meaning of Scripture, and hence a myriad of Protestant sects appeared basing their allegiances on charismatic preachers or rigid interpretations of selected scriptural passages. There was no challenge here to the idea of the supernatural: whether demonstrated through the powers of devils or God, it loomed as large as it had always done.

It was hardly surprising that the challenge to the supernatural, and hence a return to the Greek view of the primacy of the natural world as it could actually be observed, came from within Italy. The Italian city states had maintained a precarious independence between emperor and papacy. They flaunted their republican identity and defence of *libertas*. They had achieved the highest levels of wealth, literacy and craftsmanship in Europe. In the fifteenth century the revival of classical learning, the movement known as humanism, allowed a creative tension between Christian and secular texts, between alternative forms of the ideal life, between philosophy and theology.[4]

This was an important contrast to the scholastics ensconced in the rarefied atmosphere of Paris or Oxford where 'in the Middle Ages reason was employed in an abstract and often *a priori* manner, and was frequently applied to hypothetical arguments and examples with little relevance to the real world'.[5] The Italians were engaged in reasoning on a practical level. The fluid nature of political life, notably the suspicion of absolutism within the city-states, meant that law held a prominent place. The assessment and applicability of evidence in everyday situations honed logical skills. In the same cities, the rise of commerce went hand in hand with advanced knowledge of mathematics and this was transferred into government. The complex taxation systems of the Italian city-states could never have worked without such expertise. Again the Italians excelled in the application of practical reasoning skills in manufacture and technology.

This provided the background for the gradual erosion of belief in the miraculous. As we have seen, there was already increasing scorn among the more educated, even within the Church, for the endless proliferation of relics whose authenticity was unproven and whose power to cure was suspect. While the Church was committed to supporting the idea of supernatural intervention, one senses that for many pragmatic members of the Italian city-states, it was no longer a serious issue. Miracles might exist but one could hardly risk depending on them in the everyday cut and thrust of political and commercial life in fifteenth-century Italy.

As yet, however, this apathy had not been focused into a reasoned attack. The first major critique of the miraculous comes from the philosopher Pietro Pomponazzi (1462–1525), almost an exact contemporary of Erasmus.[6] Pomponazzi had been born in Mantua, educated at the university of Padua where he also taught for many years, and ended his life teaching at the university of Bologna, best known for its law faculty. He stands out for the independence of his thought, although he drew heavily on Aristotle and the philosophy of Plato and the Stoics now that these were gradually becoming available to humanists such as himself. It was his championing of Aristotle that first got Pomponazzi into trouble.

The pagan Aristotle had been welcomed into Christian thought by the theologians Albertus Magnus and Thomas Aquinas in the thirteenth century, but not without difficulty.[7] The whole tenor of Aristotle's approach, with its emphasis on the gathering and classification of empirical evidence and his determination to remove the miraculous from the understanding of natural phenomena, fitted uneasily with the God-centred cosmos of the medieval theologians. There were specific beliefs of Aristotle, the view that the soul was an integral part of the body and not immortal and that the world had no separate moment of creation, that were anathema to Christians. Yet Aristotle survived within the universities and many of the scholastics wrote commentaries on his works, unfortunately to the extent of obscuring the vitality and breadth of his thought. Scholastic Aristotelianism was to retard intellectual progress until well into the seventeenth century.

Even two hundred years after the rediscovery of Aristotle, any philosopher who reasserted his original teachings was likely to face the wrath of the Church. In 1513 Pope Leo X had asserted in a bull that the soul was immortal and individual to each human being. This was a counter to Aristotle's view on the soul. In 1516 Pomponazzi published a response to Leo. He breathed new life into Aristotle's view that the body and soul were inseparable. Like an image on a coin, which gives the coin its identity, the soul was an intrinsic part of the body, and if the body died so did the soul. Pomponazzi made the brave assertion that there was no good reason for believing in the existence of the soul as an entity anywhere after death and so nothing to suggest punishment in hell or reward in heaven. Pomponazzi stressed that his argument involved 'leaving aside revelation and miracles, and remaining entirely within natural limits' but he must have realised how controversial his views were. In the closing paragraphs of his *On the Immortality of the Soul*, he accepts that faith requires him to accept the immortality of the soul although it could not be proved! Even so his work aroused fury, was burned as heretical in Venice, and it was only thanks to the protection of Cardinal Pietro Bembo, the great humanist churchman, that he escaped a similar end himself.

Yet Pomponazzi was much too vigorous and independent a thinker to be suppressed so easily. He moved on to challenge the idea of the miraculous itself. His *On Incantations* was written in 1520 but Pomponazzi dared to circulate it only in manuscript. One of his arguments in his treatise on the soul had been that supporters of the immortality of the soul had given instances of souls having been 'seen'. Many of these cases, he argued, were tricks of the imagination or even fraudulent. In *On Incantations* he goes on to discuss the vast number of other miracles that, as we have seen, pervaded Christian literature, among them cures, resurrections of the dead and the appearance of *stigmata*. He notes that objects often have unseen powers that do cause physical changes. So some herbs cure specific illnesses but it is impossible to observe what is in them that has this effect. A magnet can have a dramatic effect on steel, again without an observable cause. Pomponazzi had heard of fish (electric eels?) that can numb a man's foot. He noted how the human body could react physically to shock and shame or would salivate when offered food. This was just the kind of empirical approach required to undermine the need for divine intervention as a cause of events.

Pomponazzi singled out Cecco d'Ascoli (1257–1327) as a scholar who had investigated such phenomena in depth. In his *Acerba* Cecco had examined the properties of metals and the stars, and studied dew and fossils. He may even have been aware of the circulation of the blood. Innovative and outspoken, Cecco had been condemned by the Church for his 'impiety' and burned in Florence in his seventieth year. (He is remembered with enough respect for there to be a lunar crater named after him.)

If inanimate objects or the lower forms of animals can have such effects, it should follow that human beings also have special powers of which they might not be aware. Indeed, there do seem to be some human beings who are able to cure others and there is no reason to regard it as a miracle of God when they do so. One possibility was that certain humans had unseen vapours that they could pass on to others – not in itself an impossible idea when we think of the transmission of germs. Pomponazzi goes on to explore another phenomenon that he has observed – the power of imagination. This is what would now be called the placebo effect – the simple belief that a cure will be effected is enough to bring it about. He applies this to relics. It is possible that bones might have some occult powers, but in cases where relics are fraudulent, say the bones of a dog rather than those of a saint, the cure can only be one induced by imagination.

Nevertheless, confronted by so many miracles, Pomponazzi has to admit that some are difficult to explain. The people of L'Aquila had endured days of rain. They prayed to their patron saint Pope Celestine V, who was buried in the city (see earlier p. 199). The rain ceased and an image of Celestine appeared in the sky. Were there vapours coming collectively from the crowd, or was it merely their collective imagination that caused the image? It might even be possible that it was the influence of the stars. Pomponazzi was determined that there should be a natural explanation, but whatever it is he is sure that it cannot be the result of prayer. Praying is not wrong but its primary aim is to purify the heart of the believer, not to achieve miraculous change. He follows Aristotle (and Plato) in arguing that God is a changeless divine essence that cannot hear or respond to human demands.

To explain the seemingly inexplicable without destroying his unchanging God, Pomponazzi has to devise a structure for the world. Yes, there is an Unmoved Mover (Aristotle's conception of God) but he does set the world in motion through the actions of the stars and the Intelligences. It is these that bring about changes on earth and Pomponazzi argues that eventually unusual happenings will be comprehensible as the outcome of these movements. In the same way, today we could argue that natural phenomena we do not yet understand, and that might in some quarters be seen therefore as miraculous, will eventually become comprehensible once science has illuminated them. Pomponazzi goes on to speculate that even the rise and fall of empires and the fates of individual monarchs might eventually be charted through a fuller understanding of the cosmos. Here, and in his other writings, he insists that the rational faculty enjoyed by humans operates independently of any influence from the universe. Man still has areas in which he is able to exercise free will.

So Pomponazzi postulates a world in which the miraculous is impossible. Since, for the committed Christian, the virgin birth, the Incarnation of Jesus and the Resurrection can all be seen to be miracles, he seems to have distanced himself entirely from Christianity. Pomponazzi cannot quite face this consequence and he claims that he is still prepared to submit to the faith of the Church. He is reluctant to follow the logic of his argument into the land of unbelief.

Pomponazzi's solution is an ingenious one. He returns to an idea that is rooted in the classical philosophy of Stoicism, that the world moves in cycles of birth, growth, decay, collapse and rebirth. He applies this to religion. He looks back to the birth of Judaism, the pagan religions of the classical world, Christianity and Islam. Each of these religions goes through a similar cycle. As one religion, say paganism, dies and another, Christianity, takes over, there is inevitably a great upheaval and it is then that the movement of the cosmos spawns events that are perceived as miraculous. Yet with time the cosmos settles into a new phase and the movement of the Intelligences and the stars is not powerful enough to effect untoward events. Gradually, a religion winds down and remarkably this is what Pomponazzi sees happening around him. 'This is why today in our religion everything grows cold, "miracles" cease or they are invented or stimulated, because its end seems near.' So, he is implying that Christianity has no unique status. It is merely one of many religions that follow one from another and, in this case, it is near the end of its natural life.

However, Pomponazzi was not so committed an empiricist as Aristotle. He did not gather evidence from the natural world to support his argument that most phenomena had their own causes independent of an interventionist God. In this he was typical of his age. The medievalists had shown comparatively little interest in the natural world. This was all to change. The shock of Christopher Columbus's discovery of America in 1492 challenged their preconceptions. In fact, it has been argued that Copernicus was jolted into his own discoveries by seeing the first map of the Americas, the Waldseemüller map of 1507.[8] The sixteenth century saw the birth of a new interest in the natural world that was slowly to wear away at the idea of everyday miracles by offering observable and testable explanations for untoward events. So far as religious belief was concerned, Pomponazzi was initiating a process that was to reach much more radical forms in the writings of Spinoza in the seventeenth century and in the works of David Hume in the eighteenth.[9]

The assault on the miraculous was perhaps inevitable as societies, and the individuals within them, took control of their own destinies. Any mentality that relies on miracles to heal or protect can hardly confront the challenges of life with much chance of success. It had always been the teaching of the Catholic Church that the grace of God, whether in effecting salvation or bestowing miracles, could not be demanded or relied on, and so the rising commercial classes chose not to rely on miracles. In this sense Pomponazzi was responding to the wider changes he must have observed around him, just as Augustine's changing attitudes to the miraculous nine hundred years before were probably a response to the rise in the popular adulation of the saints and martyrs. Yet the Catholic Church was not giving up easily. It was now ready to mount a rearguard action against the denigration of cults. When Pomponazzi's *On Incantations* was eventually printed in 1556, just over thirty years after his death, it was soon placed on the papal Index of Prohibited Books, a fate also enjoyed by every one of Erasmus's works. Old patterns of behaviour were to be reasserted.

CHAPTER TWENTY-FIVE

Reasserting the Miraculous

The holy bodies of holy martyrs, and of others now living with Christ, which bodies were the living members of Christ . . . and which are by Him to be raised unto eternal life, and to be glorified, are to be venerated by the faithful; . . . those who affirm that veneration and honour are NOT due to the relics of saints; or, that these, and other sacred monuments, are uselessly honoured by the faithful; and that the places dedicated to the memories of the saints are in vain visited with the view of obtaining their aid; are wholly to be condemned, as the Church has already long since condemned, and now also condemns them.[1]

So spoke the assembled bishops at the Council of Trent in December 1563. The Reformation had shaken the Catholic Church. Yet there was some vigour in its response. While the inquisitions conducted by medieval Dominican preachers against heretics had often been amateurish, the Roman Inquisition set up by Pope Paul III in 1542 was better equipped to define heresy and carry out formal trials. An Index of Prohibited Books, a massive compilation in its first edition of 1559 of the entire works of 550 authors, was in itself a sign of bureaucratic efficiency. A new order, the Jesuits, married the austerity of their founder, Ignatius Loyola (1491–1556), to intellectual rigour to provide the shock troops of what is usually known as the Counter-Reformation. The Jesuits made education and confrontations with Protestantism their priorities, and they had soon spread to three continents as the Spanish and Portuguese imposed Catholicism on their subjects overseas. Meanwhile, the authority and doctrine of the Church was proclaimed by the Council that met over several years (1545–63) at Trent in the Italian Tyrol.[2]

At Trent there were to be no compromises over traditional teaching. The Council's very first decree, in 1546, proclaimed that the Catholic doctrine might rest on the Scriptures but only according to the Church's interpretation of them. In Italy vernacular translations of the Bible were placed on the Index – in 1606 Pope Paul V was heard to say that too much reading of the Scriptures ruined the Catholic religion. The Council went on to decree that there were alternative truths, passed down from the Apostles, that again only the Church knew how to interpret. So, as one might expect, traditional teaching on relics and indulgences was reaffirmed, in decrees passed right at the end of the Council during its twenty-fifth session in December 1563.

The Council's decree on indulgences accepted that abuses had taken place, although it was vague about what these were, blaming them on 'superstition, ignorance and irreverence'. 'All evil gains for the obtaining thereof' were to be 'wholly abolished'. The principle of granting indulgences was retained under a new argument – that Christ himself had instituted them. So the whole structure of purgatory, the saints and indulgences that might shorten one's time there – the structure that brought pilgrims to shrines – remained in place.

The decree on the veneration of relics and images traced the practice back to the early Church. The Church Fathers and the early Councils of the Church, it was claimed, supported intercession through the saints. So it is confirmed that the saints live with God in heaven and can approach God, through Christ, to obtain benefits from him on behalf of intercessors. Anyone who argued that the saints could not help by passing on prayers to God through Christ or that intercession through them was idolatrous was to be condemned. The importance of images was reasserted. They reminded the faithful of the benefits and gifts bestowed on them by God and also the miracles that God has performed through the saints. Also restated was the teaching that the relics and images were only those means through which the saints could be reached or commemorated, and not the instruments of miracles themselves. They could not be sold. There was some recognition that feast days of saints had got out of hand. Images must be treated with respect, not associated with revelry, and must not incite lascivious feelings (thus were genitals painted over, classical statues fig-leaved and the breasts of the Virgin Mary covered). From now on only a bishop could confirm that a miracle had taken place or that a new relic was genuine.

None of this prevented an outburst of flamboyant and opulent display in the churches of the late sixteenth and seventeenth centuries. There was something both magnificent and appalling about the shrines of the period, especially when, in Rome, it was a time of economic decline (with a massive increase in poverty in the city during the seventeenth century). The Jesuit church in Rome, the Gesù, is unashamed in its splendour and there can be no greater contrast between the ascetic life of Ignatius Loyola and his shrine that is swathed in lapis lazuli, gold and marble. A magnificent balustrade in front of the altar encloses statues of *Religion Triumphing over Heresy* and *Barbarians Adoring the Faith*. One of Ignatius's companions, St Francis Xavier, is commemorated in the chapel opposite his. St Francis died in Goa in 1552 but one of his arms was brought back to Rome and placed there in a silver-gilt reliquary. Images took on an emotional intensity that was far removed from the strictures of the Council of Trent that lascivious feelings were to be avoided. The great sculptor Gianlorenzo Bernini must have had his mind elsewhere when he created his superlative 'image' of Teresa of Àvila (1515–82) swooning in erotic ecstasy on contemplation of her God in the Cornaro chapel of Santa Maria della Vittoria in Rome (1647–50).

More far-seeing churchmen (not least in France where papal assertion was seen as threatening the power of the monarchy) saw the Council's decrees and the palpability of old Catholic practices and display as a loss of opportunity to make some kind of reconciliation with the Protestant churches or, at least, to move towards the conciliar Church that many medieval theologians had hoped for. The condemnation of every one of the Catholic Erasmus's works in 1559 was the symbolic moment when the Church retreated from free intellectual enquiry and positioned itself back within medieval theology. The elimination of any forms of liberalism and dissent in Italy, the home of most of the bishops at Trent, allowed the new regime to consolidate itself. When challenged by scientific advance in the shape of Galileo Galilei (1564–1642), its response was confused and finally condemnatory. Galileo was only one of many scientists and philosophers whose name appeared on the Index of Prohibited Books. While the opening of the New World gave the Church opportunities for expansion it was not slow to exploit, it remained embedded in the theology of Augustine. Faith continued to trump reason.

And it had to. With the Protestant assault on all Catholic rites as the sorcery of the Devil, the Catholic Church could hardly play into the hands of the Protestants by rejecting these practices wholesale. Although the Counter-Reformation brought with it Catholic intellectuals who questioned the superstition of the shrines, they were unable to impose absolute control over local practices. Instead, the saints were staunchly defended in their role of defeating sorcery.[3] The Catholic theologian Albrecht Hunger of Ingolstadt (1545–1604) prepared a series of theses for a student disputation in 1574, with Thesis 88 stating:

> Sorcery is also repelled without doubt by the merits and intercessions of the saints: it is repelled by the signing of the holy cross, by adjuration, exorcisms, prayers, and by the most holy blessings of the Church, which is the column and foundation of the truth (although heretics may deride this) if we use, in complete faith and entire devotion of the mind, these and the other things called sacramentals of the Church, as for instance sprinkling with holy water and so bravely resist the wickedness of the demons.

The Jesuit demonologist Martin Delrio (1551–1608) was even more expansive in his *Magical Disquisitions* of 1603. He listed a vast array of objects, relics, amulets, holy bells, as well as incantations and intercessions to Christ and the saints, signs of the Cross and works of penance, all of which, Delrio claimed, could be shown to have, on occasions, repelled demons, cured illness and protected against other misfortunes. Just as early Christians had claimed that they could effect miracles when pagans could not, now Delrio produced cases when Catholic priests had exorcised demons that had resisted Protestants. Catholics and Protestants alike were preoccupied with the restless activity of the Devil and how to combat it.

So there remained much work for the saints to do. The renewal of confidence in their power was marked in 1588 by the first papal canonisation for sixty-five years, of a Spanish Franciscan missionary, Diego of Alcalá.[4] There were to be another fourteen by 1665; nothing compared to the exuberant saint-making of Pope John Paul II in the late twentieth century, but one more sign that the old ways were still respected. There was even a dramatic 'holy theft' in 1580 when the body of St Benno of Meissen (canonised in 1523) was seized by the Wittelsbachs of Bavaria from Protestant Saxony and taken back to their capital Munich. In 1554 the Jesuits had assumed responsibility for the shrine of the Virgin's House at Loreto and they used it as a base from which to spread the cult of the Virgin back into Germany as Catholicism regained the initiative in some areas.

There was no slackening off in the restless activity of venerating the saints. When the Jesuit Jean Bolland began a detailed compilation of saints' lives in 1643, he found that 1,170 were still recognised by the Church. There were twenty-eight saints' and feast days listed in the Roman breviary for January 1568 alone. In Milan, the city where Ambrose had founded the cult of relics through his championship of Gervasius and Protasius, Archbishop Carlo Borromeo, consecrated in 1565, tied his obsessively authoritarian regime in with the veneration of the saints, martyrs and pious former archbishops of the city in a massive stage-managed procession of communal adoration in May 1582. In 1578 the catacombs had been rediscovered in Rome and there was an inexhaustible supply of fresh relics, while many bishops now began energetic searches of their own ancient burial grounds. In Sardinia an enormous cache of the bodies of some supposed 338 martyrs was discovered in 1614. There was a major distribution of them throughout Italy, twenty bodies and eighty-eight further relics going to Piacenza and the body parts of eighty-six martyrs going to Alassio in Liguria. The saints played as prominent a role in the Americas. The Christianity of the converted Nahua people (of modern Mexico) appears to have gone little further than the adoption of the European saints, who were revered as their 'parents' and the real owners of their community's land.

It is interesting that Venice, resolutely independent of the papacy, and a city that even successfully defied a papal excommunication in 1606, also saw a revival in the veneration of its impressive relic collection.[5] An inventory of relics in the city made in 1631 put Venice as second only to Rome in the size of its collection, which included the complete bodies of forty-nine saints. The plagues and famines that hit Venice in the late sixteenth and early seventeenth century played a major role in consolidating traditional cults. Fortuitously, a large cache of 'new' relics, including samples of Christ's blood and fragments of the True Cross, were 'found' in the sanctuary of St Mark's early in the century and a great procession was organised to flaunt them. Once again the Piazza San Marco provided a wonderful setting for the display and the Scuole went out with their own sacred objects. On three occasions the procession came to a ceremonial halt and the relics were put forward for veneration to the crowds. Claudio Monteverdi provided the music for the basilica's choir. Like most of the Italian economies, that of Venice was now in a long period of decline and it is possible to argue that there is some correlation between economic stagnation and the vigorous reassertion of traditional cults that centred on sacred 'display' objects such as relics.

Essentially, therefore, the Catholic Church preached the continuity of worship according to traditional rituals, and one can see this in the persistence of relic cults in Spain whose contribution to the Counter-Reformation had already proved substantial.[6] The country had produced the founder of the Jesuits, Ignatius Loyola, and his companion Francis Xavier, and spearheaded the expansion of Catholicism overseas. There was a hard edge to Spanish Catholicism that had been honed in the repression and expulsion of Islam and Jews in the fifteenth century. It was shown in a harshness and aggression that was driven by the devout Catholicism of Spain's rulers. The Spanish Inquisition was tied to the secular power of the monarchy and so had an impact that outclassed in ferocity the easily thwarted and often derided inquisitions of the medieval Dominicans. Between 1481 and 1488, it ordered the burning of 700 'Judaisers' in Castile alone. The pretensions and independence from Church control of the Spanish Inquisition was such that, in 1559, it even arrested the primate of the Spanish Church, the Archbishop of Toledo, Bartolomé Carranza.

Spain achieved the height of its European, and Catholic, power under Philip II, who had inherited Spain, in 1559, among many other territories as the heir of the Habsburgs. He added Portugal and its colonies to his empire in 1580. English historians have traditionally painted Philip as a severe and withdrawn man, conscious of his immense duties as a Catholic ruler with the power traditionally inherent in the Spanish monarchy to deal with heresy and ready to suppress opposition. More recently a more expansive and sympathetic Philip, a man who travelled widely in and beyond his immense empire, who was attracted by as sensual an artist as Titian and who moderated the more extremist of his ministers, has replaced the Protestant view that was fashioned in the afterglow of Queen Elizabeth I's lucky escape from his invading armada. While the burning of convicted offenders by the Inquisition in the *autos-da-fé* were spectacular dramas attended by thousands, the actual rate of execution was far below the levels of the late fifteenth century.

Philip maintained the medieval tradition, started by Charlemagne, and followed by many devout rulers since then, of accumulating a relics collection. It was housed in the Escorial, a vast and austere royal palace-monastery outside Madrid completed in 1584, where Philip isolated himself, poring over the hundreds of incoming documents that he refused to delegate to others. The palace was dedicated to St Lawrence, possibly to commemorate a victory over the French that took place on St Lawrence's feast day, and the ground plan reflected the grid-shaped grill on which the martyr had been roasted. One contemporary observer, Baltasar Porreno, saw the driving force behind the building as Philip's obsession with the insults against the Catholic Church and its relics:

> So great was his devotion to relics and churches that in order to offer them the highest reverence he built the magnificent temple of San Lorenzo el Real, which merits the first place among the Seven Wonders of the World. He began to build this great temple and house of God when the enemies of Christ, showing contempt for the Catholic Church and all holy relics, would burn and destroy temples, desecrate churches, abuse images, destroy sanctuaries, silence praises to God, and remove the Holy Sacrament from the altar.[7]

It was essentially a bastion of the Counter-Reformation.

Philip began his search for relics as soon as his building began taking shape and, appropriately enough, one of his first acquisitions was a tooth of St Lawrence sent to him from Montpellier in France.[8] He did eventually gain a larger piece of St Lawrence from the church of John Lateran in Rome but only after he had donated some fine silver statues in return. It was typical of his desire to consolidate every aspect of Spanish life under his own control that he also fought to get the bones of St James transferred to the Escorial from Compostela. He pleaded that king and patron saint needed to be together in a place that was more central and safe from the ravages of English pirates, but he received a stern rebuff from the guardians of the lucrative shrine. Philip next launched an expedition to Germany and the Low Countries to salvage relics from Protestant iconoclasm. Among them was a host that had bled when stamped on by a Dutch Calvinist. They were gathered at Cologne, packed into crates and then had to fight their way through hostile Protestant areas into Italy and from there to Madrid, where they were greeted with ecstasy by Philip who was now seriously ill. His collection now numbered between seven and eight thousand relics.

Philip's last weeks, spent at the Escorial, were excruciating for him and those who cared for him. He was racked with pain, covered in ulcers and could hardly move or be moved. One of his few comforts was his relics. Every day part of the collection was brought in for him. So, shortly before his swollen knee was due to be lanced, he asked for the knee of the martyr St Sebastian, which was complete with its bone and skin, to be placed against his own. He was meticulous in ensuring that each relic was properly tagged as if terrified he might misplace his veneration. He kissed each one and then applied it to one of his lesions and was furious with the attending clerics if the pile became muddled or any were missed. As Philip neared death a rib of the English martyr St Alban was brought forward. This had been sent to Philip by Pope Clement VIII and had been imbued with a special papal indulgence that would release Philip's soul from purgatory. The relic was only revealed at Philip's last moments so that it would be sure of achieving its aim.

Philip died on 13 September 1598. His final agonies and his submission to them were seen as symbolic of the inevitable fate awaiting all human beings and here, as in much else, the monarch had to show his people how to endure them. In Spain the 'good' death, embellished with last sacraments and confessions and intense concentration on God, was celebrated with an obsessive attention to ritual that extended to the funeral and the masses associated with the soul in heaven. Philip's devotion to his relics was lauded as an example to all of the reverence they should inspire.

This mystical quality of religious life was profoundly Spanish and had been exemplified by the life of one of Spain's greatest saints, St Teresa of Àvila.[9] Teresa (1515–82) came from converted Jewish stock and she had entered a convent of Carmelite nuns at Àvila in Castile at the age of nineteen against the wishes of her father. She was a restless woman, tormented by profoundly disturbing visions that she entangled with Solomon's Song of Songs. Her fellow mystic, John of the Cross, whom she used as a confessor for her nuns, had the same obsession with the Song and there was an erotic tone to the way in which both envisaged their relationship with Christ (powerfully captured in Teresa's case by Bernini's sculpture in Rome). Yet Teresa was also a leader. After the bull of 1566, in which Pius V ordered that all female religious communities be enclosed, 'Teresa became the embodiment of the ideal female religious, tirelessly (and visibly) rendering women invisible in enclosed and reformed convents'.[10] She renovated the Carmelites through a new Order of both nuns and monks who expressed their poverty by wearing no shoes (the Discalced Carmelites). Even so, her outbursts of mystical fervour and her determination to impose her will on her convents appalled many, and it was probably only Philip II's own support that saved her from some form of condemnation. It was Philip who prompted the first inquest into her life as a preliminary to a campaign for her canonisation.

Teresa, now well into her sixties, died in October 1582 at one of her foundations, Alba de Tormes near Salamanca. All the accounts see her death, as Philip's sixteen years later, as an exemplary process in which she seemed to be merely stepping into the presence of God. Indeed the nuns attending her later reported visions, of Christ and a multitude of angels at the foot of her bed, or a brilliant flash of light, as she died. A barren fruit tree outside the window suddenly filled with blossom even though it was winter. In another of her convents, articles she had once touched began emitting a sweet fragrance and several nuns saw her in heaven, as one of a crowd of virgins dressed in white or with Francis of Assisi or St Joseph. The compilers of these accounts assured any sceptical readers that such phenomena had often been reported in the lives of medieval saints and so they could be assured that they were authentic.

So the experiences of Teresa's body in the years that followed need to be seen as a reaffirmation of Catholic tradition as much as an affirmation of her own sanctity. As with medieval saints, Teresa's body underwent a spiritual transformation after her death. 'Her face became more beautiful and without a single wrinkle, in spite of the fact that she had many before her death; her body was also free of wrinkles and very white, like alabaster; her flesh became very soft, and as tractable as that of a two-to three-year old child.' It was said that this was just how St Francis of Assisi's body had been, another sign that she was conforming to the precedents set by earlier saints. As might be expected, the body also exuded a sweet fragrance that spread throughout the convent. The body began to effect its own miracles. A nun who kissed her feet was cured of the headaches that had bothered her; another was relieved of intense pain in her eyes.

The problem facing the nuns of Alba was that Teresa had died far from home and they knew they would challenged for possession of her remains by the nuns of Àvila. It was decided to bury the body as deeply as possible within the nuns' chapel and to cover the grave with a heavy mix of stones, bricks and lime. Even so her presence remained in the chapel. If a sister fell asleep during prayer, angry knockings would be heard and the fragrance of the saint persisted, especially on her birthday.

After nine months concern grew over the hasty burial. If this was truly a saint then surely the body required greater respect, the process that in the medieval period traditionally led to a *translatio* from the first place of burial. The provincial responsible for the Order, Father Jerónimo Gracián, acquiesced in its recovery and was present when, with much difficulty, the site was excavated and eventually the coffin, shattered by the weight of stones placed above it, emerged. Miraculously, the body was still uncorrupted and such a strong smell of sanctity came from it that some were overwhelmed by it. This was seen as confirmation of Teresa's virginity, as a body that had been in any way contaminated by sexual activity would never have remained so whole.

Father Gracián's motives were not so pure as the body he had recovered. As far back as 1577, he had signed an agreement that if Teresa died away from Àvila her body would be returned there. All along he had plans for a *translatio* to Àvila. To start with he cut off Teresa's left hand and took a finger from this for himself. Then the rest of the body was reburied although not so deeply as it had been. He sealed up the dismembered hand and presented it to the convent of Àvila on condition that the container would not be opened. This was only a preliminary gift. In November 1585 Gracián reappeared at Alba, this time with the Provincial Vicar of Castile, Gregorio Nacicenceno, and, although the Àvila nuns did not know of it, approval from the chapter of male Discalced Carmelites that the body be moved. They ordered the body to be exhumed yet again and then announced to the distressed nuns that they were taking the body with them. As compensation, Father Gregorio sliced off the left arm for the nuns to keep and proclaimed it a miracle that it had come away so easily from the rest of the corpse. Then they made off with the body, secretly conveying it from inn to inn until it arrived at Àvila to the great excitement of the nuns, many of whom had known Teresa well. A coffin decorated in silver and gold was made for it. Here it underwent yet another inspection. This time not only was the incorruptibility of the body confirmed – the flesh was so tractable that it would dent and spring back when pressed – but the body weighed no more than that of a two-year-old, a sure sign that it had achieved 'the agility of the resurrected body of the blessed'.

Alas, the saga was not over. The Dukes of Alba had greater power and influence than any other family in Spain outside royalty. The duke of the day had been away at the time of the theft from Alba but he was furious when he heard of it. One of his family, Don Fernando de Toledo, had left money in his will to help fund the canonisation campaign and the duke was adamant that the honour of his family had become tied up with Teresa's presence at Alba. There was one authority that the duke could appeal to, the Pope, Sixtus V. Sixtus acquiesced in the demand and ordered the return of the body to Alba where the dukes commissioned another sumptuous tomb for her that quickly became a pilgrimage site. Once the body was back there, the nuns of Àvila grumbled that the body was continually raided for more parts and that flesh was handed out by their sisters in Alba to those who asked for them. Certainly the heart was removed and rumours spread that it had been found shattered by the ultimate mystical experience of Teresa seeing God at the moment of her death. This again echoed accounts of medieval dissections of bodies in search of their sanctity. Those with parts of Teresa's body claimed that they continually exuded oil, again a phenomenon recorded of saints in medieval times. Hundreds of healing miracles were recorded in the thirty years after Teresa's death. In case the relic of St Alban had not performed as promised, one of these ensured that her patron Philip II spent no more than fourteen days in purgatory.

Teresa was canonised in 1622 and is seen as one of the quintessential saints of the Counter-Reformation. In 1970 she was made a Doctor of the Church, one of only three female saints with the privilege.[11] The way that her body and miraculous activity conformed to medieval precedents of sainthood was a particularly powerful way of reconfirming the protection of God for his Church and its saints. But Teresa was also a representative of Spain, one of the country's most prestigious patron saints. Her relics received an accolade like no other when her hand, 'rescued' from the Republicans during the Spanish Civil War, was awarded a medal by General Franco, *La Cruz Laureada de San Fernando*. By this time she was being seen not only as a patron saint of Spain but also of the pure Spanish blood, *La Santa de la Raza*. She had been manipulated to serve the needs of the nation.

The patterns of relic worship that began many centuries before – the fragrances of the saintly body, its power to effect miracles, the use of relics as status symbols and healing artefacts – were as powerful as ever. For over thirteen hundred years the same rituals had been followed, the same enthusiasm aroused and the power of the saints' bodies to bring miracles continually reasserted. This was to continue in the centuries to come with some of the greatest pilgrimages ever known taking place in the sixteenth and seventeenth centuries. The essentials of Catholic sainthood, the recognition of a saint's place in heaven through the grant of miracles, remain in place today.

Within the Community
of the Supernatural

In 1413 a skeleton was found in a lead sarcophagus in a graveyard in the city of Padua, home of one of Italy's oldest universities and a centre of humanism. A scholar, Sicco Polenton, came out to see it and enthusiastically proclaimed that it was no other than the body of the Roman historian Livy.[1] At the news sightseers came flocking out of the city and students reverently took some of the teeth as a memorial.[2]

For a monk that was watching this was no more than an act of idolatry. Whatever the merits of Livy as a historian, he was, after all, a pagan. The monk began smashing up the skull to stop more being removed. In the scuffles that followed, the rest of the bones were rescued and placed in a casket that was then covered in laurel leaves, the traditional Roman symbol of triumph. A procession of the leading dignitaries of the city was formed and Sicco was delighted to see that it included artisans, butchers and shoemakers, a cross-section of the citizens of Padua. There were plans for a shrine, with a statue of Livy on a column, but eventually, in 1426, there was a more restrained *translatio* in which the bones were placed in a niche in a central gateway of the city, complete with a portrait bust and an epitaph in gold lettering.

What a society considers sacred changes with context. In fifteenth-century Italy many of the great names of antiquity reappear and are honoured in statues, on palace facades, in libraries and in frescos. None of them, however, bring miracles and they are certainly not clothed in gold. Relics are rare and reverence is token. The statues are often backdrops, giving dignity to a building or lined along the tops of library shelves.

One reason why these figures – historians, philosophers, generals and statesmen – had limited resonance is that they were known only to the educated elite, recovered from the texts that were being read for the first time in a thousand years. Christian relics, on the other hand, had originated in the bodies of the martyrs and these came from every walk of life. Many such relics were recovered as decayed fragments after Christianity became tolerated in the fourth century, although, whatever their actual condition, they were, of course, soon said to be fresh and uncorrupted. The crucial difference was that every level of society, from kings and bishops to the very poor, were involved in the miraculous. Even the intellectual Augustine turns from sceptic to enthusiast. Once the potency of the relics was accepted, it is astonishing how quickly their power spread, not only across the Mediterranean world but to every kind of object. To the martyrs are added relics of Christ's life and Passion, the Virgin Mary and the Apostles, and even Old Testament figures. Then there are the *brandea*, objects that have touched relics and obtained power of their own. By the time of Charlemagne some shrines have enormous accumulations of relics, representing the whole span and richness of Christian history. They play the role of consolidating a continuous narrative of the Christian past in material form.

Relics go much further than merely providing a narrative. They weave in and out of medieval society. They are used blatantly as prestige items by kings. Bishops assert their authority as impresarios for their own shrines. They are bought and sold, stolen and traded. They are looted in their hundreds from Constantinople after the schism between east and west legitimates them as plunder. They provide an explanation for the birth of Gothic architecture and hence some of the finest buildings in Europe. The great processions of bejewelled bones and flesh, with music and ceremony to match, provide the theatre of the age. Relics are intrinsic to the self-identity of the Italian city-states and, as such, are actually used against the power of the institutional Church. The popes try, with little immediate success, to use the control of canonisation as one of the means of asserting their authority. The Eucharistic 'relic' is used to consolidate the clergy as an isolated spiritual elite. In fact, relics become pawns in almost every power struggle of medieval Europe.

Yet they did bring their benefits. There was never any possibility of religious uniformity in medieval Europe. There were too many foci of worship: the distant and sometimes resented papacy; rulers who claimed their own brand of sacred power; well-endowed and independent monasteries;

bishops, many of them of great personal wealth and influence; and the preaching orders with their obsessive denunciations of human wickedness. Underneath these conflicting powers lay deep, sometimes unrecognised, spiritual needs, not least relief from the fear of intense and eternal suffering in hell. The shrines responded to this by offering homes for personalities, real or imagined, who fulfilled different kinds of functions, above all as antidotes to the forbidding power of Christ. The saints were more accepting of human frailty than was the Church and so maintain an identity that is, in many ways, independent of it. The Virgin Mary, who extends her cloak over her people to save them from the plague arrows of her own Son, is a paradigm here. A resilient and fruitful polytheism emerges that is all too often overlooked in the history of medieval Christianity.

It is the intensity of worship at the shrines that stands out. The Middle Ages are often termed an 'Age of Faith' but it was certainly not 'faith' in the certainty of a loving God who would bring salvation. One of the bestsellers of the period, *On the Contempt of the Worlds,* by Innocent III, the Pope who has featured so often in these pages, confirmed that this was not a church that believed in the dignity of human beings. 'Man has been conceived in the desire of the flesh, in the heat of the sensual lust, in the foul stench of wantonness. . . . His evil doings offend God, offend his neighbours, offend himself. . . . Accordingly, he is destined to become the fuel of the everlasting, eternally painful hellfire: the food of the voracious consuming worms'. Not everyone might have been taken in by such bluster, but a burden of desperation had been laid on the backs of believers.[3] The belief that God actually permitted the Devil to work his evil simply compounded the despair.

It was just possible that God or Christ might relent. As the shattered body on the crucifix reminded the medieval observer, Christ was certainly angry at the suffering that he had undergone for the sins of humanity as a result of the long-distant sin of Adam and Eve, but he might, in individual cases, be persuaded to grant sinners remission, even admit them to paradise. He was not an abstract, rational being. God and rational behaviour do not go hand in hand in the Middle Ages – what could be more irrational than to forgive some sinners but not others on a purely arbitrary basis or let them off years of purgatory on the purchase of an indulgence – yet his irrationality meant that he might be cajoled by the intercession of his saints.[4] An extraordinary spiritual economy was born in which the shrines became centres of bargaining. They were noisy and emotionally charged places. Many accounts stress the howls of anguish with which the exposition of a relic was greeted. The people of Chartres who call on their priests to beat them in the hope of bringing the Virgin Mary's succour are typical. There is what appears to be a 'darkly erotic aesthetic of pain', in which self-diagnosed sinners inflict as much humiliation on themselves as they can in the hope of attracting the notice of Christ.[5] It is the vivid descriptions of the self-abasement of supplicants at the shrines that provide the best documentary evidence for the impact of the medieval Church's profoundly pessimistic portrayal of humanity.

There was something yet more profound. For centuries there was virtually no questioning of the power of relics. One of the few treatises against relics, that of Guibert of Nogent, is more about his distaste of the clamour of the shrines than the practice of veneration. What we have instead is a society that lives collectively and individually in a place 'between heaven and earth'. A modern mind can become irritated with the belief in so many stories of resurrections, healings and rescuings for which there can be no 'scientific' explanation. Yet if the supernatural is treated as a 'real' world, on a different level, its events, or lack of them, can be accepted as easily as they were in the natural world we can see or touch. Fantasy perhaps, but it is an imagined world that balances the harshness of the material one.

By the fifteenth century the authority of the shrines as the gateway to the supernatural is being challenged. The shock of the Black Death and the void of authority in the Catholic Church must have had their effect. The constant hawking of indulgences undermined any idea of personal responsibility for ethical behaviour. Something began to crumble. The wealth of the shrines now became offensive. There were the first challenges to their efficacy. The theology behind the cults suddenly appeared hollow. While Catholic intellectuals began to question the superstitions of the shrines, it was the Protestant preachers who most effectively galvanised the masses, especially the commercial classes who had been alienated from the institutional Church, and oversaw their destruction.[6] While medieval Europe had never experienced religious cohesion, there were now conflicting paths to 'the truth', each with its own concept of the supernatural. An alternative approach, that the supernatural might be a figment of the imagination, was being formulated for the first time but its definition, notably in the Enlightenment, lies far beyond the scope of this book.[7]

'The community of the supernatural' formed a very real part of the medieval world. Tracing the rise, fall, appearance and veneration of relics is a rich and important story that provides important fresh perspectives on medieval Europe. The presence of relics at every different level gave psychological cohesion to the complex and bustling world of the supernatural. Relic cults made up a landscape, a language and a set of beliefs that were common to all. Relics had their presences, in the parish church, the great cathedrals and the famous pilgrimage sites. Sometimes they were arrayed in their hundreds, at other shrines a single relic glittered from a gold reliquary. They are so pervasive that they are often mentioned only in passing, their ubiquity assumed. Relics provided the sacred consciousness that infused medieval Christianity.

Notes

I have included the main sources for each chapter under each chapter heading together with supplementary footnotes when appropriate. I have not footnoted quotations where the author is cited and the quotation is essentially descriptive. All books cited here together with others I have found useful are listed in the Select Bibliography.

PREFACE

1. A good survey of the present state of research on the Turin Shroud is to be found in James Beresford, 'When Faith and Science Collide', in *Minerva* 21:4, July/August 2010, pp. 42–4. For Calvin on relics see pp. 236–8 above.
2. Robert Orsi, *Between Heaven and Earth: The Religious Worlds People Make and the Scholars Who Study Them*, Princeton and Oxford, 2004.

PROLOGUE: THE MAKING OF A MARTYR

1. Anne Duggan, *Thomas Becket*, in the Arnold Reputations series, London, 2004, is a good introduction to the main issues in Thomas's life and subsequent reputation. I have used Michael Staunton (ed.), *The Lives of Thomas Becket*, in the Manchester Medieval Sources series, Manchester 2001, for the original sources quoted in this chapter. The background to this period is well covered in Robert Bartlett, *England under the Norman and Angevin Kings, 1075–1225*, in *The New Oxford History of England*, Oxford, 2000.
2. Quoted in Julia Smith, 'Saints and their Cults', in Thomas Noble and Julia Smith (eds), *Early Medieval Christianities, c.600–1100: The Cambridge History of Christianity, Volume Three*, Cambridge, 2008, p. 592.
3. Benedict of Peterborough's account, p. 204, in Staunton, *op. cit.*
4. A good account is to be found in Allan Doig, *Liturgy and Architecture: From the Early Church to the Middle Ages*, Aldershot, UK, and Burlington, Vermont, 2008, pp. 177–82. There are apparently some minor earlier examples of Gothic style in Cistercian abbeys.
5. Most of these details of the *translatio* come from 'The Origins of Shrines: Canonisation and Translation', Chapter 1 in Ben Nilson, *Cathedral Shrines of Medieval England*, Woodbridge, UK, and Rochester, New York, 1998. A figure for the percentage of income appears on p. 182 where Nilson notes that few other English cathedrals obtained more than 10 per cent of their income from shrine offerings.
6. Quoted in Jonathan Sumption, *Pilgrimage: An Image of Mediaeval Religion*, London, 1975, p. 155.

Chapter One: How the Christian Relic Emerged

1. From Book 23 of Homer's *Iliad*, *c.*725 BC. Translation: Robert Fagles.
2. The second-century AD Greek historian and biographer Plutarch gives the details in his *Life of Cimon*.
3. See Ramsay MacMullen, *The Second Church. Popular Christianity AD 200–400*, Atlanta, 2009 for details. MacMullen suggests that as many as 95 per cent of Christians may have worshipped outside the institutional church.
4. Jas Elsner and Ian Rutherford (eds), *Pilgrimage in Graeco-Roman and Early Christian Antiquity: Seeing the Gods*, Oxford, 2005, has good introductory essays on these themes. See also Claudia Rapp, 'Saints and Holy Men', Chapter 22 in Augustine Casiday and Frederick Norris (eds), *Constantine to c.600: The Cambridge History of Christianity, Volume Two*, Cambridge, 2007, p. 542.
5. Edward Grant, *Science and Religion, 400 BC to AD 1550*, Baltimore, 2004, p. 37.
6. Paschasius Radbertus (*c.*790–865) quoted in Rachel Fulton, *From Judgment to Passion: Devotion to Christ and the Virgin Mary, 800–1200*, New York, 2002, p. 15.
7. Quoted in Charles Freeman, *The Closing of the Western Mind: The Rise of Faith and the Fall of Reason*, London, 2002, and New York, 2003, p. 316.
8. The full flow of Augustine's pessimism can be found in the closing chapters of his magisterial *The City of God*. Most of these issues are well explored in John Rist, *Augustine: Ancient Thought Baptised*, Cambridge, 1994.
9. Quoted in Georgia Frank, 'From Antioch to Arles, Lay Devotion in Context', Chapter 21, in Casiday and Norris (eds), *The Cambridge History of Christianity, Volume Two, op. cit.*, p. 542.
10. I have tried to keep within the context of medieval relics, but there are interesting ideas that explore the issues in more depth in many of the essays in David Morgan (ed.), *Religion and Material Culture: The Matter of Belief*, London and New York, 2010.

Chapter Two: The Incorruptible Flesh of the Martyrs

1. Ambrose is well covered by Neil McLynn, *Ambrose of Milan, Church and Court in a Christian Capital*, Berkeley and London, 2004; Chapter 4 for the 'crisis' of 386.
2. On the transformation of the flesh, I have relied heavily on Caroline Walker Bynum, *The Resurrection of the Body in Western Christianity, 200–1336*, New York, 1995, especially Chapter 1, 'Resurrection and Martyrdom: The Decades Around 200', and Chapter 2, 'Resurrection, Relic Cult and Asceticism: The Debates of 400 and Their Background'. The quotation from Augustine comes from *The City of God*, Book XXI:8.
3. Quoted in Bynum, *op. cit.*, pp. 40–41.
4. Quoted in David Hunter, *Marriage, Celibacy and Heresy in Ancient Christianity: The Jovinianist Controversy*, Oxford, 2007, p. 278.
5. Quoted in Charles Freeman, *A New History of Early Christianity*, New Haven and London, 2009, p. 213, where the wider context of Christian martyrdom is described in Chapter 20. A good general survey is Lucy Grig, *Making Martyrs in Late Antiquity*, London, 2004. Grig shows how martyr cults were created and portrayed by the early Christian communities.
6. Quoted in Freeman, *op. cit.*, p. 213.
7. Quoted in Rowan Greer, *The Fear of Freedom: A Study of Miracles in the Roman Imperial Church*, University Park and London, 1989, p. 99.
8. In Book IV, Chapter 15 of the *Exposition of the Orthodox Faiths* by John of Damascus.
9. This subject is covered in Mary Douglas's celebrated study, *Purity and Danger: An Analysis of the Concepts of Pollution and Taboo*, London and New York, 1966.

10. Quoted in Cynthia Hahn, 'What do Reliquaries do for Relics?' in *Numen* 57: 3–4, 2010, pp. 284–316.

CHAPTER THREE: CREATING A CHRISTIAN LANDSCAPE

1. Quoted in Colin Morris, *The Sepulchre of Christ and the Medieval West: From the Beginning to 1600*, Oxford, 2005, p. 53.
2. The *Itinerarium Egeriae*, the surviving part of Egeria's pilgrimage account and time in Jerusalem, is easily accessed in online translations. See also R.A. Markus, 'How on Earth Could Places Become Holy? Origins of the Christian Idea of Holy Places' in *The Journal of Early Christian Studies* 2:3 (1994), pp. 257–71. The process by which Christians came to accept opulence in the church building and decoration is well covered in D. Janes, *God and Gold in Late Antiquity*, Cambridge, 1998.
3. See Wendy Pullan, 'Ambiguity and Early Christian Pilgrimage', in Elsner and Rutherford, *op. cit.*, pp. 387ff. This is a sensitive exploration of the transition from rejection to acceptance of the Holy Places as legitimate sites of pilgrimage.
4. Jerome's pilgrimage is described in J.N.D. Kelly, *Jerome*, London, 1975, Chapter XII, 'To and Fro from Bethlehem'.
5. The full inscription with translation can be found in Tyler Lansford, *The Latin Inscriptions of Rome: A Walking Guide*, Baltimore, 2009, pp. 212–13.
6. There is a fine biography of Paulinus by Dennis Trout, *Paulinus of Nola: Life, Letters and Poems*, Berkeley and London, 1999, esp. Chapter 7 on the shrine.
7. *Praising the Saints* is available online.

CHAPTER FOUR: THE BATTLE FOR ACCEPTANCE

1. From Eunapius's *Lives of the Philosophers and Sophists*, available online, here in the 1921 translation by Wilmer Cave Wright.
2. They would have agreed with the view of Edward Gibbon, *The Decline and Fall of the Roman Empire*, Chapter XXVIII, III: 'The sublime and simple theology of the primitive Christians was gradually corrupted: and the Monarchy of Heaven, already clouded by metaphysical subtleties, was degraded by the introduction of a popular mythology, which tended to restore the reign of polytheism.'
3. G.J.C. Snoek, *Medieval Piety from Relics to the Eucharist: A Process of Mutual Interaction*, Leiden and New York, 1995, p. 254.
4. Available online and see discussion in Kelly, *Jerome, op. cit.*, pp. 286–90. See also David Hunter, 'Vigilantius of Calagurris and Vitricius of Rouen: Ascetics, Relics and Clerics in Late Roman Gaul', in *The Journal of Early Christian Studies* 7:3 (1999), pp. 401–30; Gillian Clark, 'Vitricius of Rouen; *Praising the Saints*', in *ibid.*, pp. 365–99; and Gillian Clark, 'Translating Relics: Vitricius of Rouen and Fourth-Century Debate' in *Early Medieval Europe* 10:2 (2001), pp. 161–76.
5. John Chrysostom, *Homilies on the Epistle to the Romans, Homily XXXII*.
6. Augustine's changing views are summarised in Tarcisius J. van Bavel, 'The Cult of the Martyrs in St. Augustine: Theology versus Popular Religion?' in M. Lamberights and P. Van Deun (eds), *Martyrium in Multidisciplinary Perspective: A Memorial to Louis Reekmans*, Leuven, 1995, pp. 351–61.
7. 'The philosophers are free in their choice of expressions, and do not fear to offend the ears of the religious when treating difficult subjects. But we [Christians] are duty bound to speak in accordance with a fixed rule.' Augustine, *The City of God*, Book X, Chapter 23. There are interesting essays on Augustine's attitude to the traditional genre of

dialogue in Part 3, 'Christianity and the Theological Imperative', in Simon Goldhill (ed.), *The End of Dialogue in Antiquity*, Cambridge, 2008.

8. Augustine, *City of God*, Book XXII, Chapter 8.
9. *Ibid.*, Book XXII, Chapter 9.
10. This comes from Theodoret, *Curatio affectionum graecarum*, 8.67.
11. Augustine's body itself became an object of veneration. Rescued from Hippo during the Arab invasions of the seventh century, it rested in Sardinia and was then transferred by a Lombard king to the church of San Pietro in Ciel d'Oro in the Lombard capital Pavia in about 720. The relics now rest in a richly decorated fourteenth-century shrine. The relics of his mother Monica are to be found in the church of St Augustine in Rome, where they arrived in the fifteenth century.

CHAPTER FIVE: THE VIEW FROM BYZANTIUM

1. This is one of the many western accounts that marvel at the richness of Constantinople. See Krijne Ciggaar, *Western Travellers to Constantinople: The West and Byzantium, 962–1204: Cultural and Political Relations*, Leiden, 1996.
2. Useful background material to Byzantium and its relics can be found in Cyril Mango (ed.), *The Oxford History of Byzantium*, Oxford, 2002; Judith Herrin, *Byzantium: The Surprising Life of a Medieval Empire*, London, 2007; and the sumptuous catalogue to the Royal Academy of Arts exhibition *Byzantium*, edited by Robin Cormack and Maria Vassilaki, London, 2008. For the relic cults, I have relied heavily on Holgar Klein, 'Sacred Relics and Imperial Ceremonies at the Great Palace of Constantinople', F.A. Bauer (Hrsg.), *Visualisierungen von Herrschaft, BYZAS5* (2006), pp. 79–99, available online from the University of Columbia, Department of Art History and Archaeology. Most of the quotations referring directly to relics in this chapter come from this source.
3. See Charles Freeman, AD 381, London, 2008, and New York, 2009, for the background.
4. For the growth of the cult to the Virgin in Constantinople see Vasiliki Limberis, *Divine Heiress: The Virgin Mary and the Creation of Christian Constantinople*, London and New York, 1994, and Miri Rubin, *Mother of God: A History of the Virgin Mary*, London, 2009, Chapter 5, 'Mary of the Christian Empire'.
5. The events are covered in Walter Kaegi, *Heraclius, Emperor of Byzantium*, Cambridge, 2002.
6. Icons are discussed in Hans Belting's celebrated study of images, *Likeness and Presence: A History of the Image before the Era of Art*, Chicago and London, 1994; Chapter 8, 'Church and Image: The Doctrine of the Church and Iconoclasm', deals with the campaign against images.
7. See Lee Palmer Wandel, *Voracious Idols and Violent Hands*, Cambridge, 1995, Chapter 1, 'The Image in the Churches'.
8. This is Robert de Clari's description from his *The Capture of Constantinople*, English translation from the French original by Edgar McNeal, New York, 1936.
9. See Chapter 11 in Belting, *op. cit.*, 'The "Holy Face": Legends and Images in Competition', for discussion of these images.
10. This account is taken from *Theophanes Continuatus*, a collection of eleventh-century texts now in the Vatican Library, Rome. The translation is by Paul Stephenson, who has useful online translations of this and similar sources on his website.

CHAPTER SIX: BISHOPS, MAGIC AND RELICS IN THE POST-ROMAN WORLD

1. Background material to the centuries after the fall of Rome is now provided by two excellent surveys: Christopher Wickham, *The Inheritance of Rome: A History of Europe from*

400 to 1000, London and New York, 2009 (especially Chapter 3, 'Culture and Belief in the Christian Roman World'), and Julia Smith, *Europe after Rome: A New Cultural History 500–1000*, Oxford, 2000. Specifically on Christianity, see Richard Fletcher, *The Conversion of Europe: From Paganism to Christianity 371–1386 AD*, London, 1997, and Peter Brown, *The Rise of Western Christendom*, second edition, Oxford, 2003. Volume 3 of *The Cambridge History of Christianity, Early Medieval Christianities, c.600–1100*, Thomas Noble and Julia Smith (eds), Cambridge, 2008, has much background material.

2. For those who can read French, there is a useful survey of early Irish attitudes to relics in Jean-Michel Picard, 'Le culte des reliques en Irlande', in Edina Bozóky and Anne-Marie Helvétius (eds), *Les Reliques: Objets, Cultes, Symboles*, Turnhout (Belgium), 1999.

3. See Valerie Flint, *The Rise of Magic in Early Medieval Europe*, Princeton, 1991, p. 148 for the quotation from Augustine.

4. *Ibid.*, p. 96.

5. From Euan Cameron, *Enchanted Europe: Superstition, Reason and Religion, 1250–1750*, Oxford, 2010, p. 88.

6. Flint, *op. cit.*, p. 397.

7. Quoted in Edward James, *Britain in the First Millennium*, London, 2001, p. 156.

8. John Crook, *Architectural Settings of the Cult of Saints in the Early Christian West*, Oxford, 2000, is an excellent introduction to the development of relic shrines during these centuries. See also Cynthia Hahn, 'Seeing and Believing: The Construction of Sanctity in Early Medieval Saints' Shrines', in *Speculum* 72:3 (1997), pp. 1,079–1,116. Similar attempts to maintain harmony could be seen in the way in which shrines to the same saint found a way of accommodating their rivalries. The eighth-century Irish *Collectio Canonum Hibernensis* encouraged a system by which saints' bodies could be divided up or transferred without the original church losing the honour of having once held them, although at the Last Judgement the saint would rise from the shrine where his head was kept. This seems to have been a deliberate attempt to calm rivalries between different tribal and religious groups.

9. From Chapter XXVIII:4.

10. From Chapter XXVIII:1.

11. Peter Brown, *The Cult of the Saints: Its Rise and Function in Latin Christianity*, Chicago and London, 1981.

12. A response to Brown is James Howard-Johnston and Paul Antony Hayward (eds), *The Cult of Saints in Late Antiquity and the Early Middle Ages*, Oxford, 1999.

13. See the discussion in Chapter 1 of Norman Housley, *Religious Warfare in Europe, 1400–1536*, Oxford, 2002.

14. I have drawn on Raymond Van Dam, *Saints and their Miracles in Late Antique Gaul*, Princeton, 1993, for Radegund and Martin of Tours.

15. On the *Penitentials* see Brown, *Western Christendom, op. cit.*, pp. 241–5.

16. This early trade in relics has been systematically analysed by Michael McCormick in his *Origins of the European Economy: Communications and Commerce, AD 300–900*, Cambridge, 2001, especially Chapter 10, 'Hagiographic Horizons: Collecting Exotic Relics in Early Medieval France'. I have used his findings here. On the slave trade see pp. 733–54.

17. For these thefts see Patrick Geary, *Furta Sacra: Thefts of Relics in the Central Middle Ages*, revised edition, Princeton, 1991. See also Julia Smith, 'Old Saints, New Saints: Roman Relics in Carolingian Francia', in Julia Smith (ed.), *Early Medieval Rome and the Christian West*, Brill (Leiden), 2000.

CHAPTER SEVEN: 'A BARBAROUS, FIERCE AND UNBELIEVING NATION'

1. See John Burrow, *A History of Histories*, London, 2007, Chapter 14, 'Gregory of Tours, Kings, Bishops and Others'.

2. On Anglo-Saxon Britain there is John Blair's comprehensive *The Church in Anglo-Saxon Society*, Oxford, 2005, where most of the material on the Anglo-Saxon saints has come from. Bede's *The Ecclesiastical History of the English People* is the key primary source (Oxford World Classics, 1999, edited by Judith McClure and Roger Collins).
3. Bede, *op. cit.*, Book One, Chapter 23.
4. See Blair, *op. cit.*, pp. 137–8.
5. The modern translation used here is by Jonathan Glenn. http://www.lightspill.com/poetry/oe/rood.html.
6. Fulton, *op. cit.*, p. 54.
7. I have used Bede for the stories of these saints.
8. See, for an assessment of Bede as a historian, Burrow, *op. cit.*, Chapter 15, 'Bede: The English Church and the English People'.
9. For Cuthbert, see Benedicta Ward, *Miracles and the Medieval Mind*, revised edition, Philadelphia, 1987, pp. 56–66.
10. These are listed in the document included in John Shinners (ed.), *Medieval Popular Religion, 1000–1500, A Reader*, second edition, Peterborough, Ontario and Plymouth, England, 2007, p. 195. There is a similar list of relics at Waltham Abbey; see Nicholas Rogers, 'The Waltham Abbey Relic-list', in Carola Hicks (ed.), *England in the Eleventh Century*, Stamford, 1992, pp. 157–82. Rogers notes that the monks do query some of the origins of their vast relic list but appear to accept the majority as genuine.

CHAPTER EIGHT: THE GREAT CONSOLIDATOR

1. In addition to the general histories cited for Chapter 5, note 1, there are two good biographies of Charlemagne: Matthias Becher, *Charlemagne*, New Haven and London, 2003, and Rosamond McKitterick, *Charlemagne: The Formation of a European Identity*, Cambridge, 2008.
2. On the *Libri Carolini*, see McKitterick, *op. cit.*, pp. 313, 356–8. On Charlemagne's attitudes to relics in general see *ibid.*, pp. 326–30, and Paul Fouracre, 'The Origins of the Carolingian Attempt to Regulate the Cult of Saints', Chapter 7 in Howard-Johnston and Hayward (eds), *op. cit.*
3. See the website of the St Gall Project, www.stgallplan.org, for further details and the map itself.
4. See Doig, *op. cit.*, Chapter 5, 'Carolingian Architecture and Liturgical Reform'.
5. On Hadrian I in Rome, see Richard Krautheimer, *Rome: Profile of a City, 312–1308*, Princeton, 2000, Chapter 5, 'Renewal and Renascence: The Carolingian Age'. See also John McCulloh, 'From Antiquity to the Middle Ages: Continuity and Change in Papal Relic Policy from the 6th to the 8th Century', in Ernst Dassmann and K. Suso Frank (eds), *Pietas: Festschrift für Berhard Kötting*, Münster, 1980, pp. 313–24.
6. See Geary, *op. cit.*, Chapter 3, 'The Professionals', for Deusdona.
7. On Einhard, see Wickham, *op. cit.*, Chapter 17, 'Intellectuals and Politics'; for this quotation, p. 406.

CHAPTER NINE: HOPE AND DESPERATION IN A DISORDERED WORLD

1. Quoted in Geary, *op. cit.*, p. 20.
2. R.I. Moore, 'Postscript, The Peace of God and the Social Revolution', in Thomas Head and Richard Landes (eds), *The Peace of God: Social Violence and Religious Response in France around the Year 1000*, Ithaca, New York, and London, 1992, p. 313. The essays here cover most aspects of the 'Peace of God' movement.

3. See Bernhard Töpfer, 'The Cult of Relics and Pilgrimage in Burgundy and Aquitaine at the Time of the Monastic Reform', in Head and Landes, *op. cit.*, pp. 41–57.

4. Quoted, without citation, in the Sacred Destinations website for Conques. I assume that it comes from the 'Book of Miracles' at Conques compiled by Bernard.

5. See Cynthia Hahn, 'The Voices of the Saints: What Do Speaking Reliquaries Say?', *Gesta* 36 (1997).

6. Quoted in Blair, *op. cit.*, p. 486.

7. The best account of the story is in Richard Landes, *Relics, Apocalypse and the Deceits of History: Ademar of Chabannes, 989–1034*, Cambridge, MA, and London, 1995.

8. Quoted in Barbara Abou-El-Hai, 'The Audiences for the Medieval Cult of Saints', *Gesta* 30:1 (1991), pp. 3–15.

9. Quoted in Fulton, *op. cit.*, p. 67, but see especially Chapter 2, 'Apocalypse, Reform and the Suffering Saviour'. See also Landes, *Relics*, Chapter 15, 'Ademar and the Millennial Generation: Apostolic Relics and Apocalyptic Pilgrimages', esp. pp. 309–13.

10. See the excellent R.I. Moore, 'Heresy, Repression and Social Change in the Age of Gregorian Reform', in Scott Waugh and Peter Diehl (eds), *Christendom and its Discontents: Exclusion, Persecution and Rebellion, 1000–1500*, Cambridge, 1996, pp. 19–46.

11. Landes, *Relics*, Chapter 14, 'Terrible Hopes of the Millennial Generation and the Weeping Crucifixion'. The problems of showing Christ actually dead on the Cross had always been a challenging one. In early Christian iconography he is not shown on the Cross at all, or if so, still alive. From this period on, his suffering is shown in increasing detail.

12. Fulton, *op. cit.*, pp. 222–3.

13. *Ibid.*, pp. 268–73.

14. See Sumption, *op. cit.*, pp. 115–16. Ward, *op. cit.*, discusses the miracles of James on pp. 110–17.

15. J. France (ed. and transl.), *Rodulfus Glaber: The Five Books of the Histories*, Oxford, 1989, pp. 126–7.

CHAPTER TEN: CULTS AND THE RISE OF ANTI-SEMITISM

1. R.I. Moore, *The Formation of a Persecuting Society: Power and Deviance in Western Europe, 950–1250*, Oxford and Malden, MA, 1997, pp. 148–9. See pp. 27–45 of this book for more information on attitudes to Jews in medieval Europe.

2. For the cult of William, see Simon Yarrow, *Saints and Their Communities: Miracle Stories in Twelfth-Century England*, Oxford, 2005, Chapter 5, and Ward, *op.cit.*, Chapter 4.

CHAPTER ELEVEN: FERVENT CHRISTIAN PILGRIMS

1. An excellent sourcebook with commentary is Diana Webb, *Pilgrims and Pilgrimage in the Medieval West*, London and New York, 1999. I have used Chapter 1, 'The Development of the Medieval Pilgrimage', for the introductory material. See also Chapter 4, 'Pilgrims and the Shrine', in Nilson, *op. cit.*, and Sumption, *op. cit.*

2. Quoted from Webb, *op. cit.*, pp. 28–9.

3. *Ibid.*, pp. 42–3.

4. See the maps provided at the beginning of Morris, *The Sepulchre of Christ*, and his Chapter 5, 'Towards the First Crusade', that discusses many of the copies of the Sepulchre to be found in western Europe.

5. For a balanced introduction to the Crusades, see Jonathan Riley-Smith, *What Were the Crusades?*, fourth edition, San Francisco and Basingstoke, 2009. See also Thomas

Asbridge, *The Crusades: The War for the Holy Land*, London and New York, 2010, for a full account.

6. See the discussion in John France, *The Crusades and the Expansion of Catholic Christendom, 1000–1714*, Abingdon, UK, and New York, 2005, Chapter 2, 'The Papal Monarchy and the Invention of the Crusade'.

7. Morris, *The Sepulchre of Christ*, Chapter 6, 'Latin Jerusalem, 1099–1187', covers the capture of Jerusalem and provides the quotation, from J.H. and L.I. Hills (eds), *Le 'Liber' de Raymond d'Aguilers*, Paris, 1969, pp. 150–1. See Housley, *op. cit.*, Chapter 1, for a discussion of the justification of religious warfare.

8. Katherine is comprehensively dealt with in Jacqueline Jenkins and Katherine Lewis, *St. Katherine of Alexandria: Texts and Contexts in Western Medieval Europe*, Turnhout, 2003.

9. *Mandeville's Travels*, written in Anglo-Norman French, were certainly not by anyone called Mandeville, who has never been shown to exist. They are a strange combination of tales, some mythical, some possibly based on personal experience. The section on the Holy Land is likely to be the most accurate. They were enormously popular. The most likely author is one Jehan à la Barbe, a physician from Liège.

10. The list is in Webb, *op. cit.*, p. 34.

11. The veil disappeared in the sixteenth century, possibly looted during the Sack of Rome by the troops of Charles V in 1527.

12. Many of these details come from Sumption, *op. cit.*, Chapter 13, 'Rome', but I have added personal knowledge.

13. Krautheimer, *op. cit.*, p. 207.

14. Listed in Webb, *Pilgrims*, pp. 52–3.

15. Sumption, *op. cit.*, p. 167 (a German pilgrim writing in 1494).

16. Ward, *op. cit.*, pp. 110–15, deals with the miracles of James.

17. These and similar stories come from Chapter 4 of Webb, *op. cit.*, 'Help and Hazard: The Pilgrim's Experience'.

CHAPTER TWELVE: 'THE EYES ARE FED WITH GOLD-BEDECKED RELIQUARIES'

1. Eric Fernie, 'Edward The Confessor's Westminster Abbey', Chapter 6, in Richard Mortimer (ed.), *Edward the Confessor: The Man and the Legend*, Woodbridge, UK, 2009.

2. Details are given in Nilson, *op. cit.*

3. Geary, *Furta Sacra*, pp. 107–15, for a description that I have supplemented from other sources on the wider context of the theft.

4. There are two lively accounts of Suger's exploits that I have used: Chapter 2, 'A Change of Style: The Invention of Gothic', from Philip Ball, *Universe of Stone: Chartres Cathedral and the Triumph of the Medieval Mind*, London, 2008, and Chapter 5, 'The Initial Vision', in Robert Scott, *The Gothic Enterprise*, Berkeley and London, 2005.

5. Quoted in Scott, *op. cit.*, p. 85.

6. Suger's own account can be found online and in Erwin Panofsky (ed. and transl.), *Abbot Suger on the Abbey Church of St. Denis and its Art Treasures*, Princeton, 1946, revised 1979, pp. 87–9.

7. Scott, *op. cit.*, pp. 91–2.

8. Ball, *op. cit.*, has all the background details and provides a fine introduction to the rebuilding of the cathedral in its present form.

9. This part of Haimon's account can be found in Shinners, *op. cit.*, p. 391.

10. Quoted in Ball, *op. cit.*, p. 21.

11. See Elizabeth Pastan, 'Charlemagne as Saint? Relics and the Choice of Window Subjects at Chartres Cathedral', in Matthew Gabriel and Jane Stuckey, *The Legend of Charlemagne*

in the Middle Ages: Power, Faith and Crusade, Basingstoke, UK, and New York, 2008, pp. 97–136.

12. See Colin Morris, 'A Critique of Popular Religion: Guibert of Nogent on *The Relics of the Saints*', in G.J. Cuming and Derek Baker (eds), *Popular Belief and Practice*, Cambridge, 1972. The *Treatise* can easily be found online.

13. This letter of 1125 is available under 'Bernard of Clairvaux: An Apology' in the Fordham University Center for Medieval Studies online sourcebook http://www.fordham.edu/halsall/sbook.html.

CHAPTER THIRTEEN: LOOTING THE EAST

1. See Anne Latowsky, 'Charlemagne as Pilgrim? Requests for Relics in the *Descriptio qualiter* and *The Voyage of Charlemagne*', in Gabriel and Stuckey, *op. cit.*

2. The story is told in Henry Chadwick, *East and West: The Making of a Rift in the Church*, Oxford and New York, 2005.

3. An excellent account of the Fourth Crusade is Michael Angold, *The Fourth Crusade: Event and Context*, Harlow, 2003. Thomas Madden has provided a revisionary account from Venice's perspective in *Enrico Dandolo and the Rise of Venice*, Baltimore, 2007.

4. The *Hystoria Constantinopolitana* can be found in translation in A.J. Andrea (ed. and transl.), *The Capture of Constantinople: The 'Hystoria Constantinopolitana' of Gunther of Pairis*, Philadelphia, 1997.

5. Angold, *op. cit.*, has a comprehensive account of the looting of relics, pp. 229–41.

6. Brett Edward Whalen, *Dominion of God, Christendom and Apocalypse in the Middle Ages*, Cambridge, MA, and London, 2009, pp. 133 ff.

CHAPTER FOURTEEN: LOUIS IX AND THE SAINTE-CHAPELLE

1. There is a full two-volume edition of *The Golden Legend* translated by William Granger Ryan, Princeton, 1995, and selections in Richard Hamer (ed.) and Christopher Stace (transl.) in the Penguin Classics series, London, 1998.

2. From Richard Hamer's introduction to the Penguin Classics edition, p. xvi, from which further information is drawn.

3. I recently came across a vivid depiction of Heraclius barefoot and in his shift before the gate of Jerusalem in the Capella della Croce da Giorno in the church of St Francis in Volterra, Tuscany. The frescos are by Cenni di Francesco (1410).

4. This is all covered in Daniel Weiss, *Art and Crusade in the Age of St. Louis*, Cambridge, 1988. Weiss not only provides the architectural and historical background to the chapel but shows how Louis's ill-fated crusade led naturally from it.

5. Quoted in André Vauchez, 'Saints and Pilgrimages: New and Old', Chapter 21, in Miri Rubin and Walter Simons (eds), *The Cambridge History of Christianity, Volume Four: Christianity in Western Europe c.1100–c.1500*, Cambridge, 2009, p. 325. The biographer of Louis IX is Guillaume de Saint-Pathus.

6. These details all come from Weiss, *op. cit.*

7. An anti-pope is a claimant to the papacy, established, at the time or since then, as outside the legitimate line of popes (which must stretch unbroken from Peter).

8. This is illustrated in a 'special issue' of *Connaissance des Arts*, 'The Palais de la Cité', English edition, Paris, 2008, p. 16. It is said that a set of plaited reeds now in Notre Dame in Paris and encased in a nineteenth-century reliquary is the Crown of Thorns from the Sainte-Chapelle, returned to the Catholic Church in 1801 after the French Revolution.

9. See John McManners, *Church and Society in Eighteenth-Century France, Volume Two: The Religion of the People and the Politics of Religion*, Oxford, 1998, p. 127.
10. Quoted in Weiss, *op. cit.*, p. 33.

Chapter Fifteen: Sacred Flesh Between Death and Resurrection

1. For this chapter I have drawn heavily on the work of Caroline Walker Bynum, *The Resurrection of the Body*, already cited. This quotation is at page 316.
2. *Ibid.*, p. 131. Chapter 3, 'Reassemblage and Regurgitation: Ideas of Bodily Resurrection in Early Scholasticism', offers a good view of attitudes in this period.
3. Quoted in Katherine Ludwig Jansen, *The Making of the Magdalen: Preaching and Devotion in the later Middle Ages*, Princeton, 2000, p. 282.
4. Quoted in Bynum, *op. cit.*, p. 210.
5. In societies where most people are only known through oral descriptions of them, tales that someone had died often conflicted with reports that they had been seen later alive. The reports might be about different people or the observer might have been simply mistaken, but the historian takes resurrection appearances, of which there are many hundreds in the Middle Ages, with extreme caution!
6. Quoted in the accompanying pamphlet to 'The Sacred Made Real', an exhibition of Spanish seventeenth-century art, the National Gallery, London, from 21 October 2009 to 24 January 2010. The exhibition included a seventeenth-century woodcarving of the scene.
7. Quoted in Bynum, *op. cit.*, pp. 178–9.
8. The canons of the Council are available under the heading 'Twelfth Ecumenical Council: Lateran IV 1215' online in the *Medieval Sourcebook*, Fordham University.
9. See Bynum, *op. cit.*, pp. 320–9, 'The Practice of Bodily Partition'.
10. This is from Marguerite's *Speculum* (Chapter 3), translated by Richard Pioli and included in Elizabeth Alvilda Petroff, (ed.), *Medieval Women's Visionary Literature*, New York and Oxford, 1986.
11. Book XXII: Chapter 11 onwards.

Chapter Sixteen: 'Christ's recruits . . . fight back'

1. Quoted in John H. van Engen, 'Conclusion: Christendom, *c*.1100', in Noble and Smith, *op. cit.*, p. 625.
2. As background material see Anthony Perron, 'The Bishops of Rome, 1100–1300', Chapter 2 in Rubin and Simons (eds), *op. cit.*
3. André Vauchez, *Sainthood in the Later Middle Ages*. The English translation by Jean Birrell, Cambridge, 1997, is the classic text here.
4. *Ibid.*, Part One, Chapter 3.
5. See Robert Bartlett, *The Natural and the Supernatural in the Middle Ages*, Cambridge, 2008, especially Chapter 1, 'The Boundaries of the Supernatural'.
6. Discussed in Bartlett, *ibid.*, pp. 23–6. This was a common subject in discussions on the miraculous. It is worth noting that Aaron's Rod had survived as a relic – sixteenth-century sources claimed that the Dominican church of Santa Maria sopra Minerva in Rome had it among other Old Testament relics, but it was also claimed by the Sainte-Chapelle in Paris. An earlier source had placed it in the vast collection of relics in St John Lateran.
7. Discussed in Vauchez, *Sainthood*, pp. 38–40.
8. Vauchez discusses the figures for canonisations and the criteria that seem to have led to successful conclusions in *ibid.*, Book II, Part II, 'Official Sainthood: Forms and Criteria of Christian Perfection According to Processes of Canonization'.

9. The account that follows is drawn largely from Robert Bartlett, *The Hanged Man*, Princeton, 2004, with supplementary material from Ronald Finucane, *Miracles and Pilgrims: Popular Beliefs in Medieval England*, London, Melbourne and Toronto, 1977, Chapter 10, 'The Changing Fortunes of a Curative Shrine: St. Thomas Cantilupe'.

10. See the discussion of this report in Vauchez, *Sainthood*, pp. 488–98.

11. Finucane, *op. cit.*, pp. 187–8.

CHAPTER SEVENTEEN: PROTECTORS OF *IL POPOLO*

1. See Iain Fenlon, *The Ceremonial City: History, Memory and Myth in Renaissance Venice*, New Haven and London, 2007, Chapter 1, 'Constructing a Civil Religion', for the legends of Mark and the background to the theft.

2. Martino da Canal is at present available only in an Italian translation of the French original, Alberto Limentani (ed.), *Les estoires de Venise. Cronaca veneziana in lingua francese dalle origini al 1275*, Florence, 1972.

3. The point is made by Otto Demus in his *The Mosaics of San Marco in Venice: Volume One, The Eleventh and Twelfth Centuries*, Chicago, 1984, pp. 69–70. This volume and the subsequent volume on the thirteenth century show the full range of mosaics connected to the legend of Mark.

4. Quoted in Edward Muir, *Civic Ritual in Renaissance Venice*, Princeton, 1986, p. 91. This is the classic introduction to the ceremonies of medieval and Renaissance Venice.

5. The horses are usually described as bronze but it has been known since the eighteenth century that they were cast in copper. It is now known that this was to allow them to take the gilding. See further my *The Horses of St. Mark's*, London, 2004, New York, 2010.

6. This miracle is described in Patricia Fortini Brown, *Venetian Narrative Painting in the Age of Carpaccio*, New Haven and London, 1988, pp. 141–9.

7. The miracle paintings of San Giovanni Evangelista are described in *ibid.*; for the background see pp. 139–41.

8. These cults are described in Diana Webb, *Patrons and Defenders: The Saints in the Italian City-States*, London and New York, 1996, especially Part Two, although I have supplemented them by personal knowledge based on my own visits to these cities.

9. The 'knights' had reason to be cautious. When the body of St John of Gualdo, who had died in 1170, was moved to a new altar in his monastery, Santa Maria of Gualdo Mazocco, the local archbishop delegated the task to three of his local bishops. Before the *translatio* of the body took place, they had detached parts of it to keep for themselves and their own churches.

10. Webb, *Patrons and Defenders*, pp. 216–19, for these later developments.

11. See the recent study by M.E. Bratchell, *Medieval Lucca and the Renaissance State*, Oxford, 2008.

12. See, in addition to Webb, Robert Maniura, 'Image and Relic in the Cult of Our Lady of Prato', Chapter 10, in Sally Cornelison and Scott B. Montgomery, *Images, Relics and Devotional Practices in Medieval and Renaissance Italy*, Tempe, Arizona, 2006.

13. My account comes from Richard Trexler, *Public Life in Renaissance Florence*, New York and London, 1980, especially Chapter 8, 'The Ritual of Celebration'.

CHAPTER EIGHTEEN: THE VIRGIN MARY AND THE PENITENT WHORE

1. I have based this account on Yarrow, *op. cit.*, Chapter 3, 'The Canons of Laon and their Tour of England'.

2. See Rubin, *Mother of God*, especially Parts Three, Four and Five for the variety of Marian cults between 1000 and 1500. See also Rachel Fulton, 'Mary', Chapter 18 in Rubin and

Simons (eds), *op. cit.* Marina Warner, *Alone of All her Sex*, London and New York, 1983 is a justly famous study. There is original source material in Shinners, *op. cit.*, Chapter 3, 'The Virgin Mary'.

3. Quoted in Belting, *op. cit.*, p. 285.

4. See Lisa Monnas, *Merchants, Princes and Painters: Silk Fabrics in Italian and Northern Paintings, 1300–1550*, New Haven and London, 2008, p. 222.

5. To be found in the Church of St Augustine in Rome.

6. See Belting, *op. cit.*, pp. 57–9, 'St Luke's Images of the Virgin and the Concept of the Portrait'.

7. *Ibid.*, Chapter 15, 'The Icon in the Civic Life of Rome'.

8. See the discussion in Belting, *op. cit.*, Chapter 14, 'Statues, Vessels and Signs: Medieval Images and Relics in the West', for a discussion of the relationship between statues/images and relics. See also Chapter 3, '*Elegentissima Mariola*: Early Images of Our Lady' in Richard Marks, *Image and Devotion in Late Medieval England*, Stroud, UK, 2004, for a good introduction focusing on English examples.

9. There is a good example in the oratory of Bernardino of Siena in Perugia. The plague arrow is an ancient symbol. Apollo uses it as a means of spreading plague on the Greeks in the opening section of Homer's *Iliad*.

10. For Gautier, see Warner, *op. cit.*, pp. 198–9 and Rubin, *Mother of God*, pp. 229–32. 'The Tale of the Tumbler' can be found online.

11. De Voragine's account can be found in full in Shinners, *op. cit.*, pp. 183–94.

12. The crucial book here is Katherine Ludwig Jansen, *The Making of the Magdalen: Preaching and Popular Devotion in the Later Middle Ages*, Princeton, 2000. The account given here is based on this book unless other references are given.

13. *Ibid.*, pp. 62–82. Supporters of ordination for women in the Catholic Church argue that she was, in fact, a female Apostle, appointed as such by Christ, and that this provides an important precedent for women priests.

14. The friars are included in any history of the medieval Church, e.g. Chapter 11 of F. Donald Logan, *A History of the Church in the Middle Ages*, London and New York, 2002, or the earlier but still much-respected R.W. Southern, *Western Society and the Church in the Middle Ages*, Volume 2 of the *Pelican History of the Church*, London and New York, 1970, Chapter 6, Part Three, 'The Friars'. In contrast to monks, canons preached the Gospel publicly.

15. W.A. Pantin, 'Instructions for a Devout and Literate Layman', in *Medieval Learning and Literature: Essays Presented to Richard William Hunt*, ed. J.J.G. Alexander and Margaret Gibson, Oxford, 1976, pp. 398–422.

16. Quoted in Jansen, *op. cit.*, p. 255.

17. *Ibid.*, pp. 257–8.

18. This bizarre story is told in the biography of Hugh of Lincoln by Adam of Evesham and can be found in Shinners, *op. cit.*, pp. 181–3.

19. See 'Virginity Reconstituted' in Jansen, *op.cit.*, pp. 286–94.

CHAPTER NINETEEN: THE WONDROUS BLOOD OF CHRIST

1. The key studies here are Caroline Walker Bynum, *Wonderful Blood: Theology and Practice in late Medieval Germany and Beyond*, Philadelphia, 2007, and Nicholas Vincent, *The Holy Blood: King Henry III and the Westminster Blood Relic*, Cambridge, 2001. The quotation comes from Bynum, *Wonderful Blood*, p. 2.

2. Bynum, *Wonderful Blood*, p. 4.

3. *The Book of Margery Kempe*, Book One, Section 28.

4. This story is told in Vincent, *op. cit.*

5. Sumption, *op. cit.*, pp. 30–1.
6. The Florentine painter Paolo Uccello's *Profanation of the Host*, of 1469, now in the Ducal Palace at Urbino, sets out such a story in six episodes.
7. Gavin I. Langmuir, 'The Tortures of the Body of Christ', in Scott Waugh and Peter Diehl, *Christendom and its Discontents: Exclusion, Persecution and Rebellion, 1000–1500*, Cambridge, 1996.
8. See Bynum, *Wonderful Blood*, pp. 69–72.
9. *Ibid.*, Chapter 2, for the story of the shrine that takes a central place in Bynum's study.
10. See especially *ibid.*, Chapter 4, 'Debates about Eucharistic Transformations and Blood Relics', from which the Weingarten and La Rochelle cases are taken, and Vincent, *op. cit.*, Chapter 5, 'The Scholastic Debate'.
11. Quoted in Caroline Walker Bynum, 'Late Medieval Eucharistic Doctrine', in Lynn Staley (ed.), *The Book of Margery Kempe*, New York and London, 2001, p. 295.
12. Quoted in Amy Hollywood, 'Mysticism and Transcendence', Chapter 19, in Rubin and Simons (eds), *op. cit.*, p. 305.
13. See Snoek, *op. cit.*, pp. 250–76.

CHAPTER TWENTY: RESCUERS AND DEVILS

1. A well-written and authoritative introduction to this troubled period is George Holmes, *Europe: Hierarchy and Revolt, 1320–1450, Blackwell Classic Histories of Europe*, second edition, Oxford, 2000. See pp. 59–68 on the Avignon Papacy.
2. The chronicler John le Bel, quoted in Michael Goodich, *Violence and Miracle in the Fourteenth Century: Private Grief and Public Salvation*, Chicago and London, 1995, p. 117.
3. See Goodich, *op. cit.*, especially Chapter 6, 'The Violence of Nature'.
4. See *ibid.*, pp. 130–7, 'A Cult Revived in France: Martial of Limoges'.
5. The rest of Nicholas's body was now hidden, so successfully that it was not rediscovered until 1926, but meanwhile the arms and bloodstained cloths were major relics, with indulgences granted to visitors in 1400. The arms have now been rejoined to the body and the whole lies in the crypt in St Nicholas's church in Tolentino.
6. Sumption, *op. cit.*, p. 284. Sumption deals with these other pilgrimages in Chapters 14 and 15.
7. See Richard Wunderli, *Peasant Fires: The Drummer of Niklashausen*, Bloomington and Indianapolis, 1992.
8. The sermons of Bernardino are well covered in Franco Mormando, *The Preacher's Demons: Bernardino of Siena and the Social Underworld of Early Renaissance Italy*, University of Chicago Press, 1999.
9. I have drawn here on Part Two of Cameron, *op. cit.*, 'The Learned Response to Superstitions in the Middle Ages: Angels and Demons'.
10. *Ibid.*, pp. 130–1 and 135–7, for Gerson's views on superstition.
11. *Ibid.*, p. 125.
12. *Ibid.*, p. 110.
13. Sumption, *op. cit.*, p. 274.
14. Cameron, *op. cit.*, p. 130.

CHAPTER TWENTY-ONE: 'OF FAR-OFF SAINTS, HALLOWED IN SUNDRY LANDS'

1. See Deborah Howard, *Venice and the East: The Impact of the Islamic World on Venetian Architecture 1100–1500*, New Haven and London, 2000, Chapter 7, 'The Pilgrim City', especially pp. 193–5, 'The Pre-Pilgrimage Tour'.

2. William Wey, *Itineraries of William Wey: fellow of Eton College to Jerusalem* AD *1458 and* AD *1462; and to St. James of Compostella,* AD *1456,* London 1857. This is a transliteration of the original English and Latin text without modern translation. See now Francis Davey (ed. and transl.), *The Itineraries of William Wey,* Oxford, 2010. I have also used an anonymous pilgrim's guide to the church of the Holy Sepulchre of *c.*1350, included in Shinners, *op. cit.,* pp. 200–4. See also Colin Morris, *The Holy Sepulchre, op.cit., passim* but especially Chapter 9, 'The "Great Pilgrimage" in the Later Middle Ages, 1291–1530', which provides an excellent overview, and the delightful R.J. Mitchell, *The Spring Voyage: The Jerusalem Pilgrimage in 1458,* London, 1965.

3. *The Book of Margery Kempe,* Book One, Chapters 26–9, for her pilgrimage to Jerusalem.

4. This is from a sermon *Veneranda Dies,* probably dating from the twelfth century, and urging a more austere attitude to pilgrimage. Quoted in Sumption, *op. cit.,* pp. 124–5.

5. See Sumption, *op. cit.,* Chapter 13, 'Rome', to which I have added personal knowledge.

6. *Ibid.,* Chapter 16, 'Medieval Christianity: Religion to Ritual', had much of this background material on indulgences.

7. The rebuilding of Rome from the fifteenth century is well covered in Loren Partridge, *The Renaissance in Rome,* London, 1996.

8. Sumption, *op. cit.,* pp. 290–1.

9. Quoted in Wunderli, *op. cit.,* pp. 39–40.

10. Finucane, *op. cit.,* Chapter 11, 'Shifting Loyalties: New Shrines and Old Saints at the End of the Middle Ages', provides the details for the shrines below. I have also used Chapter 7, 'The Offerings Examined', in Ben Nilson, *op. cit.,* Woodbridge and Rochester, New York, 1998.

11. This is well covered in Richard Marks, *op. cit.,* especially the Introduction. See Duffy, *The Stripping of the Altars: Traditional Religion in England 1400–1580,* New Haven and London, 1992, pp. 155–9, 'The Saints in their Images'.

12. Marks, *op.cit.,* pp. 26–7.

CHAPTER TWENTY-TWO: 'DEAD IMAGES THAT . . . MAY NOT . . . HELP ANY MAN OF ANY DISEASE'

1. There are good introductory essays on Wyclif in Part Two of Gordon Luff, *Heresy, Philosophy and Religion in the Medieval West,* Aldershot and Burlington, Vermont, 2002. See also Kantik Ghosh, 'Wycliffism and Lollardy', Chapter 28 in Rubin and Simons (eds), *op. cit.,* and 'Nominalists, Lollards, and Hussites' in Diarmaid MacCulloch, *A History of Christianity,* London and New York, 2009, pp. 564–74.

2. I am thinking especially of the controversies surrounding the 1277 Condemnations made in Paris, which dealt with many of the new ideas that had come in with Aristotle and his Arab commentators.

3. The *Arundel Constitutions* are available as one of the supplementary texts in Lynn Staley's edited version of *The Book of Margery Kempe, op. cit.,* at pp. 187–95, with an accompanying commentary by Nicholas Watson on pp. 299–301.

4. There is a good summary of Hus's ideas in Holmes, *op. cit.,* pp. 151–66. See also MacCulloch, *op. cit.,* above.

5. This series of crusades is neglected in English histories. See, as an introductory survey, 'A Crucible of Religious Warfare: Bohemia during the Hussite Wars, 1400–1436', Chapter 2 in Housley, *op. cit.* The quotation comes from a papal bull of 1421, quoted at page 43.

6. See A.G. Dickens and Whitney R.D. Jones, *Erasmus: The Reformer,* London, 1994, as a readable introduction to Erasmus's ideas.

7. *Pilgrimage for Religion's Sake* is easily available online.

8. Quoted in Anthony Levi, *Renaissance and Reformation: The Intellectual Genesis*, New Haven and London, 2002, p. 301.
9. See Diarmaid MacCulloch, *Reformation: Europe's House Divided 1490–1700*, London and New York, 2003, Chapter 3, 'New Heaven: New Earth, 1517–1524', for the details of the early Reformation.

CHAPTER TWENTY-THREE: PROTESTANTISM AND THE NEW ICONOCLASM

1. *The Exposition of the Ten Commandments.*
2. Quoted in Cameron, *op. cit.*, p. 163.
3. Readily available online.
4. From Luther's *Commentary on the Epistle to the Galatians*, quoted in Cameron, *op. cit.*, p. 166.
5. MacCulloch, *Reformation*, pp. 145–6, for a summary.
6. I have used Lee Palmer Wandel's excellent analysis, *Voracious Idols and Violent Hands*, for the events that follow. He has separate chapters on Zurich (Chapter 2), Strasburg (Chapter 3) and Basel (Chapter 4).
7. The classic essay on this is Hugh Trevor-Roper's 'Religion, the Reformation and Social Change', reproduced in his *The Crisis of the Seventeenth Century*, New York, 1965.
8. See the biography by Bruce Gordon, *John Calvin*, New Haven and London, 2009. *The Treatise on Relics* is available online.
9. It has been argued that Calvin does refer specifically to the Turin Shroud, among others he discusses. He does describe a similar one in Nice, and there is some evidence that the Shroud may have been temporarily at Nice at the time he was writing.
10. Eamon Duffy's *The Stripping of the Altars: Traditional Religion in England, 1400–1580*, New Haven and London, 1992, is the most comprehensive account of the campaign against the shrines. I have used as support Diarmaid MacCulloch's fine biography, *Thomas Cranmer*, New Haven and London, 1998. Geoffrey Moorhouse, *The Last Office: 1539 and the Dissolution of a Monastery*, London, 2008, is a survey of the Reformation in England which focuses on the monastery and cathedral of Durham. There is also helpful material in Finucane, *op. cit.*, Chapter 12, 'The Destruction of the Shrines', and Marks, *op. cit.*, Chapter 10, 'Deface and Destroy: The End of Images'.
11. Anne Duggan, *op. cit.*, deals with the campaign in Chapter 11, 'The Image Constructed and Deconstructed, 1171–1900'.
12. Allan Doig, *op.cit.*, p. 193 has the details.
13. See, for instance, his *The Voices of Morebath: Reformation and Rebellion in an English Village*, New Haven and London, 2001.
14. Quoted in Marks, *op. cit.*, p. 268.

CHAPTER TWENTY-FOUR: INTIMATIONS OF REALITY

1. Diary entry for 27 March 1511, quoted in David Chambers and Brian Pullan, *Venice, A Documentary History, 1450–1630*, Oxford and Cambridge, MA, 1992, p. 189.
2. Michael Hoskin and Owen Gingerich, 'Medieval Latin Astronomy', Chapter 4 in Michael Hoskin (ed.), *The Cambridge Concise History of Astronomy*, Cambridge, 1999, p. 88. Copernicus is important in that he moves beyond both the Bible and ancient texts. Medieval cosmography had taught that the earth was the lowest and most unstable part of the universe with the spheres of the planets ascending around it, the ultimate sphere being the perfection and stability of heaven. This rigid hierarchy was now shattered. Many date the birth of modern science from this moment. Isaac Newton was to bring this revolution to fruition by proving that the whole universe was subject to the same physical

laws, thus making redundant the medieval concept of a heaven, and, on earth, saintly bodies, as being qualitatively different in substance from the rest of the material world.

3. Edward Grant sums it up succinctly in his *God and Reason in the Middle Ages*, Cambridge, 2001, p. 14. 'During the late Middle Ages those who applied reason to the solution of problems in theology knew that, in the final analysis, reason was subordinate to faith, the Christian faith based on the revelation of fundamental truths, that were assumed to be beyond the ken of reason.' See also Levi, *op. cit.*, Chapter 2, 'The Crisis of Scholasticism'.

4. There is a vast literature on humanism. See, for instance, Charles Nauert, *Humanism and the Culture of Renaissance Europe*, Cambridge, 1995, and Jill Kraye (ed.), *The Cambridge Companion to Renaissance Humanism*, Cambridge, 1996. The many studies on aspects of humanism by Anthony Grafton are particularly important, and the field is being invigorated by the new I Tatti translations of Renaissance texts.

5. Grant, *God and Reason*, p. 290. One of the limitations of Grant's work is that he does not deal with the use of reasoning outside Paris and Oxford. Practical reasoning skills were probably, in the long run, much more important in laying the foundations of science. There is good material on the Italian achievement in Alexander Murray, *Reason and Society in the Middle Ages*, Oxford, 1978. See also Philip Jones, *The Italian City-State: From Commune to Signoria*, Oxford and New York, 1997.

6. I have used Martin Pine, *Pietro Pomponazzi, Radical Philosopher of the Renaissance*, Padua, 1986, especially Chapter 3, 'The Workings of Nature'.

7. See the excellent Richard Rubenstein, *Aristotle's Children: How Christians, Muslims and Jews Rediscovered Ancient Wisdom and Illuminated the Middle Ages*, Boston, 2003.

8. Toby Lester, *The Fourth Part of the World*, London and New York, 2009.

9. See further Richard Popkin, *The History of Scepticism from Erasmus to Spinoza*, Berkeley and London, 1979. Spinoza's *Tractatus-Theologico-Politicus* was the first modern text to express complete scepticism about the claims of revealed religion.

CHAPTER TWENTY-FIVE: REASSERTING THE MIRACULOUS

1. From the decree passed at the Twenty-Fifth Session of the Council of Trent, *On the Invocation, Veneration, and Relics, of Saints, and on Sacred Images*, December 1563.

2. A reliable introduction to all these developments is R. Po-Chia Hsia, *The World of Catholic Renewal, 1540–1770*, second edition, Cambridge, 2005. See also Christopher Black, *Church, Religion and Society in Early Modern Italy*, Basingstoke, UK, 2004, and *The Italian Inquisition*, New Haven and London, 2009. The basics are covered in Diarmaid MacCulloch, *Reformation*, especially Chapters 5, 6 and 9. See also Part III, 'Catholic Renewal', in R. Po-Chia Hsia (ed.), *Reform and Expansion 1500–1600: Volume Six of the Cambridge History of Christianity*, Cambridge, 2007. The details of the Council of Trent are to be found here.

3. This is a point well argued by Cameron, *op. cit.*, Chapter 15. 'Reformed Catholicism: Purifying Sources, Defending Traditions', *passim*, from which these examples are taken.

4. See Simon Ditchfield, 'Tridentine Worship and the Cult of Saints', Chapter 12 in R. Po-Chia Hsia (ed.), *Reform and Expansion 1500–1600*, and R. Po-Chia Hsia, *The World of Catholic Renewal*, Chapters 8 and 9 for the Church's attitude to the saints in this period.

5. See Fenlon, *op. cit.*, pp. 319–20.

6. I have used Carlos Eire, *From Madrid to Purgatory: The Art and Craft of Dying in Sixteenth-Century Spain*, Cambridge, 1995, as the basis of my account. Baltasar Porreno is quoted on p. 334.

7. Quoted in *ibid.*, p. 334.

8. See *ibid.*, Book Two, Chapter 4, 'Defending the Faith through Ritual', for an account of Philip's use of relics.
9. I have used *ibid.*, Book Three, 'The Saint's Heavenly Corpse: Teresa of Avila and the Ultimate Paradigm of Death', for my account of Teresa.
10. Hsia, *The World of Catholic Renewal*, p. 34. There is an excellent study of the problem of the female mystic with more material on Teresa in Chapter 9.
11. A Doctor of the Church is a major theologian of acknowledged saintliness. Teresa of Àvila and Catherine of Siena were the first women to be proclaimed Doctors, in 1970. Teresa of Lisieux became the third woman Doctor in 1977.

CHAPTER TWENTY-SIX: WITHIN THE COMMUNITY OF THE SUPERNATURAL

1. Livy (59 BC–17 AD) was a Roman historian at the time of the emperor Augustus who wrote a monumental history of the Roman people.
2. The story is told in Patricia Fortini Brown, *Venice and Antiquity*, New Haven and London, 1999, p. 98.
3. The distinctive and frightening quality of the Christian afterlife is not often given the serious analysis it deserves. John Casey, *After Lives: A Guide to Heaven, Hell and Purgatory*, Oxford, 2009, is particularly good at comparing the Christian view of the afterlife with those of alternative cultures. A sane and absorbing book.
4. Many scholastic theologians did attempt to use reason to understand the nature of God. However, Augustine, and most of those following him did not believe that God acted rationally in deciding who should and who should not be saved.
5. 'The darkly erotic aesthetic of pain' comes from Orsi, *op. cit.*, p. 23.
6. Trevor-Roper, *op. cit.*, sees the crucial moment as being the alienation of those who responded to the more reasoned approach to theology of Erasmus when the Catholic Church condemned him. In retrospect, this does seem to be the moment when the Church turned back from the challenges of a more progressive society.
7. The story is well told by Jonathan Israel, *Radical Enlightenment: Philosophy and the Making of Modernity 1650–1750*, Oxford, 2001, and *Enlightenment Contested: Philosophy, Modernity and the Emancipation of Man 1670–1752*, Oxford, 2006.

Select Bibliography

PRIMARY SOURCES

i. General

Texts of many of the figures dealt with here are available on the Fordham University Center for Medieval Studies online sourcebook http://www.fordham.edu/halsall.html.

Jansen, Katherine, Drell, Joanna, and Andrews, Frances, *Medieval Italy: Texts in Translation*, Philadelphia, 2009.

Petroff, Elizabeth Alvilda (ed.), *Medieval Women's Visionary Literature*, New York and Oxford, 1986.

Shinners, John (ed.), *Medieval Popular Religion, 1000–1500, A Reader*, second edition, Peterborough, Ontario, and Plymouth, England, 2007.

ii. Specific Authors

Augustine: *The City of God*, Henry Bettenson (transl.), Penguin Classics, London and New York, 1972.

Bede: *The Ecclesiastical History of the English People*, Judith McClure and Roger Collins (eds), Oxford World Classics, Oxford, 1999.

Chaucer, Geoffrey: *The Canterbury Tales*, transl. into modern English by Nevill Coghill, Penguin Classics, London and New York, 1951 (with subsequent minor revisions).

Da Canal, Martino: *Les estoires de Venise. Cronaca veneziana in lingua francese dalle origini al 1275*, Alberto Limentani (ed.), Florence, 1972.

De Clari, Robert: *The Capture of Constantinople*, English transl. Edgar McNeal, New York, 1936.

Dante Alighieri: *The Divine Comedy*, C.H. Sisson (transl.), Oxford World Classics, Oxford and New York, 1980.

Glaber, Rodulfus: *Rodulfus Glaber: The Five Books of the Histories*, J. France (ed. and transl.), Oxford, 1989.

Gunther of Pairis: *The Capture of Constantinople: The 'Hystoria Constantinopolitana' of Gunther of Pairis*, A.J. Andrea (ed. and transl.), Philadelphia, 1997.

Kempe, Margery: *The Book of Margery Kempe*, Lynn Staley (ed.), New York and London, 2001.

Suger, Abbot: *Abbot Suger on the Abbey Church of St. Denis and its Art Treasures*, Erwin Panofsky (ed. and transl.), Princeton 1946, revised 1979.

Voragine Jacobus de: *The Golden Legend*, William Granger Ryan (transl.), Princeton, 1995, and selections in Richard Hamer (ed.) and Christopher Stace (transl.), Penguin Classics series, London, 1998.

Wey, William: *Itineraries of William Wey: fellow of Eton College to Jerusalem AD 1458 and AD 1462; and to St. James of Compostella, AD 1456*, London, 1857.

SECONDARY SOURCES

Abou-El-Hai, Barbara, 'The Audiences for the Medieval Cult of Saints', *Gesta* 30:1 (1991), pp. 3–15.

Angenendt, Arnold, 'Relics and their Veneration in the Middle Ages', Chapter 2 in Anneka Mulder-Bakker (ed.), *The Invention of Saintliness*, London and New York, 2002.

Angold, Michael, *The Fourth Crusade: Event and Context*, Harlow, 2003.

Aries, Philippe, *The Hour of Our Death*, New York and Oxford, 1991.

Arnold, John, 'Repression and Power', Chapter 23 in Miri Rubin and Walter Simons (eds), *Christianity in Western Europe, c.1100–c.1500*, Cambridge, 2009.

Asbridge, Thomas, *The Crusades: The War for the Holy Land*, London and New York, 2010.

Asbridge, Thomas, 'The Holy Lance of Antioch: Power, Devotion and Memory on the First Crusade', *Reading Medieval Studies* 33 (2007), pp. 3–36.

Asztalos, Monika, 'The Faculty of Theology', Chapter 13 in Hilde de Ridder-Symeons (ed.), *A History of the University in Europe: Volume One, Universities in the Middle Ages*, Cambridge, 1992.

Baker, Derek and Cuming, G.J. (eds), *Popular Belief and Practice*, Cambridge, 1972.

Ball, Philip, *Universe of Stone: Chartres Cathedral and the Triumph of the Medieval Mind*, London, 2008.

Bartlett, Robert, *England under the Norman and Angevin Kings, 1075–1225*, Oxford, 2000.

Bartlett, Robert, *The Hanged Man*, Princeton, 2004.

Bartlett, Robert, *The Making of Europe: Conquest, Colonization and Cultural Change, 950–1350*, London and New York, 1993.

Bartlett, Robert, *The Natural and the Supernatural in the Middle Ages*, Cambridge, 2008.

Becher, Matthias, *Charlemagne*, New Haven and London, 2003.

Belting, Hans, *Likeness and Presence: A History of the Image before the Era of Art*, Chicago and London, 1994.

Benveniste, Henrietta, 'Dead Body, Public Body: Notes on Execution in the Middle Ages', in *Law and Critique* IV:1 (1993).

Beresford, James, 'When Faith and Science Collide', in *Minerva* 21:4 (July/August 2010), pp. 42–4.

Bethell, Denis, 'The Making of a Twelfth-Century Relic Collection' in Derek Baker and G.J. Cuming, (eds), *Popular Belief and Practice*, Cambridge, 1972.

Black, Christopher, *Church, Religion and Society in Early Modern Italy*, Basingstoke, UK, 2004.

Black, Christopher, *The Italian Inquisition*, New Haven and London, 2009.

Blair, John, *The Church in Anglo-Saxon Society*, Oxford, 2005.

Blanning, Tim, *The Pursuit of Glory: Europe 1648–1815*, London and New York, 2007.

Bouwsma, William, *The Waning of the Renaissance, 1550–1640*, New Haven and London, 2000.

Bozóky, Edina, and Helvétius, Anne-Marie (eds), *Les Reliques: Objets, Cultes, Symboles*, Turnhout (Belgium), 1999.

Bratchell, M.E., *Medieval Lucca and the Renaissance State*, Oxford, 2008.

Brown, Peter, *The Cult of the Saints: Its Rise and Function in Latin Christianity*, Chicago and London, 1981.

Brown, Peter, *The Rise of Western Christendom*, second edition, Oxford, 2003.

Burrow, John, *A History of Histories*, London, 2007.

Bynum, Caroline Walker, *The Resurrection of the Body in Western Christianity, 200–1336*, New York, 1995.

Bynum, Caroline Walker, 'Late Medieval Eucharistic Doctrine' in Lynn Staley (ed.), *The Book of Margery Kempe*, New York and London, 2001.

Bynum, Caroline Walker, *Wonderful Blood: Theology and Practice in late Medieval Germany and Beyond*, Philadelphia, 2007.

Cameron, Euan, *Enchanted Europe: Superstition, Reason and Religion, 1250–1750*, Oxford, 2010.

Casey, John, *After Lives: A Guide to Heaven, Hell and Purgatory*, Oxford, 2009.

Casiday, Augustine, and Norris, Frederick (eds), *Constantine to c.600: The Cambridge History of Christianity, Volume Two*, Cambridge, 2007.

Chadwick, Henry, *East and West: The Making of a Rift in the Church*, Oxford and New York, 2005.

Ciggaar, K.N., *Western Travellers to Constantinople: The West and Byzantium, 962–1204: Cultural and Political Relations*, Leiden, 1996.

Clark, Anne L., 'Guardians of the Sacred: The Nuns of Soissons and the Slipper of the Virgin Mary', *Church History* 76 (December 2007), pp. 724–49.

Clark, Gillian, 'Translating Relics: Vitricius of Rouen and Fourth-Century Debate' in *Early Medieval Europe* 10:2 (2001), pp. 161–76.

Clark, Gillian, 'Vitricius of Rouen: *Praising the Saints*', in *The Journal of Early Christian Studies* 7:3 (1999), pp. 365–99.

Coldstream, Nicola, *Medieval Architecture* (Oxford History of Art), Oxford, 2002.

Cormack, Robin, and Vassilaki, Maria, *Byzantium*, London, 2008.

Cornelison, Sally, and Montgomery, Scott B., *Images, Relics and Devotional Practices in Medieval and Renaissance Italy*, Tempe, Arizona, 2006.

Crook, John, *Architectural Settings of the Cult of Saints in the Early Christian West*, Oxford, 2000.

Davey, Francis (ed. and transl.), *The Itineraries of William Wey*, Oxford, 2010.

Demus, Otto, *The Mosaics of San Marco in Venice: Volume One, The Eleventh and Twelfth Centuries*, Chicago, 1984.

Dickens, A.G., and Jones, Whitney R.D., *Erasmus: The Reformer*, London, 1994.

Diehl, Peter, and Waugh, Scott (eds), *Christendom and its Discontents: Exclusion, Persecution and Rebellion, 1000–1500*, Cambridge, 1996.

Ditchfield, Simon, 'Tridentine Worship and the Cult of Saints', Chapter 12 in R. Po-Chia Hsia (ed.), *Reform and Expansion 1500–1600, op. cit.*

Doig, Allan, *Liturgy and Architecture: From the Early Church to the Middle Ages*, Aldershot, UK, and Burlington, Vermont, 2008.

Douglas, Mary, *Purity and Danger: An Analysis of the Concepts of Pollution and Taboo*, London and New York, 1966.

Duffy, Eamon, *Marking the Hours: English People and their Prayers*, New Haven and London, 2006.

Duffy, Eamon, *The Stripping of the Altars: Traditional Religion in England, 1400–1580*, New Haven and London, 1992.

Duffy, Eamon, *The Voices of Morebath: Reformation and Rebellion in an English Village*, New Haven and London, 2001.

Duggan, Anne, *Thomas Becket*, London, 2004.

Eire, Carlos, *From Madrid to Purgatory: The Art and Craft of Dying in Sixteenth-Century Spain*, Cambridge, 1995.

Elsner, Jas, and Rutherford, Ian (eds), *Pilgrimage in Graeco-Roman and Early Christian Antiquity: Seeing the Gods*, Oxford, 2005.

Fenlon, Iain, *The Ceremonial City: History, Memory and Myth in Renaissance Venice*, New Haven and London, 2007.

Fernie, Eric, 'Edward The Confessor's Westminster Abbey', Chapter 6 in Richard Mortimer (ed.), *Edward the Confessor: The Man and the Legend*, Woodbridge, UK, 2009.

Finucane, Ronald, *Miracles and Pilgrims: Popular Beliefs in Medieval England*, London, Melbourne and Toronto, 1977.

Fletcher, Richard, *The Conversion of Europe: From Paganism to Christianity 371–1386 AD*, London, 1997.

Flint, Valerie, *The Rise of Magic in Early Medieval Europe*, Princeton, 1991.

Flint, Valerie, 'The Saint and the Operation of the Law: Reflections upon the Miracles of St. Thomas Cantilupe', Chapter 25 in Richard Gameson and Henrietta Leyser (eds), *Belief and Culture in the Middle Ages: Studies Presented to Henry Mayr-Harting*, Oxford, 2001.

Fortini Brown, Patricia, *Venetian Narrative Painting in the Age of Carpaccio*, New Haven and London, 1988.

Fortini Brown, Patricia, *Venice and Antiquity*, New Haven and London, 1999.

Fouracre, Paul, 'The Origins of the Carolingian Attempt to Regulate the Cult of Saints', Chapter 7 in James Howard Johnston and Paul Antony Hayward (eds), *The Cult of Saints in Late Antiquity and the Early Middle Ages*, Oxford, 1999.

France, John, *The Crusades and the Expansion of Catholic Christendom, 1000–1714*, Abingdon, UK, and New York, 2005.

Frank, Georgia, 'From Antioch to Arles, Lay devotion in Context', Chapter 21 in Augustine Casiday and Frederick Norris (eds), *Constantine to c.600, The Cambridge History of Christianity, Volume Two*, Cambridge, 2007.

Freedberg, David, *The Power of Images: Studies in the History and Theory of Response*, Chicago and London, 1989.

Freeman, Charles, *AD 381*, London, 2008, and New York, 2009.

Freeman, Charles, *A New History of Early Christianity*, New Haven and London, 2009.

Freeman, Charles, *The Closing of the Western Mind: The Rise of Faith and the Fall of Reason*, London, 2002, and New York, 2003.

Fulton, Rachel, *From Judgment to Passion: Devotion to Christ and the Virgin Mary, 800–1200*, New York, 2002.

Fulton, Rachel, 'Mary', Chapter 18 in Miri Rubin and Walter Simons (eds), *Christianity in Western Europe, c.1100–c.1500*, Cambridge, 2009.

Gabriel, Matthew, and Stuckey, Jane, *The Legend of Charlemagne in the Middle Ages: Power, Faith and Crusade*, Basingstoke, UK, and New York, 2008.

Gameson, Richard and Leyser, Henrietta (eds), *Belief and Culture in the Middle Ages: Studies Presented to Henry Mayr-Harting*, Oxford, 2001.

Geary, Patrick, *Furta Sacra: Thefts of Relics in the Central Middle Ages*, revised edition, Princeton, 1991.

Geary, Patrick, 'Humiliation of Saints', Chapter 3 in Stephen Wilson (ed.), *Saints and their Cults: Studies in Religious Sociology, Folklore and History*, Cambridge, 1983.

Ghosh, Kantich, 'Wycliffism and Lollardy', Chapter 28 in Miri Rubin and Walter Simons (eds), *Christianity in Western Europe c.1100–c.1500*, Cambridge, 2009.

Gibbon, Edward, *The Decline and Fall of the Roman Empire*, available in many editions.

Goldhill, Simon (ed.), *The End of Dialogue in Antiquity*, Cambridge, 2008.

Goodich, Michael, *Violence and Miracle in the Fourteenth Century: Private Grief and Public Salvation*, Chicago and London, 1995.

Goodich, Michael, *Lives and Miracles of the Saints: Studies in Medieval Latin Hagiography*, Aldershot, UK, and Burlington, Vermont, 2004.

Goodich, Michael, 'The Politics of Canonisation in the Thirteenth Century: Lay and Mendicant Saints', Chapter 5 in Stephen Wilson (ed.), *Saints and their Cults: Studies in Religious Sociology, Folklore and History*, Cambridge, 1983.

Gordon, Bruce, *John Calvin*, New Haven and London, 2009.

Grafton, Anthony, *What was History?: The Art of History in Early Modern Europe*, Cambridge and New York, 2007.

Grant, Edward, *God and Reason in the Middle Ages*, Cambridge, 2001.

Grant, Edward, *Science and Religion: 400 BC to AD 1550*, Baltimore, 2004.

Greer, Rowan, *The Fear of Freedom: A Study of Miracles in the Roman Imperial Church*, University Park and London, 1989.

Grig, Lucy, *Making Martyrs in Late Antiquity*, London, 2004.

Hahn, Cynthia, 'Seeing and Believing: The Construction of Sanctity in Early Medieval Saints' Shrines', in *Speculum* 72:3 (1997), pp. 1,079–116.

Hahn, Cynthia, 'The Voices of the Saints: What Do Speaking Reliquaries Say?, *Gesta* 36, 1997.

Hahn, Cynthia, 'What do Reliquaries do for Relics?' in *Numen* 57: 3–4, 2010, pp. 284–316.

Hayward, Paul Antony, 'Demystifying the Role of Sanctity', Chapter 6 in James Howard-Johnston and Paul Antony Hayward (eds), *The Cult of Saints in Late Antiquity and the Early Middle Ages*, Oxford, 1999.

Hayward, Paul Antony, and Howard-Johnston, James (eds), *The Cult of Saints in Late Antiquity and the Early Middle Ages*, Oxford, 1999.

Head, Thomas, and Landes, Richard (eds), *The Peace of God: Social Violence and Religious Response in France around the Year 1000*, Ithaca, New York, and London, 1992.

Herrin, Judith, *Byzantium: The Surprising Life of a Medieval Empire*, London, 2007.

Hicks, Carola (ed.), *England in the Eleventh Century*, Stamford, 1992.

Holmes, George, *Europe: Hierarchy and Revolt, 1320–1450, Blackwell Classic Histories of Europe*, second edition, Oxford, 2000.

Housley, Norman, *Religious Warfare in Europe, 1400–1536*, Oxford, 2002.

Howard, Deborah, *Venice and the East: The Impact of the Islamic World on Venetian Architecture 1100–1500*, New Haven and London, 2000.

Hunter, David, *Marriage, Celibacy and Heresy in Ancient Christianity: The Jovinianist Controversy*, Oxford, 2007.

Hunter, David, 'Vigilantius of Calagurris and Vitricius of Rouen: Ascetics, Relics and Clerics in Late Roman Gaul', in *The Journal of Early Christian Studies* 7: 3 (1999), pp. 401–30.

Israel, Jonathan, *Radical Enlightenment: Philosophy and the Making of Modernity 1650–1750*, Oxford, 2001.

Israel, Jonathan, *Enlightenment Contested: Philosophy, Modernity and the Emancipation of Man 1670–1752*, Oxford, 2006.

James, Edward, *Britain in the First Millennium*, London, 2001.

Janes, D., *God and Gold in Late Antiquity*, Cambridge, 1998.

Jansen, Katherine Ludwig, *The Making of the Magdalen: Preaching and Devotion in the Later Middle Ages*, Princeton, 2000.

Jenkins, Jacqueline, and Lewis, Katherine, *St. Katherine of Alexandria: Texts and Contexts in Western Medieval Europe*, Turnhout, 2003.

Jones, Philip, *The Italian City-State: From Commune to Signoria*, Oxford and New York, 1997.

Jordan, William Chester, *Europe in the High Middle Ages*, London and New York, 2002.

Kaegi, Walter, *Heraclius, Emperor of Byzantium*, Cambridge, 2002.

Kelly, J.N.D., *Jerome*, London, 1975.

Klein, Holgar, 'Sacred Relics and Imperial Ceremonies at the Great Palace of Constantinople', F.A. Bauer (Hrsg.), *Visualisierungen von Herrschaft*, BYZAS5 (2006), pp. 79–99.

Krautheimer, Richard, *Rome: Profile of a City, 312–1308*, Princeton, 2000.

Kraye, Jill (ed.), *The Cambridge Companion to Renaissance Humanism*, Cambridge, 1996.

Landes, Richard, *Relics, Apocalypse and the Deceits of History: Ademar of Chabannes, 989–1034*, Cambridge, MA, and London, 1995.

Langmuir, Gavin, 'The Tortures of the Body of Christ' in Scott Waugh and Peter Diehl, *Christendom and its Discontents: Exclusion, Persecution and Rebellion, 1000–1500*, Cambridge, 1996.

Lansford, Tyler, *The Latin Inscriptions of Rome: A Walking Guide*, Baltimore, 2009.

Latowsky, Anne, 'Charlemagne as Pilgrim? Requests for Relics in the *Descriptio qualiter* and *The Voyage of Charlemagne*', in Matthew Gabriel and Jane Stuckey (eds), *The Legend of Charlemagne in the Middle Ages: Power, Faith and Crusade*, Basingstoke, UK, and New York, 2008.

Lester, Toby, *The Fourth Part of the World*, London and New York, 2009.

Levi, Anthony, *Renaissance and Reformation: The Intellectual Genesis*, New Haven and London, 2002.

Limberis, Vasiliki, *Divine Heiress: The Virgin Mary and the Creation of Christian Constantinople*, London and New York, 1994.

Lloyd, G.E.R., *The Revolutions of Wisdom: Studies in the Claims and Practice of Ancient Greek Science*, Berkeley and London, 1987.

Logan, F. Donald, *A History of the Church in the Middle Ages*, London and New York, 2002.

Luff, Gordon, *Heresy, Philosophy and Religion in the Medieval West*, Aldershot, UK, and Burlington, Vermont, 2002.

Madden, Thomas, *Enrico Dandolo and the Rise of Venice*, Baltimore, 2007.

Mango, Cyril (ed.), *The Oxford History of Byzantium*, Oxford, 2002.

Maniura, Robert, 'Image and Relic in the Cult of Our Lady of Prato', Chapter 10 in Sally Cornelison and Scott B. Montgomery, *Images, Relics and Devotional Practices in Medieval and Renaissance Italy*, Tempe, Arizona, 2006.

Marks, Richard, *Image and Devotion in Late Medieval England*, Stroud, UK, 2004.

Markus, R.A., 'How on Earth Could Places Become Holy? Origins of the Christian Idea of Holy Places' in *The Journal of Early Christian Studies* 2: 3 (1994), pp. 257–71.

McCormick, Michael, *Origins of the European Economy: Communications and Commerce, AD 300–900*, Cambridge, 2001.

MacCulloch, Diarmaid, *Thomas Cranmer*, New Haven and London, 1998.

MacCulloch, Diarmaid, *Reformation: Europe's House Divided 1490–1700*, London and New York, 2003.

MacCulloch, Diarmaid, *A History of Christianity*, London and New York, 2009.

McCulloh, John, 'From Antiquity to the Middle Ages: Continuity and Change in Papal Relic Policy from the 6th to the 8th Century', in Ernst Dassmann and K. Suso Frank (eds), *Pietas: Festschrift für Berhard Kötting*, Münster, 1980, pp. 313–24.

McKitterick, Rosamond, *Charlemagne: The Formation of a European Identity*, Cambridge, 2008.

McLynn, Neil, *Ambrose of Milan: Church and Court in a Christian Capital*, Berkeley and London, 2004.

McManners, John, *Church and Society in Eighteenth-Century France, Volume Two: The Religion of the People and the Politics of Religion*, Oxford, 1998.

MacMullen, Ramsay, *The Second Church. Popular Christianity AD 200–400*, Atlanta, 2009.

Mitchell, R.J., *The Spring Voyage: The Jerusalem Pilgrimage in 1458*, London, 1965.

Monnas, Lisa, *Merchants, Princes and Painters: Silk Fabrics in Italian and Northern Paintings, 1300–1550*, New Haven and London, 2008.

Moore, R.I., 'Postscript, The Peace of God and the Social Revolution', in Thomas Head and Richard Landes (eds), *The Peace of God: Social Violence and Religious Response in France around the Year 1000*, Ithaca, New York, and London, 1992.

Moore, R.I., 'Heresy, Repression and Social Change in the Age of Gregorian Reform', in Scott Waugh and Peter Diehl (eds), *Christendom and its Discontents: Exclusion, Persecution and Rebellion, 1000–1500*, Cambridge, 1996, pp. 19–46.

Moore, R.I., *The Formation of a Persecuting Society: Power and Deviance in Western Europe, 950–1250*, Oxford and Malden, MA, 1997.

Moorhouse, Geoffrey, *The Last Office: 1539 and the Dissolution of a Monastery*, London, 2008.

Morgan, David (ed.), *Religion and Material Culture: The Matter of Belief*, London and New York, 2010.

Mormando, Franco, *The Preacher's Demons: Bernardino of Siena and the Social Underworld of Early Renaissance Italy*, University of Chicago Press, 1999.

Morris, Colin, *The Sepulchre of Christ and the Medieval West: From the Beginning to 1600*, Oxford, 2005.

Morris, Colin, 'A Critique of Popular Religion: Guibert of Nogent on *The Relics of the Saints*', in G.J. Cuming and Derek Baker (eds), *Popular Belief and Practice*, Cambridge, 1972.

Mortimer, Richard (ed.), *Edward the Confessor: The Man and the Legend*, Woodbridge, UK, 2009.

Muir, Edward, *Civic Ritual in Renaissance Venice*, Princeton, 1986.

Mulder-Bakker, Anneka (ed.), *The Invention of Saintliness*, London and New York, 2002.

Murray, Alexander, *Reason and Society in the Middle Ages*, Oxford, 1978.

Nauert, Charles, *Humanism and the Culture of Renaissance Europe*, Cambridge, 1995.

Nees, Lawrence, *Early Medieval Art* (Oxford History of Art), Oxford, 2002.

Nilson, Ben, *Cathedral Shrines of Medieval England*, Woodbridge, UK, and Rochester, New York, 1988.

Nixon, Virginia, *Mary's Mother: Saint Anne in Late Medieval Europe*, Pennsylvania, 2004.

Noble, Thomas, and Smith, Julia (eds), *Early Medieval Christianities, c.600–1100: The Cambridge History of Christianity, Volume Three*, Cambridge, 2008.

O'Donovan, Oliver, and O'Donovan, Joan Lockwood, *From Irenaeus to Grotius: A Sourcebook in Christian Political Thought*, Grand Rapids, Michigan, and Cambridge, 1999.

Orsi, Robert, *Between Heaven and Earth: The Religious Worlds People Make and the Scholars Who Study Them*, Princeton and Oxford, 2004.

Pantin, W.A., 'Instructions for a Devout and Literate Layman', in J.J.G. Alexander and Margaret Gibson (eds), *Medieval Learning and Literature: Essay Presented to Richard William Hunt*, Oxford, 1976.

Partridge, Loren, *The Renaissance in Rome*, London, 1996.

Pastan, Elizabeth, 'Charlemagne as Saint? Relics and the Choice of Window Subjects at Chartres Cathedral', in Matthew Gabriel and Jane Stuckey, *The Legend of Charlemagne in the Middle Ages: Power, Faith and Crusade*, Basingstoke, UK, and New York, 2008, pp. 97–136.

Picard, Jean-Michel, 'Le culte des reliques en Irlande', in Edina Bozóky and Anne-Marie Helvétius (eds), *Les Reliques: Objets, Cultes, Symboles*, Turnhout (Belgium), 1999.

Pine, Martin, *Pietro Pomponazzi, Radical Philosopher of the Renaissance*, Padua, 1986.

Po-Chia Hsia, R., *The World of Catholic Renewal, 1540–1770*, second edition, Cambridge, 2005.

Po-Chia Hsia, R. (ed.), *Christianity, Reform and Expansion, 1500–1660: The Cambridge History of Christianity, Volume Six*, Cambridge, 2007.

Popkin, Richard, *The History of Scepticism from Erasmus to Spinoza*, Berkeley and London, 1979.

Radker, Gary, 'Relics and Identity at the Convent of San Zaccaria in Renaissance Venice', Chapter 9 in Sally Cornelison and Scott, B., Montgomery, *Images, Relics and Devotional Practices in Medieval and Renaissance Italy*, Tempe, Arizona, 2006.

Rapp, Claudia, 'Saints and Holy Men'. Chapter 22 in Augustine Casiday and Frederick Norris (eds), *Constantine to c.600: The Cambridge History of Christianity, Volume Two*, Cambridge, 2007.

Ridder-Symeons, Hilde de (ed.), *A History of the University in Europe: Volume One, Universities in the Middle Ages*, Cambridge 1992.

Ridyard, S.J., *The Royal Saints of Anglo-Saxon England*, Cambridge, 1988.

Riley-Smith, Jonathan, *What Were the Crusades?*, fourth edition, San Francisco and Basingstoke, 2009.

Rist, John, *Augustine: Ancient Thought Baptised*, Cambridge, 1994.

Roach, Andrew P., *The Devil's World: Heresy and Society 1100–1300*, Harlow, UK, 2005.

Rogers, Nicholas, 'The Waltham Abbey Relic-list', in Carola Hicks (ed.), *England in the Eleventh Century*, Stamford, 1992.

Rubenstein, Richard, *Aristotle's Children: How Christians, Muslims and Jews Rediscovered Ancient Wisdom and Illuminated the Middle Ages*, Boston, 2003.

Rubin, Miri, and Simons, Walter (eds), *The Cambridge History of Christianity, Volume Four: Christianity in Western Europe, c.1100–c.1500*, Cambridge, 2009.

Rubin, Miri, *Mother of God: A History of the Virgin Mary*, London, 2009.

Scott, Robert, *The Gothic Enterprise*, Berkeley and London, 2005.

Sekules, Veronica, *Medieval Art* (Oxford History of Art), Oxford, 2001.

Sharpe, Richard and Thacker, Alan (eds), *Local Saints and Local Churches in the Early Medieval West*, Oxford, 2002.

Skinner, Quentin, *The Foundations of Modern Political Thought, Volume One: The Renaissance*, Cambridge, 1978.

Smith, Julia, *Europe after Rome: A New Cultural History 500–1000*, Oxford, 2000.

Smith, Julia, 'Old Saints, New Saints: Roman Relics in Carolingian Francia', in Julia Smith (ed.), *Early Medieval Rome and the Christian West*, Brill (Leiden), 2000.

Smith, Julia, 'Oral and Written: Saints, Miracles, and Relics in Brittany, c.850–1250', in *Speculum* 65 (1990), pp. 309–43.

Smith, Julia, 'Saints and their Cults', in Thomas Noble and Julia Smith (eds), *Early Medieval Christianities, c.600–1100: The Cambridge History of Christianity, Volume Three*, Cambridge, 2008.

Snoek, G.L.C., *Medieval Piety from Relics to the Eucharist: A Process of Mutual Interaction*, Leiden and New York, 1995.

Southern, R.W., *Western Society and the Church in the Middle Ages*, Volume 2 of the *Pelican History of the Church*, London and New York, 1970.

Stalley, Roger, *Early Medieval Architecture* (Oxford History of Art), Oxford, 1999.

Staunton, Michael (ed.), *The Lives of Thomas Becket*, Manchester, 2001.

Sumption, Jonathan, *Pilgrimage: An Image of Mediaeval Religion*, London, 1975.

Swanson, R.N., *Religion and Devotion in Europe, c.1215–c.1515*, Cambridge, 1995.

Trevor-Roper, H.R., 'Religion, the Reformation and Social Change', reproduced in his *The Crisis of the Seventeenth Century*, New York, 1965.

Trexler, Richard, *Public Life in Renaissance Florence*, New York and London, 1980.

Trout, Dennis, *Paulinus of Nola: Life, Letters and Poems*, Berkeley and London, 1999.

Van Bavel, Tarcisius J., 'The Cult of the Martyrs in St. Augustine: Theology versus Popular Religion?' in M. Lamberights and P. Van Deun (eds), *Martyrium in Multidisciplinary Perspective: A Memorial to Louis Reekmans*, Leuven, 1995, pp. 351–61.

Van Dam, Raymond, *Saints and their Miracles in Late Antique Gaul*, Princeton, 1993.

Vauchez, André, *Sainthood in the Later Middle Ages*, English translation by Jean Birrell, Cambridge, 1997.

Vauchez, André, 'Saints and Pilgrimages: New and Old', Chapter 21, in Miri Rubin and Walter Simons (eds), *The Cambridge History of Christianity, Volume Four: Christianity in Western Europe c.1100–c.1500*, Cambridge, 2009.

Vincent, Nicholas, *The Holy Blood: King Henry III and the Westminster Blood Relic*, Cambridge, 2001.

Wandel, Lee Palmer, *Voracious Idols and Violent Hands*, Cambridge, 1995.

Ward, Benedicta, *Miracles and the Medieval Mind*, revised edition, Philadelphia, 1987.

Warner, Marina, *Alone of All her Sex*, London and New York, 1983.

Webb, Diana, *Patrons and Defenders: The Saints in the Italian City-States*, London and New York, 1996.

Webb, Diana, *Pilgrims and Pilgrimage in the Medieval West*, London and New York, 1999.

Weiss, Daniel, *Art and Crusade in the Age of St. Louis*, Cambridge, 1988.

Whalen, Brett Edward, *Dominion of God, Christendom and Apocalypse in the Middle Ages*, Cambridge, MA, and London, 2009.

Wickham, Christopher, *The Inheritance of Rome: A History of Europe from 400 to 1000*, London and New York, 2009.

Wilson, Stephen (ed.), *Saints and their Cults: Studies in Religious Sociology, Folklore and History*, Cambridge, 1983.

Wunderli, Richard, *Peasant Fires: The Drummer of Niklashausen*, Bloomington and Indianapolis, 1992.

Yarrow, Simon, *Saints and Their Communities: Miracle Stories in Twelfth-Century England*, Oxford, 2005.

Ziegler, Joseph, 'Faith and the Intellectuals I', Chapter 24 in Miri Rubin and Walter Simons (eds), *Christianity in Western Europe, c.1100–c.1500*, Cambridge, 2009.

Index

1/20/19
17